# LANGUAGE
# EDUCATION

# WORLD YEARBOOK OF EDUCATION 2003

# LANGUAGE

# EDUCATION

EDITED BY
JILL BOURNE & EUAN REID

KOGAN
PAGE

First published in Great Britain and the United States in 2003 by Kogan Page
Limited

120 Pentonville Road
London N1 9JN
UK
www.kogan-page.co.uk

22883 Quicksilver Drive
Sterling VA 20166–2012
USA

**British Library Cataloguing in Publication Data**

A CIP record for this book is available from the British Library.

ISBN 0 7494 3613 1

Typeset by Saxon Graphics Ltd, Derby
Printed and bound in Great Britain by Biddles Ltd, Guildford and King's Lynn
*www.biddles.co.uk*

# Contents

# List of contributors

**Mike Baynham** is currently Professor of TESOL at the University of Leeds, UK, where his publications and research focus on adult literacy. He is also Chair of the British Association for Applied Linguistics, and co-convenor of the AILA Scientific Commission on Literacy.

**Jill Bourne** is Professor of Primary Education in the University of Southampton, UK. She has led a number of research projects on educational provision in multi-ethnic schools, and most recently contributed to the drafting of the government's national 'Standards for Initial Teacher Training' in England.

**Michael Byram** is Professor of Education at the University of Durham, UK, having earlier taught French and German at secondary and adult levels. He has researched linguistic minorities and foreign language education, and is a Special Adviser to the Council of Europe Language Policy Division.

**Amitav Choudhry** works as Associate Professor in the Indian Statistical Institute in Calcutta, on the demography of languages in India, with particular emphasis on the development of public policy on language and on language education.

**Frances Christie** is Foundation Professor of Language and Literacy Education at the University of Melbourne, Australia. She has research interests in writing development, classroom discourse analysis, development of a pedagogic grammar and reading theory.

**Jim Cummins** is Professor in the Department of Curriculum, Teaching and Learning in the Ontario Institute for Studies in Education, University of Toronto, Canada. His research focuses on language proficiency and second language acquisition, with emphasis on the social and educational barriers that limit academic success for culturally diverse students.

**Maya Khemlani David** is Associate Professor of Linguistics in the University of Malaya, Kuala Lumpur, Malaysia. She was editor of the journal of the Malaysian English Language Teaching Association, and her research interests are in sociolinguistics and second language learning.

**Ingrid Gogolin** is Professor of International Comparative and Intercultural Educational Research at the University of Hamburg, Germany. Her research focuses on multicultural education, and on multilingualism in Germany and other European countries resulting from immigration.

**Subra Govindasamy** is Assistant Professor at the International Islamic University, Malaysia. He has researched extensively on English grammatical and discourse features, language acquisition, bilingualism, language policy and language planning.

**Georgii Khruslov** is head of the Professional Development section of the Pushkin Institute of Russian Language, and Senior Researcher in the Institute for Ethnic Issues in Education, both in Moscow, Russian Federation. His work focuses on comparative studies of the teaching of Russian as a mother tongue, and on multilingualism in the Russian Federation.

**Sjaak Kroon** is an Associate Professor in Babylon, the Centre for Studies of Multilingualism in Multicultural Societies at Tilburg University, the Netherlands. His main research and teaching activities are in the field of multilingualism, language education and language policy.

**Joseph Lo Bianco** is Director of the National Languages and Literacy Institute of Australia ('Language Australia'), and a visiting Professor of Education at the University of Melbourne, and of Languages and Comparative Cultural Studies at the University of Queensland. His main research interests are in language politics.

**Joanna McPake** is Deputy Director of the Scottish Centre for Information on Language Teaching and Research at the University of Stirling, UK. She researches language learning in school and employment, and has been involved in public policy development in Scotland.

**John C Maher** is Professor of Linguistics at International Christian University, Tokyo, Japan. His research centres on sociolinguistics, multilingualism and the bilingual communities in Japan. His publications include *Diversity in Japanese Culture and Language* (1994), *Language and Cultural Diversity in Japan* (1995) and *Multilingual Japan* (1995).

**Clare Mar-Molinero** is the Head of the Modern Languages Department at the University of Southampton, UK, with a particular interest in Spanish, Catalan, and Latin American Studies. She teaches sociolinguistics, especially relating to language policies in the Spanish-speaking world.

**Luiz Paulo Moita-Lopes** is Associate Professor of Applied Linguistics at the Federal University of Rio de Janeiro, Brazil. His current research interests relate to narratives and the construction of masculinities in the classroom.

**Akira Nakayama** is Assistant Editor of *Educational Studies* and a visiting lecturer at several universities and schools in Japan. His research interests are in language education in Japan, learner motivation and beliefs, and learning strategies.

**Sigmund Ongstad** is Professor of Norwegian at Oslo University College, Norway. His research interests and publications include mother tongue education, genre and Norwegian writing research. He co-convenes AILA's Scientific Commission for Mother Tongue Education.

**Carlos J Ovando** is Professor and Associate Dean for Teacher Education, and Division Director for Curriculum and Instruction at Arizona State University, United States. His work on bilingual teacher preparation and multicultural education has appeared in many publications.

**Carol A Padden** is Professor in the Department of Communication at the University of California, San Diego, United States. She has published sign language textbooks, a book about the deaf community in the United States, and on sign language structure and reading development in signing deaf children.

**Anne Pakir** is Associate Professor in the Department of English Language and Literature at the National University of Singapore. She is a sociolinguist and applied linguist, and her research interests include bilingualism and language management, language policy and planning, and English as a global language.

**Peter Plüddemann** is a researcher and teacher educator with the Project for the Study of Alternative Education in South Africa, University of Cape Town, South Africa. Current research interests include language-in-education policy implementation, and dual-medium schooling.

**Euan Reid** teaches in the School of Culture, Language and Communication, Institute of Education, University of London, UK. His research interests are centred on linguistic minorities, and on multilingual schooling, in comparative perspective.

**Terrence G Wiley** is Professor of Education and Director of the Division of Educational Leadership and Policy Studies at Arizona State University. He is author of numerous publications on language policy, literacy, biliteracy and language diversity.

# Series editors' foreword

The issues raised by the role of language in education are some of the most important and contentious ones faced by education systems across the globe. Thus we were delighted when Jill Bourne and Euan Reid, two experts in this field, agreed to edit this *World Yearbook of Education*.

Our expectations have been fulfilled. We believe that this *Yearbook* is an excellent overview of the range of educational issues raised by language in education. More, the detailed case studies show how these issues are resolved, or not, in practice. Perhaps most significantly, this book shows how the role of language in education is deeply embedded in more general debates about the nature of nationhood in an increasingly globalizing world. The issues may shift and change, as will our understanding and practice, but the fact remains that the role of language in education is a critical one. States and education systems that fail to face up to these issues do so at their peril.

Accordingly, we feel that this *Yearbook* makes a valuable contribution to this key debate and a thought-provoking and challenging one at that.

*David Coulby and Crispin Jones*
*December 2002*

# Preface

What can we expect from a *World Yearbook* with the special theme of 'Language Education' published in 2003? Our view is that what a series like this can do best is to offer a range of international perspectives on familiar problems of common concern in most parts of the world. We invited some of the most interesting people we knew from a variety of different countries, the most stimulating thinkers and writers in the various sub-fields within language education, to offer in condensed form discussion of key themes that preoccupy education ministries, researchers, teacher educators and practitioners everywhere. Our hope is that readers will find new insights, evidence and ideas that will help them find new solutions to age-old problems.

The key contextual factors in the early 21st century seem to us to be increasing globalization and the increasing mobility of populations. Every sector of language education and every education system in every part of the world is concerned in some way to balance two central elements. On the one hand, there is a perceived need to maintain – or develop for the first time – national, cultural and linguistic cohesion. This leads to a focus on what is often called 'the mother tongue', although it frequently turns out on closer inspection to be more accurately described as a 'standard national language'. On the other hand, many systems today are also acknowledging, and in the best cases actually making positive use of, the linguistic diversity to be found in every country and region. Minority languages of various kinds are finding a place in schools, as well as in public life, and in the most ambitious cases are being given a central role in bilingual, even occasionally multilingual, schooling. However, there is still a nervousness about the dangers of national disintegration should 'other languages' be given too high a status. This is easier to understand in post-colonial situations where a sense of nationhood is less secure, but it is also evident in well-established 'old countries', where it is less easily explicable. Altogether then, the many tensions and dilemmas arising from the contradictions between the desire for uniformity and the pressures for diversity – Bakhtin's 'centrifugal' and 'centripetal' forces – are at the heart of much of the discussion in the papers that follow.

There is also increasing awareness in many places of the role of language in maintaining unequal power relationships between different sectors of national populations, in encouraging participation and inclusion, or in challenging the status quo more radically. Many of the contributions that we offer here are also preoccupied by these interrelated themes. Other important contextual factors are the more general, and sometimes radical, changes in many education systems, with their own special impact on language education.

Against this background, we asked all the contributors to Part I of the volume to outline and provide commentary on what they regard as the key contemporary issues in relation to their chapter title, each reflecting on their own specialist area in the field of language education. Then, in Part II, we sought contributions that focus on the particular national implications of attempts to formulate policy and establish practice in language education. All the contributors have a close knowledge of and strong commitment to the development of enlightened language education in their regions. They were given an open brief, allowing each to provide an intuitive response to those concerns they themselves identify as currently significant in their own location. Each has selected a few overall themes around which the dilemmas and potentials of the various forms of language in education can be discussed, with reference to the cultural values and beliefs in which they are embedded. Thus there are only background treatments of the structural features of national education systems and the different provisions for different languages and language groups available within them, although the chapters are well referenced for those who wish to learn more about particular contexts.

In the light of a number of the issues raised in Part I of the book, we have organized the chapters in Part II in the following way. We start with an examination of some strong nation-states where the hegemonic dominance of one language has become naturalized and thus often unexamined. Chapter 9, on Japan, outlines the decline of the hegemony of Japanese in the face of globalization and the need for wider international contacts and understanding. Japan was once seen as perhaps the most socially homogeneous nation in the world, but the chapter reveals the dawning there of a new awareness of social and linguistic diversity, alongside the effects of a 'modernizing' school system. Chapters 10 and 11 pick up the theme of hegemony, examining the struggles to define language education policy within two English-dominant nations. Chapter 10, on the United States, draws out the implications of non-standard dialects of English within education, as well as of the nation's existing linguistic diversity for language policy and provision. With Chapter 11, on the United Kingdom, it illustrates the struggle to motivate learners and to resource the teaching of other languages in the context of the global spread of English and its current status as an international language. In contrast, Chapter 12 examines the way in which leadership in language education policy development has enabled Australians to explore notions of multiculturalism and the possibilities of new forms of national identity, despite hegemonic pressures.

Chapters 13 to 16 examine the role of language education in 'nation building', first in Spain and Russia as they respond to political and social reforms, then in post-colonial Malaysia and India. These chapters illustrate the conflicts and resolutions in language policy making and provision for 'minorities' and 'minority languages' where both regional differences in language profiles and the existence of linguistically diverse urban centres need to be taken into consideration. In these systems, the existence of minority languages is given formal status within the school systems in a variety of different ways in the different regions, but there is overarching concern, reflected in language education policy, to maintain national integration and a sense of national citizenship, and to avoid linguistic difference escalating into divisiveness. In contrast to the emphasis on nation building in the previous chapters in Part II, Chapter 17, on Brazil, returns to some of the other themes raised in Part I, reminding us of the crucial role of language education in raising the general educational attainment of disadvantaged students and in helping to provide equal opportunities and social justice for all.

This emphasis on the role of language in learning and on improving opportunities for students from disadvantaged communities is continued in Part III of the book. This offers illustrative case studies of language education policy and practice in three linguistically diverse cities in Europe, Asia and Africa respectively. Contributors to this section each provides a sense of the complex sociolinguistic profile of their city, and of the degree of 'fit' of national policy with local realities, as well as of the very different attempted solutions to language education in a world in which such multilingualism is becoming increasingly accepted as the norm.

As editors, we have greatly enjoyed our contacts with the international group of contributors to this volume, and the opportunity to learn from their different perspectives and analyses. We thank them for their patience in responding to all our requests for clarifications, and for their tolerance in submitting to necessary cuts and editorial amendments. We hope that, taken overall, this book will allow the reader a sense of some of the tensions implicit in implementing language education policy in the 'real world', in the context of current and ongoing educational, social and political reforms.

*Jill Bourne and Euan Reid*
*December 2002*

# Part I
# Key issues

# 1.   Bilingual education

Jim Cummins

At a very general level, the term *bilingual education* refers to the use of two (or more) languages of instruction at some point in a student's school career. Each language is used as a medium of instruction to teach subject matter content rather than just the language itself. Despite the apparent simplicity of this description, the phenomenon of bilingual education entails considerable complexity. Variation in the goals and implementation of bilingual education can derive from a multitude of sociopolitical, sociolinguistic, administrative and instructional factors. In addition, the use of a language as a medium of instruction in state-funded school systems confers recognition and status on that language and its speakers. Consequently, bilingual education is not simply a politically neutral instructional phenomenon but rather is implicated in national and international competition between groups for material and symbolic resources. In some contexts (eg the United States), this has resulted in major political controversy surrounding bilingual programmes. Questions related to the educational effectiveness of bilingual programmes have become hopelessly confounded with ideological issues related to national identity and unity (Crawford, 2000).

In the sections that follow, typologies of bilingual education are described and synthesized into five broad types of programme. Then the psycholinguistic research on bilingual education is reviewed and several generalizations deriving from that research are proposed. Finally, future directions are discussed in the context of economic globalization and the associated movement of people and information across national and linguistic boundaries.

## Types of bilingual education

Initially it is important to outline some basic distinctions that have been prominent in discussions of bilingual education. These distinctions represent conceptual continua rather than strict dichotomies and they overlap in obvious ways:

- *Majority/minority languages or students.* These terms refer to whether a language is the language of the numerically dominant group in a society or that of a numerically non-dominant group.

- *Dominant/subordinated students or groups.* These terms are often used inter-changeably with *majority/minority* but they refer explicitly to power and status relations between societal groups rather than to the numerical size of the groups. For example, in South Africa under the apartheid regime, the dominant group of 'white' South Africans was numerically much smaller than the 'non-white' groups who were subjected to a pattern of coercive power relations over many generations.
- *Enrichment/remedial programmes.* The term *enrichment bilingual education* refers to programmes that aim to enrich students' educational experience by strongly promoting bilingualism and biliteracy. *Remedial programmes,* by contrast, aim to remediate or compensate for presumed deficits in the language capacities that bilingual children bring to school; for example, their lack of proficiency in the school language.
- *Maintenance/transitional programmes.* Both of these terms are used in the context of programmes intended for minority group students. *Maintenance programmes* aim to help students maintain and develop their proficiency in their home language (L1) while *transitional programmes* are designed to provide a temporary bridge to instruction exclusively through the dominant language of the school and society.
- *Late-exit/early-exit programmes.* Transitional bilingual programmes are often distinguished according to the grade level at which students make the transition from the bilingual programme into mainstream regular monolingual classes. Early-exit programmes are often motivated by the assumption that students will benefit by transferring from the bilingual programme into the mainstream monolingual programme as rapidly as possible. The transition usually occurs by grade 2 or 3. By contrast, late-exit programmes, also known as *developmental programmes* in the United States, transfer students close to the end of elementary school (grade 5 or 6). The assumption is that academic outcomes in both the majority language and students' L1 will benefit from strong promotion of both languages.
- *Immersion/submersion programmes.* The term *immersion* came into wide-spread use in the context of French immersion programmes in Canada during the 1960s and beyond. In these programmes, English L1 students were 'immersed' in a French-language school environment for several years prior to the introduction of formal teaching of English (L1) (see Lambert and Tucker, 1972). These programmes are fully bilingual in so far as they are staffed by bilingual teachers, both languages are used for instructional purposes in a planned and organized way, and they aim to promote proficient bilingualism and biliteracy. They are distinguished from *submersion programmes*, which simply instruct minority children through the dominant language with minimal or no support to enable children to understand the language of instruction and access curricular content (Cohen and Swain, 1976).

As noted above, bilingual education is generally defined in terms of the *means* through which particular educational goals are achieved. Two or more languages are used for instructional purposes in order to promote certain kinds of educational outcomes. When used in this sense, proficiency in two languages is not necessarily a goal of bilingual education. For example, the most common form of bilingual education in the United States over the past 30 years, *transitional bilingual education*, aims only to promote students' proficiency in English. When it is assumed that students have attained sufficient proficiency in the school language to follow instruction in that language, home-language instruction is discontinued and students are transferred into mainstream classes taught exclusively in English.

However, the term *bilingual education* is sometimes defined in relation to *goals*, to refer to educational programmes that are designed to promote bilingual proficiency among students. When used in this broader sense, bilingual education may entail instruction primarily through only one language, as for example when instruction is delivered through a minority language in order to provide students with the maximum opportunity to learn that language. In Canada, for example, many French immersion programmes intended for English-speaking children involve initial instruction exclusively through French. Many English-speaking parents in the Montreal area choose a more radical immersion in French for their children by sending them voluntarily to the French school system. Their goal is to have their children become fully bilingual by means of monolingual instruction through a second language (Macnamara, Svarc and Horner, 1976).

That example illustrates the complexities of attempting to categorize bilingual education programmes in any rigid manner. Nevertheless, typologies can serve a useful purpose in highlighting major issues that need to be addressed in planning and implementing such programmes. Typologies of bilingual education have generated a myriad of different types depending on the combination of programme goals, status of the student group (eg dominant/subordinated, majority/minority, etc), proportion of instructional time through each language, and sociolinguistic and sociopolitical situation in the immediate community and wider society.

The typology of bilingual education proposed by Mackey (1970) remains one of the best known and most elaborate. This typology distinguishes 90 different potential varieties depending on the intersection of home language(s), curricular organization of languages, language(s) of the community and country, as well as the regional and international status of the various languages.

Another useful typology that highlights the intersections between educational and sociopolitical factors in bilingual/multilingual education for both minority and majority students is that developed by Skutnabb-Kangas (1984). This classifies programmes according to *language of instruction, programme target group(s), societal goals of the programme and linguistic aims.*

For our purposes, it is sufficient to distinguish five broad types based on the sociolinguistic characteristics of the language used in the programme and the population groups the programme is intended to serve. Four of these programme types are intended primarily for minority or subordinated group students while the fifth is intended for majority or dominant group students. These distinctions are motivated by pragmatic considerations to facilitate discussion and are not intended to represent rigid categories. Thus, there is overlap among the categories and some bilingual programmes could be located in more than one category.

Type I programmes involve the use of *indigenous or native languages* as mediums of instruction; examples are the various Native American and English language bilingual programmes in the United States (eg McCarty, 1997) and Maori bilingual or immersion programmes in New Zealand (Bishop and Glynn, 1999). The indigenous group has usually been conquered or colonized at some time in the past and the bilingual programmes are often aimed at revival or revitalization of languages that have become endangered.

Type II bilingual programmes involve the use of a *national language* together with a majority or more dominant language. The languages involved usually have long-term status in the society and often some degree of official recognition. In some cases, the national language may be the majority language of the society and is combined in the bilingual programme with a language of wider communication (eg the language of a former colonial power). In the case of Type II programmes involving minority languages, maintenance or revitalization of these languages is usually the primary goal. When the national language is the majority language in a particular context, it is usually used as a transitional or supplementary language prior to the introduction of education predominantly in the language of wider communication. Examples include programmes that use various African languages together with English in South Africa, Gaelic in Ireland and Scotland, and Welsh in Wales, as well as Basque and Catalan in Spain. The right to L1 instruction for official language minorities (both French and English) in Canada constitutes another example. Many other examples exist across the world (Baker and Prys Jones, 1998; Cummins and Corson, 1997; Skutnabb-Kangas, 2000; Zhou, 2001). Some programmes could be classified as either Type I or Type II; for example, the Basques are usually regarded as the indigenous population of the northern parts of the Iberian Peninsula and thus programmes aimed at the revitalization of Basque could also be classified as Type I.

Type III programmes involve *immigrant languages* that are the languages of relatively recent immigrants to a host country. Many of the bilingual programmes in countries such as the United States, the Netherlands, Australia or Sweden fall into this category. Most of these are transitional programmes designed to facilitate students' academic progress. In some situations Type II and Type III programmes merge into one another, as in the case of some Spanish–English bilingual programmes in the United States that may serve both long-term Spanish-speaking groups and more recent immigrant groups. In some educational jurisdictions (eg Sweden, Alberta in Canada) it has become possible for community groups to establish enrichment bilingual programmes involving immigrant languages as a result of policy changes that permit state funding to follow individual students (eg Peura, 2000).

Type IV programmes serve children who are *deaf or hard of hearing*. Bilingual/bicultural programmes for Deaf children are a relatively recent phenomenon. This is not surprising in view of the fact that the manual languages of the Deaf were widely recognized by linguists (and somewhat later by policy makers) as genuine languages only in the 1970s. Bilingual/bicultural programmes involving American Sign Language (ASL) started in North America only in the early 1990s (Gibson, Small and Mason, 1997). Scandinavian countries were more advanced in implementing bilingual/bicultural programmes for Deaf students (Mahshie, 1995). However, bilingual/bicultural programmes for Deaf children are still in their infancy in most places around the world.

Type V programmes are intended for *dominant or majority group students* and aim to develop bilingual and biliteracy skills among such students. French immersion programmes in Canada and dual language programmes in the United States are examples of Type V. Dual language programmes in the United States also fall into the categories of Type II or Type III since they also serve linguistic minority students together with English L1 students, with the goal of promoting bilingualism and biliteracy for both groups. The European Schools model (Beardsmore, 1993; Skutnabb-Kangas, 1995), which involves instruction through four languages at various points in the students' school career, also qualifies as Type V, as do Swedish immersion programmes for Finnish students in Finland (Buss and Laurén, 1995).

Although research and formal documentation of bilingual education is a relatively recent phenomenon, bilingual education itself has been implemented at least from Greek and Roman times (Lewis, 1976). Prior to the First World War, bilingual education involving German and some other languages was widely implemented in the United States (Kloss, 1977). Currently, some form of bilingual education is implemented in the vast majority of countries around the world (Baker and Prys Jones, 1998). In the next section, psycholinguistic issues related to the outcomes of bilingual education are discussed.

## Linguistic and academic outcomes of bilingual programmes

### Alternative theoretical propositions

All bilingual programmes necessarily entail less instructional time through the majority or dominant language of the society than is the case with monolingual programmes conducted through that language. Thus, regardless of bilingual programme type (I–V above), parents and policy makers have often been concerned that spending instructional time through a minority language will result in lower achievement in the majority language. If we dilute instructional exposure to the majority language, then surely students' mastery of that language will be adversely affected.

This line of reasoning has been termed the *time-on-task* hypothesis and has been used to argue against bilingual programmes for linguistic minority students in the United States (eg Imhoff, 1990; Porter, 1990). In recent years, referendums have been passed in California (June 1998) and Arizona (November 2000) that have attempted to eliminate bilingual programmes for linguistic minority students. The time-on-task hypothesis has been persuasive to many policy makers and members of the general public because it seems intuitively logical that academic and linguistic outcomes will be influenced by the amount of instructional time spent through a language. Imhoff expresses the argument as follows:

> Bilingual-education advocates also tend to dismiss the idea that practice makes perfect, expressed in educational terms as 'time on task,' and hold instead that non-English-speaking students will learn English better if less time is spent teaching it. (1990: 51)

However, as documented below, research data are unequivocal in showing that academic development in the majority language does not suffer as a result of bilingual instruction – assuming, of course, that the bilingual programme is well implemented. So why is it that less instruction in the majority language results in no adverse effects on students' development of mastery of that language? The theoretical proposition that attempts to account for these data has been termed the *interdependence hypothesis* (Cummins, 1981):

> To the extent that instruction in Lx is effective in promoting proficiency in Lx, transfer of this proficiency to Ly will occur provided there is adequate exposure to Ly (either in school or environment) and adequate motivation to learn Ly. (1981: 29)

In concrete terms, what this hypothesis means is that in, for example, a Spanish–English bilingual programme, Spanish instruction that develops Spanish reading and writing skills (for either Spanish L1 or L2 speakers) is not just developing *Spanish* skills, but is also developing a deeper conceptual and linguistic proficiency that is strongly related to the development of literacy in the majority language (English). In other words, although the surface aspects (eg pronunciation, fluency, etc) of different languages are clearly separate, there is an underlying cognitive/academic proficiency that is common across languages. This common underlying proficiency makes possible the transfer of cognitive/academic or literacy-related concepts and skills from one language to another.

In general, transfer is more likely to occur from the minority to the majority language because of the typically greater exposure to literacy in the majority language outside of school and the strong social pressure to learn it. However, when the sociolinguistic conditions are right, two-way transfer across languages *does* occur. This has been demonstrated in both minority contexts (Verhoeven, 1991) and majority contexts (Cashion and Eagan, 1990).

The empirical data from bilingual programmes in a wide variety of sociolinguistic contexts overwhelmingly refute the time-on-task hypothesis and support the interdependence hypothesis. Illustrative data from the five types of bilingual programmes outlined above are reviewed below.

## Type I. Programmes involving indigenous languages

Among the major goals of bilingual education programmes for indigenous students are the enhancement of cultural pride, development of fluency in the indigenous language and academic achievement in the majority language. Although such programmes have been implemented widely in North and South America as well as in Australia and New Zealand (Bishop and Glynn, 1999; Harris, 1990; Hornberger, 1988; McCarty, 1997; Modiano, 1973), relatively few outside of North America have been formally evaluated with respect to how well they attain these goals. The US programme evaluations reviewed by McCarty (1997) show a consistent pattern of considerable success in promoting proficiency in the indigenous language at no cost to students' proficiency in English. She cites, for example, a Navajo immersion programme at Fort Defiance, Arizona, consisting of more than half the time between K and grade 3 in Navajo followed by one hour of daily Navajo instruction in grade 4. The grades 3 and 4 immersion students performed better than the comparison group in monolingual English classes on tests of Navajo ability, English writing and mathematics. They also performed as well as monolingual English students on measures of English academic achievement.

A similar pattern emerges from a Mohawk partial immersion programme in the Kahnawake school system near Montreal in Canada (Lambert *et al*, 1984). The research focused on students in grades 1 and 3 whose parents had enrolled their children, starting at kindergarten, in the programme and compared these children to equivalent Native children in the same school but in English-only instruction.

Students in the immersion programme were individually matched with the control students with respect to both vocabulary and non-verbal reasoning and compared on end-of-year achievement in English and content areas. At the grade 1 level, children in the immersion programme who had spent more than half their instructional time through Mohawk performed at a significantly higher level than the control group in mathematics, social studies and language skills, with no differences in reading comprehension. At the grade 3 level, no differences were apparent between immersion and control students on any of the measures. At this level the amount of Mohawk was reduced to 90 minutes per day (compared to 3.5 hours for English), and French was also taught as a subject. The authors interpret these results as follows:

> This means that the immersion and control pupils, although receiving different amounts of English instructional time, are essentially alike on a large array of English language tests, ranging from measures of English reading skills and language competence, to science, math, and social studies. In other words, the greater instructional time devoted to Mohawk apparently has not disrupted the English language and academic development of the immersion pupils at the grade 3 level. This is so even when very careful controls are applied to equate immersion and control pupils on basic reasoning skills and vocabulary skill. (1984: 12–13)

The same pattern of positive outcomes with respect to promotion of cultural pride and indigenous language development at no cost to achievement in the majority language emerges from a large majority of other programme evaluations (eg Kamana and Wilson, 1996; Modiano, 1973). Clearly, these data are consistent with the interdependence rather than the time-on-task hypothesis.

## Type II. Programmes involving national languages

Bilingual programmes that involve languages with some formal or informal long-term political status in the society have been extensively implemented in countries around the world. These situations often involve a minority language together with a more powerful majority language but they also include the use of the majority language in a society together with a language of wider communication (often the language of a previous colonial power). Many bilingual programmes in Africa fall into this category. The *Encyclopedia of Language and Education*, volume 5 (Cummins and Corson, 1997), which is focused on bilingual education, reviews programmes that fall into this category in African countries, the Basque Country of Spain, Slovenia, Friesland, Ireland, Scotland, Wales, Italy, Germany, China, Canada, Singapore, Malaysia and Indonesia. Many other countries and languages could be added to this list (Baker and Prys Jones, 1998). The outcomes of these programmes show clearly that minority languages can be used as mediums of instruction in school for a significant proportion of the school day at no cost to students' proficiency in the majority or educationally dominant language. Three examples will illustrate the pattern.

Williams (1996) examined the impact of language of instruction on reading ability in L1 and L2 in Malawi and Zambia. In Malawi, Chichewa is the language of instruction for years 1–4 of primary school, with English taught as a subject. In Zambia, English is the medium of instruction, with one of seven local languages taught as a subject. Williams administered an English reading test and a local-language reading test (Chichewa in Malawi and the almost identical Nyanja in Zambia) to year 5 learners in six schools in each country. He reported no significant difference in English reading ability between students in each country, despite the huge difference in amount of English instruction. However, large differences emerged in favour of Malawi in local-language reading ability. He concludes that these results 'are consistent with research on minority groups suggesting that instruction in L1 reading leads to improved results in L1 with no retardation in L2 reading' (1996: 183).

John Macnamara's (1966) nationally representative survey of bilingual education in Ireland appears initially inconsistent with the bulk of bilingual programme evaluations. Macnamara interpreted his data as showing that grade 5 Irish students taught predominantly through the medium of Irish performed less well than comparison students in problem arithmetic, although there was no difference in their ability in calculation. The difference between these two types of test is that problem arithmetic involves linguistic presentation of problems to be solved whereas calculation just requires numerical problems to be solved. Macnamara also argued that the significantly lower performance of Irish students on English achievement in comparison to the test norming group (a UK sample) represented an indictment of the policy of spending a considerable proportion of instructional time teaching Irish (as either a medium or a subject of instruction). He proposed that there is a 'balance effect' operating in the teaching of language. This is a precursor of the *time-on-task* hypothesis and entails similar predictions: if more time is spent on one language less is left for the other and achievement will suffer.

Unfortunately, Macnamara's interpretation of his findings does not accurately represent what his data show. The finding that students in all-Irish immersion schools (80 per cent Irish, 20 per cent English) performed more poorly in problem arithmetic than comparison groups can be attributed to the fact that these students were tested through their weaker language. The effects of testing through a weaker language are confounded with the effects of instruction through a weaker language. Macnamara's data also show that students instructed in all-Irish schools (80 per cent Irish-medium instruction) were performing at the same level in English academic achievement as all other groups of students in Irish schools, including those whose instruction was predominantly through English. Thus, his data show clearly that minority languages can be promoted educationally at no cost to proficiency in the majority language. The fact that Irish students, in general, performed more poorly than students in the test norming sample in the United Kingdom can be attributed to a variety of factors (eg curriculum differences, test validity for a sample that is not part of the norming group) (Cummins, 1977).

A series of evaluations of Basque–Spanish bilingual programmes in the Basque Country of Spain (Gabina *et al*, 1986; Sierra and Olaziregi, 1989, 1991) similarly showed a minimal relationship between instructional time spent through the medium of a majority language (in this case Spanish) and academic achievement in that language. The three studies were similar in design in that each compared the Basque and Spanish achievement of elementary school students in three programme types:

- Spanish language instruction with Basque taught as a second language (Model A);
- Spanish and Basque both used for instruction about 50 per cent of the time (Model B); and
- Basque as the language of instruction with Spanish taught as a subject (Model D).

Students in Model D came from both Basque- and Spanish-speaking homes, whereas the majority of students in the other two programmes came from Spanish-speaking homes. In all three studies, stratified random samples were chosen that were representative of the population of the Basque Country.

A similar pattern of results emerged in the three studies and at both grade levels studied (grades 2 and 5). Extremely large differences were evident between Models D and A in command of both oral and written Basque, with Model B in an intermediate position. With respect to Spanish, however, the programme differences at both grade levels were minimal. For example, in the second study involving grade 5 students (Sierra and Olaziregi, 1989) there was only a six-point difference in overall Spanish scores between Models A and D (79.81, standard deviation 7.99, versus 73.77, standard deviation 9.31), compared to a 56-point difference in Basque scores (23.17 versus 79.04).

These findings are consistent with other bilingual programme evaluations in showing that instruction through the medium of a minority language for a substantial part of the school day entails no long-term academic disadvantage with respect to achievement in the majority language.

## Type III. Programmes involving immigrant languages

Studies from the Netherlands and from the United States can be used to illustrate the pattern of findings that emerge from programmes intended to address the learning needs of first and second generation immigrant students. Unlike most Type I and II programmes, these programmes focus primarily on achievement in the majority language rather than on the development of both languages.

Verhoeven reported the results of two experimental programmes in transitional L1 literacy instruction with Turkish-background students in the Netherlands. He summarizes the results as follows:

> With respect to linguistic measures, it was found that a strong emphasis on instruction in L1 does lead to better literacy results in L1 with no retardation of literacy results in L2. On the contrary, there was a tendency for L2 literacy results in the transitional classes to be better than in the regular submersion classes. Moreover, it was found that the transitional approach tended to develop a more positive orientation toward literacy in both L1 and L2. (1991: 72)

Verhoeven also reported support for the interdependence hypothesis in so far as literacy skills being developed in one language strongly predicted corresponding skills in the second language acquired later in time.

In the United States, Ramírez (1992) reported the results of a large-scale longitudinal study involving 2,352 Latino elementary schoolchildren in nine school districts, 51 schools and 554 classrooms. It compared the academic progress of children in three programme types:

- English immersion, involving almost exclusive use of English throughout elementary school;
- early-exit bilingual in which Spanish was used for about one-third of the time in kindergarten and first grade with a rapid phase-out thereafter; and
- late-exit bilingual that used primarily Spanish instruction in kindergarten, with English used for about one-third of the time in grades 1 and 2, half the time in grade 3, and about 60 per cent of the time thereafter.

One of the three late-exit programmes in the study (site G) was an exception to this pattern in that students abruptly underwent transition into primarily English instruction at the end of grade 2 and English was used almost exclusively in grades 5 and 6. In other words, this 'late-exit' programme is similar in its implementation to early-exit.

The comparison of immersion and early-exit programmes showed that by the end of grade 3 students were performing at comparable levels in English language and reading skills, as well as in mathematics. Students in each of these programme types progressed academically at about the same rate as students in the general population but the gap between their performance and that of the general population remained large.

In contrast to students in the immersion and early-exit programmes, the late-exit students in the two sites that continued strongly to emphasize primary language instruction throughout elementary school (at close to 40 per cent of instructional time) were catching up academically to students in the general population. This is despite the fact that these students received considerably less instruction in English than students in early-exit and immersion programmes and proportionately more of their families came from the lowest income levels than was the case for students in the other two programmes. It was also found that parental involvement (eg help with homework) was greater in the late-exit sites, presumably because teachers were fluent in Spanish and students were bringing work home in Spanish.

Differences were observed among the three late-exit sites with respect to mathematics, English language (ie skills such as punctuation, capitalization, etc) and English reading. Students in the two late-exit sites that continued L1 instruction through grade 6 made significantly better academic progress than those in site G who were transferred early into all-English instruction.

The report concludes that:

> Students who were provided with a substantial and consistent primary language development program learned mathematics, English language, and English reading skills as fast or faster than the norming population used in this study. As their growth in these academic skills is atypical of disadvantaged youth, it

14  JIM CUMMINS

provides support for the efficacy of primary language development in facilitating
the acquisition of English language skills. (Ramírez, 1992: 38–39)

These data are consistent with the findings of other large-scale research on
bilingual education for minority students conducted in the United States (eg
Thomas and Collier, 1997).

## Type IV. Programmes involving manual sign languages

Although manual sign languages were widely used as mediums of instruction
in Europe and North America in the 19th century, they were suppressed in
favour of an oralist approach after the 1880 International Congress of
Educators of the Deaf in Milan, Italy. Gibson, Small and Mason summarize the
effects of this change in policy:

> The suppression of sign language and decline in the number of Deaf educators
> had deleterious effects on the academic, social, cognitive, emotional, cultural and
> linguistic development of Deaf individuals and on the Deaf community. Course
> content was presented in spoken English which could not possibly be fully
> accessible to Deaf students and children's academic achievements were limited
> by and measured by their oral English ability. (1997: 232)

By the 1970s, oralist approaches had begun to give way to 'total communication' programmes that used manual coding systems based on the structure
of the spoken language. These have been widely rejected by Deaf communities, and in recent years bilingual/bicultural programmes involving the
natural sign languages of Deaf communities have been instituted in many
countries (Gibson, Small and Mason, 1997; Mahshie, 1995). Because of the
recency of these programmes and the considerable implementation challenges they entail (eg availability of teachers proficient in sign language,
curriculum development, etc), formal research on their efficacy is limited.
However, according to Gibson, Small and Mason, 'recent results from Sweden
and Denmark demonstrate that the reading, writing and overall academic
levels of their Deaf students in bilingual programmes are on a par with their
hearing peers' (1997: 236).

## Type V. Programmes intended for dominant/majority group students

Enrichment bilingual programmes intended for dominant or majority group
students came to international prominence as a result of the extensive research
on French immersion programmes in Canada. These programmes began
during the 1960s and involved use of the French language as a medium of
instruction for elementary school students whose home language was
English. However, as Johnson and Swain (1997) point out, there is nothing
new in the phenomenon of 'immersing' students in a second language
instructional environment. In fact, throughout the history of formal education

the use of an L2 as a medium of instruction has been the rule rather than the exception. The Canadian French immersion programmes, however, were the first to be subjected to intensive long-term research evaluation, although some large-scale research had been undertaken in other contexts prior to the Canadian experience (eg Macnamara, 1966; Malherbe, 1946).

Three major variants of French immersion programmes have been implemented: early immersion starting in kindergarten or occasionally grade 1; middle immersion starting in grades 4 or 5; and late immersion starting in grade 7. All are characterized by at least 50 per cent instruction through the target language (French) in the early stages. For example, early immersion usually involves 100 per cent French in kindergarten and grade 1 with one period of English-language arts introduced in grades 2, 3 or sometimes as late as grade 4. By grades 5 and 6 the instructional time is divided equally between the two languages and usually the amount of time through French declines to about 40 per cent in grades 7, 8 and 9, with further reduction at the high school level as a result of a greater variety of course offerings in English than in French.

Consistent findings have been obtained from French immersion programme evaluations across Canada. In early immersion programmes, students gain fluency and literacy in French at no apparent cost to their English academic skills. Within a year of the introduction of formal English language, arts students catch up in most aspects of English standardized test performance. Usually students require additional time to catch up in English spelling, but by grade 5 there are normally no differences in English test performance between immersion students and comparison groups whose instruction has been totally through English. There is also no evidence of any long-term lag in mastery of subject matter taught through French in early, middle or late immersion programmes.

With respect to French skills, students' receptive skills in French are better developed (in relation to native speaker norms) than are their expressive skills. By the end of elementary school (grade 6) students are close to the level of native speakers in understanding and reading of French but there are significant gaps between them and native speakers in spoken and written French. The gap is particularly evident in grammatical aspects of the language (Swain, 1997).

Similarly positive outcomes from immersion and dual language programmes for majority language students have been reported in many contexts ranging from Swedish immersion programmes in Finland (Buss and Laurén, 1995) to English immersion in Japan (Bostwick, 1999; Downes, 2001). Less intensive forms of bilingual education for majority students have also been implemented. For example, the so-called German model of bilingual education involves teaching one or two subjects at the secondary level through a second language (French or English) (Masch, 1993).

In all of these programmes, the amount of instructional time devoted to the majority language (students' L1) is largely unrelated to academic outcomes in that language. This pattern is consistent with the interdependence hypothesis and clearly inconsistent with the time-on-task hypothesis.

## Conclusion

Current trends in the implementation and expansion of bilingual programmes can be understood in the context of *globalization*, a term never far from the front pages of newspapers these days. It evokes strong positive or negative feelings depending upon whether it is being praised by the business community for opening up world markets to more extensive trade or condemned by those who associate the term with the dramatically widening gap between rich and poor nations and people.

Several aspects of globalization are contributing directly to the expansion, and controversy over, bilingual education. One aspect is the rapid spread of English as a global lingua franca. Because of this, many parents (and policy makers) in non-English-speaking countries see English proficiency as crucial to their children's prospects of social and economic mobility. This has resulted in the growth of all forms of teaching English, including bilingual and/or immersion approaches that promise greater proficiency than simply teaching the language as a subject.

Another aspect of globalization that has important implications for educators is the increasing movement of people from one country to another. Population mobility increases the economic and personal utility of bilingual and multilingual skills, a phenomenon that has resulted in increased interest in bilingual and immersion education.

Population mobility also increases the number of children from linguistic minority groups in countries around the world. For many of these groups, bilingual education has emerged as a potentially effective approach to promoting academic achievement while at the same time encouraging maintenance of home languages. However, in a number of countries bilingual education has become embroiled in volatile debates regarding the overall goals of education for minority groups. Should society adopt a pluralist approach that encourages children and communities to maintain and develop the minority language and culture in addition to acquiring the majority language, or should schools promote the assimilation of immigrants and encourage minority languages and cultures to atrophy? In these contexts, bilingual programmes are frequently seen as valuable and worthy of public funding when they are directed towards the acquisition of additional languages by dominant-group students but highly problematic when the target group is a minority or subordinated group.

A final aspect of globalization that has implications for the spread of bilingual programmes is the dramatically increased access to information available in countries throughout the world. Thus, research data on immersion and bilingual programmes are being disseminated and discussed at a policy level, and among parents, much more than was the case 20 years ago. The implications of research conducted in one context for the implementation of programmes in other contexts are not always clear, but at least options that may not have been considered before are now on the table in many countries. This research is sufficiently clear-cut in its overall trends to open up the possibility that debates on the sociopolitical dimensions of bilingual education will be more informed than has often been the case in the past.

## References

Baker, C and Prys Jones, S (1998) *Encyclopedia of Bilingualism and Bilingual Education*, Multilingual Matters, Clevedon, UK

Beardsmore, H B (1993) The European schools model, in *European Models of Bilingual Education*, ed H B Beardsmore, pp 121–54, Multilingual Matters, Clevedon, UK

Bishop, R and Glynn, R (1999) *Culture Counts: Changing power relations in education*, Dunmore Press, Palmerston North, New Zealand

Bostwick, R M (1999) A study of an elementary English language immersion school in Japan, unpublished doctoral dissertation, Temple University, Philadelphia, PA

Buss, M and Laurén, C (1995) Language immersion: teaching and second language acquisition: from Canada to Europe, *Proceedings of the University of Vaasa Research Papers, Tutkimuksia no 192*, University of Vaasa, Vaasa, Finland

Cashion, M and Eagan, R (1990) Spontaneous reading and writing in English by students in total French immersion: summary of final report, *English Quarterly*, **22** (1–2), pp 30–44

Cohen, A D and Swain, M (1976) Bilingual education: the immersion model in the North American context, *TESOL Quarterly*, **14** (2), pp 45–53

Crawford, J (2000) *At War with Diversity: US language policy in an age of anxiety*, Multilingual Matters, Clevedon, UK

Cummins, J (1977) Immersion education in Ireland: a critical review of Macnamara's findings, *Working Papers on Bilingualism*, **13**, pp 121–29

Cummins, J (1981) The role of primary language development in promoting educational success for language minority students, in *Schooling and Language Minority Students: A theoretical framework*, ed California State Department of Education, pp 3–49, Evaluation, Dissemination and Assessment Center, California State University, Los Angeles, CA

Cummins, J and Corson, D (eds) (1997) *Encyclopedia of Language and Education*, vol 5, *Bilingual Education*, Kluwer Academic Publishers, Dordrecht, the Netherlands

Downes, S (2001) Sense of Japanese cultural identity within an English partial immersion programme: should parents worry?, *International Journal of Bilingual Education and Bilingualism*, **4** (3), pp 165–80

Gabina, J J *et al* (1986) *EIFE: Influence of factors on the learning of Basque*, Central Publications Service of the Basque Country, Gasteiz

Gibson, H, Small, A and Mason, D (1997) Deaf bilingual bicultural education, in *Encyclopedia of Language and Education*, vol 5, *Bilingual Education*, ed J Cummins and D Corson, pp 231–40, Kluwer Academic Publishers, Dordrecht, the Netherlands

Harris, S (1990) *Two Way Aboriginal Schooling: Education and cultural survival*, Aboriginal Studies Press, Canberra

Hornberger, N H (1988) *Bilingual Education and Language Maintenance: A southern Peruvian Quecha case*, Foris, Dordrecht, the Netherlands

Imhoff, G (1990) The position of US English on bilingual education, in *English Plus: Issues in bilingual education*, eds C B Cazden and C E Snow, pp 48–61, Sage, Newbury Park, CA

Johnson, R K and Swain, M (eds) (1997) *Immersion Education: International perspectives*, Cambridge University Press, Cambridge

Kamana, K and Wilson, W H (1996) Hawaiian language programs, in *Stabilizing Indigenous Languages*, ed G Cantoni, pp 153–56, Northern Arizona University, Flagstaff, AZ

Kloss, H (1977) *The American Bilingual Tradition*, Newbury House, Rowley, MA

Lambert, W E and Tucker, G R (1972) *Bilingual Education of Children: The St. Lambert Experiment*, Newbury House, Rowley, MA

Lambert, W E, Genesee, F, Holobow, N E and McGilly, C (1984) *An Evaluation of a Partial Mohawk Immersion Program in the Kahnawake Schools*, McGill University, Montreal

Lewis, E G (1976) Bilingualism and bilingual education: the ancient world to the Renaissance, in *Bilingual Education: An international sociological perspective*, ed J A Fishman, pp 150–200, Newbury House, Rowley, MA

McCarty, T L (1997) American Indian, Alaska Native, and Native Hawaiian bilingual education, in *Encyclopedia of Language and Education*, vol 5, *Bilingual Education*, eds J Cummins and D Corson, pp 45–56, Kluwer Academic Publishers, Dordrecht, the Netherlands

Mackey, W F (1970) A typology of bilingual education, *Foreign Language Annals*, **3**, pp 596–608

Macnamara, J (1966) *Bilingualism and Primary Education*, Edinburgh University Press, Edinburgh

MacNamara, J, Svarc, J and Horner, S (1976) Attending a primary school of the other language in Montreal, in *The Bilingual Child*, ed A Simoes, Academic Press, New York

Mahshie, S (1995) *Educating Deaf Children Bilingually: With insights and applications from Sweden and Denmark* Gallaudet University, Washington, DC

Malherbe, E G (1946) *The Bilingual School*, Bilingual School Association, Johannesburg

Masch, N (1993) The German model of bilingual education: an administrator's perspective, in *European Models of Bilingual Education*, ed H B Beardsmore, pp 155–72, Multilingual Matters, Clevedon, UK

Modiano, N (1973) *Indian Education in the Chiapas Highlands*, Holt, Rinehart & Winston, New York

Peura, M (2000) Creating a successful minority school, in *Rights to Language: Equity, power, and education*, ed R Phillipson, pp 219–26, Lawrence Erlbaum, Mahwah, NJ

Porter, R P (1990) *Forked Tongue: The politics of bilingual education*, Basic Books, New York

Ramírez, J D (1992) Executive summary, *Bilingual Research Journal*, **16**, pp 1–62

Sierra, J and Olaziregi, I (1989) *EIFE 2: Influence of factors on the learning of Basque*, Central Publications Service of the Basque Country, Gasteiz

Sierra, J and Olaziregi, I (1991) *EIFE 3: Influence of factors on the learning of Basque: Study of the models A, B and D in second year Basic General Education*, Central Publications Service of the Basque Country, Gasteiz

Skutnabb-Kangas, T (1984) *Bilingualism or Not: The education of minorities*, Multilingual Matters, Clevedon, UK

Skutnabb-Kangas, T (ed) (1995) *Multilingualism for All*, Swets & Zeitlinger, Lisse, the Netherlands

Skutnabb-Kangas, T (2000) *Linguistic Genocide in Education – or Worldwide Diversity and Human Rights*, Lawrence Erlbaum, Mahwah, NJ

Swain, M (1997) French immersion programs in Canada, in *Encyclopedia of Language and Education*, vol 5, *Bilingual Education*, eds J Cummins and D Corson, pp 261–70, Kluwer Academic Publishers, Dordrecht, the Netherlands

Thomas, W P and Collier, V (1997) *School Effectiveness for Language Minority Students*, National Clearinghouse for Bilingual Education, Washington, DC

Verhoeven, L (1991) Acquisition of biliteracy, in *Reading in Two Languages*, vol 8, eds J H Hulstijn and J F Matter, pp 61–74, AILA Review, AILA, Amsterdam

Williams, E (1996) Reading in two languages at Year 5 in African primary schools, *Applied Linguistics*, **17** (2), pp 183–209

Zhou, M (2001) The politics of bilingual education and educational levels in ethnic minority communities in China, *International Journal of Bilingual Education and Bilingualism*, **4** (2), pp 125–49

## 2. Remedial or radical? Second language support for curriculum learning

Jill Bourne

### Introduction

As the different chapters in this book illustrate, multilingualism is the norm in most countries of the world. It is increasingly likely that at some stage of their career, teachers will work with students who have limited previous experience of the language of the school curriculum. At the same time, their classrooms may contain children who have grown up confidently speaking two or more languages, and switching between them for different purposes and in different contexts. Yet these special strengths of young bilinguals are too rarely recognized in the classroom, or built on in supporting the development of the second language and literacy of their more newly arrived peers. It has been far more common to define the needs of minority group children whose home language differs from that of their school in terms of a deficit, sometimes in need of urgent remediation, requiring the 'silver bullet' of intensive language classes away from their peers. In this chapter I pose the following questions. First, in making provision in schools for second language learners from minority linguistic group backgrounds, should the emphasis be on setting up remedial programmes, or is a more radical programme required, one that entails a reappraisal of all mainstream 'good practice' and of the role of the 'normal' class and subject teacher? And second, using the terminology explained by Cummins (this volume, Chapter 1), how might it be possible to integrate supportive 'immersion' strategies for minority second language learners into the mainstream classroom, while avoiding the danger of 'submersion', where the learner is simply left to sink or swim?

In discussing these questions, I have drawn on a range of international examples, although taken mainly from the English-speaking world. As in foreign language teaching (Byram, this volume, Chapter 5), the literature on provision of English as a second language dominates research on the development of second language teaching methodology globally, not least because of the rapid spread of English through education systems across the world, together with the greater possibilities of publication and dissemination in English.

## Why is second language support necessary?

The scale and rapidity of the changes in demography that are facing school systems in the Western world as a result of globalization are illustrated by the example of the United States. Census figures show that between 1980 and 1990 the population speaking a language other than English at home grew by 38 per cent, compared to a total population growth of only 10 per cent. One in every six middle and high school students now speaks a language other than English at home, is a newcomer to the United States, or both. Nor is this simply a bilingual situation that might be addressed by increasing bilingual education; although the majority of new arrivals are Spanish speakers, others are drawn from the former Soviet Union, Iran, Poland, Germany and Portugal, from Vietnam, the Philippines, Korea and other parts of Asia, from the Pacific Islands, and Arabic speakers from the Middle East and North Africa (Waggoner, 1999).

The need to address the academic needs of second language learners in multilingual contexts is not just an issue for the West, and not simply an issue of population mobility, but also a consequence of policies of nation building around a selected 'national language'. In Mozambique, for example, the national language is Portuguese, but this is estimated to be a first language for only 1 per cent of its multilingual population, with students from many different local language backgrounds sharing schools in urban areas (Norton Pierce and Ridge, 1997). Similar situations exist throughout Africa and parts of Asia.

The internationally agreed UNESCO 1990 Jomtien Declaration on Education for All, reaffirmed in the Dakar Framework for Action (WEF, 2000), recommends education in the mother tongue or other familiar language in the initial years of schooling, before transition to a second language if necessary. However, there is otherwise no internationally agreed language policy, with the choice of the language medium for education seen as the prerogative of the nation-state. A fortunate few are able to access mother tongue or bilingual education at least in the early years of schooling, if not throughout their education, but for large numbers of students, across the world, the majority of their learning takes place in a second, or third, language.

The linguistic diversity of many schools and the dispersal of language speakers across geographical areas make formal approaches to bilingual education (see Cummins, this volume, Chapter 1) impractical in many contexts worldwide. Even in the United States, where there has been considerable research interest in bilingualism and where there are many schools with substantial numbers of shared Spanish/English-language speakers, bilingual education touches the lives of relatively few learners. To teach the full minority school age population bilingually, even if politically acceptable, would require a massive teacher recruitment programme (Macias, 1989). In California, where the Spanish-speaking population has reached a majority, there is a 58 per cent shortfall of bilingual Spanish–English teachers for the Spanish-speaking school population (Gold, 1997). The lack of qualified bilingual teachers is likely to be even greater in relation to the variety of languages of Asian origin now widely spoken by US students. Yet Merino (1999), using data from national school enrolment information, claims that of the 40 million schoolchildren in the United States, almost 2 million, or 5 per cent, are 'limited in their proficiency in English'. Most of these students will continue receiving instruction through the medium of English from their regular 'mainstream' classroom teachers for the greater part of the school day.

Whatever the strength of arguments for bilingual education, learning through a second language is often the choice of the elite, as well as a necessity for many of their poorer peers within most national education systems. Parents act as 'invisible planners' (Pakir, this volume, Chapter 19), using available economic muscle to select an education for their children in the language medium they feel will benefit their future chances most, as the following dialogue from South Africa suggests:

*Woman*: I want he must go to a proper English school. I do not want Xhosa school...
*Researcher*: But not to forget Xhosa, because in Xhosa are his roots?
*Woman*: Yes, in Xhosa are his roots, he must have a little bit of Xhosa, but a lot of English. Because you can't get anywhere in life without it. (Prinsloo and Kell, 1997)

## Avoiding stereotypes

It is important for educational researchers and policy makers not to adopt a monolingual perspective and assume that operating in a second or third language is necessarily difficult and problematic. As Crystal put it, 'Multilingualism is the natural way of life for hundreds of millions all over the world' (1995: 360). Graddol (1997) argues that globally there are now more second language speakers of English than those born into families using it as their main medium of communication. New arrivals from different parts of the world who enter an English-speaking environment such as the United Kingdom, Australia or the United States bring with them different levels of contact with and proficiency in English, in different domains of use, depending on their experience of English in communication in their daily lives. Studies of educational outcomes also show that while certain linguistic minorities underachieve in relation to 'majority group' peers from the same socio-economic background, other groups achieve at the same or higher levels (Vallet and Caille, 1999; Gillborn and Gipps, 1996).

Length of settlement in a particular language-dominant environment, previous level of education, age, gender, the closeness of the ethnic community within the neighbourhood, and the educational history of family elders are just some of the factors that play a part in creating diversity within as well as between language minority groups and that seem to play out differently within different minority communities. In UK Asian communities, there is evidence to suggest that over half of 16- to 29-year-old pupils of Indian and African-Asian origin, and nearly half of those of Pakistani background, have English as their main spoken language, although tending still to use a familial language in speaking to the older generation. In contrast, only a fifth of another minority group, those of Bangladeshi origin, currently had English as their main language (Madood *et al*, 1997).

These differences between large and well-established minority groups are amplified when we come to look at the diversity of language use and language needs among more recently arrived linguistic minority groups such as asylum seekers and refugees from areas of the world suffering war and famine. These new arrivals come from a range of different socio-economic and educational backgrounds. Some may be highly educated, while others have missed out on years of schooling, and so have very different needs.

Ethnic identities, educational experiences and linguistic strengths in the context of globalization and population mobility, then, are highly complex. Statistics on numbers of minority ethnic students should therefore be treated with care in determining the extent of second language teaching provision that may be required. It is important to avoid viewing language minority students stereotypically as having second language learning needs above and beyond the usual language and literacy development needs of their majority ethnic group peers, or as potentially the objects of special policy and provision. Instead, it is important to recognize the great diversity of origins, social dialects and socio-economic positions that impact on the educational attainment of all students.

## Making provision for second language learners

The diversity in levels of receptive and productive knowledge of the language of the school curriculum makes the setting up of special language teaching classes for minority group, immigrant and refugee children problematic. Their needs to develop the language of the school curriculum are to varying extents shared with peers from the dominant language community itself. Their diversity of backgrounds makes the formation of homogenous groups within schools for clearly targeted 'second language teaching' difficult to implement. Structured traditional foreign-language teaching curricula and methods are inappropriate given this mixed group's varied levels of understanding and skill, and the urgency of their need to acquire access to the school curriculum, no matter how intensive the course. There is simply not the time available for early-stage second language students to first master the language before tackling the school curriculum. Research suggests it takes a beginner five to seven years to reach the language level required to tackle the school curriculum on a level with their peers (Cummins, 1984; Collier, 1987). By that time, many older students would be beyond school leaving age, while younger students would be five years behind their peers, with little hope of catching up.

Nevertheless, the setting up of separate language classes for second language learners has tended to be the first resort of many schools worldwide when faced with increasing numbers of students with limited proficiency in the language of the school system. However, this has proved to be a problematic strategy in raising the attainment of minority group students. Minicucci and Olsen (1992), in a study of 19 high schools in the United States, found that where immigrant students were segregated from other pupils, they were offered fewer and inferior academic opportunities, focusing almost exclusively on English as a second language. Similarly, in the United Kingdom, the Commission for Racial Equality (1986) found that separate induction arrangements for newly arrived pupils were discriminatory in effect, lowering attainment by limiting pupils' access to school curriculum subject areas and specialist teachers. Not providing any language support, however, would risk failure in the school system. Educationalists have therefore looked for ways in which students can be supported to access the full school curriculum while at the same time developing their second language skills.

Since the 1980s, theories of second language acquisition and teaching have suggested that it is not necessary for learners to follow a structured, sequential language learning syllabus, but that language learning is more efficient when learners focus on meaning rather than form, as long as the 'input' they receive is made comprehensible to them and where they have opportunities to engage in meaningful language use in a relaxed environment (Krashen, 1982). More cautiously, others have argued also for the back-up of supporting sessions focused on language form and structure for developing 'accuracy' as well as 'fluency' (Brumfit, 1984).

Initially, these theories tended to focus more on spoken than written language. This connected with classroom teachers' concerns in engaging with newly arrived and early-stage language learners in their classrooms, with a focus on providing learners with the basic tools of communication necessary for effective classroom management by teachers. Second language, or 'reception', classes aimed to give students enough basic spoken language to 'get by' in the second language environment of the school. However, Cummins (1984) argued influentially that surface fluency in spoken, everyday language is not enough for learners to succeed in curriculum learning, but that they need ongoing support throughout the school years to acquire the cognitive, academic language proficiency required by school curriculum subjects. As first language speakers also need to develop the new abstract and written forms of the subject curriculum (Christie, this volume, Chapter 7), this opened the door to the return of second language learners from special and separate second language learning classes to language learning through the curriculum in a supportive, language-aware mainstream classroom, alongside their peers.

Critiques of separate 'remedial' forms of second language provision have led many educationalists to transfer their focus from second language learners themselves to reforming the wider context in which those learners must operate: the mainstream school itself. In the United Kingdom, influential strategies for integrating second language learners into the mainstream school curriculum, alongside their English language peers, had emerged by the early 1980s, led from the 'grass roots'. Since the early 1980s, groups of teachers have sought inclusive ways of teaching for their 'mixed ability' classes in primary and comprehensive schools. Teacher-produced materials were often not formally published, but spread through newsletters, in-service sessions and national and international conference presentations. Published examples include materials produced by the Schools Council (1983) and Davies and Sturman (1988), with a focus on structuring peer group talk and directed group activities so as to support reading and writing in the language of the subject curriculum. The language development activities produced were designed to benefit all students, not only second language learners, who were seen as the 'barium meal in the X-ray', showing up deficiencies in the schooling system that affected the progress of many other students (Levine, 1990).

The aim was to develop 'normal' classroom processes that were 'hospitable' (Levine, 1990) to children from minority groups. Respecting and accepting their home languages and cultures within the classroom was deemed important in order to achieve the cognitively positive 'additive' bilingualism (Lambert, 1980) that research on bilingualism suggests is necessary for academic success. The focus was on adapting the mainstream classroom and therefore on training and supporting mainstream class and subject teachers to respond to the needs of students from a diversity of language backgrounds as the norm. Much attention has therefore been given to developing cooperative, team teaching strategies between class teachers, second language specialists and bilingual support teachers or assistants (Bourne, 1989), and even to reforming whole-school organizational structures in ways that would encourage these adaptations (Bourne and McPake, 1991).

While UK education policy has embraced integration into the mainstream classroom with subject teacher responsibility for second language learners' progress, across Europe specialist second language teaching in separate 'reception' classes for new arrivals in the country appears still to be the more common approach, with rather more attention paid in research and pilot projects to the provision of separate classes for mother tongue language teaching than on strategies for teaching the dominant language of the host country and school curriculum (Reid and Reich, 1992; Kroon, Gogolin, this volume, Chapters 3 and 18). Despite such 'mother tongue' language provision being made within many schools, concerns have been raised about the continuing lack of awareness of language and cultural diversity in main-stream classrooms on the part of other curriculum subject teachers (Gogolin, 1994; Jaspaert and Ramaut, 2000; Kroon, this volume, Chapter 3). Developments in linking language development strategies with curriculum content teaching appear to have impacted mainly on those teachers opting for specialist second language teacher training courses (EUNIT, 1998).

In the United States, too, approaches to the integration of early-stage second language learners into the mainstream classroom have been more cautious than in the United Kingdom. Second language classes taught by trained second language specialist teachers appear still to be the norm for newly arrived and early-stage second language learners. However, within these special classes there has been a concern to develop 'content-focused teaching' (Crandall, 1993) that introduces students to the language of the school subject curricula, and engages with written texts, so supporting students' transition to the mainstream and to effective engagement with the school curriculum.

Crandall (1993) lists a number of ways in which the integration of language and content instruction takes place in the United States. In the first, 'content-based language instruction', sometimes also called the 'cognitive academic language learning approach' (CALLA), second language teachers, working with second language groups of learners, use content-based texts and tasks as the vehicles for developing both knowledge of language and of curriculum content. In the second, 'sheltered' or 'language-sensitive' subject teaching, subject teachers work with second language groups of learners by adapting the language of their texts and tasks to make them more accessible, as is also done in bilingual 'immersion' programmes. The third approach, 'language across the curriculum', attempts to integrate language instruction into all curriculum subject planning, often employing cooperative teaching between subject and second language teacher, as in the UK model.

Such a mix of short-term, separate, specialist teaching with long-term strategies for improving mainstream teacher training, so as to impact on all lessons, seems appropriate for achieving the best results possible for learners in contexts where mainstream classrooms and subject teachers are still inade-quately prepared for dealing with linguistic diversity. However, with a diverse population becoming the norm in most countries, it seems clear that even where separate second language classes are offered to students initially, or for some parts of their school day, training in second language methods and techniques will need to become an integral part of all teacher training, in order for class and subject teachers to meet the needs of all the students facing them each day in their classrooms.

## Is there still a role for the 'second language specialist'?

In view of the need for all teachers to adapt their strategies to meet the needs of linguistically diverse classrooms, it seems fair to ask, with Creese (2000), if there is any content specific to the second language class, and any expertise left that is specific to the second language specialist. Leung explains:

> The concept of curriculum content is reasonably clear to teachers when it is used to refer to subject content such as science and mathematics. The subject content represents a body of specialist knowledge… and skills… which are, to various extents, manifested through language. It is far more complex when this term is used with reference to [second language learners]. (1997: 29)

Leung argues that the expertise of the second language teacher does not lie in the planning of a separate syllabus of instruction, but rather in the ability to analyse how language is used in different curriculum subject tasks and what second language learners have to be able to do to accomplish those tasks; and to prepare effective supporting materials based on these analyses. The task (whether taking place in the mainstream or in the second language learning classroom) provides the focal point for the analysis and planning of language teaching. (For detailed explanations of task-based learning and teaching, see Mohan, 1986.)

Underlying the integration of content and language instruction and the implementation of task-based learning are a number of widely used teaching strategies. These include setting up cooperative group learning activities that are carefully planned and selected by the teacher to include language learning objectives, and where students, often of different language backgrounds or at different levels of proficiency in the second language, work together on a common task. Here talk and reading are used to support written production, as students jointly construct shared understandings. Following Cummins (1984), the aim is to provide activities with high cognitive demand but with lowered second language demands for curriculum learning, alongside complementary activities that lower the cognitive demand and allow students to focus on the new language structures.

The focus on developing 'academic language' in second language instruction has received significant support from mainstream literacy research in Australia, analysing the different 'genres' of written language in use in different school subjects (Christie, this volume, Chapter 7). The Australian Disadvantaged Schools Program (1994) drew out the implications of this research for planning second language learning support, making explicit the ways in which the different text types necessary for academic success in the Australian school system are constructed. Suggested activities carefully link talk, reading and writing (Hammond, 2001; Gibbons, 1991, 2002), moving back and forth across the spoken–written language continuum. For example, students have opportunities to share a real experience together, discuss it, and carry out some research from books or the Internet to extend their under-standing and gain models of academic prose. They then can go on to write a report, recount or other appropriate written genre, perhaps with the aid of written models or outlines provided by the teacher as appropriate for their level of second language proficiency. Although the analyses of text types are limited to academic writing in English, the examples of practice outlined by these authors offer a rich resource for any teacher of second language learners.

The expertise of a language specialist in this context would include extra training in the systemic functional grammar (Halliday, 1994) underlying the analysis and teaching of different text types, a training potentially open to all teachers, but which the additional time involved in training for a language specialism will enable to be more fully and usefully developed. In this way, the language specialist would have the expertise to be a real resource of advice and support to class and subject teachers on language across the curriculum for all students in multilingual schools.

## Teacher training

While the implications of this chapter suggest the continuing need for well-trained language specialists to support mainstream class and subject teachers in meeting the diverse needs of students from a range of language back-grounds, there is also a clear need for all teachers, whatever their subject back-ground, to receive training in assessing the language demands of their subject areas, designing appropriate tasks and texts for learners, and in employing a range of appropriate teaching strategies in the classroom. When linguistic diversity is the norm, it is no longer acceptable for mainstream teachers to believe that supporting second language learners is not an essential part of their responsibility. In the United States, states with large numbers of minority linguistic group students have begun to make additional requirements of teachers. In California, for example, teachers are required to add a 'Cross Cultural Language and Academic Development Certificate' (CLAD) to their qualifications (Merino, 1999). This certificate covers the minimal knowledge and skills required by all teachers to teach those learning English as a second language.

In Europe, some efforts are also being made to include preparation for the support of increasingly linguistically diverse classes in generalist teacher training. A set of shared competences have been prepared, which set out an agreed set of teacher skills and abilities against which to evaluate all teaching in multilingual schools and classrooms (EUNIT, 1998). In England, the focus has moved away from seeing learning in a second language from a deficit perspective, towards a focus on providing equal opportunities in the main-stream and raising the attainment of every student in the school, with high expectations for all. Government legislation (DfEE/TTA, 2001) sets out a range of statutory requirements for the pre-service training of new teachers in order to prepare them for meeting the needs of second language learners in mainstream classes. The National Curriculum also explicitly requires that every teacher in every subject must be responsible for teaching language/literacy across the curriculum. The National Literacy Strategy in-service training materials incorporate strategies that mirror approaches that research suggests are also good for second language learners (Gregory, 1996). All these initiatives in England are subject to a programme of inspection to ensure implementation.

## Bilingual support for learning across the curriculum

With the focus on subject learning and higher attainment across the curriculum, new and important work on the contribution of students' first languages to second language development, and on using the students' full linguistic repertoire, including their ability to code-switch between languages and translate, is emerging from multilingual contexts. In South Africa, for example, code switching is increasingly being promoted as a learning and teaching resource in classrooms where both students and their teacher are bilingual in the same languages (Setati *et al*, 2002). In such schools, the second language remains the main medium of instruction because

> Parents' memories of Bantu education, combined with their perception of English as a gateway to better education, are making the majority of parents favour English from the beginning of school, even if their children do not know the language before they go to school. (NEPI, 1992: 3)

The aim is to support a move from informal exploratory talk (and perhaps writing) in students' usual everyday language (often in small groups) towards formal, subject-specific talk and writing in the second language. Exploratory talk enables learners to explore ideas and concepts in a comfortable environment, and for the teacher, where he or she shares the language, to listen to learners and pick up on any misconceptions. Where such use is common among the students, the exploratory language will naturally include code switching. While acknowledging teachers' initial anxiety about code switching in the classroom (see also David and Govindasamy, this volume, Chapter 15), Setati *et al* (2002) suggest that mixed language use is valuable in clarifying concepts both among students working in groups, and between teacher and students. However, they found that it was crucial that teachers moved on from merely encouraging mixed-code exploratory talk to following this up with explicit teaching of the formal discourse of the subject required for abstract concept formation (see also Fradd and Lee, 1999; Rollnick and Rutherford, 1996).

The mainstream school and classroom organization to enable this new and complex form of bilingual language support for curriculum learning to work successfully remains problematic (Bourne, 2001; Kroon, this volume, Chapter 3). For both second language support and bilingual support work in mainstream classrooms to be effective, there is a need for substantial teacher training involving all mainstream class and subject teachers as well as language specialists. Monolingual classroom and subject teachers need to understand the contribution which first language use, non-standard dialects and code switching can make to exploratory talk in small groups between students sharing the same languages. Bilingual teachers need encouragement to draw on their own bilingual resources, and time to consider the use of bilingual support strategies – for example, in judging when to shift into a first language or dialect to reformulate a concept, and how and when to move from exploratory talk into more formal discourse in the standard language of the school curriculum. There has been little research in this field of bilingual support in multilingual contexts. One way forward would be for school staff to be supported in carrying out action research themselves, where possible with the support of trained researchers to help document and disseminate the process. Rarely has such an innovative form of teaching as bilingual support for subject learning in the mainstream classroom been introduced with so little support for teacher development. Yet in the work emerging from South Africa, with its recognition of the role of mixed language use in learning and teaching, there are lessons to be learnt for second language provision in many countries.

## Conclusion

In this chapter I have attempted to outline the ways in which second language learners can be given access to the school curriculum and to the academic language through which it is constructed. Fundamental to this is the recognition of the training needs of mainstream subject teachers if they are to understand and meet the language and learning needs of all students in their multilingual classes. I have also outlined the contribution that could still be made by well-trained teachers specializing in language development across the curriculum, working inside or outside the classroom, both with students and with their teacher colleagues, depending on the very different needs of different groups of students and on variations in existing teacher expertise within the school. There is no one model of 'good practice' for second language support; it crucially depends on the ability to analyse shifting local needs and innovate to meet them. Finally, I have argued for the need to develop new forms of bilingual support for learning that are open to students' own everyday forms of bilingual language use, including non-standard dialects, code switching and mixing, in the process of ensuring access to the forms of academic language used in abstract concept formation.

## References

Bourne, J (1989) *Moving into the Mainstream: LEA provision for bilingual pupils in England and Wales*, NFER-Nelson, Windsor

Bourne, J (2001) 'Doing what comes naturally': how the discourses and routines of teachers' practice constrain opportunities for bilingual support in UK primary schools, *Language and Education*, **14**, pp 1–18

Bourne, J and McPake, J (1991) *Partnership Teaching: Co-operative teaching strategies for English language support in multilingual classes*, HMSO, London

Brumfit, C (1984) *Communicative Methodology in Language Teaching: The roles of fluency and accuracy*, Cambridge University Press, Cambridge

Collier, V (1987) How long? A synthesis of research on academic achievement in a second language, *TESOL Quarterly*, **23** (3), pp 509–31

Commission for Racial Equality (CRE) (1986) *The Teaching of English as a Second Language*, CRE, London

Crandall, J (1993) Content-centred learning in the US, *Annual Review of Applied Linguistics*, **13**, pp 111–26

Creese, A (2000) The role of the language specialist in disciplinary teaching: in search of a subject? *Journal of Multicultural and Multilingual Development*, **21** (6), pp 451–70

Crystal, D (1995) *The Cambridge Encyclopaedia of the English Language*, Cambridge University Press, Cambridge

Cummins, J (1984) *Bilingualism and Special Education: Issues in assessment and pedagogy*, College-Hill, San Diego, CA

Davies, A and Sturman, E (1988) *Bilingual Learners in Secondary Schools*, Inner London Education Authority, London

Department for Education and Employment/Teacher Training Agency (DfEE/TTA) (2001) *Standards for Initial Teacher Training*, DfEE, London

Disadvantaged Schools Program (1994) *Write It Right: Exploring literacy in school English*, New South Wales Department of School Education, Sydney

European Network of Intercultural Teacher Training (EUNIT) (1998) *Skills and Abilities Required for Teaching in Multilingual Schools*, Waxmann, Münster and New York

Fradd, S and Lee, O (1999) Teachers' roles in promoting science inquiry with students from diverse language backgrounds, *Educational Researcher*, **29** (5), pp 14–20

Gibbons, P (1991) *Learning to Learn in a Second Language*, Primary English Teaching Association (PETA), Newtown

Gibbons, P (2002) *Scaffolding Language, Scaffolding Learning: Working with ESL children in the mainstream elementary classroom*, Heinemann, London

Gillborn, D and Gipps, C (1996) *Recent Research on the Achievements of Ethnic Minority Pupils*, OFSTED, London

Gogolin, I (1994) *Der monolinguale Habitus der multilingualen Schule*, Waxmann, Münster and New York

Gold, N (1997) *Teachers for LEP Students: Demand, supply and shortage*, State Department for Education, Sacramento, CA

Graddol, D (1997) *The Future of English?* The British Council, London

Gregory, E (1996) *Making Sense of a New World: Learning to read in a second language*, Paul Chapman, London

Halliday, M (1994) *An Introduction to Functional Grammar*, 2nd edn, Edward Arnold, London

Hammond, J (ed) (2001) *Scaffolding: Teaching and learning in language and literacy education*, PETA, Newtown, NSW

Jaspaert, K and Ramaut, G (2000) Don't use English words in Dutch: portrait of a multilingual classroom in Flanders, in *Man screibt, wie man spricht*, eds I Gogolin and S Kroon, pp 27–40, Waxmann, Münster

Krashen, S (1982) *Principles and Practice in Second Language Acquisition*, Pergamon, Oxford

Lambert, W (1980) The social psychology of language, in *Language: Social psychological perspectives*, eds H Giles, W Robinson and P Smith, Pergamon, Oxford

Leung, C (1997) Language content and learning process in curriculum tasks, in *English as an Additional Language: Changing perspectives*, eds C Leung and C Cable, pp 28–39, National Association for Language Development in the Curriculum (NALDIC), Watford

Levine, J (1990) *Bilingual Pupils and the Mainstream Curriculum*, Falmer, London

Macias, R (1989) *Bilingual Teacher Supply and Demand in the United States*, USC Center for Multilingual, Multicultural Research and the Tomas Rivers Center

Madood, T, Berthoud, R, Lakey, J, Nazroo, J, Smith, P, Virdee, S and Beishon, S (1997) *Ethnic Minorities in Britain: Diversity and disadvantage*, Policy Studies Institute, London

Merino, B (1999) Preparing secondary teachers to teach a second language, in *So Much to Say: Adolescents, bilingualism and ESL in the secondary school*, eds C Faltis and P Wolfe, pp 225–54, Teachers College Press, New York

Minicucci, C and Olsen, L (1992) *Programs for Secondary Limited English Proficient Students: A Californian study*, National Clearing House for Bilingual Education, Washington, DC

Mohan, B (1986) *Language and Content*, Addison-Wesley, Reading, MA

NEPI (1992) *Language*, Oxford University Press, Cape Town

Norton Pierce, B and Ridge, S (1997) Multilingualism in Southern Africa, *Annual Review of Applied Linguistics* 17, 170–90

Prinsloo, M and Kell, C (1997) Literacy on the ground: a located perspective on literacy policy in South Africa, *Literacy and Numeracy Studies*, 7 (2), pp 83–101

Reid, E and Reich, H (1992) *Breaking the Boundaries: Migrant workers' children in the EC*, Multilingual Matters, Clevedon, UK

Rollnick, M and Rutherford, M (1996) The use of mother tongue and English in the learning and expression of science concepts: a classroom-based study, *International Journal of Science Education*, 18 (1), pp 91–103

Schools Council (1983) *Language in the Multicultural Primary Classroom*, broadsheets, Schools Council, London

Setati, M, Adler, J, Reed, Y and Bapoo, A (2002) Incomplete journeys: code switching and other language practices in mathematics, science and English language classrooms in South Africa, *Language and Education*, **16** (2), pp 128–49

Vallet, L and Caille, J (1999) Migration and integration in France: academic careers of immigrants' children in lower and upper secondary school, paper prepared for the ESF conference 'European Societies or European Society? Migrations and inter-ethnic relations in Europe', Obernai

Waggoner, D (1999) Who are the secondary newcomer and linguistically different youth?, in *So Much to Say: Adolescents, bilingualism and ESL in the secondary school*, eds C Faltis and P Wolfe, pp 13–41, Teachers College Press, New York

World Education Forum (WEF) (2000) *The Dakar Framework for Action: Education for All*, UNESCO, Paris

# 3. Mother tongue and mother tongue education

Sjaak Kroon

## Introduction

Without going into much historical detail, in this chapter I will try to shed some light on the intricacies connected with concepts of 'mother tongue' and 'mother tongue education' – henceforth 'MT' and 'MTE'. In this task I take the mosaic of contemporary multilingual societies as a main frame of reference, since it is in this context above all that the concepts just referred to are gaining importance. The chapter starts by distinguishing analytically between different meanings of MT and MTE . Then it gives an account of two different versions of MTE, from a majority and a minority perspective respectively. It then outlines the difficulties that the process of inclusion of MTs in multi-lingual classrooms has to face. The final section deals with MTE and linguistic human rights. In its examples, and maybe in its basic thinking, this chapter may well reflect a Western European, especially a Dutch, bias. It is hoped, however, that the concepts and practices dealt with will be recognizable in other contexts as well.

## Mother tongue and mother tongue education

Historical and contemporary meanings of MT and MTE are explored by Gagné *et al* (1987). They distinguish at least three different meanings that turn out to be intricately intertwined: meanings stemming in turn from a primary-socializational, a politico-cultural and an educational viewpoint. I will elaborate below on these distinctions.

First of all I identify a linguistic perspective that includes the historical-linguistic definition of mother tongue as a 'language from which others spring' (*The Concise Oxford Dictionary of Current English*, 1976 edition, p 711), as well as the primary-socializational perspective proposed by Gagné *et al* (1987). In the socializational concept, a major role is played by first language acqui-sition, which is part of the process of primary socialization. MT then refers to one's native language – that is, the language of one's mother or, more generally, the language that is used by a child's first carers in the home, without any contribution from educational institutions – hence 'home language'.

Given the fact that in a growing number of families several languages are in active use, it is quite conceivable that the home language of a child differs from its mother's mother tongue. As Kaplan and Baldauf (1997: 19) put it, referring to the example of a child born to a Tamil-speaking mother in Malaysia possibly acquiring Tamil, Straits Malay and/or Straits Chinese, and/or Bahasa Melayu, and/or English, 'One may be a native speaker of a language even though one's mother was not... It is impossible to designate that individual's MT except in the literal sense, and it is not so useful to do so... It is not a useful term, but it is, nonetheless...widely used.'

It goes without saying that the socializational use of the term MT does not distinguish between minority and majority, regional and national, indigenous and non-indigenous languages. It refers to the only 'real' MT of a speaker.

We come now to a language policy perspective leading to a politico-cultural concept of MT, such a concept being closely related to national or regional identity formation or state formation. The awareness or invention of a common mother tongue plays a central role in the attempt to establish and develop the awareness of a common fatherland, ie a nation-state. A fatherland needs a mother tongue, which education has to supply, and generally speaking, this is done by selecting, standardizing and teaching a so-called national or official language. In the process of state formation in 19th-century Western Europe, this language was in most cases a standardized variety of the MT of the nation's dominant group. A well-known example here was the role of the German language in the development of the German state.

The obvious exceptions to this general rule are former colonies where the non-indigenous colonial language was selected as the official language of the independent state. An example here is Angola, where after the colonial period Portuguese was selected as the official language. Other exceptions are contemporary multilingual states where a language policy decision leads to having more than one official language or no official language at all. Examples here are post-apartheid South Africa, which in its 1996 constitution designated 11 official languages, and Eritrea, where in the 1997 constitution no single language was designated as an official or national language, and all nine languages of the country are used as media of instruction. It will be clear that in the politico-cultural use of MT it is mainly integrating tendencies that are in the foreground – whether or not under the slogan of 'unity through diversity', as in Eritrea. These integrating forces, however, can all too easily turn into separatist tendencies, leading to the potential marginalization and (sometimes self-chosen) exclusion of the MTs of indigenous and non-indigenous minorities.

Finally, seen from an educational perspective the concept of MT has to do with the intertwining of knowledge of the world in terms of its social construction, and the way in which this knowledge is made accessible and has to be mastered through language in education. MT, then, refers to the official standardized language variety that is used as a school language – that is, that serves as the medium of teaching and learning in educational contexts. In this 'language across the curriculum' perspective, teachers of maths and history too can be considered as mother tongue teachers. As a consequence mainly of external democratization processes in education, of social mobility and of immigration movements, more and more children come to school and experience a gap between their MT and the school's medium of instruction. Their MT in a socializational sense can be a regional or social dialect of the standard language, a totally different indigenous or non-indigenous language or language variety, a language variety that resulted from a process of second language acquisition, or some combination of these. It is the official language that they have to learn as a school subject, and that is the language in which they are supposed to acquire and develop knowledge, without the school as an institution really being aware of that fact, let alone taking explicit account of it in the learning and teaching processes that it sets up.

The analytical differences in meaning between the three notions of MT generally speaking do not correspond with the use of the term in ordinary speech. It is likely that everyday understanding of 'mother tongue', quite apart from connotations such as the language known best, used most, liked best, etc, contains all three aspects at the same time of the meanings just discussed – which of course does not exclude the possibility of one being more prominent in specific cases.

With respect to the use of the term MT in a multilingual context in particular, it is important to be aware of its possible negative political connotations. Baker and Prys Jones (1998: 50) state that

> the term 'mother tongue' when applied to different ethnic groups often reveals a bias and a prejudice. When Maori peoples in New Zealand, or Finns in Sweden, or Kurds from Turkey in Denmark, or Mexican Spanish speakers in the United States, or the speakers of different Asian languages in Canada and England are referred to in terms of their 'mother tongue', the expression may refer to minorities who are oppressed. The term has then taken an evaluative meaning – symbolizing migrant workers, guest workers, oppressed indigenous peoples and language minorities. 'Mother tongue' tends to be used for language minorities and much less so for language majorities. The term therefore tends to be a symbol of separation of minority and majority, or those with less, as opposed to those with more, power and status.

## Mother tongue education from a majority perspective

Although the notion of MT in contemporary discussion seems to be connected mainly with a minority language position, historically speaking it is primarily related to majority contexts, one of its main characteristics being its relationship to emancipatory movements. Ahlzweig (1994) shows that the concept *lingua materna* in its earliest appearances refers to the language of the uneducated people, as opposed to *lingua latina*, the language of the educated scholarly elite. This democratic and emancipatory concept of MT spread over Europe from the 12th century onwards. After centuries of schooling in Latin, the European lingua franca since the Middle Ages, in 16th-century Europe the vernacular became the language of instruction – although not for the masses, of course, since compulsory education only started to gain ground at the end of the 18th century (Tulasiewicz and Adams, 1998).

As an example of the role of the MT in this respect, reference can be made here to the first Dutch school grammar, *Twe-spraack vande Nederduitsche letterkunst* (Dialogue on the art of Dutch grammar), published in Leyden in 1584 and believed to have been written or edited by Hendrik Laurensz Spiegel. Spiegel *cum suis* not only wanted to formulate some linguistic rules for the Dutch language, but also intended through these rules to cultivate this *moedertaal* (mother tongue), to show that it had at least as good qualities as the 'sacred languages', Hebrew, Greek and Latin. The plan was to make it available in the end as a language of instruction for the sciences, which would save the pupils from the time-consuming task of first having to learn Latin (Bakker and Dibbets, 1977).

In 18th- and 19th-century Europe especially, the mother tongue played an important role in nation building, yet another emancipatory process. According to Heller (1999), having a shared language is central to this process in two ways. First, sharing a language facilitates the construction of the shared values and practices that lead to unity. Second, a shared language contributes to legitimizing the nation in such a way that it is possible to argue that a group legitimately constitutes a nation because it shares a language.

Education plays an important role in the status-planning process of providing a nation with a national language. But in order to function as an instrument of national unification and to be used in education, the mother tongue itself has to be to some extent 'unified'. This process of standardization is in fact well known, and has been documented for many languages (Clark, 2001). As a consequence mainly of its unifying and educational function, once mainly oral vernaculars became written standardized languages in many countries, following very strong prescriptive rules of grammar and style derived from classical Latin. These in the end lead to rather 'unnatural' invented varieties of language.

As a reaction to this kind of written language, at the end of the 19th century a new, and again emancipatory mother tongue movement emerged. In the Netherlands this was marked by the publication in 1893 of a pamphlet entitled *Pleidooi voor de moedertaal, de jeugd en de onderwijzers* (Plea for the mother tongue, the youth and the teachers), in which the author, J H van den Bosch, argued against the classicist unnaturalness of the written school language and proposed his 'language is sound' philosophy, allowing for a great deal of mainly phonetically based language variation.

It has been under Van den Bosch's seminal banner of 'mother tongue education' that many theorists and practitioners in the educational field have argued right into the present period for changes in the teaching of Dutch as a mother tongue that would lead to greater freedom, better communication, and the acceptance of linguistic and cultural variation. In the 1970s in particular, publications on the teaching of Dutch proclaimed that the teaching of Dutch should become 'mother tongue education'. With hindsight, the term MTE in this context seems to have had a mainly exhortatory function: speaking about MTE meant that you were in favour of the principle of linking language teaching with the child's home language. That language often differed from the school language and the language that predominated in text-books, and research had by then already made abundantly clear that an approach that neglected the pupils' home language could lead to serious problems. The aim of 'linking up with the pupils' home language' – that is, reducing the problems of speakers of languages and language varieties other than the standard language – has to be valued positively. The usefulness of the term MTE when referring to this aim, however, does not alter the fact that this actual term in no way covers what still happens in the so-called MT classroom. What is referred to as MTE in most cases turns out to be standard language teaching – that is, teaching in the standard language and aiming to give the learners better proficiency in that language.

The greater the number of pupils taking part in the educational process who have other indigenous or non-indigenous languages or language varieties as their home language, the more the term MTE, although its use gained impetus from the presence of these very children, becomes a contradiction in terms. For dialect-speaking children, mother tongue education would be education in a regional or social dialect; for immigrant pupils from Turkey it would be education in Turkish or Kurdish; and for Moroccan pupils it would be education in Berber or Moroccan Arabic. Neglecting for a moment the specific characteristics of language across the curriculum, it would only be pupils who speak the national standard language at home for whom MTE would really be mother tongue education (Kroon, 1985).

## Mother tongue education from a minority perspective

Nineteenth- and 20th-century nationalism did not only result in nation-states and national languages; according to Heller (1999:15), one of its by-products was the construction of national minorities. It was after all the nation-state with its dominant national identity and language that gave indigenous minorities and their languages their minority status. The interesting paradox here is that indigenous minorities, faced with the problem of their own legit-imacy, base their claims on the logic of linguistic identity, on the right of a people identified by its common language to self-determination. They use exactly the arguments that led to the development of nation-states in the first place. From this perspective it comes as no surprise that they have always strongly focused on securing their institutional position within the nation-state.

In this respect the establishment of institutional provisions for indigenous minority language teaching – the teaching of 'lesser-used languages' – has been a largely successful enterprise in Europe. The relatively strong position of languages such as Frisian, Welsh and Breton in Western Europe, as well as the still improving position of languages such as Altai and Bashkir in the Russian Federation Republics of Altai and Bashkortostan (see Khruslov, this volume, Chapter 14), has been established mostly through hard-fought political struggles for recognition of the languages on a territorial basis. This recognition is usually codified in national language laws or international documents such as the Council of Europe's 1992 European Charter for Regional or Minority Languages and 1994 Framework Convention on National Minorities (Extra and Gorter, 2001). This is not to say, of course, that indigenous minority languages and indigenous minority language teaching are not under constant pressure. Particularly in the context of contemporary large-scale modernization and globalization processes, they run the risk of being considered obsolete and therefore no longer eligible for state support by the dominant society. In a Europe of regions on the other hand, as opposed to a Europe of nations, indigenous minority languages and dialects might thrive (de Bot *et al*, 2001).

A major difference between indigenous national minorities and non-indigenous immigrant minorities and the position they are able to acquire for their respective languages has to do with political power. Generally speaking, indigenous minorities are citizens of their country of residence, whereas non-indigenous minorities are not. The latter implies a considerable limitation on political participation and, consequently, a considerably weaker institutional position for their languages.

Among other ways, this is shown by the abundance of terms referring to languages seen in a minority perspective. Anthologies such as the one edited by Extra and Gorter (2001) may contain terms like 'native language', 'mother tongue', 'own language', 'home language', 'vernacular language', 'community language', 'ancestral language', 'heritage language', 'language of origin', 'non-indigenous minority language', 'allochthonous language', 'immigrant language', 'ethnic minority/group language', 'lesser-used language' and 'language other than English' – but they are all euphemisms intended to signal that they are not the majority language (Kaplan and Baldauf, 1997: 21). It would take too long to discuss fully here the pros and cons of all these terms. However, in what follows I will use the term 'community language', to avoid unwanted minoritizing perspectives and to indicate that the language in question is not necessarily acquired by each individual or used in every home, but is related in various ways to a particular – originally immigrant – community.

This terminological debate, however, pales as compared to the political, educational and societal struggle about the curricular position of the languages that as a consequence of migration have considerably enriched traditional language variation patterns in most West European societies. Making decisions about the position of community languages in the curriculum has to deal with the twofold issue of using these languages as media of instruction and offering them as subjects in their own right. The former can be done through various forms of transitional or two-way bilingual education, which affects the whole construction of the curriculum. The latter only involves providing for an additional language subject within or outside the curriculum, depending on the languages' officially accepted status (Kroon and Vallen, 1997). The conceptual and practical discussion about these approaches is often blurred by lack of clarity about their stated objectives, and the main perspectives on this question are multilingualism seen as a problem, as a resource or as a right (Baker, 2001). The different options may lead to giving community languages a place in the curriculum (as a medium of instruction and/or as a subject) in order to improve the pupils' proficiency in the dominant school language and their school achievement in general, or (as a subject only) to improve the pupils' proficiency in their community language as an intrinsic goal.

In the following these options are illustrated from the Netherlands. The current 1998 Dutch community language teaching legislation, enshrined in the Primary Education Act, sections 171–176, combines the instrumental and autonomous perspective by offering so-called language support and community language teaching as a subject at the same time. During language support lessons, community languages are used by a community language teacher within school hours in order to support the pupils in mastering regular curriculum subjects. Pupils who are selected for language support are withdrawn from the mainstream class for a limited number of hours each week and get extra help of various kinds, during which in principle the community language can be used as a language of instruction and a resource. Community language teaching as a subject, for which the pupils' parents have to apply explicitly, takes place outside school hours. Decisions regarding the languages that are on offer are taken by the municipal authorities on the basis of, for example, a home language survey. Community language teaching of both kinds is financed by the Ministry of Education and under the control of the Schools Inspectorate.

The first evaluations of both versions of community language teaching in the Netherlands have not been very positive. They first of all make clear that the Dutch educational authorities and schools seem to prefer the instrumental function of community language teaching, so that the intrinsic function has thereby lost status. At the same time it remains rather unclear what the instrumental function really entails. As of August 2002 the law defines 'language support' as all teaching activities that, with the aid of a community language, contribute to learning Dutch and as such to achieving the attainment targets of

primary education. The way in which this is to be accomplished is not specified, and explanations of the supposed beneficial relationship between Dutch
as a target language and a community language as a language of instruction
are rather ambiguous. The history of community language teaching in the
Netherlands, which started in the 1970s and since then has been characterized
by unclear goals, underlying rationales and ideologies on the one hand, and
unsatisfactory practices on the other, seems to be repeating itself yet again.

## Including the mother tongue in the curriculum

Although the theoretical possibilities for including community languages in
the curriculum of the kind discussed so far might appear as more or less
convincing in an academic discussion, educational reality is quite another
matter. Data from a growing number of case studies in multilingual classrooms illustrate the different attitudes to community languages in the schools.
In order to complement the theorizing here, I will give a brief account of some
key incidents taken from multilingual primary school classes in the
Netherlands (for methodological detail, see Kroon and Sturm, 2000). As well
as an example taken from a language support lesson, I will also include two
examples from mainstream multilingual assimilation classrooms: these after
all, in spite of all the arguments for multilingual and multicultural education,
still reflect the dominant approach in most countries.

### *Forbidding community languages in the mainstream classroom*

Imagine a multilingual classroom where eight-year-old pupils are sitting in a
circle telling the class about the weekend's events. Turkish Ertugrul has almost
finished his story and Turkish Canan really wants to tell her story before
sharing time is over. In order to achieve this aim she whispers to Ertugrul in
Turkish to select her as the next speaker. Unfortunately, the Dutch boy Kees
hears her do this and informs the teacher: 'Miss, Canan was just speaking
Turkish to Ertugrul.' The teacher is very angry and says to Canan that she is a
naughty girl. 'We talked about that already many times. Do you remember?
Why is this naughty, not nice of you?' 'Because the other children cannot
understand me,' Canan replies. 'Yes,' the teacher continues, 'because Kees
probably thinks that you are saying very nasty things. I have been explaining
this to you already for five years and I find it a little bit strange that you still
don't know.' Canan nods, and the teacher asks Ertugrul to pick someone else.

  In this classroom it is clearly forbidden to speak Turkish and the pupils
know that. According to the teacher, the main reasons for this are didactic (the
pupils should speak as much Dutch as possible in order to improve their proficiency) and communicative (when working together one should be able to
understand one another and that is not the case when Turkish is used).

Keeping to this rule, apparently, is more important than keeping the rule that whispering and snitching are forbidden in the classroom and the rule that pupils are not allowed to ask for a turn in sharing time (Canan) or to speak before they have been given a turn (Kees). The use of Turkish undermines the monolinguality of the sharing time routine as a Dutch-medium teaching situation, and potentially loses its general functionality as a teaching–learning situation. By referring to the rule that forbids Turkish in the classroom, the teacher attempts to re-establish the normality of monolingualism in the classroom, in what is a clear example of the kind of linguistic homogenization found all over Europe at least (Gogolin and Kroon, 2000).

### Linking up with community languages in the mainstream classroom

Imagine a lesson of language awareness in a multicultural classroom with eight-year-old pupils in which the teacher explicitly tries to link up with the pupils' community languages in a lesson on interethnic communication problems. The conversation is on confusing food names. The teacher asks for the name of peanut butter in languages other than Dutch: 'How do you say that in, let's say, Turkish?' A Turkish pupil responds, 'We simply say "peanut butter" [using the Dutch term].' The teacher again: 'You simply say "peanut butter" in Turkish? Yes? Ilias, do you know a word in Turkish or do you just say "peanut butter"? Ayse?' And the answer: 'Peanut butter!'

The next word, 'cauliflower', leads to the following dialogue. Teacher: 'Who knows how to say it in their own language? Most of you do know what a cauliflower is, don't you?' A pupil from former Yugoslavia answers, 'A cauliflower [again using the Dutch word]'. Again the teacher asks, 'In Yugoslavian?' And the pupil replies, 'I don't know, my mother always says "cauliflower". She always says "cauliflower" in Dutch.'

What this incident shows is that community languages are not necessarily the mother tongues of the pupils coming from the communities involved. As a consequence of processes of language loss and incomplete learning, the pupils' proficiency in their community language may be limited. Linking up with their assumed 'mother tongue' knowledge therefore can easily turn out to be a very embarrassing experience for the pupils. Already they don't know Dutch very well, and now they turn out also to have only a limited proficiency in their 'mother tongue'. On top of that, this lesson, which was explicitly intended to combat linguocentrism, seems to communicate that languages such as Turkish and 'Yugoslavian' don't even have words for such simple things as peanut butter and cauliflower (Kroon, 1990; Leung, Harris and Rampton, 1997).

### Using community languages as a medium of instruction outside the mainstream classroom

Imagine a 'language support' lesson with seven-year-old Moroccan pupils, two of whom, according to the teacher, are speakers of Berber; they understand

Moroccan Arabic but find it difficult to answer questions in it. One child is fluent in Berber and Moroccan Arabic. All the parents are fluent in Arabic, but their home language is Berber. The teacher does not speak Berber but he claims to use Dutch if necessary to explain things to the pupils. The language of instruction is Moroccan Arabic, and the class is working on reading strategies.

The teacher asks (italics indicate switches to Dutch), 'If Miss or Sir gives you an assignment, what *do you have to do* first, Jamila?' Jamila answers in Dutch: '*Read the title.*' The teachers first repeats the answer in Dutch, but when Nawar continues in Dutch, saying, '*And then…*', he interrupts and says in Moroccan Arabic, 'Say it in Arabic.' Nawar does so: 'If you read it and don't understand it, then you have to read it once again.' The teacher continues in Moroccan Arabic, but at the end switches again to Dutch: 'Yes, how many times do we have to *read*?' Nasira answers in Dutch '*Two times*', which is confirmed by the teacher, first in Dutch, but at the end again in Moroccan Arabic: '*Two times or three times, if something,* if we cannot understand something.'

Within this teacher-guided classroom conversation the teacher, as well as the pupils, in 9 out of 11 turns switches to Dutch. This shows the complex language use patterns in a 'language support' lesson where it is not in fact the pupils' 'mother tongue' Berber that is used, but Moroccan Arabic. The ultimate question to be answered here is whether and if so how this type of community language teaching can contribute to better proficiency in Dutch and to achieving general educational attainment targets (see also Bezemer and Kroon, 2001).

## Mother tongue education and linguistic human rights

As early as 1953 the famous UNESCO report *The Use of Vernacular Language in Education* asserted that 'it is axiomatic that the best medium for teaching a child is his mother tongue'. This may well be one of the most frequently quoted and at the same time most frequently contested recommendations in the field of mother tongue education ever, and the line of argument proposed by UNESCO has been extended, recently mainly in the work of Skutnabb-Kangas and Phillipson with Rannut (1995: 2). They developed the concept of 'linguistic human rights' on an individual level – that is, the idea 'that everyone can identify positively with their mother tongue, and have that identification respected by others, irrespective of whether their mother tongue is a minority or majority language' – as well as on a collective level – that is, the right of minority groups 'to enjoy and develop their language and… to establish and maintain schools and other training and educational institutions, with control of curricula and teaching in their own languages'. Violation of this right, they assert, should be considered as a violation of human rights.

Recent years have witnessed a number of declarations that in one way or another seem to be inspired by a linguistic human rights position. Two examples from different parts of the world, related to instrumental and autonomous functions of mother tongue teaching in a broad sense, are:

• the 2000 Asmara Declaration on African Languages and Literatures, which stipulates in Article 5, that 'all African children have the inalienable right to attend school and learn in their mother tongues. Every effort should be made to develop African languages at all levels of education' (in Blommaert, 2001: 132);
• the 2000 Declaration of Oegstgeest: Moving Away from a Monolingual Habitus, which stipulates in Article 6 that 'education in regional, minority and immigrant languages should be offered, supervised and evaluated as part of the regular curriculum in preschool, primary and secondary education' (in Extra and Gorter, 2001: 448).

The linguistic human rights paradigm has meanwhile been challenged from different directions. Blommaert (2001), for example, although sympathetic to the basic principle of linguistic rights, argues against it where it automatically leads to implementing the right of every citizen to enjoy social opportunities in and through the mother tongue by provision of education in the mother tongue. Using the mother tongue as a medium of instruction, although it may sound very appealing as a principle, can turn out to be counter-productive unless due attention is given to the complexities it presents, and may not lead to equal opportunities for the speakers of these languages in real-life situations.

Equal participation in society for minorities is a result of emancipation, and this emancipation process – of the 'illiterate masses' in the 19th century as well as of 'pupils at risk' in the 21st – is clearly a central task for education. However, the value that is given to linguistic products on the linguistic market depends on what is considered 'legitimate language' (Bourdieu, 1982), and it is above all by teaching the dominant language that education facilitates societal participation. The introduction of the 'national' mother tongue in the curriculum in the 19th century is from this perspective as understandable as the exclusion from the mainstream curriculum of the immigrant 'mother tongue' in the 20th century. A 'non-exclusive acknowledgement of the existence of these (regional, minority and immigrant) languages as sources of linguistic diversity and cultural enrichment' (Extra and Gorter, 2001: 447) may be a congenial position, but without a fundamental change of societal power relations, these languages have only a very limited chance of becoming a real part of the dominant curriculum.

## References

Ahlzweig, C (1994) *Muttersprache – Vaterland: Die deutsche Nation und ihre Sprache*, Westdeutscher Verlag, Opladen
Baker, C (2001) *Foundations of Bilingual Education and Bilingualism*, Multilingual Matters, Clevedon, UK

Baker, C and Prys Jones, S (1998) *Encyclopedia of Bilingualism and Bilingual Education*, Multilingual Matters, Clevedon, UK

Bakker, D M and Dibbets, G R W (eds) (1977) *Geschiedenis van de Nederlandse taalkunde* (A history of Dutch linguistics), Malmberg, Den Bosch

Bezemer, J and Kroon, S (2001) Dealing with multilingualism in the primary school curriculum, paper presented at the Third Conference of the International Association for the Improvement of Mother Tongue Education, Amsterdam, 10–13 July

Blommaert, J (2001) The Asmara Declaration as a sociolinguistic problem: reflections on scholarship and linguistic rights, *Journal of Sociolinguistics*, **5** (1), pp 131–55

Bot, C de, Kroon, S, Nelde, P H and Van de Velde, H (eds) (2001) *Institutional Status and Use of National Languages in Europe*, Asgard, St Augustin

Bourdieu, P (1982) *Ce que parler veut dire*, Fayard, Paris

Clark, U (2001) *War Words: Language, history and the disciplining of English*, Elsevier, Amsterdam

Extra, G and Gorter, D (2001) *The Other Languages of Europe: Demographic, sociolinguistic and educational perspectives*, Multilingual Matters, Clevedon, UK

Gagné, G, Daems, F, Kroon, S, Sturm, J and Tarrab, E (eds) (1987) *Selected Papers in Mother Tongue Education / Études en pédagogie de la langue maternelle*, Foris Publications, Dordrecht, the Netherlands

Gogolin, I and Kroon, S (eds) (2000) *'Man schreibt wie man spricht': Ergebnisse einer international vergleichenden Fallstudie über Unterricht in vielsprachigen Klassen*, Waxmann Verlag, Münster

Heller, M (1999) *Linguistic Minorities and Modernity: A sociolinguistic ethnography*, Longman, London

Kaplan, R B and Baldauf, R B Jr (1997) *Language Planning from Practice to Theory*, Multilingual Matters, Clevedon, UK

Kroon, S (1985) Moedertaalonderwijs of onderwijs Nederlands (Mother tongue education or Dutch), *Spiegel*, **3** (1), pp 87–92

Kroon, S (1990) Over de pretenties en de zinvolheid van interculturele taalbeschouwing (The pretension and usefulness of multicultural language awareness), in *Meertaligheid op school: bijdragen aan de ontwikkeling van een taalbeleid* (Multilingualism at school: contributions to the development of language policy), eds W L M van Galen, J Jongerius and R Kabdan, pp 77–89, Groningen: Wolters-Noordhoff, Groningen

Kroon, S and Sturm, J (2000) Comparative case study research in education: methodological issues in an empirical-interpretive perspective, *Zeitschrift für Erziehungswissenschaft*, **3** (4), pp 559–76

Kroon, S and Vallen, T (1997) Bilingual education for migrant students in the Netherlands, in *The Encyclopedia of Language and Education*, vol 5, *Bilingual Education*, ed J Cummins and D Corson, pp 199–208, Kluwer Academic Publishers, Dordrecht, the Netherlands

Leung, C, Harris, R and Rampton, B (1997) The idealised native speaker, reified ethnicities, and classroom realities, *TESOL Quarterly*, **31** (3), pp 543–60

Skutnabb-Kangas, T and Phillipson, R with Rannut, M (1995) *Linguistic Human Rights: Overcoming linguistic discrimination*, Mouton de Gruyter, Berlin

Tulasiewicz, W and Adams, A (1998) *Teaching the Mother Tongue in a Multilingual Europe*, Cassell Education, London

# 4.  The expansion of sign language education

Carol A Padden

Alexander Graham Bell is best known to the world as the inventor of the tele-phone, but he is known to deaf Americans as the husband of a deaf woman, and a frequent commentator on the subject of deafness and deaf education. In 1878, at the invitation of the headmaster of a deaf school in upstate New York, Bell paid a visit to the school and then was interviewed by a local newspaper. Bell was quoted as congratulating the headmaster for his policy prohibiting sign language at the school, adding that 'I think the use of the sign language will go entirely out of existence very soon' (Scouten, 1942). Whatever Bell's genius regarding telephonic communication, it evidently did not extend to prognostications about sign language. Today sign language education has become more broadly used than Bell could have imagined – or desired.

At the time Bell made his prediction, sign language education was under threat both within the United States and throughout the world, a turn of events that Douglas Baynton (1996), a social historian, describes as resulting from a broad social move towards rational and technological ideas of language and human nature. Many schools in Europe had begun undertaking reform projects to replace sign language education for deaf students with education in speech only (Fischer and Lane, 1993; Lane, 1992; Plann, 1997), an endeavour that has left a long legacy of speech education for deaf children that remains to this day in many parts of the world.

The US legacy is somewhat different, mainly because of the durability of its sign language institutions: the survival of schools with deaf teachers, the presence of Gallaudet University exclusively for deaf students, and the efforts of political organizations headed by deaf people. Today sign language education for deaf children in the United States remains prominent. A recent survey of language policies used in programmes with deaf and hard of hearing children in the United States reported that about 55 per cent of the programmes use sign language in some form (Gallaudet Research Institute). This figure accounts for about half of the children surveyed for this report who are considered 'severely or profoundly deaf'; the remainder have lesser degrees of hearing loss, and typically would be directed to more speech-oriented programmes. Of the state-supported schools for the deaf in the

United States, like the one Bell visited in Rochester, New York, and others founded throughout the 19th century, nearly all have sign language as the policy of education. Many public school districts also offer sign language education as one of several 'parental options', along with the choice to attend regular public school classes with hearing children with or without a sign language interpreter.

Recently there have been experiments in bilingual education for deaf children in the United States and elsewhere. A few experimental schools have been established in the United States, free from control of either traditional deaf schools or public school districts and explicitly promoting education in written English and American Sign Language (ASL). In Denmark and Sweden the national schools for deaf children openly bill their philosophy as bilingual in the national written language as well as the sign language of the country (Mahshie, 1995). But perhaps most intriguing of all are new programmes in the United States that are experimenting with primary education conducted in English and ASL for deaf as well as hearing children. Though the experiment sounds modern, there was in fact a similar brief experiment in 1852 when a small school in Connecticut was established for deaf signing children and their hearing siblings. The experiment did not last long, and by 1861 the school was closed for lack of financial support (Van Cleve, 1993).

## Sign language education for deaf children

Baynton explains in his history of 19th-century deaf education in the United States (Baynton, 1996) that the ascendancy of Alexander Graham Bell and others like him who actively campaigned against sign language in education came as a result of a significant shift of ideas about language and human behaviour. When the first school for deaf children in the United States was founded in 1817 in Connecticut, quickly followed by new schools in New York (1818) and Philadelphia (1820), sign language was generally accepted as the mode of communication among the students and their teachers. Indeed, the first admissions records at the Pennsylvania Institution for the Deaf and Dumb made little note of whether the children used sign language at the time they arrived at the school, preferring instead to record details about the child's family and whether the parents could afford to pay the expense of educating the child. Pennsylvania had just embarked on an ambitious programme of public education for all its citizens, and state funding of these various endeavours depended on keeping meticulous records of where in the state the deaf children lived, who referred them to the school, and their age in order to determine for how long the school would need to be responsible for their care. Sign language is mentioned casually among the earliest records of the Pennsylvania Institution – it was accepted that deaf children used it, and it was rarely discussed as an object of concern or question.

It would take an intellectual shift, from thinking about humans and language as 'natural' in the romantic sense of the term, to a more 'rational' view of the world, to force sign language to become an object of controversy. Baynton argues that seeds of the anti-sign perspective were already present in early US history, but by the end of the 19th century these sentiments became expressed in full force, especially by very public and influential individuals like Alexander Graham Bell. He opposed sign language because he viewed its gestural form as indicative of a more primitive world, less rational and forward-seeking. Educating deaf children without sign language and wholly in speech was the more advanced goal, since it would incorporate them in mainstream culture. This goal could be reached through 'new scientific' methods of speech education that would overcome the dependence on signing and gesturing. If teachers could be properly trained, and if deaf children spent enough time working on their training tasks, speech could be taught to even the most profoundly deaf child. These would be the themes that Bell and those that followed him would repeat: sign language represents an earlier, more naive existence where humans do not strive to overcome their tendencies, but instead fall victim to them.

Indeed, these sentiments would spread throughout Europe and elsewhere, as schools for the deaf closed down their sign language programmes in favour of expanding rigorous training in oral language. In part to combat the alarming rise of oral sentiment in European and US schools and to push for recognition within the United States, deaf people founded their first national organizations, including the National Association of the Deaf (NAD), during this time. The NAD held its first meeting in 1880 and remains today the leading advocacy organization for deaf people in the United States. The position of the NAD and other organizations through the beginning of the 20th century was to argue, as did their president (Veditz, 1913), that 'sign language was the noblest gift God gave to deaf people', but they were persisting in the rhetoric that Baynton says was no longer in vogue. Bell and others ridiculed 'naturalness' as meaning backwardness and persistence in old ways. 'Natural' tendencies, particularly the fondness that deaf people have for sign language, could be overcome by training and perseverance. The scientific endeavour would reward its forward-looking citizens by bringing them into the advances of modern society.

Through the first half of the 20th century, oralism made inroads into deaf education in the United States, leading to dramatic changes in school curricula (Van Cleve and Crouch, 1989) and pitting oralists against 'manualists'. But by the 1960s, campaigners in support of sign language began to shift to a new rhetoric, one that embraced rather than countered the scientific–rational theme, and argued that there were studies showing that sign language education had a positive effect on the development of intelligence, academic performance and psychological well-being (Mindel and Vernon, 1971; Schlesinger and Meadow-Orlans, 1972). Their argument was a revision of an earlier rhetorical tradition: that sign language was natural, not in the sense that it descended from ancient times, but in the sense that it was easy to use, and that it promoted normal development in addition to supporting communication within families. They were part of a growing chorus of educators who wanted to advocate sign language education to parents of deaf children.

## A new science of sign language

The first sign language classrooms of the 1960s and 1970s in the United States were populated by those with a vested interest in deaf education: hearing parents of deaf children, teachers, psychologists and other staff. Locales of sign language classrooms were in church basements or deaf schools. Sign language books were basic vocabulary books made up of pictures or illustrations of signs, with some notes on how to combine signs together to make sentences (Madsen and Lehman, 1982; O'Rourke, 1980; Riekehof, 1963). None of the books published at this time were grammar books, for the simple reason that there was not yet a concept that sign languages had a grammar.

During this same period, sign language education of deaf people and of hearing professionals who worked with them was almost perfectly convergent. Sign language was learnt largely by those with a personal or professional interest in deaf education. The convergence mirrored the segregation of deaf education and the deaf community. Few deaf children attended schools with hearing children; instead they attended large state-funded schools for deaf children, often located at great distance from their homes. They would be boarded at the schools, returning to their homes infrequently through the school year. Sign language teachers were typically individuals who worked at schools like these, or at churches for the deaf. They taught students who would be expected to have interest in either education or religious services for deaf people. Classes were small, and informally conducted. Training of sign language teachers was nonexistent, mainly because the subject was not believed to be complicated. Sign language teachers taught vocabulary lists of signs, and gave advice about how to construct sentences. Byron Burnes, the editor of *Silent Worker*, the official organ of the National Association of the Deaf, wrote in an editorial that though sign language had no grammar, there were expectations and guides to 'good signing' that should be followed by all those using the language (Burnes, 1950). He complained that he saw an erosion of quality of signing, but at the time there was no expectation of a sign language grammar or structure.

The prominence given to sign language in the fields of linguistics and anthropology represented a rapid change, and very recent, occurring only within the past 40 years. As with the first transformation of rhetoric about sign language, it would take another social and intellectual shift to complete this ascendancy. A great deal of credit for this shift is ascribed to William C Stokoe, who, when newly hired as a professor of English at Gallaudet University, had begun reading in cultural and linguistic anthropology. Not having been trained in deaf education, or having had any meaningful contact with deaf people before arriving at Gallaudet, Stokoe viewed sign language with completely new eyes. He wondered if the sign language he was beginning to learn and use with his students might not be a foreign language after all (Stokoe, 2001).

He had spent time in Edinburgh during the 1950s and worked hard to learn the Lallans Scots dialect while there, and it struck him that the language of his students and of the deaf community at Gallaudet was just as hard to learn, and ought to be accounted for on its own terms. He set out, with his colleagues Dorothy Casterline and Carl Croneberg (1965), to write a dictionary and grammar of what he called 'the American sign language', a new term for what had been called simply 'the sign language'. Stokoe is credited with many things, but especially with obstinacy and an ability to endure ridicule, both of which he called upon in great measure as he fought against surprising opposition to publish his dictionary of American Sign Language. As he explains, he found that instead of embracing his project, many hearing educators and even his deaf colleagues at Gallaudet thought he was deluded or wrong, accusing him of embarking on a vanity project.

The dictionary was unlike anything published before; it proposed that signs could be reduced to a set of discrete 'cheremes' or sub-lexical units: the handshape, the movement of the handshape, the hand's orientation, and the location of the hands in a sign (Stokoe et al, 1965). Instead of listing signs according to their English translations, he grouped them according to handshape, and then he coded each sign using a notation system he himself developed (which is still in use today by sign language linguists and bilingual educators of deaf children). Stokoe also published a description of grammatical categories in American Sign Language, and principles of syntax. It was not detailed, but it was startling in what it proposed.

A simple history would credit Stokoe single-handedly for this revolution of ideas, but by his own admission he was inspired by his reading in cultural and linguistic anthropology and was inspired by the work of those who sought to describe little-known languages around the world. He conceived the idea of a dictionary at a pivotal moment in linguistics. As Frederick Newmeyer explains in his history of linguistics (1986), the post-Second World War generation of linguists – those whom Stokoe had been reading – shared two views of languages: that they could be described according to structural properties proposed by Ferdinand de Saussure (which is why they were called structuralists), and that all languages shared the same properties. Stokoe had been reading the work of George Trager and Henry Smith, who described languages according to their phonological structures. Stokoe thought he would try his hand at describing sign language using the same principles: to discover what units combine to form a word, and how they are arranged in sequence.

At almost the same time that Stokoe published his grammar of 'the American sign language', a new National Theatre of the Deaf was founded in the United States made up of deaf actors who for the first time performed outside the deaf community on professional stages throughout the world. As I have discussed elsewhere, the act of performing before the hearing public spurred the creation of a new self-consciousness by deaf actors about their language (Padden, 1990; Padden, in press). Once on stage, deaf actors became more reflective about their language and experimented with ways to explain themselves to the larger hearing public. They began to echo Stokoe's structuralism in the content of their performances. In a scene from the first original production of the National Theatre of the Deaf, called *My Third Eye*, deaf actors Freda Norman, Ed Waterstreet, Richard Kendall and Linda Bove explained that their language was made up of signs distinguished from one another by their handshapes and movements (Padden and Humphries, 1988). It was a sign language lesson from the stage, blended together with evocative pieces about the actors' experiences of oppression of those using sign language in their deaf schools. The deaf actors were articulating a new voice, one that deaf people in the community began to assume, that their language should have a status equal to that of all other human languages of the world.

At the same time that deaf actors began to rework their public performances, there came an explosion in the science of sign languages throughout the world, one that would deeply influence sign language education at the turn of the 21st century. William Stokoe's work was occupied with the systematic description of sign language structure. Soon other scientists would emerge on the scene, and like Stokoe they had little or no background in deaf education. Furthermore, they would profess to no involvement in deaf education. Their scientific goals lay elsewhere, in the fields of psychology, neurolinguistics and theoretical linguistics (Bellugi and Studdert-Kennedy, 1980; Klima and Bellugi, 1979; Poizner, Klima and Bellugi, 1987). Where Stokoe's contribution was to propose a structural analysis of sign languages, that of Ursula Bellugi and Edward Klima was to move sign languages squarely into the centre of modern debate about the nature of language, the brain and cognition, a very powerful place to be at the turn of the century (Emmorey and Lane, 2000).

The new field of sign language linguistics would expand throughout the world, in much the same fashion as within the United States, and as it reached language and cognition laboratories in Europe, South America and Asia, it would become a means for advocating sign language development in these and other areas. Today there are sign language laboratories in numerous universities around the world, from Bristol University in the United Kingdom to Stockholm University in Sweden and the University of Haifa in Israel, to name only a few. Studies of sign language structure across sign languages of the Americas, Asia, Europe, Africa and Australia can be found in a number of recent volumes, ranging from grammar to language acquisition and reading development (Ahlgren et al, 1994; Brentari, 2001; Chamberlain et al, 2000; Fischer and Siple, 1990; Lucas, 1990; Siple and Fischer, 1990).

## Sign language education in colleges and universities

The scientific study of sign languages had broad reach beyond the sciences alone; it had an impact on the teaching of sign languages to adults. Until the 1970s, sign languages were usually taught in deaf education or in churches, and occasionally at colleges and universities, but not with equal status to that of foreign languages. As academic interest in sign languages increased in major research universities across the United States, courses have begun to appear in academic departments, sometimes alongside offerings in Spanish, French, German and other languages. In Europe and Asia the growth of sign language classes has also been notable, driven both by academic interest and by government projects to increase the availability of sign language interpreters for deaf people. In Japan and Scandinavia, sign language classes are not offered in colleges or universities; instead they are taught in interpreter training programmes run by community organizations and funded by the government (Y Osugi and A Bergmann, personal communication). In the United Kingdom, sign language classes are taught both as a further education (ie adult education) subject and in some universities as a higher education (ie university) subject (G Turner, personal communication).

In the United States the expansion of ASL education has been one of the most surprising consequences of the recognition of sign languages by the sciences. The language now ranks behind Spanish as the most common foreign-language choice at some universities, ahead of French and other languages that held that rank through to the end of the 20th century. It is a popular language of choice for students in adult education and community colleges, state teaching colleges and even in research universities like the University of California, San Diego. Many students taking ASL classes have never met a deaf person before, and do not plan careers in deaf education or with deaf people. Indeed, the sheer numbers of students of ASL each year (variously estimated at around 200,000) would exceed the capacity of deaf schools, deaf organizations or social service agencies to absorb them.

The motive of students taking ASL classes seems to be entirely different from that in the last generation. Students view ASL as an exotic example of the human language capacity and want to study the language on its own terms. Other students say they choose ASL as a second language because they think there is greater likelihood that they will meet an ASL signer than an Italian speaker within the United States. One might decry the shift of interest away from learning about other nations and languages of the world, but it has been argued that the 'cognitive revolution' that brought human language and cognition to the forefront of intellectual enterprise at the start of the 21st century has made its way to foreign language education as well. Students are taking foreign languages, including ASL, because they want to learn how languages work and how they are used by communities of users. Indeed, the teaching of foreign languages has changed to include cognitive and structural topics as well as language education per se. University students may or may not be contemplating careers in the foreign language, but in choosing ASL their motives are academic and professional.

The popularity of ASL classes has even extended to the high school level, with many high schools offering ASL classes as electives, alongside other special subjects. Again the motives of high school students are similar to those of college students: they are attracted to the unusual properties of sign languages and use the modality of the hands and eyes as a way to learn about languages and communication. And even more recently, a few elementary schools have begun offering after-school classes in ASL, along with music and sports, in part driven by literature in popular media suggesting that early education in a sign language may afford communicative and verbal advantages to babies and young children.

Marilyn Daniels (2001) has proposed that pre-schoolers and children attending kindergarten can benefit from a small amount of sign language instruction in the school curriculum, using evidence from a small-scale study comparing US children who were exposed to instruction of ASL vocabulary to those who had no such instruction. The children who learnt some signs scored better on the Peabody Picture Vocabulary test, a measure used to determine the size of a child's spoken language vocabulary. She also claims a benefit for literacy development, since larger vocabulary size is correlated with success at learning to read. It is not clear whether her result is due to instruction in sign language specifically, or to any kind of second language instruction (say in Spanish) that can help children learn new vocabulary. Daniels argues that it is specifically the physical and visual nature of sign languages that helps with vocabulary learning, a claim that is so novel that it needs to be evaluated carefully in other research. But her work has drawn attention from the popular media, and hearing parents of hearing children have grown interested in the possibilities of sign language, a very unusual turn of events considering the status of sign languages 30 or 40 years ago.

## The future of sign language education

The model of education for most deaf children throughout the world until the 1970s was in segregated schools. In the United States, each state had its own state-supported boarding school, sometimes more than one, which attracted large numbers of deaf children. Similar policies of grouping deaf children together in special schools were supported in Europe, Asia and South America (Fischer and Lane, 1993). Spurred on by disillusionment with residential institutions, the United States and many other countries in the world undertook a massive shift to move deaf children out of boarding schools and into mainstream school settings. Indeed, by 1990 almost 75 per cent of all deaf children in the United States were educated in public schools and not in the older school settings (Van Cleve, 1993). Against the wave of integration, deaf schools began to be viewed as anachronisms, their architecture too reminiscent of older institutional models of education. Some of these schools would close, and others would reinvent themselves, no longer boarding schools but regional schools serving cities and areas within the state, as in California, New York, and Maryland.

Many of the reinvented regional schools redesigned their curricula, integrating sign language education explicitly into the design of classrooms, the hiring of teachers and revision of their curricula. In many, though not all, the revised curricula are called 'bilingual', where instructional materials and techniques use both written English and ASL. Teachers are required to be bilingual themselves, and to teach not only English but ASL structure as well in a curriculum designed to encourage language development and literacy in both languages. In public schools with special programmes for deaf children, the use of sign language is less explicitly acknowledged. Most public school programmes use a blended system of sign language and spoken English called 'total communication'. Some of these programmes also use an engineered sign language that incorporates novel manual vocabulary invented to represent English. For this reason, Baynton (1996) points out that the sign language revolution in education at the end of the century needs to be qualified: the language of the deaf community in the United States, ASL, is often not named as the language of instruction in most public schools programmes; instead, the official policy is more likely to be 'total communication' that includes some form of sign language.

Counterbalancing the efforts of public schools are a few novel experiments, particularly in charter schools around the United States to experiment with bilingual approaches. Examples of these can be found in Colorado, Minnesota and Utah. There is currently a bilingual charter school for deaf children in Tucson, Arizona, where hearing children are permitted to enrol, reviving the brief 19th-century experiment to educate deaf children together with their hearing siblings (Van Cleve, 1993). Most of the hearing children have some connection to the deaf community, either because their parents are deaf and ASL signers, or because they work in the community, and the parents desire a broad language education for their children in ASL as well as English. There are also day care and pre-school programmes in both ASL and spoken English, including deaf and hearing children from the local community in places around the country. These are very small-scale efforts, not likely to overtake the educational order as it currently stands in the United States, but like the experiments to teach sign language vocabulary to pre-schoolers and children attending kindergarten (Daniels, 2001), they are motivated by a different conception about sign language education. Whether this novelty will be sustainable in the long run, or will fail again as the 19th-century experiment did, it is too soon to tell.

It is easy to recognize how dramatic changes have been in acceptance of sign language and interest in the language. Where hearing parents were once counselled not to use sign language, many schools and programmes now offer early infant education programmes where parents can learn sign language while their children are still very young. Scandinavian countries have aggressive programmes to teach sign language to hearing parents of young deaf children (Mahshie, 1995). Sign language classes in the United States as well as elsewhere show no sign of abating in popularity, with enrolments in colleges and universities having continued to increase for over 20 years. Hearing children in the United States can take pre-school classes alongside deaf children where the medium of communication is ASL as well as spoken English.

Despite these remarkable changes, Baynton offers no cheery predictions about the future (1996). While it is true that sign language has reached a level of unprecedented recognition, he observes that the sentiments that opposed sign language education have not disappeared. The same scientific–rational impulse that led Bell to advocate oral training for deaf children has transmogrified into a techno-rational campaign where the rhetoric of technology and biomedicine has made deep inroads into sign language education, notably in schools and programmes for deaf children. Children who receive cochlear implants, a device surgically placed inside the cochlea to provide amplified sound, are commonly directed to programmes without sign language so that they can fully focus on speech and auditory training. When Bell visited the Rochester School in 1878 he was impressed with the headmaster's method of using only the manual alphabet in all school communication, to the exclusion of sign language. The policy was a good one, Bell argued, because the presence of sign language distracts children from the task of learning English. Sign language's ease of use was not seen as a desirable quality; indeed, it would lead the children astray because they would succumb to their instincts (Van Cleve, 1993).

The same argument applies again almost unchanged nearly 120 years later, that children with implants should not acquire sign language or meet other signers because doing so might compete with their ability to learn to speak and use their device to hear. If the scientific study of sign languages had fully advanced their cause, sign languages would be not seen as burdens or distractions; instead they would be viewed as additional languages that could be learnt without risk to the acquisition of the other language. But as it remains now, the scientific study of sign languages has yet to reach its pinnacle: of achieving, in scientific as well as popular realms, universal acceptance of sign languages.

It is hard to know whether the conflicting trends are because of an unfinished project – that is, that sign languages have not yet been fully brought into the world of human languages and more research needs to be done to convince parents and school directors – or because the move to embrace sign languages and recognize their uniqueness will always exist alongside the drive to celebrate spoken language, or certain spoken languages, above all other languages. We can only hope that universal acceptance prevails, because above all, we can then celebrate genius in all its different forms, not just in a few.

# References

Ahlgren, I, Bergman, B and Brennan, M (1994) *Perspectives on sign language: papers from the Fifth International Symposium on Sign Language Research*, International Sign Linguistics Association, Deaf Studies Research Unit, University of Durham, UK

Baynton, D C (1996) *Forbidden Signs: American Culture and the Campaign Against Sign Language*, University of Chicago Press, Chicago, IL

Bellugi, U and Studdert-Kennedy, M (1980) *Signed and spoken language: Biological constraints on linguistic form*, Verlag Chemie, Weinheim

Brentari, D (2001) *Foreign vocabulary in sign languages: a cross-linguistic investigation of word formation*, Lawrence Erlbaum Associates, Mahwah, NJ

Burnes, B (1950) *Silent Worker*, p 2

Chamberlain, C, Morford, J P and Mayberry, R I (2000) *Language acquisition by eye*, Lawrence Erlbaum Associates, Mahwah, NJ

Daniels, M (2001) *Dancing with words: signing for hearing children's literacy*, Bergin & Garvey, Westport

Emmorey, K and Lane, H (2000) *The Signs of Language Revised: An Anthology to Honor Ursula Bellugi and Edward Klima*, Lawrence Erlbaum Associates, Mahwah, NJ

Fischer, R and Lane, H (eds) (1993) *Looking Back: A Reader on the History of Deaf Communities and their Sign Languages*, Signum Press, Hamburg, Germany

Fischer, S D and Siple, P (1990) *Theoretical issues in sign language research* (*Vol. 1: Linguistics*), University of Chicago Press, Chicago, IL

Gallaudet Research Institute (2000) *Regional and National Summary Report of Data from the 1999–2000 Annual Survey of Deaf and Hard of Hearing Children and Youth*, GRI, Gallaudet University, Washington, DC

Humphries, T (1996) Of deaf-mutes, the strange, and the modern deaf self, in *Culturally affirmative psychotherapy with deaf persons*, eds N S Glickman, M A Harvey *et al*, Lawrence Erlbaum Associates, Mahwah, NJ

Klima, E and Bellugi, U (1979) *The signs of language*, Harvard University Press, Cambridge MA

Lane, H (1992) *The Mask of Benevolence: Disabling the Deaf Community*, Alfred A Knopf, New York

Lucas, C (1990) *Sign language research: theoretical issues*, Gallaudet University Press, Washington, DC

Madsen, W J and Lehman, L A (1982) *Intermediate conversational sign language: American sign language with English translations*, Gallaudet College Press, Washington, DC

Mahshie, S (1995) *Educating Deaf children Bilingually: With Insights and Applications from Sweden and Denmark*, Pre-College Programs, Gallaudet University, Washington, DC

Mindel, E D and Vernon, M (1971) *They grow in silence; the deaf child and his family*, National Association of the Deaf, Silver Spring, MD

Newmeyer, F J (1986) *The politics of linguistics*, University of Chicago Press, Chicago, IL

O'Rourke, T (1980) *ABC: A Basic Course in Manual Communication*, National Association of the Deaf, Silver Spring, MD

Padden, C (1990) Folk explanation in language survival, in *Collective Remembering* ed D Middleton, Sage, Los Angeles, CA

Padden, C (in press) Afterword, in *Signing the Body Poetic: Essays in ASL Literature*, eds D Bauman, J Nelson and H Rose, University of California Press, Berkeley, CA

Padden, C and Humphries, T (1988) *Deaf in America: Voices from a Culture*, Harvard University Press, Cambridge, MA

Peters, C (in press) Deaf American theatre, in *Signing the Body Poetic: Essays on American Sign Language Literature*, eds D Bauman, J Nelson and H Rose, University of California Press, Berkeley, CA

Plann, S (1997) *A Silent Minority: Deaf Education in Spain, 1550–1835,* University of California Press, Berkeley, CA

Poizner, H, Klima, E S and Bellugi, U (1987) *What the hands reveal about the brain*, Mit Press, Cambridge, MA

Riekehof, L L (1963) *Talk to the deaf; a manual of approximately 1,000 signs used by the deaf of North America*, Gospel Pub. House, Springfield, MO

Schlesinger, H S and Meadow-Orlans, K P (1972) *Sound and sign; childhood deafness and mental health.* University of California Press, Berkeley, CA

Scouten, E L (1942) *A revaluation of the Rochester method*, The Alumni Association of the Rochester School for the Deaf, Rochester, NY

Siple, P and Fischer, S D (1990) *Theoretical issues in sign language research (Vol. 2: Acquisition)*, University of Chicago Press, Chicago, IL

Stokoe, W, Croneberg, C and Casterline, D (1965) *A dictionary of American Sign Language on linguistic principles*, Gallaudet College Press, Washington, DC

Stokoe, W C (1960) *Sign language structure: an outline of the visual communication systems of the American deaf*, Department of Anthropology and Linguistics University of Buffalo, Buffalo

Stokoe, W C (2001) *Language in hand: why sign came before speech*, Gallaudet University Press, Washington, DC

Van Cleve, J and Crouch, B (1989) *A Place of Their Own: Creating the Deaf Community in America*, Gallaudet University Press, Washington, DC

Van Cleve, J V (1993) The academic integration of deaf children: A historical perspective, in *Looking Back: A Reader on the History of Deaf Communities and their Sign Languages* eds R Fischer and H Lane, Signum Press, Hamburg, Germany

Veditz, G (1913) *The preservation of the sign language* [Film]. National Association of the Deaf, Silver Spring, MD

# 5. Foreign language education in context

Michael Byram

Three fundamental functions of all national education systems, and of compulsory education in particular, are to create the human capital required in a country's economy, to develop a sense of national identity, and to promote equality, or at least a sense of social inclusion. In various degrees and forms these have been educational aims since the foundation of national education systems in Western Europe and North America and were exported, together with the forms of schooling, to other parts of the world by the colonial powers in the 19th and 20th century. The learning of a foreign language was in the early stages of this development rather anomalous. It was not essential to the economy since it was, above all, colonial languages that were used in trade or supplemented by knowledge of other languages by a few intermediaries. It did not function in policies of equality or social inclusion but rather was anti-thetical to these since only an elite learnt foreign languages. And it was, if anything, a potential threat to national identity because it introduced learners to different beliefs and values. However, in practice the threat was minimized by teaching methods based on translation, which by definition involves seeing another language and the values and beliefs it embodies through the framework of one's own language, and one's own beliefs and values.

Some of the purposes and forms of education remain unaltered, but social changes of the late 20th and early 21st centuries that are encapsulated in the words 'globalization' and 'internationalization' have given new meaning and significance to foreign language learning. One example of this is to be found in Western Europe, and increasingly in Central and Eastern Europe. The creation of a single market in Europe is a microcosm of globalization and has led to increased mobility and frequent interactions among people of different languages. This in turn has led to a political will to develop a new concept of identity, a European identity, which is fostered by increased foreign language learning. A second example is China, where entry into the World Trade Organization is creating a demand for language learning on a major scale but where access to international communication, particularly through the Internet, is perceived as sufficiently threatening to national values and beliefs to lead to censorship.

Foreign language education is thus no exception to the need to locate all education in its social, economic and political context. There are factors to be considered both in the educational purposes as sketched above, and in the analysis of the content and methodology of teaching. Prior to this, however, there are also factors to be taken into account in the definition of 'foreign' language education.

## Defining foreign language education

From a psychological perspective on the processes of language learning, there may be no useful distinction between 'second' and 'foreign' languages, since it can be argued that the acquisition processes are identical. In an educational and political context, however, the status of a language in a given society is important, and the distinction significant. Consider the case of French, for example. In the anglophone provinces of Canada, French is taught as a second language, being one of the two official languages of the country. Across the border in the United States it is a foreign language with no official status but considerable prestige. In Australia, too, it is a foreign language but its prestige is being threatened by other foreign languages from countries such as Japan, which are more important than France in a geopolitical sense. In India, French is present in the curriculum of the Central Institute of English and Foreign Languages, the major university for languages, but is not a significant language in India, whereas in some African countries it is an official language. Yet in both cases French is clearly a non-indigenous language – in one 'foreign', in the other 'official'. Finally, in France, French is taught as the national language and assumed to be the 'mother tongue', even though there are many French citizens for whom it is chronologically their 'second' language since they have learnt, for example, Arabic in the home. Furthermore, it may not be perceived by some citizens as their 'national' language because, for example, they attribute this status to Breton, the language of an indigenous ethnic minority.

A second issue in the definition of foreign language education is the importance of distinguishing 'learning' from 'education'. It is evident that in most countries, people learn more than one language in the course of their lives. They do so in many settings, of which educational institutions are only one. They also learn in many ways, of which being taught in a classroom is only one. What distinguishes foreign language education is that it has social and political purposes reflected in the formalities of an educational institution and embodied more or less explicitly in the learning aims and objectives attributed to the institution by governments at local or national level.

As a consequence of globalization and internationalization, these educational policies and aims have changed, or more accurately the emphasis has changed. Although there was a famous call for change in aims in the late 19th century, when in the so-called 'Reform Movement' Viëtor said, 'Der Sprachunterricht muss umkehren' ('Language teaching must start afresh'), the fresh start took almost 100 years to be accepted. The change was from aims of acquiring a foreign language for purposes of understanding the high culture of great civilizations to those of being able to use a language for daily communication and interaction with people from another country. As this change became accepted, ultimately under the banner of 'Communicative Language Teaching', the aims of language teaching in educational institutions began to coincide with the aims of most people learning languages in many other ways and locations. Foreign language education is now largely focused on the purposes of language learning, which seem self-evident to learners, and has to meet their expectations of success. Those expectations are high because they see people around them, especially young children, apparently learning languages quickly and successfully in non-educational settings and through interaction with other children and through exposure to mass media. To what extent their expectations are justified and how often they are fulfilled varies from country to country and is an issue to which we shall return below.

To what extent the shift of focus in educational aims is satisfactory is still under debate. The shift within compulsory education seems to be almost complete. For example, in Japan in 1993 a Government Commission on Foreign Language Policy Revision for the Twenty-first Century proposed fundamental structural change in syllabus, teacher training, public examinations exchange programmes and so on, to improve learners' communication skills. In the United States the publication in 1999 of *Standards for Foreign Language Learning: Preparing for the 21st Century* moved away from a framework of four skills (listening, speaking, reading and writing), where the focus is on language as a system to be acquired, and substituted goal areas (communication, cultures, connections, comparisons and communities), where the focus is on what can be accomplished through a foreign language. The underlying principles are provided by three modes of communication – interpersonal, interactive and presentational – which describe the ways of functioning in a language. Similarly, the *Common European Framework of Reference for Languages: Learning, teaching, assessment*, developed by the Council of Europe in the 1980s and 1990s, proposes an approach based on an analysis of how languages are used in communication, on the 'functions' people use them for, and the 'notions' they use them to express, instead of an analysis of the grammatical system.

All of these are influential documents on which new curricula and teaching methods are being constructed in the new century throughout the First World. The Second World of the former Soviet bloc is also quickly moving from traditions of language learning based on linguistic analysis and is in fact overtaking many First World countries by moving more quickly to this new position without passing through intermediary phases of language teaching methods such as the audio-lingual method. Changes in the Third World are, however, much slower. Modern methods require hardware and teaching materials, which are costly. Methods that rely on minimal equipment that can be used in large classes, with emphasis on grammatical analysis, are still wide-spread. On the other hand, 'new' methods of using a language as a medium of instruction in other subjects, which are currently being (re)discovered in Western Europe and imported from immersion programmes in North America, have been current in many African countries for many decades. This is, however, a necessity rather than a choice because foreign, ie non-indigenous, languages (English and French above all) are the official languages of many African countries and therefore automatically the languages of instruction. Children acquire them as a consequence simply of attending school.

The shift of emphasis to communication aims is thus largely unchallenged in compulsory schooling and vocational education but is disputed in university education. Language teaching in universities for non-majors is following the shift in emphasis on aims and methods with little hesitation, and the formation of an association to support this kind of teaching in Europe (the Confédération Européenne des Centres de Langues dans l'Enseignement Supérieur) is a symptom of the recognition of this function of university education. On the other hand, 'study' of languages, as opposed to language learning, for language majors and their lecturers seems to be caught between the poles of language as 'a means to an end' and language as 'an end in itself'. When language is a means to an end, the purpose has traditionally followed that of the study of classical languages – Chinese, Greek, Latin, Sanskrit, Arabic – that is to gain access to great texts, often literary but not exclusively so. In some countries the literary canon has been expanded to include, or has given way absolutely to, the study of cultures and societies, drawing on a range of disciplines such as anthropology, sociology, economics, history, and not just literary history and criticism. A striking example of this is the growth in interest in British Studies or British Cultural Studies in departments of English in many countries where previously the study of English literature (or sometimes all literature written in English) was the norm. Similar developments are taking place in other language 'disciplines' and have, for example, fostered a debate in German Studies in the United States. One of the issues is precisely whether language study is a 'discipline' with clear definition of an object of study, a methodology and an epistemology, or whether it is an 'area' whose boundaries are in fact 'fuzzy' and, in the contemporary post-modern world, appropriately so (Di Napoli, Polezzi and King, 2001).

## Foreign language education policies

As foreign language learning has become more important for societies responding to globalization and internationalization, governments have paid more attention to policy making. In many cases the focus is on the teaching and learning of English, and English as a Foreign Language (EFL) is almost synonymous with foreign language learning in many countries. This is a consequence of British colonialism continued by US dominance of world affairs.

The role of English thus often dominates the development of language education policies, and the teaching of English has been a major influence on the methods of teaching all foreign languages. The most significant factor in policy making for EFL is the relationship English has with native-speaker communities. As an 'international language', there should be in principle no priority accorded to British or US English, or in fact any other country where English is the national or official language. Yet there is still a strong tendency in many countries to pay allegiance by accepting British or US norms of language use, of pronunciation, of grammatical correctness, of dictionary definitions of meanings. Despite the special circumstances of English being spoken by many more non-native than native speakers, native-speaker norms are thus taken as international norms, in spite of the questioning of the whole concepts of 'nativeness' in this sense. For example, in Singapore, government has formulated an explicit policy of maintaining external norms against the development of Singaporean English, not least for fear of Singaporeans losing competence in the major medium of international trade.

Native speakers, and the governments and cultural institutes of native-speaker countries, have a vested interest in promoting attitudes of deference to native-speaker norms in that they thereby continue to dominate communication and gain advantage in negotiation. Academic analysis has suggested that there is both conscious and unconscious 'linguistic imperialism' (Phillipson, 1992) beneath these processes. On the other hand, there is growing evidence that the dominance of native speakers, for example as teachers setting and embodying linguistic and cultural norms, is being challenged (Medgyes, 1994). It is evident that international users of English are taking ownership of it for their own purposes (Canagarajah, 1999).

Other languages and their native-speaker communities have not been criticized as vehemently as English. Nonetheless the institutionalization and promotion of French, German and Spanish (in the Alliance Française, the Goethe-Institut and the Cervantes Institute) is an indicator of the significance of the teaching of their languages in the foreign policies of the countries in question. The Cervantes Institute, for example, was founded in 1991, embracing the aims of language teaching for communication, and the significance of Spanish continues to grow in the commercial development of South America, and also as the second language of the United States. The Goethe-Institut plays a crucial role in the teaching of German because German does not have a substantial place in school-level education but is learnt by adults, and adult education is seldom a priority for governments. The Goethe-Institut thus offers a systematic base for the learning of German, and it too has embraced communicative aims for language learning.

Policy responses to the evolving significance of language learning, and in particular the dominance of English, are mainly based on acceptance of the trend towards English. Politicians in democratic societies, at whatever level they operate, follow the perceived demands and needs of their publics who seek every opportunity to learn English, to have English introduced to their children at an early age, to use English for work and leisure. These perceptions may not be as well founded as they seem and the future of English may be less dominant, evolving simply as one of a number of languages an individual speaks (Graddol, 1997). Furthermore, as the case of education in France demonstrates, the choice of foreign language by parents for their children can sometimes support languages other than English since the choice of a 'difficult' or 'less widely used' language ensures that a pupil is placed in a good learning environment and among an elite. Nonetheless, here too the tendency is for a reduction of diversity as most parents 'play safe' and choose English (Puren, 2000).

Policies to encourage diversity in non-anglophone countries thus run against the trend and are difficult to sustain in a democracy. On the other hand, there is some recognition in policy making that language teaching is a necessary but not a sufficient response to change, and needs to be accompanied by 'internationalization' of the whole curriculum in compulsory education. Examples include Japan, South Korea, Sweden and Denmark, where an explicit policy has been formulated by national ministries of education. This typically means that teachers of all subjects are expected to make explicit the international dimension; for example, science teachers might draw attention to the nationality of well-known scientists and the places and circumstances in which their discoveries were made, or mathematics teachers might draw out the historical origins of mathematics in the Arabic-speaking world. Visits and exchanges with other countries are seen not simply as an opportunity to practise foreign languages but as occasions for cross-curricular projects and comparative studies.

The European Union is the only example of a supra-national polity that believes that it needs to develop a language education policy. As a political entity with 11 'official and working languages' functioning in its institutions, it has formulated a policy that all citizens of its member states should learn three of these languages: their own national language and two foreign languages (European Commission, 1995). This is seen as crucial to the development of the economy and a sense of identity, not unlike the policies of nation-states:

> Proficiency in several Community languages has become a precondition if citizens of the European Union are to benefit from the occupational and personal opportunities open to them in the border-free single market. This language proficiency must be backed up by the ability to adapt to working and living environments characterised by different cultures.
>
> Languages are also the key to knowing other people. Proficiency in languages helps to build up the feeling of being European with all its cultural wealth and

diversity and of understanding between the citizens of Europe. (European Commission, 1995: 67)

The Council of Europe is similarly a supra-national body but focused on cultural cooperation. It embraces more than 45 member states, as compared to the 15 of the European Union, and it too has formulated a policy to promote linguistic diversity. It has not committed itself to a specific number of languages but has recognized that diversity is a function of each particular situation and should be pursued as an over-arching principle. In both cases the wish to promote diversity stems partly from a recognition of the economic value of plurilingual individuals able to move freely in a multilingual market-place, and partly from a concern to sustain the culturally diverse heritage of European countries.

A comparable policy in nation-states would be to promote continuing cultural as well as commercial relations with a wide range of countries, not just those where English is the native or official language. Understanding of other cultures, for example of China or Arabic-speaking countries, presupposes acquisition of Chinese or Arabic in order to have access to significant texts. A policy that encourages diversity in language learning for these reasons would in fact be a revival of earlier aims of language learning for cultural purposes. Although it would be perceived as incompatible with communication aims and emphasis on major languages, above all English, it is in fact a complementary function since political and economic affairs often founder not on a lack of linguistic competence but on a lack of cultural understanding.

The policy dilemmas in anglophone countries are different. Despite what might appear to be the advantages of 'linguistic imperialism', the US President's Commission on Language Learning was established in 1978 and found 'a serious deterioration in this country's language and research capacity at a time when an increasingly hazardous international military, political and economic environment is making unprecedented demands on America's resources, intellectual capacity and public sensitivity' (*Strength through Wisdom*, 1979: 1). Language teaching and learning is here again part of foreign policy. British governments have reacted much more slowly, and it was necessary for a privately sponsored commission to be formed in the late 1990s before a substantial policy review could be inaugurated (*Languages: The next generation*, 2000).

The case of Australia is different in that foreign language education policy has developed within a broader national language policy. This has arisen from the recognition of the multilingual composition of the Australian population itself, comprising people of Aboriginal origins and languages, and others of European and East Asian emigration from non-anglophone countries. Language policy from the 1970s encouraged multiculturalism rather than assimilation to an anglophone norm, including provision of opportunity to learn second and foreign languages. In the 1990s increased emphasis was placed on the relevance of some languages more than others to the competitiveness of the business community; these were particularly Japanese, Chinese, Korean and Indonesian. Thus, despite the different policy content, the significance of languages in foreign policy is again evident.

## Content and methods

We have seen that the contemporary re-definition of foreign language education can be traced to social, political and economic change, to forces external to education and language teaching. Internal factors have also been influential, but more at the level of detail: methods of teaching, learning processes and assessment. Within the language teaching profession, the phrase 'communicative language teaching' (CLT) has encapsulated internal changes since the 1970s. CLT was in part a response to external change and in part a development in pedagogical theory where it was argued that language learning cannot be successful for purposes of communication in real time if learners and teachers concentrate exclusively on acquiring linguistic competence – that is, ability to produce grammatically and phonetically correct sentences. Theorists (Hymes, 1971; Savignon, 1997), argued that when we acquire our first language we acquire both linguistic and sociolinguistic competence – that is, the ability to use a language in ways appropriate to any given situation – and that learners of foreign languages must do the same. Language was conceived as social behaviour that could be analysed on a number of dimensions that could then be used to guide syllabus planning and course design. Two influential analyses were published independently in Europe and North America (Canale and Swain, 1980; van Ek, 1986) with some overlap on the analyses of communicative competence they presented. They both emphasize, first, strategic competence: the ability to identify and cope with gaps in one's language knowledge and skill; second, sociolinguistic competence: the ability to use the appropriate language for a given social situation; and third, linguistic competence: mastery of language rules. Van Ek's definition also included pragmatic competence: the ability to handle different structures of discourse above the level of the sentence; and sociocultural competence: knowledge about a country or countries where the language being learnt is spoken natively.

Of the two, the North American version of CLT has been more influential on a world scale because it was cited in the work of theorists and teachers of EFL. It can be argued that this too led to an imperialism of methodology that was not always appropriate (Holliday, 1994). The native-speaker teacher, and teacher-trainer, brought certain presuppositions about how learners should be managed, what techniques are likely to be successful and what norms should be used in assessment.

The European version of CLT has been established by theorists and practitioners working under the aegis of the Council of Europe. Their influence has been largely restricted to member states of the Council – some 45 states throughout Europe – partly because publications have remained internal until recent years. Their work constitutes a body of research and publication that defines the content and objectives for learning specific languages at a number of levels from beginner to advanced. The 'Threshold' level defines the language needed to transact the business of everyday life adequately and establish and maintain social contacts, and has been produced for more than 20 European languages (both regional and national languages – for example, for Catalan as well as Spanish). Other levels are described as 'Waystage' (below Threshold) and 'Vantage' (above Threshold), and an initial 'break-through' level is being developed. Subsequently, a *Common European Framework of Reference for Languages: Learning, teaching, assessment* was published in English and French (Council of Europe, 2001a, b) and embodies the pedagogical philosophy of the Council of Europe as it has evolved over 30 years. It defines levels of language proficiency and discusses processes of learning and teaching as well as assessment. It does not recommend specific methods of teaching but attempts to provide a framework for reflection on teaching. Similarly, it does not propose a specific theory of learning since it is argued that 'there is at present no sufficiently strong, research-based consensus on how learners learn' (p 139).

In short, in the development of CLT there has been much attention given to content and objectives or expected outcomes, and considerable consensus that 'communicative competence' includes, but is more complex than, linguistic competence. The question of how the competence as a whole or sub-competencies within it are acquired, and therefore what methodology teachers should adopt, is a much more open and debated question.

The lack of consensus on learning theory is a disappointment for many teachers in many countries. Although there is a significant field of research on 'Second Language Acquisition' (SLA), it is not primarily concerned with helping teachers. It is far more focused on explaining what is known about acquisition of languages in all kinds of situations, of which the classroom is only one (Bremer *et al*, 1996). It does not claim to be a theory of teaching, predicting the results of particular methods. Furthermore, SLA is concerned with the acquisition of linguistic competence rather than other dimensions of communicative competence, such as strategic or sociocultural competence.

This leaves language teachers to make their own decisions for their language classrooms, and a number of teaching methods have developed under the label of CLT. Many of these argue that communicative competence can be best acquired by using a language as a medium rather than studying it as an object. Such methods include 'content-based instruction' or 'bilingual education' or 'immersion programmes', in all of which learners are taught subjects other than languages through the medium of a foreign language. Such approaches are to be found in many countries as methods more and less formally constituted. Most publicized and researched are 'immersion programmes' in Canada, where for example English-speaking Canadian children are taught from the beginning of compulsory schooling for significant proportions of their schooling through the medium of French. Programmes labelled as 'bilingual' exist in Germany, where learners begin to study some but not all of their subjects in secondary education in a foreign language. In Bulgaria and the Czech Republic there have existed for many years specialist secondary schools where learners are given intensive courses in a foreign language for up to one year and then begin to study the whole of their curriculum in that language.

These and similar methods are conceived as means of improving language learning and communicative competence. They have in common a rejection of methods that focus on language itself, either in the shape of grammatical analysis and translation, the so-called grammar–translation method, or in the shape of instilling linguistic behaviour in the audio-lingual and audio-visual methods. The emphasis on language use also means that such methods can be compared with the informal methods of teaching a language experienced by learners in many countries, namely the obligation to attend a school where the language of instruction is different from the language they have learnt in their home. In the latter case, however, teachers often pay little attention to the fact that their learners are simultaneously learning a content and the medium in which it is presented. In the former, teachers are aware of potential difficulties and therefore attend to the medium and its forms as well as the content. In this respect, they do not reject entirely the focus on language itself, which has dominated language teaching and is still widely prevalent.

For the question of whether it is better to focus on form or meaning is by no means resolved. It is therefore still common to find grammatical analysis and translation in language teaching in many countries, for example China and Japan. It is also possible to find methods associated with CLT focusing on language use present in one sector of an education system, and grammar and translation being preferred in another sector. The former is the case in primary and secondary education in most West European countries, and the latter is present in language teaching in the universities of those countries.

The debate is likely to continue but is in some respects a false one. On the one hand, there is a view that it should be possible to establish fundamental principles for teaching since learning is assumed to have some universal characteristics. On the other hand, it is argued that methods need to be in harmony with culture-specific factors in schooling and in learning experiences (Holliday, 1994). For example, CLT techniques involve much emphasis on pairwork and other classroom activities that presuppose a willingness on the part of the learners, whereas learners may wish to learn individually, to be allowed to use their own time and methods to learn rather than being put under the spotlight. There is doubtless some truth in both positions and therefore a need to resolve the debate about methods differently in different contexts, even within the same education system.

The 'modernization' of language teaching is thus a constant process of advances in theory but reassessment of past and present practices. Progress involves looking backwards as well as forwards. Modernization is also evident in the use of technology. The invention of audio recording, for example, allowed techniques of teaching pronunciation to be developed and 'language laboratories' to appear. New technologies are now integrated into self-access language or media centres where learners can work at their own pace and in their own time. This presupposes, however, an ability to organize one's own learning, and the vision of the autonomous learner who 'learns to learn' has become part of the methodology of many teachers (Little, 1991). Furthermore, the potential for learning at a distance is also provided by Internet and computer links, either under the guidance of a teacher or in programmes that exploit the potential of multimedia sources such as video discs to guide learners through independent learning. The options offered by computers have long been evident (Kenning and Kenning, 1984) and are constantly being revised (Cameron, 1998), but have not resolved the issues of language learning theory and practice that have already been mentioned in connection with traditional classroom learning. On the other hand, the Internet and electronic mail open up possibilities of interaction among learners in quick and easy ways – in contrast with the difficulties of postal correspondence in the past. The evidence is that here too the teacher still has a role to play in maintaining motivation by offering a structure of tasks and activities, but the immediacy of Internet communication may be the only way in which many learners will have direct interaction with speakers of other languages.

Finally, a recent development internal to foreign language education but, like others, also a consequence of social change, is to refine the definition of 'communicative competence' to include the concept of intercultural competence. Researchers have re-analysed the ways in which learners use their foreign languages in interactions with 'the other' – that is, with people of different linguistic and cultural identities. Based both in empirical analysis of the capacities of those with considerable experience of mobility, and in conceptual analysis of relationships between different cultural groups – notably nation-states – they have argued that the successful person is the one who can act as a social mediator between groups. Such a person can occupy a 'third space', being neither in his or her own group nor attempting to be a native of the other group (Kramsch, 1993). The implications for foreign language education are, it is then argued (Byram, 1997), that new objectives must be defined that include intercultural competence as well as communicative competence. This leads to further implications for teaching and assessment, but as with the discussion of linguistic competence, a lack of a consensual view of learning processes means that methods are being developed above all by trial and error, on the basis of a few conceptually argued principles (Byram, Nichols and Stevens, 2001).

## Evaluation and planning of foreign language education

The growing importance of foreign language education in social, political and economic terms is leading to more attention being paid to its efficiency. Investment of time in the formal curriculum of compulsory education and of money in the materials to support it, particularly the use of information and communication technology, calls for evaluation. Decisions about which languages to teach, how many, at which points in education, both compulsory and post-compulsory, and in particular a general policy to encourage linguistic and cultural diversity lead to more conscious planning of foreign language education.

Detailed planning and policies for language education are, as we saw earlier, beginning to be taken seriously by politicians. Evaluation of the success of policies is still rare at national and international level, and tends to be limited to the collection of statistics (for a recent example at an international level, see Eurobarometer, 2001). An exception to this are the studies carried out by the International Association for the Evaluation of Educational Advancement (IEA) in the 1970s. These considered policies, human and material resources and institutions in English teaching in 10 countries and French teaching in seven countries. Rather than making comparisons among countries, which is almost impossible because of the variations and complexities of different systems, these studies allowed insight into such factors as the length of time spent on learning and the intensity of courses, and the identification of important independent variables. The amount of time spent on learning is crucial, but the starting age is not. Exposure to a foreign language outside the classroom leads to higher achievement than where a foreign language is a school-based subject (Cumming, 1996: 1, 5). Further studies of this kind planned during the 1990s were not completed, and international evaluation has therefore not been brought up to date.

Evaluation studies on a smaller scale are more frequent, and methods have been developed as part of a wider concern with educational evaluation. Important distinctions are made between formative and summative evaluation, between quantitative and qualitative techniques of data collection, and among the different foci for evaluation: teaching methods, teachers, materials. The inclusion of language teaching in the development of quality management and the use of 'benchmarks' as part of public accountability for financial investment is evident in Western countries and will doubtless spread. In Hong Kong, for example, teachers of English have been required to take tests to establish whether their competences meet predetermined benchmarks. In Britain the definitions of what levels students of languages in universities can be expected to reach are being negotiated.

## Conclusion

Although the focus in this chapter has been on foreign language education, it is important that it be seen in a context of language education in general. The difficulty of defining a *foreign* language is an indication of this need. The interest in *Second* Language Acquisition research in the relationship between processes of acquisition of first and subsequent languages is a further indication. Educationalists have argued that learners' understanding of languages and themselves as language people requires an integrative approach to teaching all languages (Hawkins, 1984; van Lier, 1995). 'Awareness of language', as this perspective is called, or in French *réveil aux langues*, also helps learners to become more effective because they are conscious of how languages can be learnt and skills transferred from one language to another, and policy making should also take this into account in order to ensure more return on investment in time and other resources. The ability to learn languages, to become a plurilingual 'language person' with a range of competences to different levels in different languages, needs to be the focus of language teaching just as much as the ability in a particular language being taught at a particular time.

Foreign language education must also be seen against a social and political background. Internationalization and globalization are forces that are not yet fully understood, but there is no doubt that both the ability to use several languages for various purposes and the capacity for empathy and understanding are crucial. People are interacting with each other face to face or at a distance, they are being told about and shown to each other by mass media, but neither real-time experience of others, nor increased exposure to information, necessarily leads to empathy and understanding. Language education needs to develop in the future towards a greater conscious inclusion of political and social purposes. What has been seen largely as a training in skills is in fact inevitably concerned with values and critical understanding of others, ourselves and how we interact together as individuals and groups. Language teachers of all kinds are under-prepared for this task because so much emphasis has been placed on technical matters of selection of content, theory of learning, and options for 'delivery' of teaching through old and new technologies. These remain significant because the problems are yet to be solved, but the challenge for language educators is above all to educate, to promote an ability to change perspective and to relativize what is taken for granted. The great German educator Wilhelm von Humboldt described this as long ago as the early 19th century:

> By the same act whereby [man] spins language out of himself, he spins himself into it, and every language draws about the people that possess it a circle whence it is possible to exit only over at once into the circle of another one. To learn a foreign language should therefore be to acquire a new standpoint in the world-view hitherto possessed, and in fact to a certain extent is so, since every language

contains the whole conceptual fabric and mode of presentation of a portion of mankind. But because we always carry over, more or less, our own world-view, and even our own language-view, this outcome is not purely and completely experienced. (von Humboldt, 1836/1988: 60)

We can never escape our own language, but in taking a different perspective, language learners of any age or disposition can be brought to a greater critical awareness of themselves and others and thereby become more adequately educated for an international world. This is the real challenge for all language education.

## References

Bremer, K, Roberts, C, Vasseur, M-T, Simonot, M and Broeder, P (1996) *Achieving Understanding: Discourse in intercultural encounters*, Longman, London

Byram, M (1997) *Teaching and Assessing Intercultural Communicative Competence*, Multilingual Matters, Clevedon, UK

Byram, M, Nichols, A and Stevens, D (eds) (2001) *Developing Intercultural Competence in Practice*, Multilingual Matters, Clevedon, UK

Cameron, K (ed) (1998), *Multimedia CALL: Theory and practice*, Elm Bank Publications, Exeter

Canagarajah, A S (1999) *Resisting Linguistic Imperialism in English Teaching*, Oxford University Press, Oxford

Canale, M and Swain, M (1980) Theoretical bases of communicative approaches to second language teaching and testing, *Applied Linguistics*, **1** (1), pp 1–47

Council of Europe (2001a) *Common European Framework of Reference for Languages: Learning, teaching, assessment*, Cambridge University Press, Cambridge

Council of Europe (2001b) *Cadre européen commun de référence pour les langues: apprendre, enseigner, évaluer*, Didier, Paris

Cumming, A (1996) IEA's studies of language education: their scope and contributions, *Assessment in Education*, **3** (2), pp 179–92

Di Napoli, R, Polezzi, L and King, A (eds) (2001) *Fuzzy Boundaries? Reflections on modern languages and the humanities*, CILT, London

Eurobarometer (2001) *Europeans and Languages: a survey*, European Commission, Brussels [Online] http://europa.eu.int/comm/education/languages

European Commission (1995) *Teaching and Learning: Towards the learning society*, European Commission, Brussels

Graddol, D (1997) *The Future of English?*, British Council, London

Hawkins, E (1984) *Awareness of language: An introduction*, Cambridge University Press, Cambridge

Holliday, A (1994) *Appropriate Methodology and Social Context*, Cambridge University Press, Cambridge

Hymes, D (1971) Competence and performance in linguistic theory, in *Language Acquisition: Models and Method*, eds R Huxley and E Ingram, Academic Press, London

Kenning, M J and Kenning, M M (1984) *An Introduction to Computer Assisted Language Learning*, Oxford University Press, Oxford

Kramsch, C (1993) *Context and Culture in Language Teaching*, Oxford University Press, Oxford

*Languages: The next generation* (2000) Nuffield Foundation, London

Little, D (1991) *Learner Autonomy: Definitions, issues and problems*, Authentik, Dublin

Medgyes, P (1994) *The Non-native Teacher*, Macmillan, London

Phillipson, R (1992) *Linguistic Imperialism*, Oxford University Press, Oxford

*Strength through Wisdom: a critique of US Capability. A report to the President from the President's Commission on Foreign Language and International Studies* (1979) Washington, DC

Puren, C (2000) France, in *Routledge Encyclopedia of Language Teaching and Learning*, ed M Byram, Routledge, London

Savignon, S J (1997) *Communicative Competence: Theory and classroom practice*, McGraw-Hill, New York

van Ek, J (1986) *Objectives for Foreign Language Learning*, vol 1, *Scope*, Council of Europe, Strasbourg

van Lier, L (1995) *Introducing Language Awareness*, Penguin, Harmondsworth

von Humboldt, W (1836/1988) *On Language*, Cambridge University Press, Cambridge

# 6. Standard language education in transition

Sigmund Ongstad

## Mother tongue education as standard language education?

Just a few decades ago it was quite common to make most of the following assumptions when designing curricula in European monolingual national states:

- that one nation, more or less, meant one language;
- that mother tongue education (MTE) and standard language education (SLE) were roughly the same thing;
- that MTE was a phenomenon that existed around the world.

However, these nationalistic, Eurocentric and monolingual premises and ideologies are no longer valid, if they ever were. Not only has the gap in meaning between MTE and SLE become clearer, but our understanding of each separate element of SLE has also changed dramatically. Altogether, then, the paradigm of the field currently looks very different.

According to a definition recently proposed by AILA, MTE can be understood as:

> the teaching and/or learning within an educational system of the so-called mother tongue, be it a standard language of a nation state that statutorily accepts it as such, the language of education or the language of primary socialization (a child's first own and/or home language). It is concerned with learners' curricular enculturation to language, literature and culture, and focuses on the disciplinary teaching and/or learning of signs, texts, utterances and their contexts, in particular reading, speaking, writing and listening. (AILA, 2001)

This chapter will be concerned mainly with standard languages as school subjects, historically established for a state's or nation's native mother tongue speakers, but now challenged by multicultural developments (see Kroon, this volume, Chapter 3). The discussion will be presented in three parts. First, the idea of a 'standard' will be discussed in relation to regionalization, language differences and nation building, processes with a potential impact on how the notion 'standard' is perceived. Second, the notion of 'language' itself will be problematized in relation to shifting perceptions of language. Third, 'education' will be looked at in relation to new curricular trends. Finally, the discussion will be summarized in the light of the increasing interest in international comparative studies of education.

## 'Standard' languages

Currently there are probably more than 6,000 spoken languages in the world but by 2000 there were 'only' approximately 140 standardized languages (ISO, 2001). So there is a significant imbalance and a direct conflict between the many oral and the rather few written languages, not only in terms of numbers, but also in terms of power (Skutnabb-Kangas, 2002).

If we focus on the power aspect, the term 'standard' may at first glance lend an aura of authority to the concept of SLE: a nation's normative fixing of its official language may seem both sensible and 'natural'. Such a simplification of complex sociolinguistic realities may be related to important historical shifts, such as the transition from predominantly oral cultures to literate ones (Ong, 1982), the spread of standard typographies, and the establishment of nation-states with a need for a governing language. Thus, on the one hand there are technical and practical reasons for standard languages. On the other hand there are political and ideological factors that support much stronger and deeper tendencies towards the maintenance of diversity.

A standardized written language is a prime mechanism for and a symbol of nationalism, a very powerful influence in the 19th century, especially in Europe. This led to an extensive and patriotic use of the nation's 'own' adjective for the language and for the school subject in question – 'Italian' in Italy, 'German' in Germany, and so on. The standard language forms were seen as representing the authentic voice and spirit of the people.

However, even when national languages were regional, like Castilian from the central region in Spain; 'imported' and moderated, like written Danish in Norway; or class based, as in England, in the same nationalistic spirit curricular documents often implied that the national language was 'pure', homogeneous and universally acceptable, ignoring the fact that there was often huge diversity. Such national languages pushed aside Latin as the main language in schools all over Europe, and became a cornerstone in nation building (Steinfeld, 1986), although, for example, what in Norway is represented by 'Norwegian' or 'MT' has altered greatly over the past 150 years, and similarly in Bulgaria the terms 'Bulgarian' and 'MT' have been used very differently at different stages over the past 40 years (Johnsen, nd; Kütchukov, 1995).

In an English-language dictionary overview of the terms used for main languages in 170 countries, the term for the standard language in 50 countries was related semantically to the name of the country, as in Albanian, Bulgarian, etc (Delbridge and Bernard, 1988: 1202–04). For a majority of the other states, however, the standard languages have been imported through colonization, and function either as national language, such as English in Australia, or as a lingua franca, such as English in Singapore. In such cases these languages may, in the long run, develop independently of the language of origin, establishing new versions of, for instance, French, English or Arabic.

The authority connected to the term 'standard' is problematic, since it veils tacit processes of harmonization and homogenization; in fact, a language is never a clear-cut and easily definable entity, especially at a national level. Nevertheless, the use of the term brings to the surface the existence of 'non-standard' versions of spoken languages and dialects, although it does not express the kind or degree of normativity and oppression that standardizing as a process can represent. The provocative distinction favoured by some sociolinguists – 'A language is a dialect with an army and a navy' – was seemingly first formulated in 1945 by the linguist Max Weinreich in Yiddish: '*A shprakh iz a diyalekt mit an armey un a flot.*' Today the educational system, especially SLE, is the army and the navy.

The issues raised by this state of affairs led to the founding of the research group known as the International Mother Tongue Education Network (IMEN), which had its origin in attempts to deal with SLE internationally. The group's first publication makes clear that

> By using the term 'standard language teaching' the editors have wanted to draw the reader's attention to the fact that mother tongue teaching still appears to be mainly or almost exclusively concerned with the standard language of the country or 'language area' under consideration – at least in the majority of the schools. (Herrlitz and Peterse, 1984: 10)

The two authors here explicitly state that their use of the term 'standard' does not imply a rejection of the relevance of dialects and minority languages as part of a broad understanding of mother tongue, but for them the two concepts 'mother tongue teaching' and 'standard language teaching' seem to be practically interchangeable.

## Early and recent standardizations and education

In general, written languages in so-called great nation-cultures, such as French, English and Arabic, have undergone early codification. Over the centuries oral forms have continued to develop and created a gap or even a conflict between the spoken and written varieties of the languages, so that slowly the written forms have become the norm for the oral and not vice versa. The written forms have become the standard, and in many countries the upper and the middle class have used SLE to achieve standardization of their spoken language as well. But as a result, millions of young learners have to spend time learning to deal with the differences, a problem causing major educational debate.

Nevertheless, even continuity of written language forms is important. Most Icelanders, for instance, having the advantage of one of the oldest continuing written cultures in the world, are able to read their almost 1,000-year-old sagas, while many Norwegians have trouble reading their own current national constitution, which was originally written in 1814: new sections are kept in the standard language form of the late 19th century in order to maintain legal consistency in the standard language from the past. Hence Icelandic school curricula in the subject 'Islandic' contain original texts from the past, while older Norwegian texts in Norwegian as SLE have to be modernized, or studied as language history.

Some languages, such as Finnish, thanks to a late codification of the written language, enjoy relatively high correspondence between phonemes and graphemes, and from an international perspective on SL education such correspondences are interesting. Burnaby (1997) presents different research on how differences in writing systems affect literacy, and finds that even if different systems may have different advantages and disadvantages in the short run, as for instance in the Finnish case, it is hard to find research that can demonstrate an overall durable significant difference in the long run. Stevenson studied children from the United States, Taiwan and Japan who learnt (respectively) alphabetic, logographic and syllabic scripts, and concluded that it is difficult to accept the hypothesis that problems in reading are closely linked to different writing systems (Stevenson, 1987: 148; Burnaby, 1997: 65).

As far as oral standardization is concerned, the new National Curriculum in England and Wales (in effect since the year 2000) calls English both as a subject and as a language simply 'English'. It is required, under the heading 'Standard English', that 'Pupils should be introduced to some of the main features of spoken standard English and be taught to use them' (www.nc.uk.net/servlets/NCP). There is a huge gap between the English curricular aims and the Norwegian ones in this respect, a point that a superficial reading of the Norwegian SLE documents may conceal (see the Internet references at the end of the chapter). The new English curriculum demands early conformity to both oral and written Standard norms. In Norway, on the contrary, since the 1880s a special law has protected children's local dialect from being imposed on by oral standardization carried by the teacher. However, although this right is embodied in the law, it is only implicitly present in the curriculum. Corson (1997), having discussed research on non-standard varieties, and addressing the question of transmission of standard varieties, claims rather pessimistically:

> Since teachers and teachers-in-training are forced by the archaic structures of most forms of formal education to follow conservative patterns of professional behaviour, it is difficult to see widespread future change occurring rapidly. This is especially so since schools will always tend to accept that their role is to pass on the cultural heritage, including the standard version of the culture's language. (Corson, 1997: 238)

It seems inevitable that something that is defined as 'standard' will tend to overlook diversity. Hence Gogolin (2002) claims that the ideology embedded in monolingual European nationalism has the refusal of diversity as its basic condition. Gogolin even says, 'in fact the negative connotations of diversity are the result of strategies used in the process of nation building itself' (Gogolin, 2002: 125). Thus it seems fair to claim that from this perspective an SLE curriculum is still one of the most important means of direct nation building, even in today's Europe.

## The problem of contesting SLs

There are many national varieties of SL constellations. Homogeneous nation-states such as Iceland may have just one standard language that is the mother tongue for a large majority. Others may have two or more closely related languages such as Norway (*bokmål* and *nynorsk*), former Czechoslovakia (Czech and Slovak) and former Yugoslavia (Serbian and Croatian). Some states, such as Canada and Finland, have two significantly different standard languages in addition to their indigenous languages. However, more often countries have a number of SLs.

Two or more SLs creates a significant political problem: who will decide the choice of 'main' language – the individual or parents, the local community, or the state? One answer is that many federal states have decentralized educational systems, and even if there are several official standard languages in a country, each sub-state may have the right to adopt different SLEs, as in Switzerland (www.educa.ch/dyn/1916.htm). Furthermore, a country may have one official nationwide standard language, but local communities and municipalities may have the right to choose a different language for their SLE. Hence the local Norwegian municipality of Guovdageaidnu (among others) has Sami as its 'main' standard language, and in Norway generally the right to choose the main orientation of SLE is local, and even individuals can still choose from the two Norwegian languages at secondary level (one as main language and the other as 'bi-language'). However, this choice is within the school subject 'Norwegian' (*norsk*); in other words, there are two SLs within SLE.

To illustrate what kind of problems the presence of two main languages can cause, the situation in Estonia is interesting. Before the Soviet invasion in 1940 less than 10 per cent of the population was Russian speaking, but by the end of the Soviet period 50 years later, the proportion had reached almost 40 per cent. Some of the Russian-speaking people live in enclave-like cities where they are a majority of the population, and in one such city, Narva, many Russian parents recently wanted their children to begin in the only Estonian school, as Estonian is now emerging as the dominant public language. This school at first refused to take any Russian students, but finally admitted some first-grade children who could speak Estonian. However, a researcher has now found that after only a few years, these children are already dramatically educationally retarded, compared to the Estonian children, an effect apparently caused by the small part Estonian plays in the Russian children's lives outside school (Leino, 2002).

To conclude this section, it looks as if standardization as a process resulting from nationalism, urbanization, industrialization and centralization is inevitable. At the same time, however, there is a growing awareness of the value and the necessity of paying attention to difference and variation. Hence a crucial, but so far unanswered question is: at which point is it functional for a country's population to stop expecting greater conformity to a given standard, and instead start adapting to a range of new forms?

## Changes in understandings of 'language'

Along with developments in linguistics, understanding of how language functions changed throughout the 20th century. As a result there has been a long-lasting pedagogical tug of war about where the main focus should be in SLE – at the level of phoneme, syllable, morpheme, word, sentence, text or context? So it is argued, for instance, that Chinese written characters are so subtle and precise that even the slightest errors in writing them may distort their meaning. It follows that the pedagogy used here of focusing on form tends to be firm and governed, characterized by repetition, memorization and careful copying (Wong, 1992; Edwards, 1997: 51). At the other end of the scale the Danish SLE curriculum has minimized formal grammar in favour of attention to text and context. The degree of emphasis on SL formalities, as opposed to text orientation, is probably one of the clearest indicators of difference between curricula in an international perspective.

In general it seems fair to suggest that developments in many countries are shifting the emphasis in SLE from the smaller to the larger entities. However, there still seem to be major national differences in this respect (Herrlitz *et al*, 1984; Delnoy, Herrlitz and Kroon, 1995; Aarsæther, 1997). It should be obvious that as long as there is a strong emphasis on formal correctness of written characters and oral sounds, this emphasis will function as part of nation building. Giving priority to the text level, on the other hand, looking at genres, discourses and contexts, giving primacy to text competence and discursive understanding, etc, will probably tie SLE less directly to a particular country and may in the long term function as a supra-national tendency. If this is the direction in which SLEs move, the relevance of the very concept of SLE as a means for developing distinctive national ideologies is fundamentally challenged (Ongstad and Ven, 2002).

Studies of written language in the first part of the 20th century were, roughly speaking, dominated by the dualism of syntax and semantics, a dichotomy that was challenged in the 1960s and 1970s by the emergence of pragmatics (Ongstad and Ven, 2002). At the turn of the millennium most theorists seem to see the three aspects as basically reciprocal. However, historically speaking, the linguistic foregrounding of particular language levels at the expense of others has often at the next stage had direct paradigmatic pedagogical consequences, as will be argued later (Nystrand, Greene and Wiemelt, 1993).

Historically, homogenization has been strong. Ven (1986, 1987) found that definitions of MTE/SLE until 1900 (and sometimes beyond) were dominated by a grammatical–literary definition characterized by the study of grammar, spelling, stylistics and the literary canon. This was expressed mainly on the rhetorical level, but in practice the conception is probably still valid.

In primary schools, at least in Northern Europe, formalism was still dominant between the two world wars. For instance, the curriculum for SLE for primary schools in Norway from 1939 (which was in use until the 1960s) had extremely formalistic aims and foci. The set of goals for Norwegian as SLE is quoted here:

*Norwegian: The goal is to teach the children:*

1. to speak their mother tongue naturally, straightforwardly and clearly – without major phonetic or grammatical mistakes;

2. to read both *bokmål* and *nynorsk* [the two Norwegian written languages], with distinct pronunciation and fairly correct accent, to understand and retell what they read, and to be able to obtain knowledge by reading;

3. to write straightforwardly, naturally and fairly correctly (and with fairly correct punctuation marks) about topics appropriate to the field of experience and knowledge for this year level. (KU, 1940: 48, my translation and added comment)

Such goals would most likely lead to a more standardized Norwegian language and therefore the 1939 curriculum deserves the label 'SLE'.

This formalist paradigm was gradually challenged by, and often merged with, a more semantically oriented view during the 1950s and 1960s, with a focus on preciseness of meaning, explicitness, logic, understanding, knowledge, logic of sentences, content in writing and literature – in other words, the perspective was essentialist. This tendency coincided with and was fuelled by Piagetian psychology and cognitive pedagogy in teacher education, which favoured a focus on knowledge and thinking (Ongstad and Ven, 2002).

The breakthrough for a more functional paradigm is connected to theorists such as Wittgenstein, Austin, Searle, Halliday and Habermas. During the 1970s and 1980s action-oriented approaches invaded standard language teaching in many West European countries. Language was language in use (Doughty, Pearce and Thornton, 1971). Besides, people gradually realized that moving from a form–content dichotomy to a functional perspective also implied a shift in emphasis from the levels of word and sentence to the levels of text and context. Recognizing and controlling text-forms (genres and discourses) now became crucial in SLE, and accordingly the traditional divide between language and literature could be bridged, partly at least.

Another implication was a shift in educational ideology. 'Use' is a rather intractable aspect of language and points more to a general 'world' rather than to a specific 'nation'. It follows that a paradigmatic move from form/content towards function would not only represent a shift of linguistic foci, but would even reduce the role for educational standardization of language. Hence language has been challenged from within. Its 'autonomous' nature is disputed and it has had to adjust to more complex understandings. During this change the appropriateness of core notions such as 'language', 'mother tongue' and 'standard language' has been contested. Not only is the national paradigm questioned (Ehlich, 2000), but 'standard' and 'national' make less sense once the focus has shifted to the text-context aspects of language.

## Second language educations: heading in different directions?

The implications of thinking about 'education' across times, cultures and national borders are not yet entirely clear. Historically, education has been for elites, for privileged groups and classes, for men, for a certain kind of social reproduction, for maintaining or gaining power. In today's world there is still an enormous difference, for example, between Canada and Bangladesh regarding general and gendered access to education. At the same time, with a development in Western countries from elite to mass education, there has been an increased commodification of education (Barnett and Griffin, 1997). Such diverse general tendencies result in ambiguities about the functions of education. What is school's main role: as a place to learn or a place to be? What is the 'real' value of schooling: for lifelong growth or to provide marketable certification? Who is education ultimately supposed to benefit: the individual, the academic disciplines or society?

Such questions, dilemmas and tensions also permeate the educational sub-elements such as 'discipline' and 'subject'. In different cultures and languages these notions may have different interpretations. Inspecting SLE elements over time, over borders, and with shifting political regimes and professional ideologies, it is clear that many elements have over the years been defined into and out of MTE/SLE. These include national literature, 'world' literature, cultural knowledge (German *Heimatkund*), cultural history, handwriting, literacy and literacies, film, drama, ICT, SLE for second language learners, writing across the curriculum, library knowledge, rhetorics, oracy, etc. The way these and other aspects of education are distributed in different SLEs makes it hard to see SLE around the world as a single phenomenon (Herrlitz and Peterse, 1984; Delnoy, Herrlitz and Kroon , 1995).

To give just one important example: referring to standard *language* education is often misleading, since literature in many countries is a dominant part of the MTE/SLE curriculum, while in other countries, such as the Netherlands, SLE is only language education; literature is a different discipline and does not only focus on Dutch literature (Ven, 1996; Ongstad and Ven, 2002). In contrast, in Norway, *Norsk*, at least in upper secondary schools, is dominated by literature – but almost exclusively Norwegian literature (Ongstad and Smidt, 1995).

The goals for education may further be linked to rather different and quite complex overall ideological concepts. Two significant examples of such concepts are *Bildung* in Germany, and 'literacy' more widely. Thus in some national curricula the rhetorical will to follow goals for *Bildung* is significant, and subject plans and syllabuses in SLE have to be subordinate to the general goals formulated for this wider *Bildung*. The written curriculum for the subject German in Schleswig-Holstein's primary schools, for example, begins as follows: 'The contribution of the subject German to basic education grows from the specific learning content of the teaching and learning of German' (Ministerium für Bildung, Wissenschaft, Forschung und Kultur des Landes Schleswig-Holstein, 1997: 51, my translation). Even if this sentence may be seen as pointing largely to a formal connection between the general and the disciplinary part of the written curriculum, it nevertheless represents a real hierarchical regulation between them.

*Literacy* has changed as a concept over the past few decades and is now often written about in the plural, as literacies (see Christie, this volume, Chapter 7). There are many reasons for this tendency, of which one is that students are kept in the educational system longer, and have to learn to cope with discursive and social skills over a longer period. Each 'literacy' can then be seen as containing different goals that point to sets of specific competencies.

*Bildung*, more conservatively, seems to warn against a mad rush towards isolated skills and knowledges, and to argue for the coherence and integration of the curricular elements, perhaps more in 'vertical' hierarchies, while literacies are more horizontally distributed. Whether SLE comes under the influence of such different ideological goals as those implied by *Bildung* or 'literacies' will give very different configurations of the subject.

Both ideologies point to classical dilemmas such as those about student development or year progression. In England and Wales a particular kind of developmental thinking has found it possible to define certain stages along an expected subject development, instead of the traditional system based on year levels (www.nc.uk.net/servlets/NCP). Through formal evaluation a student can now be placed on a more advanced level – in principle, irrespective of the age group the student belongs to. In other words, the student can advance faster through the educational system, or, correspondingly, more slowly, or even have to leave school at one of the lower levels. At the moment England and Wales do not seem to have many followers in this tendency.

Another dilemma in all curricular construction of any school subject is how content elements should be outlined, in relation to study years. According to

Aarsæther (1997), in a comparison of syllabuses for the Scandinavian countries used in the late 1990s, Sweden and Norway differ significantly in this respect. The Norwegian curriculum, L97, carefully builds up a delicate skyscraper of content elements designed for everyone, with a year by year progression; the Swedish curriculum on the other hand explicitly rejects this idea and argues that, for instance, as far as knowledge of text-types is concerned, all children argue, narrate and reflect, even from a very early age, and that there are no clear hierarchies between language functions.

Discursive awareness, or 'reflexivity' is another significant new goal in some curricula. The curriculum for 'Norwegian' 1–10 in L97 will stimulate students to use their own writing in SLE to reflect upon their own learning and learning processes both in the discipline and in general. A major new goal is 'to make pupils conscious participants in their own learning processes, provide them with insight into their own linguistic development, and enable them to use language as an instrument for increasing their insight and knowledge' (TRMERCA, 1999: 126). This goal represents a radical *didaktization*[1] of SLE knowledge, since it transfers teaching and learning responsibilities to students, making them auto-didakts (Ongstad, 1999). SLE now has a meta-epistemological purpose. All of this amounts to a significant paradigmatic shift from the massive formalism of the 1939 curriculum to the new pedagogical aims of SLE in the 1997 curriculum. International comparisons rarely take such basic contextual shifts of curricular ideology into account, and therefore risk their basic validity.

One clear new trend is increased student-centredness, visible as ideas of constructivism in many school subjects. There is a clear shift in many curricula from stating what teachers should teach to a description of what the students shall do. This is an interdisciplinary trend, and so in SLE it takes the shape of a certain discursive syntax, a rhetoric about how goals in the written curriculum are to be presented: 'The students shall…: conduct interviews…, work on spelling according to individual needs…, listen to samples of dialect and try to locate them' (TRMERCA, 1999: 127–33). Thus the overall tendency to put the students and their learning more in focus is, at least at the rhetorical level, yet another example of how didaktization of MTE/SLE has weakened the role of the 'pure standard national language' as the common ground for understanding what happens within MTE/SLE internationally.

## Conclusion: comparing within contexts of stability and change?

The many new trends discussed have affected different SLEs in different ways, and have thus created new discursive contexts that have a major influence on what kind of international comparative studies can be conducted. As illustrated above, the effects of 'Dutch' and 'Norwegian' SLE cannot properly be tested comparatively, given that their contents differ so fundamentally. And the two school subjects German in German-speaking countries and English in the United Kingdom differ not least because of the strong underlying *Bildung* tradition in Germany.

SLE in most countries is changing rapidly, so that disciplinary openness and dynamism are necessary conditions for MTE/SLE to survive in a changing world. In earlier times many SLEs/MTEs were based for longer stretches on fixed standard languages, canonical texts and lasting cultural traditions. The vanishing stability in many countries will make international comparisons an even more problematic enterprise in future.

## Notes

1. This word is deliberately spelt with a 'k' here to make it clear that in most Northern European and many Latin countries this very basic concept does not have the negative associations that didactic, with a 'c', often has in English (Gundem and Hopmann, 1998).

## References

Aarsæther, F (1997) 1990-åras danskfag, norskfag og svenskfag: tre nordiske læreplaner (Danish, Norwegian and Swedish as school subjects in the 1990s: three Nordic written curricula), *Nordisk Pedagogik*, 1, pp 43–55

Association Internationale de Linguistique Appliqué (AILA) (2001) www.aila.ac/ (accessed 2002)

Barnett, R and Griffin, A (eds) (1997) *The End of Knowledge in Higher Education*, Cassell, London

Burnaby, B (1997) *Writing Systems and Orthographies*, in *Encyclopedia of Language and Education*, vol 2, *Literacy*, eds V Edwards and D Corson, Kluwer, Dordrecht, the Netherlands

Corson, D (1997) Non-standard varieties and educational policy, in *Language Policy and Political Issues in Education*, eds R Wodak and D Corson, Kluwer, Dordrecht, the Netherlands

Delbridge, A and Bernard, J (eds) (1988) *The Macquarie Concise Dictionary*, The Macquarie Library Pty, Sydney

Delnoy, R, Herrlitz, W and Kroon, S (eds) (1995) *European Education in Mother Tongue: A second survey of standard language teaching in eight European countries*, IMEN, Nijmegen, the Netherlands

Doughty, P, Pearce, J and Thornton, G (1971) *Language in Use*, Edward Arnold, London

Edwards, V (1997) Reading in multilingual classrooms, in *Encyclopedia of Language and Education*, vol 2, *Literacy*, eds V Edwards and D Corson, Kluwer, Dordrecht, the Netherlands

Ehlich, K (2000) Europäischen Sprachen im Zeitalter der Postnationalität, *Mitteilungen des Deutschen Germanistverbandes*, **47** (2/3), pp 186–95

Gogolin, I (2002) Linguistic and cultural diversity in Europe: a challenge for educational research and practice, *European Educational Research Journal*, **1** (1), pp 123–38

Gundem, B and Hopmann, S (eds) (1998) *Didaktik and/or Curriculum: An international dialogue*, Peter Lang, New York

Herrlitz, W and Peterse, H (1984) The International Mother Tongue Education Network, in *Mother Tongue Education in Europe: A survey of standard language teaching*, eds W Herrlitz *et al*, IMEN, Enschede, the Netherlands

Herrlitz, W *et al* (eds) (1984) *Mother Tongue Education in Europe: A survey of standard language teaching in nine European countries*, IMEN, Enschede, the Netherlands

IAWE (2001) www.we.pdx.edu / conf.html

ISO (2001) *ISO 639 Standard Language Codes*, www.amazesoft.com / iso639.htm

Johnsen, E B (1992) Omkring betydningen av ordet morsmål (On the meaning of the word mother tongue), unpublished manuscript

KU (1940) *Normalplan (mønsterplan) for landsfolkeskulen*, Aschehoug, Oslo

KUF (1996) *Læreplanverket for den 10-årige grunnskolen*, KUF, Oslo

Kütchukov, H (1995) Teaching Bulgarian as a mother tongue in Bulgarian schools, in *European Education in Mother Tongue: A second survey of standard language teaching in eight European countries*, eds R Delnoy, W Herrlitz and S Kroon, IMEN, Nijmegen, the Netherlands

Leino, M (2002) Russian and Estonian children at Estonian school, paper given at NERA's conference in Tallinn, Estonia, 7–9 March

Ministerium für Bildung, Wissenschaft, Forschung und Kultur des Landes Schleswig-Holstein (Schleswig-Holstein: written curriculum) (1997) [Online] http:/ /lehrplan.lernnetz.de/html/lehrplan.htm (accessed 2002)

Nystrand, M, Greene, S and Wiemelt, J(1993) Where did composition studies come from? An intellectual history, *Written Communication*, **10** (3), 267–333

Ong, W (1982) *Orality and Literacy: The technologizing of the word*, Routledge, London

Ongstad, S (1999) Sources of 'didaktization': on defining disciplines and their '(fag-)didaktik' across borders, illustrated with examples from Mother Tongue Education (MTE), in *Didaktik/Fachdidaktik as Science(s) of the Teaching Profession?*, vol 2, no 1, eds B Hudson, F Buchberger, P Kansenen and H Seel, TNTEE Publications, Umea, Sweden

Ongstad, S and Smidt, J (1995) Norwegian: a dynamic battlefield, in *European Education in Mother Tongue: A second survey of standard language teaching in eight European countries*, eds R Delnoy, W Herrlitz and S Kroon, IMEN, Nijmegen, the Netherlands

Ongstad, S and Ven, P H van de (2002) Mother tongue education: Fachdidaktik, in an electronic textbook on Fachdidaktik and Didaktik [Online] http:/ /ive.pa-linz.ac.at/emdid/default.html

Skutnabb-Kangas, T (2002) Education and maintenance of linguistic diversities, keynote address at NERA's conference in Tallinn, March

Steinfeld, T (1986) *På skriftens vilkår: et bidrag til morsmålsfagets histori* (In terms of the script(ure): a contribution to the history of mother tongue (as discipline)), Landslaget for norskundervisning / Cappelen, Oslo
Stevenson, H W (1987) Children's problems in learning to read in Chinese, Japanese and English, in *The Future of Literacy in a Changing World*, ed D Wagner, Pergamon, Oxford
TRMERCA (1999a) *The Curriculum for the 10-year Compulsory School in Norway*, National Centre for Educational Resources, Oslo
TRMERCA (1999b) *Rammeplan og forskrift: Allmennlærerutdanning* (Frame curriculum and regulation: general teacher education, Norgesnettrådet, Oslo
Trudgill, P (1999) Norwegian as a normal language, in *Language contact and language conflict*, ed U Røyneland, Ivar Aasen Institute, Volda, Norway
Ven, P H van de (1986) Some histories about mother tongue teaching, *Western Europe: Mother Tongue Education Bulletin*, **2** (2), pp 40–49
Ven, P H van de (1987) *Stability and Change in Mother Tongue Education*, PU series 87, University of Lund, Lund
Ven, P H van de (1996) *Moedertaalsonderwijs: Interpretaties in retoriek en praktijk, heden en verleden, binnen en buitenland* (Mother tongue education: interpretations in rhetoric and practice, present and past, at home and abroad), doctoral thesis, University of Utrecht, Wolters-Noorhoff, Groningen
Wong, L Y-F (1992) *The Education of Chinese Children in Britain and the USA*, Multilingual Matters, Clevedon, UK

## Internet references/resources

http://www.nc.uk.net/servlets/NCP (UK curriculum)
http://skolenettet3.ls.no/L97_eng/curriculum/ (Curriculum for Norwegian)
http://www.educa.ch/dyn/1916.htm (Information on Swiss education)

# 7.   Initial literacy: extending the horizon

Frances Christie

## Introduction

This chapter will begin with some discussion of general issues relating to the emergence of mass education in the 20th century, and the significance attaching to literacy in this emergence, in both developed and developing countries. It will be suggested, first, that while the spread of mass education as a global phenomenon has not been uniformly successful, the aspiration to offer a literacy programme to all as an aspect of its emergence has become a concern in all countries, developed and developing. Second, it will be suggested that in the global trend towards extending literacy provision to all, a premium has attached to teaching what is sometimes referred to as 'initial literacy', where this has been understood as a phenomenon of the early years of primary schooling. Third, it will be argued that while the commitment to the teaching of initial literacy is itself a laudable thing, it is in fact misleading to see its teaching as the province only of the early years of schooling. While the research on literacy development in the various languages of the world no doubt remains to be fully undertaken, it is already clear, as I shall suggest later from available research on English literacy, that adequate provision of 'initial literacy' is a matter involving several years of education, and requiring considerably more than the rudimentary introduction to literacy that can be afforded in the first years of the primary schools. Initial literacy requires for its teaching all the years of a typical primary school education, and what might be termed 'mature' or 'advanced' literacy is a phenomenon whose mastery belongs at the earliest to the years of adolescence.

## The significance of mass education as a global phenomenon and the role of literacy

One of the most significant of the sociopolitical changes of the 20th century was the spread of mass education programmes. While the trend towards provision of such programmes appeared first in the affluent Western countries, by the turn of the 21st century mass education had become an issue of great significance in the various developing countries, causing governments of various political persuasions to devote resources to it, and attracting a considerable share of the national budgets, even in poor countries. By the mid-20th century, the Western nations – stimulated in part by the needs and consequences of two world wars – had accepted the principle that all children should have an education that covered at least the elementary or primary years, and ideally, a junior secondary education. During the latter half of the century, the Western countries extended the periods of time students were to be in school, so that, at least in the English-speaking world, the age of 16 became the minimal age for leaving school, though opportunities were provided for further education in technical colleges, colleges of advanced education and universities. The pattern was rather different in those nations that became known as the 'developing countries'. For the most part these remained colonies of the Western powers until the Second World War, and it was in its aftermath, when the governments of many new nations were grappling to come to terms with the needs of newly developing nations, that education emerged as a matter of vital concern, linked to national growth. In some countries the drive for a mass education was seen as a tool for forging a united country whose people might share common aspirations for their future. In others, the extension of education was linked closely to the goal of achieving an educated workforce whose people might build their country's economy and break the patterns of poverty, malnutrition and maladministration that had come to blight so many developing countries. In many cases, of course, the concerns for building a politically united people and a skilled workforce have been held in common, as indeed they are to this day in the affluent Western countries as well.

Overall, by the turn of the 21st century, both the developed and developing nations had come to attach great significance to the provision of mass education, while international agencies, most notably UNICEF and UNESCO, had come to devote considerable resources to educational programmes, along with programmes devoted to such matters as the improvement of health, and provision of infrastructural resources to support agriculture and new industry. By the start of the 21st century, the provision of mass education had thus become a global phenomenon. It does not follow that the provision of such education has been uniformly successful, or that its benefits have been felt equally well, even in the affluent nations such as the United Kingdom, the United States or Australia. Plainly, in many parts of the world, educational provision is of variable quality, while many students achieve poor educational attainments. Currently, in the affluent countries, it tends to be boys who do poorly in school, often failing to achieve adequate literacy skills; the reasons for this are not always well understood, and remain matters of continuing research. By contrast, it is girls who fare badly in the developing countries, since they are often withdrawn from school to do domestic and rural work.

Acknowledging, as we should, on the one hand, the rather variable nature of the educational provision offered, and on the other hand, the equally variable levels of educational attainments achieved, the fact remains that the principle has been accepted internationally that countries should provide an education to all. And critical to educational provision anywhere in the world is the commitment to the central role of literacy as a tool for living and for learning. Literacy became a major issue in educational theory and research in the 20th century, its significance gaining as the century proceeded. This was because of the vital role that literacy came to assume in the mass educational programmes that emerged. Today, all societies attach significance to the teaching of literacy, and all aspire to see their students achieve at least a minimal literacy level, even though, as noted, the aspiration is not always fulfilled.

## The term 'literacy'

Literacy programmes became an issue of some significance in the aftermath of the Second World War, as developed and developing countries alike sought to extend educational opportunity to all. All countries intended that their students should learn to read and write. But the term 'literacy' itself was often not in wide use, and as a term in policy and in research it has had only fairly recent currency. In some developing countries, such as Indonesia, for example, no term for 'literacy' actually exists in the language. Thus, though the national curriculum documents that emerged in that country after independence in 1947 sought to develop programmes that would teach children to read and write, no term such as 'literacy' was available, or is indeed available to this day. Even in the English-speaking world, the term 'literacy' was not in wide use in educational discussions until recent years, even though the word was known. From the 19th century on, curriculum guidelines for the primary school had sought to teach reading and writing. Right down to the 1960s and 1970s, primary teachers trained for the teaching of the 'language arts', while secondary teachers of English trained to teach 'English', where the latter included interests in reading and writing. Developments in the 1970s and early 1980s, at least in the English-speaking world, led to increasing significance attaching in curriculum guidelines and textbooks to the four language modes of listening, speaking, reading and writing.

By the early 1990s the world had changed. The decade commenced with the International Literacy Year (ILY) in 1990. Talk of 'literacy', rather than of 'language arts' or 'reading' and 'writing', began to achieve widespread acceptance in curriculum documents, in teacher education programmes and in government policy statements of many kinds. The ILY itself did much to extend international interest in literacy provision, and to alert the various nations, both developing and developed, to the importance of literacy in the modern world.

In Australia, for example, by the early 1990s, we began to talk of 'language and literacy programmes', or 'language and literacy education'. As the decade proceeded, literacy as a theme achieved greater prominence, so that both the federal and the state governments gave, and continue to give, considerable financial support to the development of various literacy programmes and strategies. Under the Labour Government in Britain in the 1990s the 'National Literacy Strategy' became a key element in the government's educational policies, attracting significant funds for its development and implementation. Both the Clinton and Bush administrations in the United States have attached importance to federal support for literacy programmes.

As for the international community of researchers, today in the English-speaking world a great deal of research attention is devoted to literacy, and to literacy education, rather than to 'reading' and 'writing'. The term 'literacy' has achieved currency because its use serves to underscore the important truth that reading and writing are two aspects of the same phenomenon – namely, control and use of literate language – and that effective educational programmes will always recognize this and build upon it in their teaching and learning. To put the matter at its most succinct, if you want to make a good reader, make a good writer, and vice versa. The two are very intimately linked, and students need to move constantly between reading and writing activities as they learn to recognize, interpret, manipulate and, if necessary, challenge what it is they read, while also reflecting carefully upon what it is they write.

Literacy provision as a matter of government policy is associated primarily with literacy in the national language. Thus, for example, in the United Kingdom, the United States and Australia, modern literacy programmes focus on the teaching of English, and indeed English is the medium of instruction, while various community and/or foreign languages are taught as subjects in the curriculum. Equally, Vietnam, Indonesia, China and Thailand, to name some countries with which I have first-hand experience, for the most part focus on literacy programmes in the national language. In practice, in many countries this means that some students are asked to learn literacy in a language other than that which is their mother tongue. This can be a challenge not only for students, but also for teachers for whom the national language is not their own, as Agustina (in preparation) has demonstrated in a study of Indonesian language and literacy programmes. The policy of teaching the national language is justified on the grounds that teaching modern Indonesian is itself a force for unification, but the policy is sometimes compromised by a teaching force that is poorly trained and lacking a strong grasp of the language. Elsewhere, as for example in Thailand, modern literacy programmes have been developed specifically to focus on teaching the national language to ethnic minority groups. Rattanavich of the University of Srinakharinwirot in Bangkok, together with colleagues, has pioneered programmes for teaching Thai literacy to ethnic minority children (see Rattanavich and Christie, 1993; Rattanavich and Walker, 1996), while she has also extended her work to training teachers in the same principles for teaching literacy among teachers in their national languages in Bangladesh, Brazil,

India and South Africa. Vietnam claims reasonably high levels of literacy in its own people, and it is also currently committed to extending literacy in the national language to its ethnic minorities, though, with UNICEF support, it has also developed programmes to promote literacy in certain of the ethnic minority languages spoken in the more remote parts of the country (Woolley, Pigdon and Molyneux, 1995, 1996; Woolley, Pigdon and Hartman, 1998). In modern China, literacy in Mandarin – also referred to as *Putonghua* – is an issue of concern; in many regions dialects of various kinds are spoken, and an effort is being made to standardize the teaching of what has become the national language.

Literacy education thus rates very highly in the countries quickly reviewed, and the curriculum is developed in such a way that significant proportions of the school week are devoted to teaching reading and writing. It is impossible to generalize about literacy programmes in the various countries of Asia and South-East Asia, though for the most part, since schools are often poorly resourced, the classes large and the teachers often not well trained, the teaching and learning are not always very effective. In the Western nations, while class sizes are smaller and resources generally better than in the developing world, the pattern remains very variable, and not all schools are necessarily well resourced in their endeavours.

As for the impact of literacy in the modern world overall, it is apparent that it has enormous significance. Literacy is generated and communicated in volumes and at a speed hitherto quite unthinkable. The World Wide Web, electronic mail and the fax machine, to name some obvious examples, have all transformed the nature of literacy and its many modes of delivery. For this reason alone the various educational systems have a major responsibility to offer the best literacy programmes they can provide, and opportunity to learn literacy should be seen as a right, not a privilege, as it often was in the past.

## The notion of 'initial literacy'

While in both the developed and the developing worlds the drive to extend and enhance literacy provision is officially seen as a matter of concern for students of all ages, there can be no doubt that the primary focus of attention has been the earliest years of schooling – the years of a primary education, when establishing initial literacy is seen as the major issue. My brief in this chapter is to discuss the teaching of initial literacy, and as I have already indicated above, I shall argue that while a concern for the teaching of literacy in the first years of schooling is indeed a very proper one, the notion of an initial literacy is sometimes confused by a tendency to see literacy and its learning as uniquely the province of the first years of schooling. The learning of 'initial literacy', however we conceive that, is, I shall suggest, only part of the quite complex business of learning literacy that lasts through all the years of schooling. Furthermore, for reasons not always understood or acknowledged in educational programmes, the nature of literacy changes quite fundamentally as students grow older. Indeed, as I have argued elsewhere (Christie, 2002), what might be termed the 'advanced literacy' characteristic of adult life does not start to emerge till students are in the secondary school. Hence it is that schools need to have an appropriate sense of the nature of the literacy to be learnt at all levels of schooling, and primary schools in particular need to be aware of those forms of literacy that still lie ahead for children to master beyond the years of a primary education. In order to develop the argument, I shall inevitably have recourse to discussion of matters to do with literacy in the English language, though I shall suggest that the general principles that I shall argue with respect to literacy and its development in that language have relevance when considering literacy in all languages.

By way of commencing the discussion with respect to literacy itself, I shall start by saying a little of what is known of the nature of language learning by the time children arrive at school. I shall go on to sketch in some sense of the nature and patterns of literacy that emerge as students take their first steps in learning literacy, and I shall also briefly consider something of the literate patterns that children will need to master in order to enter secondary school as well as adult life.

## Children's language development

The decades from the 1960s and 1970s on saw a great deal of very useful research in many parts of the world into young children's language learning. What the research said tended to vary, depending upon the particular paradigm selected for considering the language system and its role in human development. Suffice it to note, however, that a general understanding emerged that in the years from birth young children devote a great deal of their energies to mastering the mother tongue, where this involves learning a great deal of its meanings, its grammar, its lexis and its phonology. They also learn something of the possible range of registers available in their communities: they learn, for example, about ways to elicit information and support, and ways to negotiate and build relationships with family, peers and members of the community, encountered, for example, in the household, the shopping centre, play group, church or sporting context, to name a few. All the understandings just quickly sketched in are a necessary prerequisite for the entry to formal schooling and the associated entry to literacy. The point may seem self-evident, though it is worth stressing, and not only because it points to the need to build strong linkages between the learning of the pre-school years and the initial years of schooling. Among other matters, we should note that the learning of literacy presupposes considerable prior knowledge in children of what language is and what it does for them. But the entry to literacy involves more than the presence of such prior knowledge, essential though that is. It also involves development of a steadily growing understanding of how very different from speech is the written mode. The latter understanding takes many years to develop. Hence, as already suggested, what we mean by the notion of 'initial literacy' needs to be defined partly in terms of the ultimate goal of achieving what we might term 'mature literacy', towards which children will strive for some time.

Language is necessarily learnt as speech and in the daily interplay of human interaction at all sorts of levels. Hence it is that while young children learn a great deal of what their language can do for them, this knowledge is most fundamentally based on an understanding of the grammar of speech, rather than of writing. Of course, it is true that most young children are also to some extent aware of the significance of written language. They are, after all, constantly exposed to it in public advertisements, sign boards and television programmes, and, in many households, they are also often read to by care givers. These are important matters, developing a sense of a world in which literacy is a feature of significance. Nonetheless, it remains true that young children's most profound knowledge of language is as speech, and this has consequences for the developmental steps they will need to take in achieving control of literacy.

## First steps in learning literacy

Whether their first steps in gaining some grasp of literacy are taken before the entry to school or within the school itself, inevitably a great deal of young children's attention is devoted to learning to recognize and eventually use the handwriting, spelling and punctuation systems. Even command of the conventions by which, in English, the writing goes from left to right across the page, and by which spaces are left between words, takes some time. It is for understandable reasons easy to become preoccupied with the teaching of all these matters, and to lose sight of issues of meaning and functions in using literacy. Indeed, on occasion a tendency creeps into public discussions to see literacy as mainly about spelling, handwriting and punctuation, so that a view emerges that these things, once mastered, will simply be recycled for the rest of one's life in some essentially unproblematic way. Literacy, in this view, is mainly about spelling, handwriting and punctuation. The truth is that control of literacy is considerably more than control of these matters, essential though they all are. It is unfortunate if the issues here are allowed to become clouded. Spelling, handwriting and punctuation are the most visible of the essential aspects of learning literacy; the less visible aspects, to do with the grammatical organization of literacy and its meanings, take longer to learn, and they are in fact the more difficult features of literacy.

The point is perhaps best understood if we recall the matters briefly addressed above in considering early language development. Language is learnt in human interaction and because it serves important human purposes in living and in learning. In this sense, early language and early language learning are always to be understood as meaningful. It follows then that children's predisposition in learning literacy will be to look for meaning and purpose in literate language. The spelling and handwriting systems must indeed be mastered, but primarily because they are means to the end of controlling literate language, not because they constitute ends in themselves. The general understanding about language and its meanings and purposes, based on the research that had been done on young children's language learning a few years earlier, led such writers as Smith (1978), Goodman (1986) and Cambourne (1988) to propose various 'natural learning theories' for teaching literacy. Thus, it was suggested that if children learnt their oral language 'naturally' in 'immersion' and in interaction with others, then the most successful literacy would provide similarly 'natural' learning opportunities to promote the learning of literacy in the classroom. The role of the teacher in this theory is that of 'facilitator', serving to give support, but essentially operating in a non-interventionist role as children come to terms with learning literacy themselves. The theory has a certain attractiveness, emphasizing, among other things, the need for supportive classroom environments in which children can take their first steps in literacy, and often allowing them opportunity to play with spelling and handwriting in constructive ways.

Yet as the years have passed, the various 'natural learning' theories have been challenged (eg Gray, 1987, 1999; Cazden, 1992; Freebody and Luke, 1990; Oakhill and Beard, 1999), primarily because it is clear that teachers will need to intervene in various ways, shaping their students' learning of literacy, and guiding them towards new understandings. There are at least two reasons for this. First, no child – even in the most literate of households – is ever exposed to the model of literate language to the same extent that he or she is exposed to speech, and for that reason alone it cannot be assumed that literacy can be learnt in the same way. Second, written language is actually grammatically very different from speech, and the learning of literacy involves learning to recognize and use very different patterns of grammatical organization, which take years to master, and which require the intervention of a mentor to assist students to learn. The point holds for even the most privileged of students whose families provide a great deal of support in the learning of literacy. However, the point is of critical importance for the many disadvantaged students, who without carefully developed literacy programmes that meet their needs across the years of a primary education will make little progress in their learning. The point has been very successfully demonstrated by Gray (1999), one of Australia's authorities on indigenous education, who is currently developing programmes in Aboriginal schools in various parts of Australia, and showing impressive gains in students' literacy learning and hence in their general performance in school learning.

Gray has demonstrated that the most successful strategies for teaching reading and writing to young children, and to older underachieving children, begin with reading texts to the children, developing confidence and familiarity with them, and gradually breaking the texts into their elements: words, word groups and phrases. In turn, these are eventually broken up to examine the ways they are spelt. It is a model that has sometimes been called a 'top-down model' in the past, in that it starts with the text as a meaningful unit and proceeds by stages to break it down into ever smaller elements, all of which require careful direction and guidance from the teacher. However, since 'top-down' models have sometimes been criticized for their alleged inattention to the 'basics' of spelling, phonics and punctuation, it needs to be stressed that in Gray's model quite exacting attention is paid to all these matters, though always as a consequence of engaging with the meanings of the overall text.

Parallel strategies for teaching writing are a necessary aspect of a successful early literacy programme. Good teaching programmes in the very early years, of the kind Gray and others advocate, actively involve children, among other activities, in watching and learning along with the teacher as she 'scribes' for them, creating sustained passages of written language as the children observe and contribute to the content that is written down. The latter activity has a number of benefits: the children watch the teacher form the letters, thereby developing some understanding of the principle of their formation; they learn to sound out the words as she writes for them, so they develop some sense of the sound–letter correspondences involved; and most important of all, they learn that meanings can be shaped in the written code. These are all important steps for the learning of literacy. Yet even allowing for these things, the first texts that children write for themselves reveal the considerable effort involved. A consideration of this should alert us to how considerable is the act of learning literacy. The first texts young children write are considerably less complex than is the language they can speak, so that in this sense their language development actually regresses.

Consider, for example, the following texts written by very young children (in which, by the way, the spelling is corrected):

*Text 1*
*We went to see the lost dogs' home and I saw a cat and I saw a dog.*

*Text 2*
*I went to the bowling alley. I like the bowling alley.*

*Text 3*
*I have a kitten and I call it Sooty.*

The grammar is in all three cases very simple, and in order to demonstrate the point I shall employ a functional grammar (see Halliday, 1994; Eggins, 1994; Thompson, 1996, for discussions). Thus, each little text constructs very simple information, constructed around a process (realized in the verbs, such as *went*, or *have*), simple participants (realized either in first-person pronouns, singular or plural, *I* and *we*, or in simple noun groups, such as *the lost dogs' home, a cat* or *the bowling alley*. The grammar is not in fact that of speech, since it is written down, but it is closer to that of speech than to the grammatical organization of written language of the kind the children will need to learn. The children who produced all these written texts were capable of much more complex expressions in talk, though such was the challenge of learning to write, these were what they could write at the time. One further matter I should draw attention to in Texts 1–3, because of its relevance for what will be argued later, is the relative sparsity of the language items per clause. There are few language items in each clause, and what items are there, as already noted, are simple: the clauses do not, in other words, carry much 'content'. Yet the tendency of the written language of secondary school and also of adult life will be that it is relatively dense, compressing and hence communicating a great deal of information in reasonably economic ways.

One of the children who wrote Texts 1–3, when a little older, and in Year 2, was able to write the following, about a class visit to a park outside her city, having both an ancestral home and a zoo in its grounds.

*Text 4: Werribee Park*
*We went to Werribee Park when we got off the bus we went in the mansion. I liked the beds and the loungeroom and the stairs after that we went to the garden and I liked the flowers and the colours. Then we went to the bus we got our lunch and ate it all. Then we went to see the animals and we saw lambs sheep ducks a kangaroo emus goats camels water buffalo pigs guinea pigs zebras rhinoceros and after that we played on the swings and then we went to the island and we climbed the island and when Mandy and I climbed it the mud was all slippery and we had to come down and go on to the top and we found a cave and there was a door in the cave and there was steps on the island and nearly everyone went into the cave and Stephen and I was the monster and it started to rain so we went home and all of us were tired. The end.*

A child capable of writing such a sustained piece of writing has made considerable progress in her control of written language and its purposes, compared with the progress made in Texts 1–3. Text 4 constitutes a written recount whose function is to reconstruct aspects of personal experience in a manner making them intelligible to others. The most distinctive feature of the text type here is its strong sense of sequence of events, established very clearly through the series of additive and temporal conjunctive relationships between clauses, as in:

*Then we went to the bus*
*we got our lunch*
*and ate it all.*
*Then we went to see the animals*
*and we saw lambs sheep ducks…*

It is this characteristic, more than any other, that reveals that this text was the work of a young writer. An older writer – even one writing a recount of personal experience – would demonstrate greater facility in creating a series of interconnected clauses. The older reader of the text probably finds the particular series of conjunctive relationships rather repetitive, though they are not in fact especially unusual in speech, even among proficient adult speakers, as Plum (1998) revealed when he investigated oral storytelling in adults. The fact is that when a young child writes a recount of the kind exemplified by Text 4, the child is again modelling the grammatical organization used much more on the grammar of the speech he or she hears and uses than on the model of written language. Such patterns are indeed often practised in the morning news sessions in which many early childhood teachers encourage their students to participate.

Text 4 is both like and unlike the other texts in other ways. It is like them in that it makes extensive uses of processes of action (realized in verbs such as *went, played, climbed*), and participant roles realized in pronouns and nouns identifying class members (*I, we* and *Mandy*). Interestingly, however, and showing that the young writer has a developing control of the resources of language for the purposes of writing, she makes greater use of circumstantial information realized in prepositional phrases (eg *then we went to the bus; we played on the swings; we went to the island*). The issue is not of course that young children can't use such expressions in speech: rather, the issue is that they don't use them very much in writing for a time. Even in matters such as this, it seems that emergent control of the resources of writing takes some time in the development. The effect, incidentally, of the greater use of prepositional phrases, as well as the larger number of participants identified, is that the text is denser, clause by clause, than were Texts 1–3.

Consider how cleverly controlled and effective is the use of prepositional phrases providing circumstantial information in the writing of Anthony Browne when writing for children of the age of the writer of Text 4. Browne (1986) begins his story *Piggybook* thus (where I have underlined the prepositional phrases that realize the circumstances):

> *Mr Piggot lived with his two sons, Simon and Patrick, / in a nice house / with a nice garden, / and [with] a nice garden / in the nice garage. Inside the house / was his wife.*

The prepositional phrases here depend for their effect, in the case of the first sentence, on the repetition of *nice*, as well as on their sequence. In the case of the second sentence, the prepositional phrase depends for its effect on the meaning suggested by putting it first, in a marked position: *inside the house was his wife*, rather than the more usual or unmarked choice in English: 'his wife was inside the house'.

One would not expect writers as young as the child who wrote Text 4 to produce something as artful as Browne's text, even though they will probably experience little difficulty in comprehending the story when it is read to them.

Young children will comprehend a great deal of written language when it is read to them, or when they are assisted to read it, and the language will often be of a kind that they are not yet able to produce themselves in writing. The model of the text as it is read helps to build a growing sense of the nature of the literate mode and of its possibilities for meaning-making.

Overall, initial literacy programmes should aim to build a growing sense of confidence in handling the spelling, handwriting and punctuation systems, while they simultaneously develop a growing sense of the meanings and organization of literate texts as well as the values of written language. The responsibility of the teacher will be to challenge young learners, encouraging them on the one hand to command the various visible manifestations of literate behaviour, and on the other hand, to explore and extend their understandings of what literacy can do for them.

## Expanding horizons in learning literacy

The expansion into understanding literacy in new ways should involve young children in reading widely, even when, as is sometimes the case, the children will need to have texts read to them before they can embark on independent reading activity. In this context, the various sets of basal readers still sometimes found in early years education are quite unsatisfactory: they sacrifice meaning and hence any emotional or intellectual excitement for the young reader, focusing instead on rather mindless repetitions of spelling principles. They offer little challenge to the interested young reader, and they certainly offer nothing to persuade the reluctant reader of the values of learning to read.

While stories will remain a major source of pleasure and excitement throughout the years of schooling, reading and writing activities should also take children into exploring the world of 'uncommonsense knowledge' – knowledge that is beyond what is immediately known – and into the world of unfamiliar experience. It is here, as children move into the less familiar knowledge of schooling, that they will need to learn to handle patterns of English grammatical organization that take them further away from speech. The writer of Text 5 (from Aidman, 1999) demonstrates some of the capacities in recognizing and deploying the grammatical features of written language that will be needed.

*Text 5*
*On Monday 29th April Grade 3V went to Science works. We went to a science show. The lady [[that put on the show]]\* showed us experiments with liquid nitrogen. One of them was with a flower. She put the flower in the liquid nitrogen and then put it on the table. The flower died. She did the same thing to a squash ball but <<when she warmed it up >>† it went back to normal. And that shows that non-living things can go back to normal but living things cannot after being put in liquid nitrogen.*

(* [[ ]] the squared brackets indicate an embedded clause that is used to expand the noun group: *The lady [[that put on the show]]*.

† The symbols << >> indicate what is termed an enclosed clause, which differs from an embedded clause. An enclosed clause is a dependent clause that would normally be placed in another position – for example, it would read thus: 'She did the same thing to a squash ball but it went back to normal when she warmed it up'.)

Text 5 marks considerable development upon the kind of text we examined above in the case of Text 4 (it is, by the way, by a different writer). It is an instance of a procedural recount (Veel, 1997), and reasonably common in scientific writing even in the adult world. Like Text 4, Text 5 makes frequent use of processes of action (eg *went, put*), and though initially the text appears to foreground personal experience, using the first person (*We went to a science show*), the text then adopts the third person to record the scientific events that occurred (*the lady [[that put on the show]], she, the flower*). The third person is retained for the rest of the text, including the important concluding element in which the significance of the events is reported, starting: *And that shows....* This young writer has moved into construction of the impersonal writing of a great deal of written language, not only that of science. Other matters of interest in revealing the developing control of written language include:

- the capacity to expand the noun group in the expression *the lady [[that put on the science show]]*, demonstrating a growing awareness of the capacity of noun groups to be expanded to 'pack in' relevant information;
- the use of several prepositional phrases creating important circumstantial information (eg *one of them was <u>with a flower</u>; she put the flower <u>in the liquid nitrogen</u>; then put it <u>on the table</u>; she did the same thing <u>to a squash ball</u>*);
- the capacity to vary the ways language items are introduced and later rein-troduced in clauses, to help link them to what has been said before, and to carry the text forward: *The lady [[that put on the show]] showed us experiments with*

                                    ➞ *liquid nitrogen.*

*One of them was with a flower*
➞

*She put the flower in the liquid nitrogen*
➞

*and then put it on the table.*
➞

*The flower died.*

Such control of the developmental progression of the text avoids the apparent repetitiveness of texts such as Text 4, as well their heavy reliance on use of temporal and additive conjunctive relationships. It also shows considerable understanding of the grammar of writing, of a kind that will stand the young writer in good stead as she grows older:

- the use of the dependent clause *when she warmed it up*, in a marked position, to signal an important step in the logic of the unfolding of the information;
- the use of the general referent *that* in the clause that starts the final element, referring back in a summarizing way to all that has been recorded of the events, and also signalling, along with *and*, the start of this section;
- the relative density of the content of the clauses, compared with the first texts we examined, brought about by the combined effect of the factors mentioned above.

Such features of written language are not merely arbitrary. They represent important choices that need to be learnt if students are to control the features of written language and the meanings constructed in these. The learning of them requires a great deal of thoughtfully planned wide reading, as well as modelling of the text features, and here skilled teaching has an important role to play.

And what of the patterns of literate language in the last years of a primary schooling? Consider Text 6 (from Sandiford, 1997), an explanation of eclipses.

*Text 6*
*There are two different eclipses and scientists discovered a long time ago how eclipses occur.*

*An eclipse is when the earth or moon blocks out the light of the sun.*

*Solar eclipse*
*A solar eclipse occurs when the moon moves in front of the earth and blocks the sun but the sun is not completely blocked because the outer atmosphere of the sun flashes and can still be seen, and that is called the corona. This can only be seen in some parts of the earth and happens for a few minutes.*

*Lunar eclipse*
*A lunar eclipse occurs when the earth is between the sun and the moon. The earth blocks the light to the moon and the earth's shadow falls on the moon and this shadow is called the umbra. The moon doesn't disappear completely when there is a lunar eclipse but grows darker and changes colour to a reddish glow. Lunar eclipses happen three times a year.*

The language here is now very impersonal, indicating that the child is aware he is reporting researched knowledge: no references to self appear and indeed no human agency appears either. Of course, these features are a characteristic of the kind of text being written, and the particular demands the construction of that text makes upon the language system. Other features that reveal the relative maturity of the young writer include:

- the confident uses of the various items of technical language employed, creating the participant roles in the text (*eclipses, a lunar eclipse, the corona, the umbra*), and associated processes of action (*the moon blocks out the sun; a solar eclipse occurs….; the moon doesn't disappear*) and other identifying processes helping to build technical definitions (eg *that is called the corona; this shadow is called the umbra*);
- the frequent uses of prepositional phrases to create circumstantial information (eg *the moon moves in front of the earth; this happens for a few minutes; the earth is between the sun and the moon; the earth blocks the light to the moon*);
- the variety of conjunctive relationships set up between clauses (eg *a solar eclipse occurs when the moon moves in front of the earth and blocks the sun but the sun is not completely blocked because the outer atmosphere of the sun flashes and can still be seen, and that is called the corona*);
- the capacity, rather reminiscent of that we saw in part in Text 5, to vary the ways language items are introduced and later reintroduced, thereby linking them to what has been said before, and carrying the text forward:

*A lunar eclipse occurs*

*when the earth is between the sun and the moon.*
———————>
*The earth blocks the light to the moon*
———————>
*and the earth's shadow falls on the moon*
———————>
*and this shadow is called the umbra.*

Text 6 represents what some successful children can do towards the end of a primary education. Such a text is very different from Texts 1–3, looked at much earlier in this discussion, and the difference lies in more than simple length. The difference lies in an overall developing capacity to deploy the linguistic resources of the written mode in order to create a text whose language is impersonal and relatively dense clause by clause, while it employs technical language well. Such features are much more a characteristic of writing than of speech. Once the writer of Text 6 enters the secondary school there will be other developments that should occur in the emergent control of written language, though these matters are beyond the scope of this chapter. Suffice it to note that while there are some critical early years of schooling in which much of the basic understandings of spelling, handwriting and punctuation should be taught and learnt, it is simply misleading and wrong to imagine either that 'initial literacy' is the province of only the early years, or that literacy itself is no more than mastery of such matters as spelling, handwriting and punctuation. The learning of 'initial literacy' takes all of the years of a

primary education, as students move increasingly away from the grammatical
features of speech towards those of writing, and as they prepare themselves
for entry to the more advanced forms of literacy that characterize a secondary
education and adult life.

## Conclusion

While the discussion has been based upon a consideration of literate texts in
English, I would suggest that the general principles I have argued have relevance for a consideration of the teaching of initial literacy in all parts of the
world and in all languages. It does not follow, of course, that all languages are
grammatically alike. Indeed, the particular challenges of learning literacy and of
developing literacy programmes in the various parts of the world will always
remain quite properly the concern of those responsible both for describing the
languages in the many countries, and for developing their literacy policies.
However, all the available evidence suggests that the many languages of the
world change grammatically with the shift from the spoken to the written
mode. One would expect that, since writing evolved to fulfil functions that
speech cannot fulfil. It is the difference in functions that accounts for the grammatical differences. Studies undertaken on languages as various as Russian
(Aidman, 1999), Spanish (Colombi, 2001), Indonesian (Agustina, in preparation)
and Chinese (Shum, in preparation), to name a few, have in different ways
revealed that the written mode in all cases differs markedly from the spoken
one, having consequences for the development of educational policies, and for
the implementation of the initial literacy programmes of the future.

## References

Agustina, L (in preparation)
Aidman, M (1999) Biliteracy development through early and mid-primary
    years: a longitudinal case study of bilingual writing, unpublished PhD
    thesis, University of Melbourne, Melbourne
Browne, A (1986) *Piggybook*, Walker Books, London
Cambourne, B (1988) *The Whole Story: Natural learning and the acquisition of
    literacy in the classroom*, Ashton, Sydney
Cazden, C (1992) *Whole Language Plus: Essays on literacy in the United States and
    New Zealand*, Teachers College Press, New York
Christie, F (2002) The development of abstraction in adolescence in subject
    English, in *Developing Advanced Literacy in First and Second Languages*, eds
    M Schlepegrell and C Colombi, Lawrence Erlbaum, Hillsdale, NJ
Colombi, C (2001) Grammatical metaphor in the sciences and the humanities
    in Spanish, paper given at the 28th International Systemic Functional
    Congress on Interfaces: Systemic Functional Grammar and Critical
    Discourse Analysis, held at Carleton University, Ottawa, 22–27 July

Eggins, S (1994) *An Introduction to Systemic Functional Grammar*, Pinter, London

Freebody, P and Luke, A (1990) 'Literacies' programs: debates and demands in cultural context, *Prospect*, **5** (3), pp 7–16

Goodman, K (1986) *What's Whole in Whole Language?*, Scholastic, Toronto

Gray, B (1987) How natural is 'natural' language teaching: employing holistic methodology in the classroom, *Australian Journal of Early Childhood*, **12** (4), pp 3–19

Gray, B (1999) Accessing the discourse of schooling: English language and literacy development with Aboriginal children in mainstream schools, unpublished PhD thesis, University of Melbourne, Melbourne

Halliday, M A K (1994) *An Introduction to Functional Grammar*, 2nd edn, Arnold, London

Oakhill, J and Beard, R (eds) (1999) *Reading Development and the Teaching of Reading*, Blackwell, Oxford

Plum, G A (1998) *Text and Contextual Conditioning in Spoken English: A genre-based approach*, Monographs in Systemic Linguistics no 10, Department of English Studies, University of Nottingham

Rattanavich, S and Christie, F (1993) Developing text-based approaches to the teaching of literacy in Thailand, in *Papers in Mother Tongue Education 1*, eds G Gagné and A C Purves, pp 97–110, Waxmann, Münster

Rattanavich, S and Walker, R F (1996) Literacy for the developing world, in *Some Contemporary Themes in Literacy Research*, eds F Christie and J Foley, pp 17–45, Waxmann, Münster

Sandiford, C (1997) Teaching explanations to primary school children: the how and the why, unpublished MEd thesis, University of Melbourne, Melbourne

Shum, M (in preparation) Learning report writing in senior secondary Chinese classes in Melbourne and Hong Kong: a cross cultural case study, unpublished PhD thesis

Smith, F (1978) *Reading*, Cambridge University Press, London

Thompson, G (1996) *Introducing Functional Grammar*, Arnold, London

Veel, R (1997) Learning how to mean – scientifically speaking: apprenticeship into scientific discourse in the secondary school, in *Genre and Institution: Social Processes in the Workplace and School*, eds F Christie and J R Martin, pp 161–95, Continuum, London

Woolley, M, Pigdon, K and Hartman, D (1998) *Report on a Writing Camp Held at Lao Cai*, World Bank Primary Education Project, Multigrade and Bilingual Education Sub-component, UNESCO Office, Hanoi (Ho Chi Minh City)

Woolley, M, Pigdon, K and Molyneux, P (1995) *Report on Development of Modules 4, 5 and 6 for Multigrade Teacher Training Program, Hoa Binh, Vietnam*, UNESCO Office, Hanoi (Ho Chi Minh City)

Woolley, M, Pigdon, K and Molyneux, P (1996) *Report on Development of Modules 7 and 10 for Multigrade Teacher Training Program, Nha Trang, Vietnam*, UNESCO Office, Hanoi (Ho Chi Minh City)

# 8.  Adult literacy

Mike Baynham

## Introduction

There are few areas of language education, excepting perhaps bilingual education, that have had the same potential for evoking controversy and contestation as adult literacy. Indeed, a literature has developed, building on the seminal work of Graff (1979, 1996), that documents the recurrent perceptions in the late modern period of crisis and falling literacy standards that have marked public policy making and debate in relation to literacy (Freebody, 1998; Freebody and Welch, 1993; Lo Bianco and Freebody, 1997). This recurrent perception of crisis of course applies equally to initial schooled literacy, the topic of another chapter in this volume, but here my emphasis is on adult literacy learning, post-school or out of school. On a regular basis, adult literacy (or its lack) has been variously linked to both personal and social development and recidivism, to economic regeneration, employment/unemployment and crime. Here is an Australian example of this stance:

> There are direct links between poor literacy, school drop out rates and youth unemployment... It is now clear that education policy and practice has failed to improve the literacy standards of a significant proportion of young people. The social and economic consequences of persistent literacy problems are so serious that literacy must be addressed as a matter of priority. (DEETYA, 1996a: 1, cited in Black, 2001)

So the 'literacy debate' is underpinned by a dark imagery of educational failure, drop-out rates, unemployment, crime. As I write this chapter, for example, a publicity campaign in the United Kingdom to promote literacy learning is explicitly linking, in a series of dramatic images on billboards, lack of literacy to a tendency to resort to crime.

In this chapter I will outline some of the interdisciplinary trends that have led, over the past two decades, to a critique of this simplistic indexing of literacy levels with various forms of social disadvantage and corresponding claims that literacy improvement will promote economic growth and social regeneration, a critique which has led to the establishment of more nuanced and complex relationships between adult literacy and other social processes. I will review significant theoretical developments over these decades, linking these to shifts and developments in social policy, most notably in a shift from discourses of social redress, access and opportunity as the underpinning justification for adult

literacy education and training towards discourses that articulate human
capital arguments for adult literacy, in relation to the macro-economic social
goals of economic rationalism (Lee and Wickert, 1995).

## The social turn in adult literacy research

A number of seminal studies in the early 1980s suggested a new direction for
adult literacy research, shifting away from both its development focus and its
reliance on theoretical perspectives drawn from the source discipline of
psychology. Scribner and Cole (1981) in psychology documented a theoretical
shift towards a more situated account of literacy that questioned the universalist
claims in the earlier literature on literacy (Goody and Watt, 1968, for instance),
which argued for profound cognitive restructurings brought about by the
advent of literacy. Street (1984) from anthropology developed this critique in his
memorable distinction between *autonomous* and *ideological* models of literacy.
Contributions from the sociologist Levine (1986) and the social historian Graff
(1979) emphasized the socially produced, contingent nature of literacy practices. Graff's historical study, as mentioned above, was particularly influential
in critiquing, on the basis of historical evidence, the simplistic indexing of
literacy with development. Heath's (1983) study of the literacy practices of three
communities in the Piedmont Carolinas is another such landmark study.

   The trend in the two decades since these studies has been a move away from
the broad-scale claims about the effects of literacy of the earlier studies.
Ironically, though, these theoretical shifts have not dispelled 'the literacy
myth' in the world of policy formation, and it will be seen that the simplistic
indexing of literacy with development underpins current economic rationalist
arguments in favour of adult literacy provision, continuing, on both a
personal and social level, the claims about the socio-economic if not the
cognitive consequences of literacy development of earlier studies. I will
briefly outline the development of this social perspective on adult literacy and
will then go on to review work in a number of domains where research
activity has been and is currently significant: literacy in development, adult
literacy in community contexts, adult literacy in the workplace and the impact
of new technologies and multimodal means of communication on conceptualizations of adult literacy and adult literacy teaching and learning. I will then
review a context where these arguments over what counts as literacy have
again become controversial: in debates over the measurement of literacy
levels through the International Adult Literacy Survey (IALS). I will conclude
by suggesting that the social turn taken by adult literacy research has to some
extent de-emphasized the research focus on adult literacy teaching and
learning, re-emphasizing social contextual factors. I will finally suggest that
recent developments in situated cognition, sociocultural theory and activity
theory provide a basis for reintegrating the cognitive with the social in adult

literacy teaching and learning without losing the insights afforded by the macro and micro social perspectives on adult literacy that have been pioneered over the past two decades of research, suggesting that this is one of the directions research should increasingly go in over the next decade.

## Situated perspectives on adult literacy: the New Literacy Studies

Originally introduced in the early 1990s in the work of Gee (1990) and Street (1993), the term 'New Literacy Studies' (NLS) is used to characterize the work of literacy researchers who have taken the social turn and a discourse-analytic turn in their research. Gee (2000) explores this convergence of theoretical interests, across a range of work in situated cognition, connectionism, socio-cultural theory, ethnomethodology and conversational analysis, ethnography of communication, the sociology of science and technology, and post-structuralist theory, arguing for a broad theoretical congruence based on social and discourse-analytic perspectives used to investigate literacy.

The New Literacy Studies perspective involves a turn away both from *a priori* specification of categories of people, such as 'literates' and 'illiterates', and from the attachment of 'typical' outcomes, to membership of such static categories and from simplistic claims about the role of literacy in promoting personal and social development. The New Literacy Studies perspective promotes the theorization of everyday social practice, based on the premise that literacy practices are always and already embedded in particular social forms of activity. Such literacy practices are mutually constructed, and are also shaped by both institutionalized and informal relations of power (Baynham and Prinsloo, 2001).

Barton and Hamilton (2000: 7–15) identify the characteristics of the New Literacy Studies approach on literacy:

- Literacy is best understood as a set of social practices; these are observable in events that are mediated by written texts.
- There are different literacies associated with different domains of life.
- Literacy practices are patterned by social institutions and power relations, and some literacies are more dominant, visible and influential than others.
- Literacy practices are purposeful and embedded in broader social goals and cultural practices.
- Literacy is historically situated.
- Literacy practices change and new ones are frequently acquired through processes of informal learning and sense making as well as formal education and training.

## Literacy in development

As I suggested above, Street's (1984) critique of the autonomous model of literacy grew in part out of a reaction against the extravagant universalistic claims for the effects of literacy on personal, social and economic development. Interestingly, after some 15 years of emphasis on situated literacy research, informed by ethnographic approaches, Street (2001) returns to the development theme in a collection that presents case studies of how the insights of ethnographically based research on literacy can inform development projects. From the ethnographic perspective, the commitment to intervention and improvement is not diminished, but the emphasis is on informed intervention. In an afterword to the collection, Rogers suggests that ethnographically based models of literacy problematize not just the models of literacy current in development rhetoric, but the nature of development interventions themselves. This shift in the conceptualization of the relationship between literacy and development has thus been accompanied by a reconceptualization of the moral and political bases for development interventions. This provides another sense in which literacy cannot be abstracted from context, and in fact involves what Lee (1997) terms a co-productive relationship with other forms of social practice.

## Literacy in the community

The focus on non-hegemonic literacy practices that has typified some research in the NLS paradigm has pointed attention to community-based uses of literacy – in other words, forms of literacy that are not institutionalized and institutionally sanctioned, that may indeed be resistant and oppositional to the culturally dominant forms. The work of Barton and Hamilton (1998) is an instance of such a community-based study; it reports on longitudinal ethnographic research in Lancaster in the United Kingdom. Another is Heath's classic (1983) study. Baynham and Masing (2000) report on Masing's research in Vanuatu on the literacy practices in Bislama of a village community (Masing, 1992). The Social Uses of Literacy (SoUL) project (cf Prinsloo and Breier, 1996) investigated literacy practices in South Africa in a range of communities and workplaces. Horsman (1990) and Rockhill (1993) research women and literacy.

## Multilingual literacies

The hegemonic status of English in language education worldwide has meant that a great deal of research is based on English, and adult literacy research is no exception to this tendency, with a great volume of research studies in the United States, the United Kingdom and Australia. Some of the key early studies, however, were conducted in multilingual settings, with languages other than English (eg Scribner and Cole, 1981, in Liberia, with literacies in Vai, Arabic and English; Street, 1984, based on fieldwork in Iran). There is a significant focus on adult literacy research in Brazil (Signorini and Kleiman, 1994; Signorini and Dias, 2000). Wagner and his associates (Wagner, 1993) have researched literacy in Morocco, as have Zubair (2001) in Pakistan, Stites (2001) in China, Papen (2001) in Namibia. The SoUL project (Prinsloo and Breier, 1996) researched literacy practices in multilingual South Africa. Jones (2000a, 2000b) has researched the bilingual literacy practices of Welsh farmers. In other areas, adult literacy research finds common cause with research on bilingualism and bilingual education (Martin-Jones and Jones, 2000), language maintenance and language planning (Hornberger, 1996; Burnaby, 1998). Hornberger's continua of biliteracy construct (Hornberger, 1989; Hornberger and Skilton-Silvester, 2000) has been influential in bringing together research on bilingualism and adult literacy. Virtually all the studies presented in Street (1993, 2001) are case studies of literacy activity in languages other than English. Clearly, a research agenda for the next decade must be to extend the scope of adult literacy research to encompass a wider range of languages and contexts.

## Shifts in the policy landscape: adult literacy and economic rationalism

I have mentioned earlier the shift from rights-driven conceptualizations of adult literacy provision to those driven by human capital agenda, which became a significant driving force of adult literacy programmes in the 1990s. We can see this from one perspective as a new iteration of the literacy = development equation, this time placed at the service of economic transformation:

> The link between literacy and economic rationalism has a long, if not altogether distinguished, history. The claim that increased levels of literacy are necessary and sufficient was a product of the Industrial Revolution. Rises in basic literacy levels, it is still claimed, will lead to increased economic productivity and social equity. (Luke, 1992: 3)

The increased prominence of adult literacy in public policy led to increased levels of funding and diversification of provision, mainly in the service of policy initiatives designed to reduce long-term unemployment and increase the effectiveness of the workforce. Another product of this shift has been increasing levels of regulation of adult literacy programmes, through national policy, curriculum and assessment frameworks, as Lee and Wickert (1995: 136) suggest:

> The consequences of these kinds of policy shifts for adult literacy and basic education workers include an increasing regulation of their work by bureaucratic management practices. The operation of what has been termed 'corporate federalism' is the manifestation of increasing centralist control through the development of national policies and strategies and the consequent establishment of national initiatives such as curriculum and reporting frameworks (Lingard, 1993).

Kell (2001) discusses the implications of this in terms of the South African National Qualifications Framework, while Hamilton (2001) points to the international dimension of this process, talking of 'a solidifying international "regime of truth" which is developing through techniques of standardised assessment and testing and which in turn is organizing national and local knowledge about what literacy is' (Darville, 1999).

So what we see in the early years of the new millennium is the continued sharpening of the debate as to what counts as literacy. This is an issue I will take up again in relation to the International Adult Literacy Survey (IALS).

## Adult literacy and the 'New Work Order'

Much recent attention in adult literacy research has focused on adult literacy in the workplace (cf for example Gowen, 1992; Hull, 1997), in part, as suggested above, because of the increase in the influence of the economic rationalist, human capital arguments for adult literacy provision, in terms of increased productivity and improvements to health and safety (cf Lo Bianco, 2001). A significant factor here has been the actual or perceived impact of changes in work practices on the literacy demands of the workplace (see Mawer, 1999). The dramatic changes to the post-Fordist workplace, stereotypically associated with flatter management structures, work teams with devolved responsibilities, continuous quality monitoring and routine requirements to manipulate symbolic systems, has been dubbed 'the New Work Order' by Gee, Hull and Lankshear (1996). Critical literacy theorists, such as Gee, Hull and Lankshear and others, have sounded a note of caution in relation to the extravagant claims of the new workplace and the multiskilled worker (cf Luke, 1992, above). Black (1998, 2001) provides a case study of the impact of New Work Order rhetoric on low-paid, unskilled workers in Sydney, Australia and Black (1995) of literacy and the unemployed. Hull has been carrying on long-term ethnographic research on the impact of changes in work practices on communication practices, including literacy in Silicon Valley, California.

## Adult literacy and technological change: shifts in the multimodal landscape

It has become a truism that technological change is reshaping communicative practices on a global basis, producing what Street (2001), Lankshear (1997), Kress and van Leeuwen (1996, 2001) and others have called 'the new communicative order'. Castells (1996) provides an overview of the communicative reshaping being brought about by new media, not least in the reconfiguring of the relationships between spoken and written language being brought about through highly interactive technologies such as e-mail and text messaging. Critical literacy theorists such as Lankshear, Snyder and Green (2000) emphasize the need for a critical vigilance, a determination to read the hype of hypertext critically for evidence of coercion, distortion, exclusion. Kress and van Leeuwen (1996) argue that another mode shift involves a shift of the relationship between visual and verbal text, with a re-emphasizing of the visual, arguing in a series of influential publications for the notion of multimodal texts. These mode shifts have enormous implications for adult literacy learning, which are brought out in a programmatic way by Warschauer (1998) and Murray (2000). In terms of empirical studies, a collection of recent research-informed papers is edited by Hawisher and Selfe (1999). Warschauer (1999) presents a series of case studies of online literacy practices in a range of educational settings in Hawaii. Merchant (2001) reports on a study of teenage girls' communication practices in chatrooms. While there have clearly been such shifts historically, the development of writing systems being one, the advent of the printing press being another, these current changes in communication practices present a huge research opportunity to document reflexively such changes in progress. No doubt literacy research in the next decade will show an exponential increase in such studies.

A common thread in the literature is the emphasis that textual change is not driven by technological change in a simplistic way, but that both are produced in complex social conditions. This idea resonates well with the Barton and Hamilton tenets of New Literacy Studies work presented above. Snyder characterizes this as 'the spurious premise that technology is directly responsible for changes that inevitably affect social relations' (1997: 133). This is an important insight and points the way to a research agenda that examines the social production of online literacy practices in both classrooms and bedrooms.

## Adult literacy pedagogies: critical, constructivist and apprenticeship perspectives

A significant theoretical influence on pedagogical issues in adult literacy has been critical theory, most notably in the work of Freire (1973), which was formative among a generation of adult literacy practitioners and theorists committed to a social perspective on adult literacy pedagogy. At present the theoretical landscape is more diverse, with a wider range of theoretical influences in play, including the work of Bourdieu, Bernstein (see Collins, 2000) and Foucault, all with somewhat different versions of the social world. Yet Freire's thinking remains influential in the work of those who take a critical theory perspective on adult literacy, such as Lankshear (1997), Auerbach (1999) and Shor and Pari (1999).

Strong Freirean approaches suggest that the appropriate pedagogical stance is not the transfer of knowledge from teacher to student (the banking concept), but rather a jointly constructed learning endeavour, erasing strong distinctions between teacher and learner. However, perspectives that emphasize the unequal distribution of power and knowledge from a Foucauldian viewpoint, for example, point to a pedagogy of access into powerful discourses, implying some kind of apprenticeship into the ways of knowing of particular discourse communities. Bernstein (1996), for example, contrasts the acquisition of horizontal and vertical discourses, with horizontal discourses as likely to be acquired through 'local activities, segmentally structured, often but not always tacitly acquired, through demonstration and exemplar modelling, eliciting and structuring'; and vertical discourses where knowledge is acquired in a structured and sequential way, typically a pedagogical progression. (For a discussion of the relevance of Bernstein's work to literacy, see Collins (2000), Kell (2001) and Moss (2000, 2001).)

One of the impacts of the policy, curriculum and assessment frameworks described above, combining both access and human capital arguments, has been the development of such vertical trajectories for adult literacy learning in the shape of frameworks for progression from basic literacy into vocational education – training at work – generally conceptualized in terms of a qualifications framework and progression through levels. These suggest a number of interesting areas for research from a New Literacy Studies perspective: first, in the general theoretical critique of restricted skills-based conceptualizations of literacy that may inform such frameworks, as I will elaborate in the discussion of the International Adult Literacy Survey below; second, at a more micro level in the validation of literacy 'outcomes' or 'competences' acquired in terms of real-world literacy uses in workplaces, classrooms and daily contexts; and third, in the integration of literacy into vocational and content area learning.

Finally, the rapidly changing communications environment and the demands of the new knowledge economy have led some theorists of literacy learning to propose more radical departures from traditional transmission pedagogies. The New London Group has elaborated a programmatic pedagogy for multiliteracies combining Situated Practice, Overt Instruction, Critical Framing and Transformed Practice (New London Group, 1996: 82). Another significant pedagogical theme is that of cultural diversity. Gutiérrez, Baquedano-López and Tejeda (1997) and Gutiérrez, Baquedano-López and Turner (2000) elaborate the Vygotskyan notion of the Zone of Proximal Development, suggesting ways of theorizing dialogicality and multi-voicedness in classroom practice in terms of a third space. Gutiérrez and her associates are looking at learning in schools, but there are obvious applications in adult literacy learning.

## Issues and controversies: the International Adult Literacy Survey

Ongoing debate in relation to the International Adult Literacy Survey (IALS) has currently crystallized some of the issues of what counts as literacy identified in the discussion above. For a summary of the scope and theoretical underpinnings of the IALS, as well as critical perspectives on it, see Hamilton (2001). The IALS (OECD, 1995) was based on a functional literacy test that provided a rating of literacy levels in 20 countries. According to Hamilton, 'the IALS test and findings are increasingly being used to underpin national policies for basic skills'. As Levine (1998: 58) points out, the IALS model of literacy is informed by perspectives from cognitive psychology:

> The academic commitment is to cognitive psychology, and this debt is freely acknowledged by Jones (1997: 22), one of the principal IALS authors, in his contribution to the debate... From the viewpoint of cognitive psychology, literacy appears to be a unified skill underpinned by an individual's information-processing capacity. This capacity is generic and transferrable, so that once acquired, it can operate across different contents, media, genre, practices, and cultural contexts. (Anderson *et al*, 1996, 1997)

This is a particularly clear articulation of the generic transferable skills model of literacy, underpinning much of the current policy developments in adult literacy curriculum and assessment frameworks worldwide. Underlying this is a quite clearly articulable controversy on the nature of literacy: is it generic transferable skill or situated social practice? As suggested at the beginning of this chapter, this is most frequently framed as a disciplinary controversy between cognitive psychological constructions of literacy and the social constructions outlined above, reiterating one of the basic cleavages in the intellectual landscape of the late modern period between psychological and social theory. (This epistemological dynamic clearly extends well beyond the current topic of adult literacy, evoking as it does basic assumptions as to what counts as knowledge.) In the final section of this chapter, I will treat it rather as a controversy within cognitive psychology, arguing that there are trends and tendencies within cognitive psychology more congruent with the social perspective on literacy that provide promising possibilities of a more integrated account of literacy from both social, discursive and cognitive perspectives.

## Research prospects for reintegrating the cognitive with the social: connectionism, situated cognition and sociocultural theory

Gee (1992) was a pioneer in revisiting the cognitive dimensions of literacy from a New Literacy Studies perspective with his book *The Social Mind*, which explores the potential of connectionism for retheorizing the psychological/social binary. More recently (2000) he points as well to other influences in sociocultural theory, including the situated cognition theory of Lave and Wenger (1991), the neo-Vygotskyan work of Wertsch (1985, 1991) and the activity theory of Leonte'ev (1978) and Engestrom (1990). All these perspectives emphasize the situated, interactively constructed characteristics of both knowing and learning in ways that are congruent with the socially situated perspectives of the New Literacy Studies. As Gee (2000: 181) suggests, from these perspectives 'knowing is a matter of being able to participate centrally in practice and learning is a matter of changing patterns of participation (with concomitant changes in identity)'. Sociocultural theory becomes a bridge to reactivate the connection with teaching and learning, de-emphasized in the earlier work of the New Literacy Studies, which sought to establish an empirical base for arguing the situated nature of literacy.

## Conclusion

In conclusion I would like to suggest that while many of the theoretical underpinnings of the New Literacy Studies are well established empirically, there still remains the issue of how these theoretically rich perspectives dialogue productively with public policy formation, for example in relation to curriculum and assessment regimes. These issues are addressed in recent papers by Hamilton (2001), Kell (2001) and Lo Bianco (2001). The initial move in the New Literacy Studies was a promising turning away from the classroom towards the social world in a comprehensive retheorization of what counts as literacy. I think this is perhaps the moment for a return of the research focus to the classroom, or perhaps more broadly to sites of literacy teaching and learning, diverse as these may be, in order to meet a further challenge of how to elaborate a theoretically rich account of teaching and learning to counter the more reductionist, skills-based versions of literacy circulating in public policy discourse. Developments in sociocultural theory provide a promising basis for this.

## References

Auerbach, E (1999) Teacher, tell me what to do, in *Critical Literacy in Action: Writing words, changing worlds*, eds I Shor and C Pari, Heinemann, Portsmouth, NH

Barton, D and Hamilton, M (1998) *Local Literacies: Reading and writing in one community*, Routledge, London

Barton, D and Hamilton, M (2000) Literacy practices, in *Situated Literacies: Reading and writing in context*, eds D Barton, M Hamilton and R Ivanic, pp 7–15, Routledge, London

Barton, D and Hamilton, M (2000) The International Adult Literacy Survey: what does it really measure?, *International Journal of Education* **46** (5), pp 377–89

Barton, D, Hamilton, M and Ivanic, R (eds) (2000) *Situated Literacies: Reading and writing in context*, Routledge, London

Baynham, M and Masing, H L (2000) Mediators and mediation in multilingual literacy events, in *Multilingual Literacies*, eds M Martin-Jones and K Jones, pp 189–207, John Benjamins, Amsterdam

ADULT LITERACY

119

Baynham, M and Prinsloo, M (2001) New Directions in Literacy Research: Language and Education, vols 2 and 3
Bernstein, B (1996) Pedagogy, Symbolic Control and Identity, Taylor & Francis, London
Black, S (1995) Literacy and the Unemployed, Research Report 1, Centre for Language and Literacy, University of Technology, Sydney
Black, S (1998) Teamwork, Discourses and Literacy, Research Report 4, Centre for Language and Literacy, University of Technology, Sydney
Black, S (2001) Literacy as critical social practice: a challenge to dominant discourses on literacy and (un)employment, unpublished PhD thesis, University of Technology, Sydney
Burnaby, B (1998) Literacy in Athapascan languages in the Northwest Territories, Canada: for what purposes?, Written Language and Literacy, 1 (1), pp 63–102
Castells, M (1996) The Rise of the Networked Society, vol 1, The Information Age: Economy, society and culture, Blackwell, Oxford
Collins, J (2000) Bernstein, Bourdieu and the New Literacy Studies, Linguistics and Education, 11 (1), pp 65–78
Darville, R (1999) Knowledges of adult literacy: surveying for competitiveness, International Journal of Educational Development, 19, 273–85
DEETYA (1996a) Alarming new literacy results, media release, Dr Kemp, Canberra, 22 October
Engestrom, Y (1990) Learning, Working and Imagining: Twelve studies in activity theory, Orienta-Konsultit, Helsinki
Freebody, P (1998) Assessment as communal versus punitive practice: six new literacy crises for Australia, Literacy and Numeracy Studies: An International Journal in the Education and Training of Adults, 7, pp 5–17
Freebody, P and Welch, A R (eds) (1993) Knowledge, Culture, and Power: International perspectives on literacy policies and practices, Falmer, London
Freire (1973) Pedagogy of the Oppressed, Penguin Books, London
Gee, J (1990) Social Linguistics and Literacies: Ideology in discourses, Falmer, London
Gee, J (1992) The Social Mind: Language, ideology and social practice, Bergin & Harvey, New York
Gee, J (2000) The New Literacy Studies: from 'socially situated' to the work of the social, in Situated Literacies: Reading and writing in context, eds D Barton, M Hamilton and R Ivanic, pp 180–96, Routledge, London
Gee, J, Hull, G and Lankshear, C (1996) The New Work Order: Behind the language of the new capitalism, Allen & Unwin, St Leonards, NSW
Goody, J and Watt, I (1968) The consequences of literacy, in Literacy in Traditional Societies, ed J Goody, Cambridge University Press, Cambridge
Gowen, S (1992) The Politics of Workplace Literacy, Teachers College Press, New York
Graff, H (1979) The Literacy Myth, Academic Press, New York

Graff, H (1996) The persisting power and costs of the literacy myth, *Literacy across the Curriculum*, **12** (2), pp 4–5

Gutiérrez, K, Baquedano-López, P and Tejeda, C (2000) Rethinking diversity: hybridity and hybrid language practices in the third space, *Mind, Culture, and Activity*, **6** (4), pp 286–303

Gutiérrez, K, Baquedano-López, P, and Turner, M G (1997) Putting language back into language arts: when the radical middle meets the third space, *Language Arts*, **74** (5), pp 368–78

Hamilton, M (nd) Commentary on the NFER Report *Progress in Adult Literacy* [Online] http://www.niace.org.uk/Organisation/advocacy/adultliteracy.pdf

Hamilton, M (2001) Privileged literacies: Policy, institutional process and the life of the IALS, in *New Directions in Literacy Research: Policy, Pedagogy, Practice*, eds M Baynham and M Prinsloo, special issue of Language and Education, vol 15, no 2 & 3, pp 178–96.

Hawisher, G E and Selfe, C (eds) (1999) *Global Literacies and the World Wide Web*, Routledge, London

Heath (1983) *Ways with Words*, Cambridge University Press, Cambridge

Hornberger, N (1989) Continua of biliteracy, *Review of Educational Research*, **59** (3), pp 271–96

Hornberger, N (1997) *Indigenous Literacies in the Americas: Language planning from the bottom up*, Mouton de Gruyter, Berlin

Hornberger, N and Skilton-Sylvester, E (2000) Revisiting the continua of biliteracy: international and critical perspectives, *Language and Education*, **14** (1), pp 18–44

Horsman, J (1990) *Something in My Mind Besides the Everyday: Women and Literacy*, Women's Press, Toronto

Hull, G (ed) (1997) *Changing Work, Changing Worker: Critical perspectives on language, literacy and skills*, State University of New York, New York

Jones, K (2000a) Becoming just another alphanumeric code: farmers' encounters with literacy and discourse practices of agricultural bureaucracy at the livestock auction, in *Situated Literacies: Reading and writing in context*, eds D Barton, M Hamilton and R Ivanic, pp 70–90, Routledge, London

Jones, K (2000b) Texts, mediation and social relations in a bureaucratised world, in *Multilingual Literacies*, eds M Martin-Jones and K Jones, pp 209–28, John Benjamins, Amsterdam

Jones, S (1997) Ending the myth of the 'literacy myth', *Literacy across the Curriculum*, **12** (4), pp 10–17

Kell, C (2001) Ciphers and currencies: literacy dilemmas and shifting knowledges, *Language and Education*, **15** (2/3), pp 197–211

Kress, G and van Leeuwen, T (1996) *Reading Images: The grammar of visual design*, Routledge, London

Kress, G and van Leeuwen, T (2001) *Multimodal Discourse: The modes and media of contemporary communication*, Arnold, London

Lankshear, C (1997) *Changing Literacies*, Open University Press, Buckingham

Lankshear, C, Snyder, I and Green, B (2000) *Teachers and Technoliteracy: Managing literacy, technology and learning in schools*, Allen & Unwin, St Leonards

Lave, J and Wenger, E (1991) *Situated Learning: Legitimate peripheral participation*, Cambridge University Press, New York

Lee, A (1997) Working together? Academic literacies, co-production and professional partnerships, *Literacy and Numeracy Studies*, **7** (2), pp 65–82

Lee, A and Wickert, R (1995) Reading the discourses of adult basic education teaching, in *Understanding Adult Education and Training*, ed G Foley, Allen & Unwin, St Leonards

Leonte'ev, A N (1978) *Activity, Consciousness and Personality*, Prentice Hall, Englewood Cliffs, NJ

Levine, K (1986) *The Social Context of Literacy*, Routledge, London

Levine, K (1998) Definitional and methodological problems in the cross-national measurement of adult literacy: the case of the IALS, *Written Language and Literacy*, **1** (1), pp 41–61

Lo Bianco, J (2001) Policy literacy, *Language and Education*, **15** (2/3), pp 212–27

Lo Bianco, J and Freebody, P (1997) *Australian Literacies: Informing national policy on literacy education*, Language Australia, Melbourne

Luke, A (1992) Literacy and work in 'new times', *Open Letter*, **3** (1), pp 3–15

Martin-Jones, M and Jones, K (eds) (2000) *Multilingual Literacies*, John Benjamins, Amsterdam

Masing, H Lobanga (1992) Literacy practice in a small, rural ni-Vanuatu village, unpublished MA TESOL dissertation, University of Technology, Sydney

Mawer, G (1999) *Language and Literacy in Workplace Education: Learning at work*, Longman, London

Merchant, G (2001) Teenagers in cyberspace: an investigation of language use and language change in Internet chatrooms, *Journal of Research in Reading*, **24** (3), pp 293–306

Moss, G (2000) Informal literacies and pedagogic discourse, *Linguistics and Education*, **11** (1), pp 47–64

Moss, G (2001) On literacy and the social organization of knowledge inside and out of school, *Language and Education*, **15** (2/3), pp 146–61

Murray, D (2000) Changing technologies, changing literacy communities? *Language Learning and Technology*, **4** (2), pp 43–58 [online]. Available at llt.msu.edu/vol4num2/murray/default/html

New London Group (1996) A pedagogy of multiliteracies: designing social futures, *Harvard Educational Review*, **66**, pp 60–92

Organization for Economic Cooperation and Development (OECD) (1995) *Literacy, Economy and Society: Results of the first International Adult Literacy Survey*. Paris: OECD, Paris, and Statistics Canada, Ottawa

Papen, U (2001) Literacy – your key to a better future?: literacy, reconciliation and development in the National Literacy Programme in Namibia, in *Literacy and Development: Ethnographic perspectives*, ed B Street, Routledge, London

Prinsloo, M and Breier, M (eds) (1996) *The Social Uses of Literacy*, John Benjamins/SACHED, Amsterdam

Rockhill, K (1993) *Gender, language and the politics of literacy*, in *Cross-cultural Approaches to Literacy*, ed B Street, Cambridge University Press, Cambridge

Scholtz, S and Prinsloo, M (2001) New workplace, new literacies, new identities, in *Journal of Adolescent and Adult Literacy*, **44** (8), pp 710–13

Scribner, S and Cole, M (1981) *The Psychology of Literacy*, Harvard University Press, Cambridge, MA

Shor, I and Pari, C (1999) *Critical Literacy in Action: Writing words, changing worlds*, Heinemann, Portsmouth, NH

Signorini, I and Dias, R (2000) 'Até agora, só ferrada, cara!' O cognitivo, o afetivo e o motivacional na alfabetização de jovens, in *O ensino e a formação do professor: alfabetização de jovens e adultos*, eds A B Kleiman and I Signorini, Artmed, Porto Alegre

Signorini, I and Kleiman, A B (1994) When explaining is saying: teacher talk in adult literacy classes, in *Education as Cultural Construction*, ed A Alvarez and P Del Rio, Fundación Infancia y Aprendizaje, Madrid

Snyder, I (ed) (1997) *Page to Screen: Taking literacy into the electronic era*, Allen & Unwin, Sydney

Stites, R (2001) Household literacy environments as contexts for development in rural China, in *Literacy and Development: Ethnographic perspectives*, ed B Street, pp 171–87, Routledge, London

Street, B (1984) *Literacy in Theory and Practice*, Cambridge University Press, Cambridge

Street, B (ed) (1993) *Cross-cultural Approaches to Literacy*, Cambridge University Press, Cambridge

Street, B (ed) (2001) *Literacy and Development: Ethnographic perspectives*, Routledge, London

Sullivan, P and Dautermann, J (eds) *Electronic Literacies in the Workplace: Technologies of writing*, NCTE and Computers and Composition, Urbana, IL

Vygotsky, L S (1978) *Mind and Society*, Cambridge University Press, Cambridge

Wagner, D (1993) *Literacy, Culture and Development: Becoming literate in Morocco*, Cambridge University Press, New York

Warschauer, M (1998) Online learning in sociocultural context, *Anthropology and Education Quarterly*, **29** (1), pp 68–88

Warschauer, M (1999) *Electronic Literacies: Language, culture and power in online education*, Lawrence Erlbaum, Mahwah, NJ

Warschauer, M and Lepeintre, S (1997) Freire's dream or Foucault's nightmare? Teacher–student relations on an international computer network. Language learning through social computing, *Occasional Papers of the Applied Linguistics Association of Australia*, pp 67–90, ALAA and the Horwood Language Centre, Melbourne

Welch, A R and Freebody, P (1993) Crisis and context in literacy education, in *Knowledge, Culture and Power*, eds P Freebody and A R Welch, Falmer, London

Wertsch, J (1985) *Vygotsky and the Social Formation of Mind*, Harvard University Press, Cambridge, MA

Wertsch, J (1991) *Voices of the Mind: A sociocultural approach to mediated action*, Harvard University Press, Cambridge, MA

Zubair, S (2001) Literacies, gender and power in rural Pakistan, in *Literacy and Development: Ethnographic perspectives*, ed B Street, pp 188–204, Routledge, London

# Part II

# Language education in policy and practice: regional and national case studies

# 9.   Language education in Japan: the multicultural challenge

John C Maher and Akira Nakayama

## Introduction

Japan in the 21st century is experiencing globalization across many terrains: economic, technological, cultural, as well as the domain of language education. Globalization is not merely the imposition of transnational capitalist structures upon local economies but is also a social relation. Thus, language – a sensitive constant of social organization and human relations – has likewise found itself the axis of dramatic change in Japan. This includes the impact of new technologies on the writing system, government reform of language teaching in schools – in particular, experiments with 'primary English' – and the crossing and hybridization of hitherto linguistically uniform local communities by 'Other' (ie immigrant) languages with their own concomitant ideological dimensions and social demands.

In the 21st century we can no longer refer, safely viewing it as a monolith, to 'the language of Japan' but are obliged rather to conjecture a more sociolinguistically complex phenomenon: perhaps 'language in Japan' or conversely, indexing new multicultural realities, 'the languages of Japan' (Maher, 1995; Shibatani, 1990). Nor can Japanese itself remain the self-regarding, self-defining entity that has long sustained its high ideological ground as *Kokugo* ('The National Language', ie 'the mother tongue'). Running symbolically with this is the demise of the term *Kokugo* itself (though still official terminology in schools) and the increasing use of its terminological alter ego *Nihongo* (Japanese language), a commonplace and paradoxically less statist terminology (*Nihon* = Japan; *go* = language) once used to label the language as taught to non-Japanese nationals but now routinely employed throughout Japan and the world and by Japanese people themselves.

Globalization in Japan is an intermingling of global and distant logics (Maher and Macdonald, 1995; Salskov-Iverson, 2000) in which the safe territoriality of the state, ideas, economies and local identities becomes blurred, redefined and recontextualized. Thus, a proposal by former prime minister Obuchi's Special Committee on Globalization in 1999 to make

English 'an official language of Japan' marked periodically and dramatically the new recontextualization of the nation's 'language in daily life' (*gengo seikatsu*). English remains pre-eminent in the pantheon of taught and learnt foreign languages: the normal vehicle of academic, scientific and cultural crossing, the thoroughfare of intermarriage, career, travel, the life of the Internet. The proposal itself was greeted with fury, delight, bewilderment and a flurry of panic publications calling the proposal linguistic treachery against the national language; and the debate continues (Inoue, 2001). Meanwhile, 2002 is a turning point in the history of language education in Japan. Foreign language teaching (English) is being formally but experimentally introduced into selected primary schools across the country, and in ordinary public schools English 'taster' classes will be offered in the context of a newly fashioned programme of 'Integrated Education' (*Sogo Kyoiku*).

The social issues of the time that tangentially impinge on language education are well known and, typically, touted in the media: the moral *crise de conscience* wrought by the expansion and collapse (*babburu hokai*) of the bubble economy; the seemingly inexplicable and different values presented by the 'new breed' younger generation (*shinjinrui*) with their new speech now referred to as 'new dialects' (*shin-hogen*); the demise of lifetime employment and the explosive rise of a part-time floating youth employment sector (*freetar*); and the problem of classroom turmoil and indiscipline and the emptying of the classrooms as a result of the drop in the national birthrate (*shoshika*). How these myriad developments influence language education is significant, subtle and can only be hinted at here. Consider one example, the phenomenon of *shoshika*: the decline in the birthrate. Slow economic growth dislocates many Japanese households and has created both unemployment and, it is said, educational discontent, but it may not cripple the country in the long run. The low birthrate, however, does threaten Japan's long-term prospects as an industrialized nation. Japanese women now have an average of 1.35 children (see Ministry of Health, Labour and Welfare, 2001), less than the 2 needed for 'statistically stable' population growth. Experts project the present population of 126 million to drop to 101 million by 2050 (*WHO Statistical Yearbook*, 2001). The classrooms, it is widely understood, have emptied and throughout the nation the upper floors of once bursting schools are silent and unused. Now, the complaint and target of language teachers in schools and colleges has long been the impossibility of teaching large classes. How can communicative skills, ran the argument, be taught and learnt in classes of 40–50 students packed into every corner of the classroom? Nowadays, with a class size of 20–30 pupils and space for movement and new methodologies, teachers must develop new strategies; no longer can 'big classes' remain the educational scapegoat for language teachers' difficulty and sometimes frank unwillingness to adopt new and challenging methodologies.

## The spirits of education past, present and future

One powerful and lingering influence has, almost spirit-like, suffused traditional approaches to language education in Japan, namely the low priority placed upon oral expression and rhetorical skills. This influence is not found, it must be stressed, in the primary school, and we are anxious to see how the 2002 introduction of language teaching in the disciplined yet remarkably free-school philosophy of the public primary school will impact upon language education at higher educational levels or overall on society. Kai (1998) cites four general historical reasons for the neglect of orality in language education in Japan. First, for over a thousand years a major component of education in Japan has been attention to an understanding of the minutiae of written Chinese language texts: Buddhist sutras, Confucian texts and other Chinese literature. Difficulty in mastering the writing system of the modern language likewise maintains ideological devotion to written language education. Second, Kai notes a strong tendency for Japanese people to hesitate to express their thoughts, formally, in public. Third, the Japanese intelligentsia have long held that genuine human qualities are developed more through the study of written texts than through ephemeral social contact. Fourth, entrance examinations for high school and university have emphasized abilities that can be objectively measured: reading ability and the retention of facts. This emphasis on written language education (ie literacy) has powered not only mother tongue education but also foreign language education (ie English language education).

The matter of language testing – methods, suitability and effectiveness – remains a central concern for language education in a nation that is test-conscious in many forms of life, from dance to calligraphy, from judo to cooking. As in other education-conscious nations, in addition to the linguistic capital involved in the possession of more qualifications, the challenge and fascination of the test also may tend to extend beyond the commonplace objective of evaluation itself. The test becomes an end in itself; tests are in abundance and school tests are likely to be pivotal in life and career (Duke, 1986); success in tests still constitutes strong social capital among the upper middle classes.

In the world of school and educational philosophy former totalizing narratives about education in Japan are being challenged. Are Japanese really 'worse' in English-speaking skills than other nationalities, or is this a folk-linguistic myth that belies a much more interesting and complex set of factors (Honna, 1995)? Even more, sociologists are returning to challenge basic social reifications such as 'the Japanese' that fuel national decisions about language policy. 'What is Japanese "society" anyway? The concept "Japanese" is undefined and is not a sociologically reliable concept" (Sugimoto, 1995: 74). However, there is no doubt that the world of education in Japan still retains, nationwide, a powerful mutuality of perceptions involving time, space, the daily routine, the overall curriculum, a common language (spoken and written), club activities, annual events (sports day, school festival), classroom cleaning, lunchtime procedures, expectations of teachers and pupils. Thus the cultural system has sustaining features (Rohlen, 1983) despite all the social turmoil of the post-war period.

At the same time, however, remarkable educational differences are on display and describable. There are the differences between public and private schools, mainstream schools and 'free schools', between the ethos of religious and non-religious schools, between schools 'with a tradition' and those with none. There are teacher differences in the realm of political consciousness and teacher militancy. Some post-war Japanese teachers have been famously left-wing militant (Duke, 1973), but there are also those who are passive or aggressively conservative. There are schools located next to volatile and controversial US military bases (Okinawa, Tokyo), schools in mountain districts and recently depopulated areas, schools in country towns and schools in the 24-hour mega-cities of Tokyo or Kansai (Osaka, Kyoto, Kobe) or Nagoya. There are teachers who view English as an imperialist nuisance in Japanese society (Tsuda, 1993) and those who view such charges as neo-fascist – a petty bourgeoisie playing to the nationalist gallery (Usui, 2000). That the United States is at its zenith of economic and cultural hegemony is a global reality. For Japan this involves US military presence in the nation's towns and ports. It is also a linguistic umbilical cord between Japan and its largest trade and military partner.

In Japan, as in many other places in the world, there is a strong inclination among children to locate 'difference' and experience difficulty with it: marked off, that is, from the observer's own prevailing framework of beliefs and assumptions. For language minorities in Japan this has created educational problems in a smoothly operated and in many respects successful educational system that has hitherto not experienced language minorities. Although there are no data to support our speculation, we suggest that this trait has to some extent hindered the empowerment of minority communities themselves who otherwise might have developed maintenance strategies for their languages. It is evident, for example, that Saturday (maintenance) schools struggle in an environment of genuine tolerance, but also one of miscomprehension concerning why people would want to bother with such an enterprise as maintaining these languages (Shi, 2002).

The following sections review the organization and practice of language education in Japan. First, with reference to mother tongue and foreign language education, the role of the 'Course of Study' (or 'National Curriculum') set out by the Ministry of Education and of the language policy of the Japanese government is briefly introduced. Later, several other aspects of language education and language policy in Japan are dealt with.

## Mother tongue education

The continuing social debate about what constitutes 'correct' Japanese is linked to social and educational norms and goals. Two observations can be made here. The empirical attack upon the stereotype of Japan as a homogeneous speech community has been pursued from the standpoint of redefining the archipelago as a fundamentally multilingual region (Maher and Yashiro, 1991; Maher and Honna, 1994; Maher, 1994a, b; Maher and Macdonald, 1995, Maher and Yashiro, 1995; Denoon *et al*, 1996). We can thus no longer employ previous ironclad variables about what constitutes a Japanese speech community. The Japanese language itself, as it evolves and is shaped in schools and colleges, is also under ideological review. Specifically, within the predictable habitus of the Japanese language itself a stripping down of assumptions about homogeneity is now under way: there is increasing serious interest in regional and social dialect variation. For example, the much-quoted gender stereotype of Japanese women's language is now being challenged as the victim of biased sampling – the fatal attraction towards the stereotype. Undoubtedly, under the impact of the ideology of gender roles, past mainstream work has consistently analysed women's language use on the basis of middle-class full-time housewives (Takano, 2000). From a focus on normative linguistic usage we now see a shift of attention to actual linguistic practice in the community (Okamoto, 1997).

Mother tongue education is conducted in accordance with the National Curriculum stipulated by Japan's Ministry of Education, Culture, Sports, Science and Technology. The guidelines define official class time, content, and specific graded goals for all school subjects during compulsory education – which consists of elementary school (ages 6–12) and secondary school (ages 13–15).

Language education is introduced with *Kokugo* (Japanese Mother Tongue) as a compulsory school subject. According to the new curriculum introduced from 2002, a total of 1,727 *Kokugo* classes – each session lasting 45 minutes in elementary school and 50 minutes in secondary school – are to be included in the nine years of compulsory education. *Kokugo* classes comprise one-fifth of the total class time in compulsory education, with just under four-fifths of them in elementary school, and no less than one-third in the first two years. The emphasis placed upon mother tongue education in the early years is evident from this framework.

Since the end of the Second World War, government-authorized textbooks have been used, and Kai (1998) groups their content into four components: Reading Comprehension, Composition, Grammar and Vocabulary, and Spoken Language. The Reading Comprehension component consists of passages from literary works and explanatory passages. Traditionally, *Kokugo* teachers have enjoyed teaching this component, and have devoted much effort and classroom time to it. Japanese classics, including poetry dating as far back as the 8th century and prose tales from the 10th century onwards, are added in secondary school.

The Composition component consists of writing essays, but this is relatively neglected in classroom teaching. The Grammar and Vocabulary component consists of exercises on the writing system, vocabulary (including Chinese characters), and the grammar of the Japanese language.

The goals of primary language education were redefined in the curriculum adopted in 1998 as follows:

> to foster pupils' ability to comprehend and use Kokugo and also communicate with each other in Kokugo, as well as thinking, imagination, and a sensibility for language; to produce deep interest and to cultivate an attitude of esteem towards Kokugo. (Ministry of Education, 1998)

The underlining that we have added demonstrates the new emphasis on oral expression in the mother tongue and upon oral communication-based teaching. However, the Spoken Language component has so far only been at the development stage, and Kai (1998) indicates that teachers have often ignored the spoken language. Thus, as a result of a system of Kokugo education in which the written language is paramount, students often do not acquire effective skills in oral expression. In an era of globalization and information technology, it is now understood that to cultivate the ability to express thoughts and feelings clearly is a highly desirable goal.

## Education for Japanese as a second language

The term Nihongo Kyoiku refers to the teaching of Japanese as a second language – 'JSL' – to speakers of other languages. With an increasing number of resident foreigners and children returning from short or long residence overseas, the importance of expansion and improvement in JSL has been re-emphasized recently. According to the Ministry of Education (2000), roughly 70 per cent of those who need JSL (a total of 18,585 students out of roughly 11 million students registered in institutions of compulsory education) are provided for in public schools.

At present the number of children from other countries on roll is under 1 per cent. However, the demographic trend towards more children coming to Japan from other countries is likely to continue upward. Since not all schools have such students, JSL teachers are allocated to schools depending on the children's levels of proficiency in Japanese. As a result, education for 'cultural literacy' is also a burgeoning area of concern in JSL education (Nishihara, 1993; Tanaka, 2000). Japanese second language learners, especially adults, want to know more about Japanese language and culture in order to develop their language and also to integrate into Japanese society.

From the practical language teacher's point of view, the main problems in cultural literacy education are to define what Japanese culture is, and then decide how to teach it – easier said than done! As Hosokawa (2000) suggests, when we make statements like 'The Japanese people are...' or 'Japanese culture is...', such totalizing concepts, drawing on some kind of average characteristics, lead to gross misunderstanding. It is now recognized to be a major challenge for current JSL education to learn how to avoid the stereotypes, and for the programme and curriculum planner to encompass individual and cultural diversity. In order to tackle these problems, Segawa (2000) proposes an approach that seeks as a central focus to deconstruct the stereotypes as well as learner beliefs about cultures and languages.

In sum, Japanese second language education now faces the fundamental problem of developing children's cultural literacy in Japanese and other languages free from the ideological wrapping of what Japanese is supposed to 'symbolize' for the nation.

## Literacy in Japanese

The issue of *kanji* (Sino-Japanese characters) and their social governance in the Japanese writing system remains an issue for 21st-century Japan and has ramifications for language education as a whole. The regulated (ie reduced) use of *kanji* initiated in 1948 during the period of the Allied occupation was motivated by a desire for the democratization of education and equal access to information. Since schools, traditionally, could not and would not teach the whole vast range of *kanji* repertoire, it was argued that this had led inexorably to the creation of a literacy exclusion zone for much of the population and a dictatorship by a literate elite.

Honna (1995) has suggested an interesting implication of *kanji* regulation. The post-war language policy was definitely instrumental in 'weakening the expressive power of *kanji* to respond to new experiences Japanese people were going through as the nation was exposed to new products, new concepts, new ways of life, and new scientific discoveries'. The result was that 'something had to fill the gap', and this became the role of *katakana* (the phonemic syllabary) loan-words from English. Even more importantly, Honna (1995: 56) theorizes, the apparent irony is that the dramatic spread of English loans was made possible by the failure of teaching English as an international language in Japan, a programme that started in junior high schools in 1947. This leads us to the situation of English in Japan, treated in the next section.

## English and other foreign language education

That Asia is the world's largest English-speaking region has not escaped the attention of scholars in Japan. These scholars view the need for greater awareness about *Ajia no Eigo* or 'varieties of English in Asia' (Takeshita, 1993, in Honna, 1990). Honna (1990) in particular has argued for a new paradigm whose axis is *Ajia no Eigo* as a dynamic factor in resetting the foundations of English language education in Japan. Likewise, as English used as an international lingua franca is increasingly variegated and de-Anglo-Americanized, this is likely to push potential Japanese speakers of English away from the native-accented perfectionism that has long underpinned both government-sponsored educational policy and the social psychology of language teaching in Japanese classrooms.

Since 2002 the National Curriculum has required foreign language education in elementary schools to be conducted within the designated Period for Integrated Study, as part of education for international understanding – a new subject added to the curriculum in 1998. In this Period, not only language education but also 'welfare', 'health' and so-called 'information education' are to be taught, depending on the local situation and location of schools. Foreign language education now starts with Year 3 students (seven–eight years old).

At secondary and high schools, foreign language education was categorized as an 'elective' subject, but in most cases English was selected as the foreign language, and commonly taught for four or five hours weekly. With the increasing internationalization of Japan, the National Curriculum was revised in 1998 so that, first, a foreign language was to be included as a required subject, and second, in principle English would be offered as the main foreign language. These two revisions embodied the goals, first, that every student ought to acquire competence for daily conversation and the exchange of ideas or information in English, in order to meet the development of international-ization in Japan; and second, that the English language must be taught in all secondary schools, given the reality that English is an international medium of communication (Hirata, 1999). From these revisions, we can observe the basics of the foreign language policy pursued by the Ministry of Education in Japan: namely, that secondary foreign language education is and must be totally committed to the English language.

Concerning the aims of 'foreign language education' within compulsory education, two things must be emphasized: the cultivation of everyday prac-tical communication and oral communication. These two developments orig-inate from the same problem: that Japanese teachers of English have relied in the past too heavily on textbook-based lessons.

In sum, foreign language education in Japan is under pressure to shift from the traditional style of teaching previously followed to a new style that will lead to the development among Japanese students of effective skills in oral communication. Oral communicative competence in English is seen as the basic tool for interpersonal communication with non-Japanese. Furthermore, such communicative competence is also gaining a role in mother tongue education. This guiding principle of symbiosis whereby communicative foreign language teaching is being used as the engine to change the style of mother tongue teaching is, we suggest, the revolutionary interface for language education in Japan as it challenges many long-held local beliefs about language pedagogy.

## The other languages of Japan

There are long-standing historical problems associated with the 'other' languages of Japan. This category involves several language communities and accompanying language issues. Specifically, we refer here to indigenous minority language education for speakers of Ainu and Ryukyu, languages traditionally spoken in Hokkaido and Okinawa respectively; language maintenance for children of immigrant families from Korea and other countries; and language support for the Chinese-speaking children of Japanese nationals who were left in China at the close of the Second World War, as well as for children who return to Japan following many years of life and education overseas (*Kikokushijo*).

The growing presence of the foreign population is now a social fact. The total number of registered foreign residents rose to 1.51 million in 1998, or 1.2 per cent of the population (Noguchi and Fotos, 2001). Thus the number of foreign-born children in Japan with at least one foreign-born parent has increased by 50 per cent over 10 years, to 32,434 in 1996 (Noguchi and Fotos, 2001). The presence of non-Japanese children in Japanese schools is now the critical issue of the next decade. Quite simply, the government has no policy to deal with this new social phenomenon legitimately, because it has no background framework of what constitutes a multilingual community – that is, no concept of Japan as a multilingual community. Only a very small number of schools, like those studied in Kanno's (2001) important ethnographic studies, are developing strategies for dealing with multilingual students. The overall picture is, however, bleak given the school system's powerful aversion to difference and emphasis upon collective behaviour.

It is national, not local, government that formulates social and educational policy for foreign residents of Japan. A key issue is the need to transfer power to local government in order to map out policies tailored to the needs of foreign residents and their families. Otherwise, education will remain in the grip of the centralized state, and the new language communities will stay in limbo, with immigrant children not even subject to compulsory education. Educating children whose mother tongue is not Japanese is a major issue in many towns and cities. Legally, foreign resident parents are not obliged to send their children to school, and indeed some parents do not do so. The situation of educational administration is confused because, as local government officials correctly complain, 'national government has no specific policy. We want the government to take concrete actions, to take this problem more seriously' (Imai, 2001), at least for the reason that 'We accepted foreign workers to alleviate our labour shortages, but we also accepted human beings – who need public services like other Japanese residents' (Itoi, 2001: 4).

There exists limited extra-curricular schooling such as Saturday schools or, typically, church-based mother tongue maintenance groups. We note that the contrast between supplementary or Saturday schools for non-mainstream languages in Japan – usually with very small numbers – compared to similar schooling sometimes on a large scale for Japanese long-term or short-term sojourners abroad (see Langager, 2001, 2002 forthcoming).

Schools for the deaf and hard of hearing in Japan use a combination of informal sign language, lip-reading, Japanese Sign Language, captions and amplification, but educational regulations do not require teachers of the deaf and hard of hearing to know sign language. The deficit/disability model is prevalent in educational policy for the deaf, not the bilingualism model. An approach that has yet to gain currency among deaf educators is that deaf education is both a component of and a springboard for bilingualism and bilingual education (Maher and Yashiro, 1995; Maher, 2001).

## Concluding remarks

Language education for the 21st century in Japan means accepting a new configuration of Japanese society. In the local communities, cultural mix and fusion continue, together with wariness about multiculturalism and political resistance to economic globalization. New hybridities are now emerging, with social expectations among the community liable to become more open. This is the case with the flowering here and there of minority communities and community languages. The old framework of discourse and common knowledge about what constitutes 'a Japanese community' has radically shifted.

Consider this example. You walk through a public housing estate in an ordinary municipality somewhere in central Japan. It is a well-kept home to 11,000 persons. Compared to a decade ago when there were none, now 3,000 Brazilian-Japanese are residents. These immigrant families speak Portuguese; many have a minimal knowledge of Japanese and some have little interest in mastering it. They send their children to local schools, teach Portuguese to locals in community centres, start up *samba* festivals and restaurants, attend a Portuguese-language mass in the local churches, park in the wrong places, mix up garbage and throw it out on the wrong days (a literacy issue since immigrants cannot read – or merely ignore – disposal instructions written in Japanese).

The current impact on education in the local schools is considerable. Among local people and organizations it sometimes provokes confusion and panic (Homi Housing Estate in Toyota City, 2001, in Itoi, 2001). Other residents are sanguine or welcoming, saying that 'this is the future' and that they are witnessing it. The issue remains how to welcome and benefit from this multilingual and multicultural challenge – the real issue facing a newly hybridized community.

In mother tongue education, in order to overcome the major recognized weakness the goals of mother tongue education in the National Curriculum set by the Ministry of Education have been redefined, while in foreign language education, English language education was made obligatory in elementary schools in 2002. These are both sea changes in the history of language education in Japan. Both theoretically and practically, we are now in a transitional period from the old fixed stereotypes of Japanese language education and culture to the emergence of new ideas. Japanese language education sees as its goal a new exploration of what constitutes (Japanese) cultural literacy, and the issue of intercultural communication arises repeatedly in educational discussion across all curricular boundaries. In the so-called globalization period the Japanese are being asked to express their thoughts in the spoken word, to reconsider what 'the Japanese people' are and what 'Japanese culture' in fact refers to. This is ever more important as cultural change and the demographics of a new, multicultural Japan emerge.

# References

Denoon, D, Hudson, M, McCormack, G and Morris-Suzuki, T (1996) *Multicultural Japan: Palaeolithic to postmodern*, Cambridge University Press, New York

Duke, B (1973) *Japan's Militant Teachers*, University Press of Hawaii, Honolulu

Duke, B (1986) *The Japanese School: Lessons for industrial America*, Praeger, New York

Hirata, K (1999) *Chugakko Shin Kyoiku Katei no Kaisetsu Gaikokugo* (The explanation of the new course of study for secondary school for foreign language education), Daiichihoki, Tokyo

Honna, N (ed) (1990) *Ajia no Eigo* (Varieties of English in Asia), Kuroshio Shuppan, Tokyo

Honna, N (1995) English in Japanese society: language within language, in *Multilingual Japan*, eds J C Maher and K Yashiro, Multilingual Matters, Clevedon, UK

Hosokawa, H (2000) The fall of 'Nihon-jijo': towards the integration of language and culture (21seiki no Nihon-jijo), *'Nihon-jijo' in 21st Century*, **2**, pp 16–27

Imai, A (2001) in A Itoi, Foreign Immigrants in Japan, *Daily Yomiuri*, 30 September, p 4

Inoue, N (2001) Where is Japanese Going and Can It Survive? [in Japanese], Kokusai Shoin, Tokyo

Itoi, A (2001) Foreign immigrants in Japan, *Daily Yomiuri*, 30 September, p 4

Kai, M (1998) Improvements in primary language education in Japan: new directions and issues, in *The National Language Research Institute. The Proceedings of the Third International Symposium: Primary language education in the world and in Japan*, pp 9–30

Kanno, Y (2001) Sending mixed messages: language minority education at a
    Japanese public elementary school, unpublished manuscripts at the
    Graduate School of Language and Educational Linguistics in the Monterey
    Institute of International Studies
Langager, M (2001) Sojourning with children: the Japanese expatriate educational
    experience, unpublished dissertation, Harvard University, Cambridge, MA
Langager, M (2002) *Nurturing on Saturdays: A hoshuko for Japanese expatriate
    children in the US*, International Christian University Publication I-A
    Educational Studies, vol 44 (in press)
Maher, J (1994a) *Japan's Language Communities: Multiculturalism in the contem-
    porary world*, National Language Research Institute, Tokyo
Maher, J (1994b) *Envisaging Multilingualism in Japan: Language Management in
    Multilingual Societies*, National Language Research Institute, Tokyo
Maher, J (1995) The Kakyo: Chinese in Japan, in *Multilingual Japan*, eds J Maher
    and K Yashiro, Multilingual Matters, Clevedon, UK
Maher, J (2001) Language policy in multilingual Japan: transition and change,
    paper presented at the Monterey Institute of International Studies,
    Monterey, CA
Maher, J and Honna, N (eds) (1994) *Towards a New Order: Language and cultural
    diversity in Japan*, Kokusai Shoin, Tokyo
Maher, J and Macdonald, G (1995) *Diversity in Japanese Culture and Language*,
    Kegan Paul International, New York
Maher, J and Yashiro, K (eds) (1991) *Nihon no bairingarizumu* (Bilingualism in
    Japan), pp 177–209, Kenkyusha, Tokyo
Maher, J and Yashiro, K (1995) *Multilingual Japan*, Multilingual Matters,
    Clevedon, UK
Ministry of Education, Japan (1998) *Course of Study for Elementary School*
Ministry of Education (2000) An investigation into the number of those who
    need Japanese language education [Online] (http://www.monbu.go.jp/
    news/00000459)
Ministry of Health, Labour and Welfare, Japan (2001) Shakaihosho shinngikai
    daiikkai jinnkoubukai gijiroku [Online] http://www.mhlw.go.jp/shingi/
    0108/txt/s0807–1.txt
Nishihara, S (1993) *Cross-cultural Pragmatics and the Japanese Language: Japanese
    correspondence course for JET participants*, book 3, Bonjinsha, Tokyo
Noguchi, M and Fotos, S (eds) (2001) *Studies in Japanese Bilingualism*,
    Multilingual Matters, Clevedon, UK
Okamoto, S (1997) Social context, linguistic ideology, and indexical expres-
    sions in Japanese, *Journal of Pragmatics*, **28**, pp 795–817
Rohlen, T (1983) *Japanese High School*, University of California Press, Berkeley
Salskov-Iverson, B (2000) The discourse of globalization, *Review of Political
    Economy*, **2** (3), pp 25–45
Segawa, H (2000) Nihon-jijo: starting with the deconstruction of stereotypes
    (21seiki no Nihon-jijo), *'Nihon-jijo' in 21st Century*, **2**, pp 28–39

Shi, J (2002) The Bilingual Children's Project: Institute for Educational Research, *Educational Studies*, **44**

Shibatani, M (1990) *The Languages of Japan*, Cambridge University Press, Cambridge

Sugimoto, Y (1993) *Hinonjin wo yameru houhou* (How to quit living as a Japanese), Chikuma Shobou, Tokyo

Takano, S (2000) The myth of a homogeneous speech community: a sociolinguistic study of the speech of Japanese women in diverse gender roles, *International Journal of the Sociology of Language*, **146**, pp 43–86

Takeshita, Y (1993) Japanese English as a variety of English and the student's consciousness, Toyo Eiwa *Journal of the Humanities and Social Sciences*, **8**

Tanaka, N (1994) *Japanese Language Teaching: Methods and practice. Japanese correspondence course for JET participants*, book 6, Bonjinsha, Tokyo

Tsuda, Y (1993) Eigo shihai eno iron (Opposition to domination of English, Daisan Shokan, Tokyo

Usui, N (2000) The Anti-English Linguistic Imperialism Movement: savior of Japanese identity or harbinger of petit nationalism?, International Christian University Publication, *Educational Studies*, **42**, pp 277–303

*WHO Statistical Yearbook* (2001) United Nations Press, Geneva

# 10. Language education in the conflicted United States

Carlos J Ovando and Terrence G Wiley

This chapter presents both a historical and a contemporary overview of the often *conflicted* nature of language education in the United States. We use the term 'conflicted' because the formation and implementation of educational language policies in the United States have often involved conflicts over the hegemony of English in the nation-building agenda, the best means of promoting instruction in English, the status and utility of languages other than English, and so-called 'non-standard' varieties of English.

These conflicts derive from a number of common myths that underlie the hegemonic, monolingual English language ideology as the basis of much of the popular understanding of educational language policies. Among these myths are:

- that language diversity in the United States is an 'abnormal' condition that is attributable to immigration;
- that past immigrants quickly and willingly learnt English, but recent immigrants resist learning English;
- that language diversity has a disuniting impact on national harmony;
- that language diversity threatens the dominance of English;
- that social and regional varieties of English weaken the purity of 'standard' English;
- that state and federally supported bilingual education is a failed programme that keeps language minorities from learning English and doing well in school; and
- that 'foreign' languages – if they are studied at all – should be taught in the higher grades.

For a more elaborated discussion of this ideology, see Kloss (1971), Macías (1985), Minami and Ovando (in press), Ovando (1990, 1999), Ovando and McLaren (2000) and Wiley and Lukes (1996).

## A US 'bilingual' tradition

There 'has always been and still is a powerful tradition upholding the merits and desirability of "one country, one language," a tradition which has been so much in the foreground that the rival tradition has been well-nigh forgotten, especially during its partial eclipse in the years after World War I' (Kloss, 1997/1998: 369). Thus a brief history of language policies in the United States and their impact on language minorities is needed as a corrective to the popular myths. One of the more prevalent myths is the belief that language diversity is *ab*normal. Although English has been the dominant language throughout US history, language diversity has always been a part of the nation's linguistic tradition. Kloss noted that it 'is justified to speak of an American bilingual tradition [but this] must not be understood to imply that it was the prevailing, let alone the, American tradition with regard to language policy' (Kloss, 1997/1998: 369).

## Early efforts to promote an American English as a national standard

As with other nations, the early period of American history saw the attempt, most passionately by Noah Webster (1758–1843), to create a unique national character defined by a common *American* English. As a staunch Federalist, Webster argued that the country's language, like the government, should be national. Although a few implausible proposals had circulated to make Hebrew or Greek the national language, for Webster the key to linguistic unity would be 'orthographic independence; by eradicating spelling variations within the United States, he hoped to build Americans' fragile sense of independence' (Lepore, 2002: 6). In 1790, by the time of the first census, about 75 per cent of the US population – a significantly lower proportion than presently – spoke English as their native tongue. Out of a population of around 4 million, 600,000 Europeans, 150,000 enslaved Africans and 150,000 Indians were native speakers of other languages (Lepore, 2002: 28). Much like those who denigrate regional and social dialects of English today, Webster was more concerned that northerners spoke differently from southerners: he believed in the need for a uniform, national standard pronunciation and to 'demolish those odious distinctions of provincial dialects' (cited in Lepore, 2002: 22).

Many of Webster's efforts to regularize English spelling were successful, largely because of his commercial influence as an authority on American English. But his aspiration to eradicate dialects through spelling reform was not to be realized. Lepore notes, 'If spelling does not dictate pronunciation [something contemporary phonics-only advocates also fail to comprehend], Webster's entire project – to eradicate dialect by standardizing spelling – makes little sense' (2002: 31).

## Native Americans: from enculturation to symbolic recognition

For American Indians, scenarios for language education were problematic. Prescribed language policies entailed a mixture of conflict, accommodation and attempts to deculturalize native peoples. During the colonial period there were some efforts to 'Christianize' Indians. German-speakers, among others, attempted to teach their language as they proselytized (Toth, 1990). During the early 19th century some of the leaders among the five so-called civilized tribes were bilingual, and some were multiracial, Indian and Anglo. Given their disadvantaged standing in treaty and legal dealings and their need to retain their ancestral lands, many native peoples recognized that they must achieve literacy in both their native languages and English if they were to deal effectively with the encroachment of whites and the threat of forced removal (Ehle, 1988; Wiley, 2000). Initial attempts at English literacy education were largely unsuccessful. In 1822, however, Sequoyah invented the Cherokee syllabary, which allowed for the rapid acquisition of Cherokee literacy and for the distribution of a weekly bilingual newspaper, which became a major voice of opposition to the removal of the Cherokee from Georgia (Weinberg, 1995). By 1838 it was estimated that approximately three-quarters of the Cherokee were literate in their own language (Lepore, 2002).

To further the goal of removing native peoples from land they wished to occupy, Thomas Jefferson prescribed that they be required to learn English and domestic skills – an imposition that would force them into economic dependency. The imposition of English was a means to *domesticate* Indians without economically and politically integrating them (Spring, 1994; Wiley, 2000). Faced with the increasing westward migration of Euro-Americans, the Cherokee and others successfully competed with them. Because of their success, President Andrew Jackson forcibly removed them in one of the largest forced relocations of native peoples in modern history (Spring, 1994; Ehle, 1988). After their resettlement in Indian Territory (in modern-day Oklahoma), by the mid-19th century the Cherokee again established their own schools and were successfully competing with white settlers in adjacent areas.

Under the direct administration of the United States Bureau of Indian Affairs, beginning in the 1880s Native American children were compelled to attend boarding schools, where they were punished for using their native languages; literacy rates plummeted as a result (Weinberg, 1995; Wiley, 2000). By the 1930s there was some relaxation of efforts at overt deculturalization, although by that time considerable language loss was occurring (Spicer, 1980). Following the late 1960s, with federal support, some promising bilingual education programmes were initiated (McCarty and Zepeda, 1995), and in 1990 the US Congress passed the Native American Languages Preservation Act. While some progress has been made, restoration efforts for many native languages have proved to be too little too late, and the loss of native languages is occurring at an alarming rate (Schiffman, 1996).

## The assault on African-American language and literacy

Africans were first forcibly brought to the British colonies in 1619, one year before the arrival of the *Mayflower*. From the colonial period to the end of the

Civil War in 1865, enslaved people of African origin were not allowed to use their native tongues, and they were prohibited from achieving English literacy through 'compulsory ignorance' laws (see Weinberg, 1995). Of the 12 million souls wrenched from their homelands during the four centuries in which the Atlantic slave trade ravaged Africa, it is estimated that between 2 and 3 million were Muslims, literate in Arabic (Lepore, 2002). A minority of these people were sent to the English colonies and, subsequently, southern states.

> [The] enslaved Muslims' literacy could be dangerous. Marked as educated, Muslim slaves may have been subject to special persecution and punishment, designed to crush any possibility of rebellion in much the same way that the ante-bellum slave codes forbade teaching slaves to write in English. (Lepore, 2002: 121)

Nevertheless, some sought to sustain their level of literacy.

The fact that some of the enslaved were literate upon arrival is often ignored in mainstream US history textbooks. Forced language shift to English was accomplished by mixing together enslaved peoples who spoke many different tongues. English quickly became their common spoken language, even as access to English literacy was denied. Among African-Americans, a creolized form of English developed, which has variously been called 'African-American vernacular English', 'Black English' and, most recently, 'Ebonics'. Although prescriptivists have ridiculed Ebonics as non-standard, linguists have long since established its rule-governed nature and its existence as a distinct language variety, with some possible West African linguistic influences.

In the 1930s Woodson lamented that in 'the study of language and schools', African-American students were taught to ridicule their own speech rather than to study their own language (1933/1990: 19). A related issue – ongoing to the present – has been the lack of knowledge on the part of many teachers and the public regarding differences in grammar and pronunciation between 'standard' English and Ebonics. This problem has been revisited a number of times but was accentuated in 1996 when the Oakland, California, school board endorsed instruction in Ebonics. The board's decision was defended by proponents of applied linguistics and sociolinguistics, but it was widely denounced by pundits and the popular media, who saw it as a concession to lower academic standards (Ovando and McLaren, 2000; Ovando, 2001; Perry and Delpit, 1998; Ramírez et al, 2000).

## Trends in foreign language education

Despite the dominance of English, schooling in other languages has been prevalent in the United States since the colonial period. Immigrant languages other than English were even carried to indigenous peoples through mission schools that were created to spread the beliefs of the encroaching Europeans. For example, Germans first arrived in the British colonies in 1683, and among the many languages carried to the colonies and the subsequent United States, by the First World War German became the second most prevalent language (Toth, 1990).

The prominence of German, particularly in education, was severely shaken by the xenophobia and jingoism of the First World War. German-Americans were persecuted in many parts of the country in those years. Between 1917 and 1919, 34 states passed laws restricting German language instruction, and many universities dropped German language requirements. Despite two Supreme Court decisions that affirmed the right to teach foreign languages in schools, both public (*Meyer* v *Nebraska*, 1923) and private (*Farrington* v *Tokushige*, 1927), the First World War period ushered in a stronger emphasis on Americanization. Spanish and French made gains at the college level, and by 1948 the percentage of high school students studying German had dropped from 25 per cent to less than 1 per cent (Leibowitz, 1971; Wiley, 1998).

The Second World War served as the first wake-up call for the United States' inadequacies in foreign language instruction. Because knowledge and skills in foreign languages, mathematics and science were essential for military, international business and diplomatic endeavours, these subjects became a high priority in the national defence agenda during the Cold War period. As a symbol of the Cold War tensions, the launching of *Sputnik* in 1957 evoked fear among US citizens that the Russians were galloping ahead technologically, thus posing a threat to national security. In response to this threat, the United States developed federal policies in foreign languages, mathematics and science, which led to the creation of the National Defense Education Act (NDEA) in 1958. The federal government awarded generous NDEA fellowships to promising language teachers to revitalize their foreign language programmes.

The National Defense Education Act promoted much-needed improvement in the teaching of foreign languages at all educational levels. Even in elementary schools there is now an increased emphasis on foreign language programmes. At the secondary and higher education levels, enrolments are up in recent years for Chinese, Japanese, Arabic, Portuguese and Hebrew, as well as for a number of less commonly taught languages. Declines have been noted for Russian, German, French, Italian, Ancient Greek and Latin (Rhodes and Branaman, 1999; Brod and Welles, 2000).

Spanish is in a special class in the United States. With the significant increase in immigration from Spanish-speaking countries, there has been a steady growth in Spanish language educational enrolments at all levels, and Spanish now accounts for more than half of all higher education foreign language enrolments, marking it as the clear second language of choice (Brod and Welles, 2000).

## Changing demographics

Although the United States has always been diverse, that diversity was constrained by US immigration policies between 1923 and 1965. Since that time

– particularly during the past three decades – US society has again become increasingly both multicultural and multilingual (Ovando, 2001). The 1990s, for instance, witnessed a rapid influx of immigrants from Asia and Latin America. A survey conducted by the US Census Bureau recently provided a new estimate of 11–12 million immigrants. The Census Bureau also increased its estimate of the country's total foreign-born population in 2000 from 28.3 million to approximately 30 million, which roughly corresponds to 11 per cent of the nation's 281 million residents (Armas, 2001). This difference was largely attributable to a higher than expected count of Hispanics; the 2000 census count of 35.3 million Hispanics nationwide was approximately 2.5 million higher than had originally been estimated. With increased immigration, the number of second- and third-generation Latino and Asian-Americans who want to maintain the language of their forebears is also increasing. Without this factor, maintenance of heritage languages might not be successful (Minami and Ovando, in press).

## Language policy development issues during the latter part of the 20th century

After the First World War, until the 1960s and 1970s, the majority of language-minority children in the United States were enrolled in 'sink or swim' mainstream instruction in English, typically without any specific support. Beginning in the late 1960s, with the rise of federally supported bilingual programmes, some students began to receive support through transitional bilingual education programmes. However, it took a decision of the US Supreme Court in 1974 (*Lau* v *Nichols*) to establish the principle that schools were required to teach English to students who did not already speak the language in order to allow them opportunities to develop it to a level that would allow for equitable learning of the broader curriculum. The court left it to the schools to determine how English was to be taught, which left the door open for either bilingual or English as a Second Language programmatic approaches.

## The attack on bilingual education

The battle against bilingual education began to gain strength during the 1980s, challenging the previous 20-year period of programme development and research activity. The politics of language during the Reagan administration provided the context for the anti-bilingual seeds that were sown during the 1980s and continued to develop into the 1990s (see also Cummins, this volume, Chapter 1). For example, reflecting a growing political opposition to education through the home language, Reagan's secretary of education, William Bennett, succeeded in promoting funding for English-only special alternative instructional programmes (SAIPS).

Further weakening bilingual education, the *Lau* compliance standards developed by the Office of Civil Rights were never published as official regulations. And the Reagan administration quickly killed the *Lau* regulations proposal, which would have mandated bilingual education programmes in schools 'where at least twenty-five LEP children of the same minority language group were enrolled in two consecutive elementary grades (K-8)' (Crawford, 1999: 52).

Beyond Washington, political activists across the nation began to press for a return to the sink-or-swim days and the ideology of the melting pot. Anti-bilingual education pressure groups such as US English, English Only and English First began to appear on the scene. In 1994 California voters approved Proposition 187, a ballot initiative designed to sharply curb illegal immigration through a variety of strong restrictions on the social and educational services that undocumented immigrants could receive. (See Laura Angelica Simón's provocative video *Fear and Learning at Hoover Elementary*.)

From the 1980s to the present, the war of words has sharpened over how long, if at all, the home language should be used before the language-minority student is transferred to an all-English classroom environment. It reached an all-time high when California voters determined in June 1998, through the passage of Proposition 227 (see PBS video *The News Hour with Jim Lehrer*, 1 February 1999), that English should be the primary medium of instruction for language-minority students. Specifically, this initiative stipulates that English language learners should remain in a sheltered English immersion programme for a period of time, which in most cases should not exceed one year. Even within this programme, instruction is to be overwhelmingly in English, with only limited support in the home language, although parents may request waivers. Upon completion of the sheltered immersion programme, students are to be placed in mainstream English-only classrooms (English for the Children, 1997).

While bilingual education has generally been under political siege from the 1980s into the new millennium, it has continued to have support in some circles. For example, in 1999 President Clinton's administration restored funding cutbacks made by the Republican-controlled Congress totalling 38 per cent between 1994 and 1996 (Crawford, 1997). English Only, US English, English First, Proposition 187 and Proposition 227 can be seen collectively as an instrument of the politics of resentment towards massive immigration from developing countries in the 1980s, especially from Asia and Latin America. The significance of Proposition 227, for example, goes beyond California. It is viewed as a harbinger of similar measures in other states, such as Arizona (eg Proposition 203), Colorado, Washington and Massachusetts.

## Current challenges to the defence of bilingual education

Given the positive evidence that quality bilingual education programmes work (see Kirk Senesak, 2002), why is there continued resistance, even hostility, towards bilingual education? Such antipathy seems to be rooted in nativistic and melting pot ideologies that tend to demonize the language and culture of the 'other'. Because bilingual education is much more than a pedagogical tool, it has become a societal irritant involving complex issues of cultural identity, social class status and language politics. Is language diversity a problem? Is it a resource? Is it a right? On the surface these issues seem quite remote from the day-to-day realities of bilingual classrooms across the United States, yet they are the basis on which bilingual education is either loved or hated (Ovando, 1990).

Along with issues of power, much of the opposition to bilingual education arises from the fact that its rationale seems to run counter to widely held popular beliefs about how humans acquire languages. Intuitively, one would think that a person learns another language by using it frequently and by avoiding use of the mother tongue. Using a new language is of course crucial to communicative and academic competence in that language. The quality of the instructional process, however, is equally important, and more time spent immersed in the new language is not necessarily associated with greater gains in that language if the student is not understanding the content of the lesson. Related to this, full cognitive development is absolutely crucial to the full development of the second language. One of the most common misconceptions is that children learn a second language with native-like pronunciation effortlessly and without pain – child's play, so to speak. Yet research suggests that young children may not reach full proficiency in their second language if cognitive development is discontinued in their primary language. Given the prerequisites for second language acquisition, older learners (approximately ages 9–25) who have built cognitive and academic proficiency in their first language are potentially the most efficient acquirers of most aspects of academic second language proficiency, except for pronunciation (Ovando, Collier and Combs, in press).

Another problem in presenting a clear case for the effectiveness of bilingual education results from the confusion between programme evaluation research and basic research. Much of the adverse publicity for bilingual education stems from a set of poor programme evaluation results. Many researchers, however, feel that it is virtually impossible to control for all the background variables associated with bilingual education outcomes. A number of variables can have a negative effect on the outcome of a particular bilingual programme: the number of qualified bilingual teachers; parental support; administrative support; material resources; time allocation for the child's first language and the second language; the sociocultural and educational background of the community; the general school curriculum and climate; and so on. Furthermore, it is not possible to have comparison groups of students – some receiving language assistance and others not – as the civil rights of the students not receiving any services would be violated. Because of these difficulties and the politicized nature of the field, researchers such as August and

Hakuta (1997) tend to favour basic research in psycholinguistics, sociolinguistics and developmental psychology rather than in programme evaluation. Researchers who are trying to get the word out about the empirical outcomes of bilingual instruction face a dilemma: to be even-handed with the results and thus run the risk of providing fuel for the critics of bilingual education, or to report findings that affirm mother tongue instruction results without providing enough empirical support for their claims (see Thomas and Collier, 1996).

So how should researchers of language-minority education respond to the above predicament: to practise even-handedness or extreme caution when sharing data on empirical studies and outcomes? On the one hand, it would be ideal if in a non-politicized world they could concentrate on conducting empirical studies that illuminate pedagogical theories and practice. On the other hand, because bilingual education has become an ideological lightning rod that tends to attract groups with a variety of pedagogical agendas, language-minority educators must become better informed and engaged in the language policy debate. To hold their ground in the debate, however, they must have a clearly articulated strategy for addressing language issues within a political context to multiple publics. The beginning of such a strategy took shape at a session of the 1999 National Association for Bilingual Education. There, in a handout titled '¿Qué pasó en California? Lessons from Proposition 227', the presenters recommended that bilingual education be linked to the larger frameworks of quality education and access for language-minority and language-majority communities (Olsen, 1999).

## Higher English standards for all

In the 1990s the goal of promoting higher literacy expectations for all students resulted in a national drive for academic 'standards' across the curriculum. Standards may have a number of positive effects as long as they are appropriate for all segments of the national population – that is, as long as they do not systematically advantage some students while disadvantaging others. However, merely having standards is insufficient if they are not fully implemented, scrutinized, and linked to the operative curriculum (Wiley with Hartung-Cole, 2000).

In recent years the International Reading Association (IRA) and the National Council of Teachers of English (NCTE) co-developed *Standards for the English Language Arts* (1996), which have been among the more representative and influential standards documents. IRA–NCTE presented 12 standards broadly applied across the curriculum, noting that 'Although we present the standards as a list, we want to emphasize that they are not distinct, separable; they are in fact interrelated and should be considered as a whole' (IRA–NCTE, 1996: 3). The document also makes an important qualification regarding the goal of educational equity: 'It is clear, however, that we have frequently fallen short of this goal with children of the poor, students from certain linguistic and cultural groups, and those in need of special education' (IRA–NCTE, 1996: 8). The document's linking of 'children of the poor' with students from 'certain linguistic and cultural groups, and those in need of special education' is typical of many documents that allude to diversity without probing its dimensions, and tend to frame it from a deficiency standpoint. However, the document does offer the important qualification that 'defining standards furnishes the occasion for examining the education' of those previously under-served.

The litmus test for such standards is that they be equitably applied to all students, which requires taking the needs of specific types of students into consideration. If particular ethnic, linguistic or social groups of students consistently fail to meet the standards, the standards themselves and the instructional process designed to implement them must be scrutinized (Wiley with Hartung-Cole, 2000). There is a need to recognize that standards, by themselves, cannot erase the impact of poverty, ethnic and cultural discrimination, family illiteracy, and social and political disenfranchisement' (IRA–NCTE, 1996: 9). If all students are to be assessed on the basis of standards, they must have access to comparable resources, their schools must be similarly equipped, and their teachers must be comparably trained.

As the 2000 presidential elections approached, testing and high standards were touted as the reason for apparent educational gains in Texas and other states. However, critics noted that it is easy to maintain high standards in states with high drop-out rates, because the standards are actually being applied to only an elite portion of the population – those who remain in school (see McNeil, 2000; Ohanian, 1999). Thus if high expectations are to be reasonably and equitably applied and achieved, all students must have an equal opportunity to reach them. In other words, schools must have comparatively equivalent resources to promote them, and students must have an equal opportunity to learn. These issues apply, for example, to Standard 8: 'Students develop an understanding of technological and informational resources (e.g., libraries, databases, computer networks, video) to gather and synthesize information and to create and communicate knowledge' (IRA–NCTE, 1996: 4).

IRA–NCTE also gave increasing recognition to linguistic and cultural diversity. For example, Standards 9 and 10 specifically addressed those elements. The fact that national model standards were finally directed towards these issues represented substantial progress. However, even as that was happening, controversy regarding Ebonics in Oakland, California, erupted in 1996, as the school district attempted to improve students' respect for their home languages. Note that IRA–NCTE Standard 9 called for such understanding: 'Students develop an understanding of and respect for diversity in language use, patterns, and dialects across cultures, ethnic groups, geographic regions, and social roles' (IRA–NCTE: 1996: 4). Nevertheless, such insight was lost on the media and the public at large (Baugh, 2000; Perry and Delpit, 1998; Ramírez *et al*, 2000).

During the 1990s, efforts to develop ESL content standards and to link those standards to academic content areas came of age. Leaders in this effort were Teachers of English to Speakers of Other Languages (TESOL), which published its own national standards, *ESL Standards for Pre-K-12 Students* (TESOL, 1997; Snow, 2000). TESOL had three broad areas of application for its standards: English in Social Settings, English in Academic Content Areas, and Culturally Appropriate English Use.

The adoption of content standards, however, also implied the adoption and appropriate use of performance standards. The contemporary emphasis on performance standards recalls the prior stress on behavioural objectives during the 1960s and 1970s, when performance objectives were designed to make specific language behaviours explicit by describing the conditions of performance, stating the standard of acceptable performance. Despite the appeal of performance standards, they were criticized previously because they equated knowing a language 'with the mastery of isolated, discrete items [that] would seem to have been disproved by the acknowledged failure of certain methods, such as audio-lingualism, which focused almost exclusively on the minutiae of language's building blocks' (Tumposky, 1984: 303). However, the recent push for standards appears to be less drastic in most US schools than the prior, more behaviouralist-oriented approaches (cf Spolsky, 1999).

## The expectation for 'native-like' proficiency

For language-minority students, 'near-native' or 'native-like' English proficiency, as called for by model standards documents (TESOL, 1997), is often presented as the ultimate goal of instruction. The importance of acquiring English is well understood by the overwhelming majority of language-minority learners and their parents. However, if the goal of 'native-like' proficiency is over-emphasized, the more important goal – for language-minority students to sustain progress in their academic subjects – can be lost. *Lau* concluded that requiring students to attain full mastery of English as a prerequisite to their study of other academic content areas makes a 'mockery of public education'. Ideally, those for whom English is a second language should be able to pursue *both* the development of English *and* grade-level mastery of academic subjects. In states where anti-bilingual education laws have been passed, such as California and Arizona, so-called English immersion programmes need to come under intense scrutiny to ensure that they are promoting both English and academic achievement (see Davis, 1999; Singh, 1998).

## Conclusions and prospects for language education at the dawn of the new millennium

As we move into the 21st century, language education in the United States remains a conflicted domain, as it has through much of its history. Although some appreciate the value of many languages as a potential national resource, language diversity continues to be a surrogate marker for race and ethnicity. Thus the new century begins, much as the previous one did during the First World War era, with a new wave of English-only initiatives and persistent opposition to bilingual education (see Tatalovich, 1995). Despite the perseverance of the attack on multilingualism, a minority US bilingual tradition remains, as do social and regional varieties of English as contested but enduring features of the US social landscape. Foreign language instruction prospers, but not at a level that poses any serious challenge to the 'land of the monolingual' (Simon, 1988), even as the hegemonic spread of English around the globe confronts local linguistic traditions that both resist and co-opt English for their own purposes. In the United States, however, language educators and policy makers face a certainty in the new millennium: the need to deal with the cognitive and academic issues involved, while making their way through a political, emotional and ideological minefield.

## References

Armas, G C (2001) Census data shows more immigrants in US, Nando Media/2001 Ap Online

August, D and Hakuta, K (eds) (1997) *Improving Schooling for Language-Minority Children: A research agenda*, National Research Council, Institute of Medicine, Washington, DC

Baugh, J (2000) *Beyond Ebonics: Linguistic pride and racial prejudice*, Oxford University Press, Oxford

Brod, R and Welles, E (2000) Foreign language enrollments in United States institutions of higher education, ADFL (the Association of Departments of Foreign Languages) *Bulletin*, **31** (2), pp 22–29

Crawford, J (1997) *Best Evidence: Research foundations of the Bilingual Education Act*, National Clearinghouse for Bilingual Education, Washington, DC

Crawford, J (1999) *Bilingual Education: History, politics, theory and practice*, 4th edn, Bilingual Education Services, Los Angeles

Davis, A (1999) Native speaker, in *Concise Encyclopedia of Educational Linguistics*, ed B Spolsky, pp 532–39, Elsevier, Oxford

Ehle, J (1988) *Trail of Tears: The rise and fall of the Cherokee nation*, Anchor, New York

English for the Children (1997) *English language education for children in public schools: California initiative statute* (certified as proposition 227 for the 2 June 1998 primary election)

International Reading Association (IRA) and National Council for Teachers of English (NCTE) (1996) *Standards for the English Language Arts*, IRA–NCTE, Newark, DE and Urbana, IL

Kirk Senesac, B V (2002) Two-way bilingual immersion: a portrait of quality schooling, *Bilingual Research Journal*, **26** (1), pp 85–101

Kloss, H (1971) Language rights of immigrant groups, *International Migration Review*, **5**, pp 250–68

Kloss, H (1977/1998) *The American Bilingual Tradition*, Center for Applied Linguistics, Washington, DC

Leibowitz, A H (1971) *Educational Policy and Political Acceptance: The imposition of English as the language of instruction in American schools*, Eric no ED 047 321

Lepore, J (2002) *A is for American: Letters and other characters in the newly United States*, Alfred A Knopf, New York

McCarty, T L and Zepeda, O (eds) (1995) Special issue: Indigenous language education and literacy, *Bilingual Research Journal* **19**(1–4)

Macías, R F (1985) Language and ideology in the United States, *Social Education* (February), pp 97–100

McNeil, L M (2000) *Contradictions of school reform: Educational costs of standardized testing*, Routledge, New York

Minami, M and Ovando, C J (in press) Language issues in multicultural contexts, in *Handbook of Research on Multicultural Education*, 2nd edn, eds J A Banks and C A M Banks, Longman, New York

Ohanian, S (1999) *One Size Fits Few: The folly of educational standards*, Heinemann, Portsmouth, NH

Olsen, L (1999) ¿Qué pasó en California? Lessons from Proposition 227, handout distributed at NABE 1999, Denver, CO

Ovando, C (1990) Politics and pedagogy: the case of bilingual education, *Harvard Educational Review*, **60**, pp 341–56

Ovando, C J (1999) Bilingual education in the United States: historical development and current issues, paper presented at the American Educational Research Association, 19–23 April, Montreal

Ovando, C J (2001) Language diversity and education, in *Multicultural Education: Issues and perspectives*, 4th edn, eds J A Banks and C A M Banks, John Wiley, New York

Ovando, C J, Collier, V P and Combs, M C (in press) *Bilingual and ESL Classrooms: Teaching in multicultural contexts*, 3rd edn, McGraw-Hill, Boston, MA

Ovando, C J and McLaren, P (eds) (2000) *The Politics of Multiculturalism and Bilingual Education: Students and teachers caught in the cross fire*, McGraw-Hill, Boston, MA

PBS video (1999) *The News Hour with Jim Lehrer*, 1 February

Perry, T and Delpit, L (1998) *The Real Ebonics Debate: Power, language, and the education of African-American children*, Beacon Press, Boston, MA

Ramírez, J D, Wiley, T G, DeKlerk, G and Lee, E (eds) (2000) *Ebonics in the Urban Education Debate*, Center for Language Minority Education and Research, California State University, Long Beach

Rhodes, N C and Branaman, L E (1999) *Foreign Language Instruction in the United States: A national survey of elementary and secondary schools*, Center for Applied Linguistics, Washington, DC

Schiffman, H F (1996) *Linguistic Culture and Language Policy*, Routledge, London

Simón, L A (1996) *Fear and Learning at Hoover Elementary* [video], distributed by Fear and Learning, 302 N. La Brea Avenue, PO Box 113, Los Angeles, CA 90036

Simon, P (1988) *The Tongue-Tied American: Confronting the foreign language crisis*, Continuum, New York

Singh, R (ed) (1998) *The Native Speaker: Multilingual perspectives*, Sage, London

Snow, M A (2000) *Implementing the ESL Standards for Pre-K12 Students through Teacher Education*, TESOL, Arlington, VA

Spicer (1980) American Indians, federal policy towards in ST Thernstrom, A Orlov and O Handlin (eds) *Harvard Encyclopedia of American Ethnic Groups*, Belknap Press of Harvard, Cambridge, CA

Spolsky, B (1999) Standards, scales, and guidelines, in *Concise Encyclopedia of Educational Linguistics*, ed B Spolsky, pp 390–92, Elsevier, Oxford

Spring, J (1994) *Deculturation and the Struggle for Equality: A brief history of the education of dominated cultures in the United States*, McGraw-Hill, New York

Tatalovich, R (1995) *Nativism Reborn? The official English language movement and the American states*, University Press of Kentucky, Lexington

TESOL (1997) *ESL Standards for Pre-K-12*, Teachers of English to Speakers of Other Languages (TESOL), Alexandria, VA

Thomas, W P and Collier, V P (1996) *Language-Minority Student Achievement and Program Effectiveness*, Center for Bilingual/Multicultural/ESL Education, George Mason University, Fairfax, VA

Toth, C R (1990) *German–English Bilingual Schools in America: The Cincinnati tradition in historical context*, Peter Lang, New York

Tumposky, N R (1984) Behavioral objectives, the cult of efficiency, and foreign language learning: are they compatible? *TESOL Quarterly*, **18** (2), pp 295–307

van Ek, J (1977) *The Threshold Level for Modern Language Learning in the Schools*, Longman, New York

Weinberg, M (1995) *A Chance to Learn: A History of Race and Education in the United States*, 2nd edn, California State University, Long Beach Press, Long Beach

Wiley, T G (1998) The imposition of World War I era English-only policies and the fate of German in North America, in *Language and Politics in the US and Canada: Myths and realities*, eds T Ricento and B Burnaby, Lawrence Erlbaum, Mahwah, NJ

Wiley, T G (1999) Comparative historical perspectives in the analysis of U.S. language policies in *Political Perspectives on Language Planning and Language Policy*, eds T Heubner and C Davis, pp 17–37, John Benjamins, Amsterdam

Wiley, T G (2000) Continuity and change in the function of language ideologies in the United States, in *Ideology, Politics, and Language Policies: Focus on English*, ed T Ricento, pp 67–85, Lawrence Erlbaum, Mahwah, NJ

Wiley, T G (2002) Accessing language rights in education: a brief history of the US context, in *Language Policies in Education: Critical readings*, ed J Tollefson, pp 511–35, Lawrence Erlbaum, Mahwah, NJ

Wiley, T G with E Hartung-Cole (2000) *ESL Standards: Questions, answers and resources*, Center for Language Minority Education and Research, California State University, Long Beach

Wiley, T G and Lukes, M (1996) English-Only and the Standard English Ideologies in the United States, *TESOL Quarterly*, 3:5, 11–30

Wilkins, D A (1976) *Notional Syllabuses*, Oxford University Press, Oxford

Woodson, C G (1933/1990) *The Mis-education of the Negro*, African World Press, Trenton, NJ [reprint: originally published by Associated Publishers, Washington, DC, 1933]

Yalden, J (1983) *The Communicative Syllabus: Evolution and design*, Pergamon, Oxford

# 11. 'Modern foreign languages' across the United Kingdom: combating 'a climate of negativity'

Joanna McPake

## Introduction

A comprehensive account of current issues and practices in language education in the United Kingdom would easily fill one volume if not several. The number of languages taught is extensive, particularly in tertiary, adult and community education contexts. At primary and secondary school levels, educational policy is devolved to the four constituent nations of the United Kingdom (Scotland, England, Northern Ireland and Wales), which traditionally have significantly different approaches to the teaching of languages. An overview of the field is complicated by fragmentation within languages education, leading to very different educational philosophies and forms of provision for 'modern foreign languages', 'classical languages', 'heritage and community languages', English as a 'mother tongue' and English as an 'additional language'. Provision for children with hearing or speech impairments is often omitted from this list, and yet some of the issues surrounding the teaching of sign languages and of augmentative and alternative communication are similar to those affecting other forms of language education.

This chapter takes one theme – recent policy development relating to languages education in the United Kingdom – to illustrate major debates currently informing provision and practice. These centre primarily on provision for 'modern foreign languages', mainly in the context of school education, but also touch on other areas of language education and raise important questions about the relationship between English as a 'global language' and other languages in use and studied in the United Kingdom.

## Why is the United Kingdom unsuccessful in producing linguists?

The 1990s saw increasing misgivings over the United Kingdom's failure to produce adults who could communicate competently in other languages in addition to English. Across the United Kingdom there is evidence of a significant decline in the number of students taking up opportunities to study languages at school and in later life (McPake *et al*, 1999; Marshall, 2000). This decline contrasts with a marked increase in the number of adults able to speak more than one language elsewhere in Europe: 52 per cent of the population of the European Union as a whole, but 33 per cent in the United Kingdom (International Research Associates, 2001).

The reasons for the decline in the United Kingdom are complex, and not all commentators are in agreement over the principal problems or solutions. There are, however, several factors that are widely considered to be significant, including the role of English as the 'global language' of communication, the ambivalent relationship of the United Kingdom to continental Europe and the nature of the provision for language teaching in schools. In addition, there is widespread apathy, and a professional crisis of confidence, towards language learning in the United Kingdom, in part a consequence of the preceding factors.

## English as a 'global language'

English is now spoken around the world by an estimated 1.5 billion people who have learnt the language either as their mother tongue or as a second or foreign language. English is, in this sense, the most widely spoken language in the world (Crystal, 1997). It has become an international lingua franca in a wide range of contexts, from air traffic control to popular music. Thus there is intense pressure on people who are not mother-tongue speakers of English to learn the language, in order for them to communicate in international contexts. In contrast, it is often argued that native English speakers have no need to learn other languages and indeed should exploit this 'natural advantage'.

Linguists have outlined a number of reasons why this notion of 'pragmatic monolingualism' is inappropriate. Crystal (1997) argues that the dominance of one global language could lead to power imbalances; that the lack of knowledge of other languages can put monolinguals at a commercial disadvantage; and also appeals to our 'ecolinguist' sensibilities, arguing that the growth of a global language such as English may bear some responsibility for the decline and death of other languages used in small communities around the world. Graddol (1997) puts forward powerful arguments against complacency, pointing out that the number of people who have learnt English as a second or foreign language is about to overtake the number of native speakers. Monolingual English speakers will be at a disadvantage, he argues, not only because they will lack the linguistic resources they are likely to need in the globalized/localized economy, but also because they will fail to understand the sophistication with which others are communicating across linguistic and cultural divides. These are intriguing but somewhat speculative arguments, hypothesizing rather than demonstrating negative outcomes of adopting the pragmatic monolingual approach. There is little evidence that such ideas have had – at least until very recently – widespread public acceptance. However, opinions may be changing following the terrorist attacks in the United States in September 2001, when some commentators identified anglophone monoculturalism both as a cause of increasing resentment towards the United States in particular, in certain parts of the world, and as an explanation for the failure of Western intelligence services to forestall the attacks (Simon, 2001; Nunan, 2001).

## The relationship of the United Kingdom to continental Europe

People in the United Kingdom often fail to perceive the importance of communicating with others, particularly their European counterparts, because of their relative geographical and cultural isolation, exacerbated by political ambivalence to the 'European project': active membership of the European Union and the Council of Europe. Right-wing politicians in the United Kingdom have traditionally distrusted the motives of European partners, fearing a loss of 'British sovereignty'; and it is notable that even under the current Blair government there has to date been little progress towards some of the key goals of the European Union, such as monetary union. (For an overview of the relationship between the United Kingdom and continental Europe, see Young, 1999, and Rosenbaum, 2001.)

In this context, the argument that language learning will enhance mobility within Europe, and lead to greater cultural and intellectual engagement with other Europeans, may backfire. Despite the increasing range of opportunities for study and work in other European countries which the European Union has provided, British students and young people will be uninterested in taking these up if they remain uncommitted to European ideals.

## Provision for languages teaching in schools

The United Kingdom devotes less time to language learning at school than its European counterparts. Eurydice, the European education information network, reports that children in the UK nations start learning a foreign language later; that the age at which foreign languages cease to be compulsory is lower in the United Kingdom; and that the amount of curriculum time devoted to foreign languages is smaller in the United Kingdom than in most other European countries (Eurydice, 2001). Thus it is not surprising that UK students fail to become as proficient in languages as their continental European counterparts.

The quality of the teaching that students experience at school is not easy to assess. Teaching approaches vary considerably. While some teachers are spectacularly successful in engaging students and producing both outstanding examination results and committed linguists, many students describe their school experiences of learning languages as dull and demotivating. If the limited amount of time devoted to languages is insufficient to enable students to develop basic competence, this may well undermine their confidence in being able to learn a language at all.

What happens in language classes at school is crucial for future success or failure in developing the language skills of the adult population. Students who have failed to acquire basic communication skills or have been turned off languages, because of the limited time devoted to the subject or because of indifferent teaching, may see themselves in later life as 'bad at languages'. They will be unlikely to return to language learning as adults, even in circumstances where they could clearly benefit. The need to improve school provision is urgent. However, initiatives that would increase the amount of time for the subject, or introduce more imaginative and more intellectually challenging approaches to language learning, have substantial resource implications and raise difficult questions about the structure and balance of the curriculum.

## Apathy and a professional crisis of confidence

UK students' motivation for continuing to study languages after they cease to be compulsory is poor. A study of the causes of decline in uptake of languages post-16 in Scotland (McPake *et al*, 1999) found that many saw language learning as 'difficult' in the sense of tedious, but also as intellectually undemanding. Furthermore, students were aware that languages were not needed to gain entry to higher education or to most careers. Thus there was little incentive to continue to study a language at school or college after the age of 16, or to choose to study languages at university level.

The study also identified a 'climate of negativity' affecting society generally. If English was believed to the global language, if people held ambivalent views about closer links with continental Europe and if their experiences of language learning at school had not been positive, it was perhaps not surprising that popular perceptions of the crisis in uptake were dismissive. The researchers found a linked crisis of confidence within the languages education profession. Teachers sought to dissuade all but the most outstanding candidates from continuing to study languages post-16 on the grounds that the examinations were too difficult. Examiners made disparaging comments on students' performance, despite the fact that this was better in languages examinations than in any other subjects except music. Successful students attributed their high grades to luck, and were unconvinced that they could communicate at all in the languages they had studied.

## Policy response

To date, there have been two types of policy response to these concerns about the United Kingdom's poor performance in other languages. The first is to argue, often by default, that market forces are at work here. If there is no demand for language skills in the UK workforce, then there is no need to stimulate production. Other subjects, such as the sciences, technology, computing, etc, have equally valid claims and demonstrate their worth in terms of their contribution to the development of UK industry and trade. If or when languages are needed, people will quickly return to study them.

The second response is that, contrary to public perception, it is important for the United Kingdom to maintain and develop a national capacity in languages other than English, for reasons that range from the economy and international trade, to cultural, social and personal benefits. Since 1998 there have been three major initiatives that take this view as their starting point and that set out specifically to change existing policy and practice in relation to languages education. The sections below briefly describe the remit of each initiative and the processes adopted to pursue these. There follows a discussion of some of the principal challenges facing policy makers and an examination of the responses from each initiative and of the impact to date of these responses.

## The Nuffield Languages Inquiry

The Nuffield Languages Inquiry (NLI) was set up in 1998 with the goal of estimating the United Kingdom's needs for capability in modern languages in the following 20 years and establishing whether existing educational provision would be sufficient. The inquiry was an independent initiative funded by the Nuffield Foundation, a charitable trust. Representatives of different language interests in the United Kingdom (at all levels of education and also from business) were invited to conduct the inquiry. NLI members began their work by commissioning a Consultative Report (Moys, 1998) that aimed to initiate public debate on a number of different issues with linguistic ramifications, such as relationships with continental Europe, global trade and the role of English as a global language. After the consultative period the NLI group produced a report (Nuffield Languages Inquiry, 2000) identifying key issues and making a series of recommendations, primarily targeting educational policy makers and providers. Following the publication of the report, the NLI sought governmental responses, from a range of departments throughout the United Kingdom, and this activity led to the setting up of the National Steering Group for Languages, coordinated by the Department for Education and Skills.

## Wales: the National Languages Strategy

The National Languages Strategy (NLS) was produced by the Welsh Assembly at the end of 2000, in response to the NLI Report. The document sought to identify the key issues for the Welsh education system, taking into account the different context for languages in Wales, including considerable success in promoting bilingualism (in Welsh and English) through the education system, but more limited provision for modern foreign languages than elsewhere in the United Kingdom. Currently still in draft form, the NLS appears to have had a relatively limited circulation to date – principally to schools and others with a clear interest in languages education. Publication in final form is awaited at the time of writing this chapter.

## Scotland: the Ministerial Action Group for Languages

The Action Group for Languages (AGL) was established in 1998 by the Minister for Education in Scotland, in response to a critical report by HM Inspectors of Schools on the standards and quality of modern languages teaching in Scottish schools (HM Inspectors of Schools, 1999). The remit of the group was 'to secure the place of modern languages in Scottish schools'. Members of the group were drawn principally from the education sector, although business interests and parent bodies were also represented. The AGL report (Ministerial Action Group, 2000) addressed the key concerns identified in this way and made recommendations. The minister responded to the report the following year (Scottish Executive, 2001).

## Three challenges for those seeking to enhance uptake and attitudes

Each of these policy initiatives faced three challenges. First, they had to find convincing arguments to counter apathy. Second, they needed to develop solutions to some of the problems of provision, outlined in the discussion above; these solutions needed to be realistic, given budgetary constraints and other limits on resources, but also to capture the imagination of the public, and particularly the students themselves. Third, they had to ensure that their proposals would be given serious consideration by those with the power and the money to make them happen. The following sub-sections examine how each policy initiative approached these challenges, and how successful they have been.

## Countering apathy and boosting confidence

All three documents recognized that if more people were to take up opportunities for language learning, then social attitudes needed to change. People had to be convinced that languages would be useful to them, and that they would be successful if they attempted to learn another language. The AGL and the NLI approached this issue in similar ways, recognizing that some form of public relations exercise was needed. The NLS is less concerned with public attitudes, partly because the strategy was drafted as a response to the NLI and therefore could assume that the awareness-raising endeavours already undertaken by Nuffield would have as beneficial effect in Wales as elsewhere.

The AGL addressed the question of public perceptions of languages by developing a *Rationale* for languages, to be distributed widely. It begins by stating conventional – yet still valid – reasons for learning languages, including developing the ability to communicate in another language, having access to other cultures through their languages and acquiring an enhanced awareness of the nature of language. However, a number of newly salient reasons for language learning are also advanced: mobility within Europe and further afield; the 'information age'; and current political concerns with social inclusion, citizenship, identity and cultural diversity. Intellectual benefits are also identified: enhanced problem-solving and memorization skills; and an improved ability to attend to detail, to make connections and to develop strategic thinking.

The NLI approach, as described above, was to circulate the consultative report widely, stimulating public debate. One of the goals of this exercise was to encourage people to identify for themselves the reasons why languages are important, and thus to create public demand for improved provision and thereby put pressure on government to take action.

How successful have these approaches been in raising public awareness of the value of languages? The NLI has pointed to a number of public relations achievements in a recent press release reflecting on developments in the year following publication of the Report (Nuffield Languages Programme press release, May 2001). Ongoing monitoring of press coverage of language issues conducted by the Centre for Information on Language Teaching and Research (CILT) in London (Blondin *et al*, 1998) shows that this increased in 2001 and was in general more positive in tone. However, whether this can be attributed to the impact of the NLI or to the fact that 2001 was European Year of Languages, the aim of which was also to generate greater public awareness and enthusiasm for language learning – or indeed to other factors – is impossible to determine. In Scotland modified versions of the AGL *Rationale* have only recently been widely circulated, other than as part of the report, via leaflets to school students and their parents. Thus it is too early to tell what the impact will be.

## *Realistic and imaginative solutions*

The second challenge for those seeking to change policy relating to educational provision for language learning is to find additional time for language learning, and to come up with solutions to problems with existing curricula, structures and resources. These solutions need to be realistic in terms of the financial and organizational demands they make on providers. They also need to be imaginative, to capture the attention of potential students, and to convince them that language learning is both feasible for those who lack confidence in their abilities, and intellectually challenging.

It is not possible in this chapter to comment on every recommendation. Instead, some of the 'big ideas' proposed in the three documents are considered here: these include the introduction of language learning at an earlier age than currently, the piloting of language immersion programmes, and the development of closer links between languages and ICT education. In each case the degree to which these initiatives can be considered to be both imaginative and realistic is considered.

*Introduction of languages in the primary school*
For some time it has been argued that an earlier start to language learning than has been traditional in the United Kingdom (ie at the start of secondary education) would have a number of benefits. It would bring the United Kingdom into line with most other European countries. It would clearly increase the period of time over which students study a language, and therefore should lead to higher levels of competence by age 16. Some commentators also argue that such a move could produce more positive atti- tudes towards language learning among UK students, because younger students are supposed to be less self-conscious about speaking other languages than those who are virtually adolescent when they start.

For reasons such as these, and because an early start to language learning is a popular idea with the public, the NLI is strongly in favour of introducing languages at primary school, recommending a starting age of seven. It points to the success of Scotland's initiative, dating back to the early 1990s, to introduce primary languages to the upper primary school, now well estab- lished. However, it has been very expensive, and a number of major obstacles remain to be overcome. These include the need for teachers to learn the languages they are to teach, for them to be trained in an appropriate pedagogy for teaching languages to young learners, and to have opportunities to maintain and develop their linguistic and their teaching skills. Retention of trained teachers has been problematic, but it has not been possible so far to include training for teaching languages in initial teacher education.

Thus although the NLI's proposal has popular appeal, it would undoubtedly be difficult and expensive to achieve in England. It is therefore surprising that a recent consultation document from the Minister for Education and Skills in England (DfES, 2002b) has taken up this proposal. This development has been viewed with some suspicion, however, given that extending provision to primary schools is linked in the document to proposals to end the period of compulsory language learning at age 14 rather than 16 (see p 167 for further discussion of these developments). In addition, the document hints that the government is not intending to fund large-scale training provision for existing and new primary teachers, as happened in Scotland, but rather will look for volunteers from outside primary education (business people, undergraduates studying languages, university staff and parents) to fill the gap.

Perhaps because of these difficulties, the NLS rejects this recommendation, electing instead to improve provision for the teaching of Welsh and English in primary schools, and to develop more explicit links between the teaching of these two languages at primary level and the teaching of modern languages at secondary level.

Given the commitment to languages at primary school in Scotland, the AGL sought to consolidate provision. It recommended a minimum 'entitlement' to languages, from at least age 10 to age 16 and of at least 500 hours, leaving it open to primary schools to introduce languages at a younger age, if resources permit, and also encouraging primaries to aim for a minimum of 15 minutes of foreign language teaching each day (or 75 minutes per week). These relatively modest goals were regarded as realistic by the AGL. Some primary schools had already introduced languages before the age of 10 and others were keen to do so when more trained teachers were in post. The amount of time spent on primary language teaching per day or per week is small by European standards but remains contentious in Scotland, where primary teachers have been complaining for some time about curriculum overload.

*Piloting partial or total immersion*
Both the NLI and the AGL recommend the experimental introduction of language immersion programmes. This approach to language teaching, whereby students study one or several other subjects through the medium of an additional language is now well established in Canada and the United States and is becoming increasingly popular in a number of European countries. (For an overview of different approaches to immersion and their impact, see Johnstone, 2000.) Immersion is not discussed in the NLS, perhaps surprisingly, given the success of this approach in Wales, in terms of anglophone students learning Welsh in Welsh-medium schools.

The introduction of immersion programmes in the United Kingdom could have two key benefits, in addition to the demonstrable gains in linguistic competence and cognitive advantage now widely attested in the research literature (Fruhauf, Coyle and Christ, 1996; Baker and Jones, 1998; Johnstone *et al*, 1999). They could increase the amount of time available for language learning without the need for a corresponding decrease in time for other subject areas. They could also constitute an imaginative solution to some students' criticism of the lack of intellectual challenge in current language courses.

Policy makers have often raised cost as a reason why immersion would be difficult to introduce. However, it seems likely that it would be considerably cheaper to introduce partial immersion programmes in secondary schools than to introduce languages at primary level, and would also be more effective. It is probable that more work needs to be done both on experimental programmes and on convincing decision makers of their value, before such ideas become widely accepted.

*Linking language and ICT education*
A third idea, discussed in all three policy documents, is to develop much closer links between the development of language and information and

communications technology (ICT) skills. International communication is clearly one of the key arenas for linguists, and therefore it is argued that it makes no sense to separate the acquisition of electronic communication skills from language learning. ICT already has an important role to play in the workplace, in terms both of gathering and disseminating information and of communicating with colleagues and customers. In addition, the use of e-mail and videoconferencing provides new opportunities for students to make contact with native speakers of the languages they are studying. This is particularly important, given the very limited opportunities that most UK students have either to visit other countries or to meet native speakers of other languages in the United Kingdom. Many school students may never have the opportunity to use their languages in a 'real' context during the entire time that they study the language (or indeed afterwards), and it is recognized that this is a demotivating factor.

While these arguments seem both valid and imaginative, the extent to which these are realistic proposals remains to be seen. Language teachers frequently report that they have very limited opportunities to make use of ICT in their teaching and decision makers who are not linguists seem to find it difficult to understand what is being proposed here, reflecting a lack of awareness not only of the changing context for languages education but also of the potential of ICT as a tool for learning.

## Convincing politicians and decision makers

Convincing politicians and decision makers to fund awareness-raising campaigns and improved educational provision for languages is a major challenge, in particular because few are themselves able to speak languages other than English. For them, the benefits that stem from enhancing individual and societal capacity to use other languages are not necessarily obvious. In order to engage politicians and decision makers, proponents need to understand how government works and how to link the issues with which they are concerned to the bigger political picture. They also need to have some insight into the way in which funds are allocated to the activities they are promoting.

One problem facing proponents of enhanced provision is the timing of changes or reforms. While proponents would prefer their recommendations to be implemented as quickly as possible, particularly given their view that languages are in crisis, politicians and decision makers are conscious of the need to choose the right moment to announce new initiatives. Thus in the case both of the NLI and of the AGL, responses from the English and Scottish education departments took several months, while ministers considered the implications.

In some cases, the effect of the responses delays still further any prospects of action. For example, in England the principal action taken to date has been to set up a National Languages Steering Group, which is considering the NLI recommendations and will report in autumn 2002. In Wales, development of the NLS (so far issued only in draft form) has been delayed for reasons that are unclear. In Scotland some of the AGL's recommendations, most notably to ensure that there is provision in initial teacher education for trainees to learn to teach foreign languages, have been deferred pending deliberations of other committees.

Beyond simply delaying developments, there is a danger that other political imperatives overtake events. This appears to have happened in Scotland and in England, where political concerns to develop a more flexible curriculum have cut across initiatives to strengthen the language curriculum. In Scotland, a circular entitled *Guidance on Flexibility in the Curriculum*, sent to Directors of Education (SEED, 2001), specifically mentions modern languages as an area of the curriculum in which headteachers can exercise flexibility. This has been widely interpreted as meaning that modern languages are no longer an essential component of the secondary curriculum, and thus the various initiatives to promote language learning put forward by the AGL on the basis that the provision itself was secure are now jeopardized. Similarly, in England, while the Languages National Steering Group was in the process of developing a strategy in response to the NLI, a consultation document on the future of educational provision for students aged 14 to 19 was issued (DfES, 2002a). This document also focuses on the need for 'a more flexible curriculum, more responsive to pupils' needs' (p 4) and also envisages removing the compulsion on students to study a foreign language after the age of 14 as a solution to the problem identified in this document: 'the large number of compulsory subjects leaves too little flexibility for other subjects and type of study such as work related or vocational learning' (p 8). The proposals made in this Green Paper are currently the subject of consultation, and therefore it is not yet definite that languages will cease to be compulsory after the age of 14. But, as in Scotland, the possibility that this may occur has interrupted discussion of the implementation of the NLI recommendations, given that provision in secondary schools, which seemed secure, is now under threat.

Lastly, there is the question of identifying funding to back recommendations. None of the policy documents gives a detailed account of costs or funding sources for the initiatives they propose. It is perhaps assumed that these questions are not the responsibility of policy development groups. It may be that they see their role as developing the ideas, while others have the task of costing proposals and identifying sources of funds. Clearly, such discussions around the kinds of budgets available to government departments and those that accompany budget allocation are complex. At the same time, budget decision makers can be helped by a clear presentation of the arguments, and those who propose innovations need to have some idea of the likely financial scope and limitations. Available evidence suggests that languages are funded markedly less generously than some other subjects such

as science and ICT. The reasons for this need to be better understood by proponents of improved provision for languages, and, if appropriate, challenged.

## Conclusions

This chapter on languages education in the United Kingdom has focused on
the development of new policies to promote and enhance languages
education, as a consequence of the decline in uptake of language courses post-
16. As several factors have contributed to this decline, these policies seek to
overcome multiple challenges, ranging from major societal changes, such as
the development of English as a global language, to specific aspects of educational provision for languages.

It is currently too early to tell how effective these policies are likely to be in
reversing the decline, but very recent developments suggest that outcomes so
far have been mixed. There is some evidence, mainly from the media, that
public attitudes are changing, becoming somewhat more positive and better
informed. However, the political argument remains to be won. Current developments across the United Kingdom give cause for concern, as arguments for
greater flexibility in the curriculum for students post-14 have been interpreted
as meaning that languages should cease to be compulsory from that age.

In the long term the principal indicator of the success of the three initiatives
discussed in this chapter will be enhanced uptake of languages post-16: it may
take between 5 and 10 years before the impact on uptake can be measured. In
addition, proponents of enhanced provision will hope to see better-informed
and more sophisticated debate concerning the future of languages in
education in the United Kingdom. The European project, the development of
English as a global language and other worldwide cultural and political
phenomena have complex implications for the linguistic practices of UK
citizens at home and abroad, and these need to be better understood.

## References

Baker, C and Jones, S (1998) *Encyclopedia of Bilingualism and Bilingual Education*,
    Multilingual Matters, Clevedon, UK
Blondin, C *et al* (1998) *Foreign Languages in Primary and Pre-school Education:
    Context and outcome*, Centre for Information on Language Teaching and
    Research (CILT), London
Crystal, D (1997) *English as a Global Language*, Cambridge University Press,
    Cambridge
Department for Education and Skills (DfES) (2002a) *14–19: Extending oppor-
    tunities, raising standards. A summary*, DfES Publications, Nottingham
    [Available online] www.dfes.gov.uk/14–19greenpaper

DfES (2002b) *Language Learning*, Nottingham: DfES Publications, Nottingham [Available online] www.dfes.gov.uk/ 14–19greenpaper

Dörnyei, Z (1994) Motivation and motivating in the foreign language classroom, *Modern Language Journal*, **78** (3), pp 273–84

Eurydice (2001) *Profile of Foreign Language Teaching in Schools in Europe*, Eurydice, Brussels

Fruhauf, G, Coyle, D and Christ, I (1996) *Teaching Content in a Foreign Language*, Stichting Europees Platform voor het Nederlandse Onderwijs, Alkmaar

Gardner, R C (1985) *Social Psychology and Second Language Learning: The role of attitudes and motivation*, Edward Arnold, London

Graddol, D (1997) *The Future of English?*, The British Council, London

HM Inspectors of Schools (1999) *Standards and Quality in Primary and Secondary Schools 1994–98: Modern languages*, The Stationery Office, Edinburgh

International Research Associates (2001) *Eurobarometer 54: Europeans and languages*, European Commission Education and Culture Directorate General, Brussels [Available online] http://europa.eu.int/comm/education/languages.html

Johnstone, R (2000) *Immersion in a Second Language at School: Evidence from international research. Report for the Scottish Executive Education Department*, Scottish Centre for Information on Language Teaching and Research, Stirling

Johnstone, R, Harlen, W, MacNeil, M, Stradling, B and Thorpe, G (1999) *The Attainments of Learners Receiving Gaelic-Medium Primary Education in Scotland. Report to the Scottish Office*, Scottish Centre for Information on Language Teaching and Research, Stirling

McPake, J, Johnstone, R, Low, L and Lyall, L (1999) *Foreign Languages in the Upper Secondary School: A study of the causes of decline*, Scottish Council for Research in Education, Edinburgh

Marshall, K (2000) The modern language student population in the UK and Wales at the beginning of the 21st century, unpublished paper presented to the University Council for Modern Languages, September

Ministerial Action Group on Languages (2000) *Citizens of a Multilingual World*, The Stationery Office, Edinburgh

Moys, A (1998) *Where Are We Going with Languages?*, Nuffield Foundation, London

National Assembly for Wales (2000) *National Languages Strategy: Draft consultation paper*, National Assembly for Wales, Cardiff

Nikolov, M (1999) Why do you learn English? Because the teacher is short: a study of Hungarian children's foreign language learning motivation, *Language Teaching Research*, **3** (1), pp 33–56

Noels, K, Clément, R and Pelletier, L (1999) Perceptions of teachers' communicative style and students' intrinsic and extrinsic motivation, *Modern Language Journal*, **83** (1), pp 23–34

Nuffield Languages Inquiry (2000) *Languages: The next generation*, Nuffield Foundation, London

Nuffield Languages Programme (2001) Response to the inquiry's report, press release, 14 May [Available online] http://www.nuffieldfoundation.org/languages/news/nw0000000316.asp

Nunan, G (2001) The answer is on the tip of our many tongues, *Washington Post*, 9 December

Rosenbaum, M (ed) (2001) *Britain and Europe: The choices we face*, Oxford University Press, Oxford

Scottish Executive (2001) *Citizens of a Multilingual World: Scottish Executive response*, The Stationery Office, Edinburgh

Scottish Executive Education Department (SEED) (2001) *Circular 3/2001: Guidance on Flexibility in the Curriculum* [Online] http://www.scotland.gov.uk/library3/education/circ3–00.asp

Simon, P (2001) Beef up the country's foreign language skills, *Washington Post*, 23 October

Young, H (1999) *This Blessed Plot*, Papermac, London

# 12. Language education in Australia: Italian and Japanese as symbols of cultural policy

Joseph Lo Bianco

## A wide scope

In its broadest sense school language education includes a wide scope of activities, policies and experiences. To speak comprehensively of such a wide-ranging field requires attention to at least the following:

- the extension of standard English-speaking children's 'home' linguistic repertoire to include literate capability (reading and writing as well as critical and imaginative literacy);
- extending the non-standard English of some communities to include spoken and written standard Australian English;
- teaching English to non-English speakers (whether of immigrant or indigenous background);
- appropriate provision for deaf, blind and other children with language-connected special needs; and
- the teaching of languages other than English.

Each of these five categories is itself broad and complex, all involving pedagogical specificities and many replete with ideology and interest. For example, the seemingly innocuous classification of 'languages other than English' is invested with contested issues, variable meanings, divergent ideologies and dynamic practices. The wide range of language classifications also suggests major policy shifts over time.

Each of the categories contains a history: the state of knowledge at a given point in time, and prevailing views about the transmission of culture and about whether education reflects social arrangements or is part of policy intervention to change them. In the Australian case public policy on languages other than English has been a prominent instrument for nation making, seeking at different times to support official multiculturalism and to advance the nation's accommodation to its Asian geography. Similarly, English teaching has been pressed into national service, but with different ideological expectations. Originally invoking identification with Britain, English norms and standards later became absorbed into a politics of assertive cultural autonomy (Australianism) and later still became enmeshed in a politics of ambivalence (simultaneous embrace and rejection) towards American influence. In the present chapter passing reference is made to each of the five categories, but most attention is devoted to the sequence of policies and issues connected with languages other than English, and more in relation to immigrant and foreign languages than to Australian (indigenous) languages.

However we define 'formal language education in Australia', it is clear that it has been a vibrant site of cultural expression, exhibiting both change and continuity. This cultural expression has been social as well as cultural. Experimentation and innovation, but also dogma and conservatism, have been motivated by aspirations for social transformation as well as reactions resisting change. English and literacy teaching have been invested with hopes from the marginalized, poor and excluded seeking either access to the norms and discourses of powerful language registers for social and economic betterment or, more radically, to undermine the extant status hierarchy in so far as language is a medium for its intergenerational reproduction. But formal language education also serves the interests of the already advantaged and can function as both practice and symbol of exclusion and domination. In these ways public policy in formal language education has oscillated between reformist zeal and conservative reproduction.

The history of language education reform movements therefore is a dynamic complex with moments of social transformation to ameliorate class inequalities, policies to inculcate attachment to Asian regionalism, moves to disengage from colonial cultural dependence, moves to validate cultural pluralism and institutionalize various minority interests, and, of course, energetic resistance to and rejection of all of these.

## Indigenous Australian languages

For most of Australia's tens of thousands of years of human occupation, some 250 languages (representing some 600 dialects) coexisted (Jupp, 2001). By contrast, in the 200 years since British settlement, many Australian languages have become extinct and all have been rendered vulnerable to extinction. Language extinction is the result of the obliteration of indigenous patterns of intergenerational socialization, the disruption of native processes of intimacy, and the erosion of the sustaining cultural contexts that scaffold languages, which then die as their speakers transfer, inexorably, to the replacing culture and language.

Today, only about 20 Australian languages are still passed on to children; only about 50,000 Aborigines and Torres Strait Islanders speak a traditional language, approximately 10 per cent of all indigenous people. Some 50–60 languages are known only by old people and are not used in communication across the generations, which usually relies on code switching. This means, then, that some 170–180 languages are no longer used at all, and about some of these languages virtually nothing is known.

## *Immigrant Australian languages*

Australians also speak more than 120 immigrant languages ('community' languages) from all parts of the world (Jupp, 2001). Community languages are spoken everywhere, but the large cities are especially multilingual. Although there had been small minority communities since the First Fleet (with vibrant German-, Chinese-, Italian-, French- and Irish-speaking populations throughout the 19th century), the immigration programme that commenced following the Second World War permanently and radically transformed the overall population mix, and, ultimately, many of its public policies.

The migration programme commenced with the admission of displaced persons from Eastern Europe but, because demand outstripped supply, moved geographically to the North of Europe and then to its South, then to its South-East (with the strategically significant admission of Turks by the mid-1960s), then to Asia, Latin America and the Middle East, and most recently to Africa. The moving geography represented a progressive abandonment in practice, and from the late 1960s in law, of the 1901 White Australia Policy. Since the 1970s Asian languages have grown in prominence, adding Indonesian, Korean, Tamil, Sinhala and Vietnamese to the Arabic, Chinese, Greek, Italian, Maltese and Turkish speech communities from earlier immigration flows.

Australian community languages are maintained intergenerationally relatively more effectively than in many immigrant-receiving nations. 'Ethnic' schools, clubs, radio, television, the Internet and newspapers, not to mention more recent possibilities of travel and immersion, have helped. But most important have been the effects of policies of official multiculturalism. However, there is still language shift over the generations, with Chinese, Greek, Italian and Vietnamese having better rates of language retention into the second and third generations than Dutch, German or Maltese (Clyne, 2001).

## Phases of formal language education policy

Language education policies and philosophies can be divided (certainly not neatly) into broad phases, each with a distinctive overarching theme and public attitude, towards linguistically expressed social difference. These themes invariably correlate with a wider social and political ideology that is not always directly about language, or even about education. From the establishment of compulsory education in the early 1870s, a recurring, if unevenly expressed, assimilation ideology prevailed in relation to indigenous and immigrant languages. This was more or less energetically pursued until the 1970s when quite radical changes were effected. The main protagonists of those changes can be described as *language interests*.

The five phases described below are broad categories; they do not represent all that was going on during the periods to which they refer, but are a sequence of distinctive policy orientations that functioned as meta-themes shaping an array of smaller actions.

## *Britishism*

Policies (laws, regulations and official texts) and practices (attitudes that constitute implicit policy) that aimed to bring about cultural homogenization for immigrants, and complete assimilation for indigenous Australians, were the operating norm between Federation in 1901 and the radical remaking of Australian identity in the early 1970s. Although a goal of universal monolingualism in an English modelled on southern British norms was rarely expressed overtly, it was the always discernible underlying objective of explicit and implicit policy in education, media, policing and law.

Britishism required the eradication of difference, and difference was often most palpably expressed in language. Southern British norms of English functioned as ideal standards for Australian speech, expressing the overarching attachments of an outpost of Empire loyalty. Great Britain's geography combined with elite European cultural values as the determiners of choice for foreign language study: literary French and 'mind-training' notions for Latin. Orientalism, with its interest in the exotic, characterized the (very minor) study of non-European languages. English teaching aimed to induct the young into the prestige of canonical literature. English beliefs in the illiberalism of overt language planning delegated to public attitudes the politics of pursuing monolingualism: languages were taught without an expectation that they would be used; the public use of minority languages was mistrusted and repressed, tolerated only in domestic spheres.

## *Australianism*

Over time, Britishism was challenged through the progressive assertion of the value of writing whose themes, idioms, style and character extolled the landscape, experience and character of Australia, contesting its judgement and representation solely through British prisms.

Often self-conscious, this movement of repudiation of British spoken norms and literary sensibilities, asserting Australian norms as the appropriate standard, was co-present with Britishism, and ultimately prevailed. Often Australianism resided within a secure attachment to a wider English-speaking sense of the world, but merged over time into a more local pluralism, and, much later still, with a sense of geography as an identity marker for

Australia: the context of embrace of Asia. Australianism was often a movement for an indigenous English to express, and to advocate, the authenticity of an Australian sensibility, for a new world to be named in its own terms. This Australianist cultural assertion, because it was internal to English (posing a national variety alternative to British), had a problematic relationship with the later emergence of multiculturalism because the latter advocated non-English ways to know and describe Australia. But Australianism also had more practical dimensions. Adult literacy, for example, was conceived mainly as 'second chance' education for mainstream community members, not immigrants. In time, Australian linguistic nationalism shifted towards including minority concerns, into constituting a new source for an original, hybrid, national identity potential for Australia (Turner, 1991) but to this day retains indications of strain with later claimants on new kinds of lingual identity for Australia.

## Multiculturalism

The multiculturalist movement conceived Australia differently from Australianism and its nationalist cultural politics. Multiculturalism imagined the nation as a multilingual and independent entity with attenuated connections to Great Britain, but it too contained strains and tensions: an uneasy accommodation of indigenous and immigrant interests, and tensions with mainstream or dominant language choices in education, originally European ones and later Asian ones. Basing its public advocacy originally on quite new notions of language rights, and later on minority languages as national resources, multiculturalism advocated language education selections based on criteria of 'community presence' and not traditions of esteem, prestige or 'foreignness'. A key justification in multiculturally advocated language policy was related to intergenerational maintenance and ethnic continuity, these ideas coinciding with moves during the late 1960s and early 1970s of connecting schools more closely to the communities they served rather than to bodies of knowledge to which society determined all learners should gain access.

In addition, multiculturalism advocated English not in a British–Australianist literary dichotomy, but as applied linguistics, second language methodologies suited to immigrant and indigenous adults and children. In relation to adult literacy, which had constituted itself as a discourse for marginalized and disadvantaged 'mainstream' Australians, multiculturalism sought a seamless provision of adult English, spoken and written, according to specific needs of learners, a tension that surfaced in the 1990s when comprehensive language policies needed to reconcile divergent advocacy and special interests. Perhaps the strongest tension of the multicultural phase was its claim to represent and reconstruct the entire nation, and its opponents' refusal to collapse the mainstream into notions of multiple and overlapping differences; they preferred instead to imagine that the mainstream would remain unchanged and new arrivals (and indigenous peoples) would have to adapt to its norms and character. Despite these complexities, cultural diversity entered political consciousness and language education as a seemingly permanent part of an evolving national compromise, which came to fuse British inheritance, ancient indigenous elements and a new demography of pluralism into a new, if not always comfortable, national norm. In this sense, multiculturalism has attained lasting success as an element in language education that has symbolized a wider remaking of cultural policy in Australia.

By the mid-1980s, advocacy of rights to the maintenance of minority languages was losing momentum. The principal reason was the realization that intergenerational language retention rests in considerable part with individual communities, and a growing view that public institutions cannot, in practice, directly intervene to support all differences of language and culture. A new manner of thinking emerged. This regarded language and cultural retention as a 'resource' rather than a right. A right involves sanction against some authority for non-compliance. A resource involves thinking about the benefits (intellectual, cultural, economic and social) of assisting young people to retain and develop a mastery of the language of their families, and the cultural knowledge that they are developing in their communities (Ruiz, 1984).

The concrete achievements of this period of intense debate and contest, in which formal language education became the locus of claims for social reconstruction, were many and lasting: the beginnings of Indigenous rights understood as cultural self-determination, a vast array of world-first policy provisions (eg public interpreting and translating), and moves towards comprehensive and explicit national language planning combining demography, geography, pluralism and cultural continuity, asserting an individuated nation in an era of global multicultural connectedness (Clyne, 1991; Ozolins, 1993; Lo Bianco and Wickert, 2001). Anglo-conformity in culture and its related aim of the eradication of language diversity were overturned by the impact of multiculturalism at home and the emergence of Asian regionalism.

## Asianism

Claims on formal language education and its role in 'signifying the nation' based on geography and economics were made powerful by the imperatives of securing new markets for Australian exports after the United Kingdom's accession to the European Common Market in the mid-1970s.

From the early 1980s, but very strongly during the 1990s, policy reports advocated the teaching of key Asian languages, and were linked with calls for pervasive transformation of the cultural orientation of public education to de-emphasize Europe-knowledge and stress what came to be called Asia-literacy. Some of this built on multiculturalism, but much of it distanced multiculturalism

(Singh, 2001), based on a view that Asia-literacy was needed for mainstream English-speaking Australia.

A significant feature of economically motivated Asian regionalism was the prominent role of champions from trade, diplomatic and political sectors, rather than the community members or language professionals who had advocated multiculturalism, or the political and cultural figures who had characterized the Australianist advocacy. Asianism was an immensely successful phase of language education policy, resulting in vast public investments in Asia-literacy and a consequent boom in enrolments and enthusiasm at all levels of education for both studies of Asia and the teaching of Asian languages.

## *Economism*

The 1990s saw the dominant language policy discourse change again, returning, in new guise, to an old pattern: the primacy of English (this time of English as literacy), but adding the new elements of a radically reconfigured notion of the role of the state and the primacy of education's contribution to economic competitiveness.

Policy and research reports indicating declining standards of English literacy coincided with a rationality of labour market connections with education sustained by the ideology of human capital theory as advanced by the Organization for Economic Cooperation and Development. The insistent advocacy of increasing English literacy standards, as measured by normalized and standardized tests, is buttressed by a discourse of enhancing young people's employment prospects in the post-industrial economic age in the context of intense economic globalization. One effect has been to make vulnerable achievements gained for multicultural and multilingual education, and even for Asia-literacy (Lo Bianco and Wickert, 2001; *Australian Language Matters*, 2 (2002)).

Economism also involves a restriction in the role of the state. As the state contracts its role, the marketplace becomes prominent. Economism makes a priority of notions of 'basics' in English literacy and numeracy, and in this new rationality, literacy, constituted as a transferable quantum of skill that public education produces, is deployed by individuals in competitive promotion in a marketplace of competence. Languages and cultural competences need to command market value to sustain their presence.

## Explicit national policy

From the late 1980s to the mid-1990s, Australianism, multiculturalism and Asianism forged an alliance of discourses and claims for public education, producing an especially prolific period for formal policy making. Policy texts included the *National Policy on Languages* (NPL) (Lo Bianco, 1987), *Australia's Language: The Australian Language and Literacy Policy* (ALLP) (Dawkins, 1992) and the *National Asian Languages and Studies Strategy* (Rudd, 1994). The first sought to be a comprehensive account of language policy. The second ostensibly aimed to be a comprehensive policy but was influenced by incipient economism and pitched nationally determined priorities against community-influenced diversity. The third enshrined a sharp priority for commercially oriented Asian languages, nominating four as priority choices: Chinese, Indonesian, Korean and Japanese. Both the NPL and the ALLP enshrined standard Australian English as the national variety of the common Australian language and both engaged with a wide range of language interests. The ALLP introduced a priority for English as literacy, making vulnerable minority language claims. All were made vulnerable in 1997 by the forceful emergence of a meta-policy of economism, that linked a notion of literacy as discrete skills to competitive economic success for individuals and the entire national economy, and combined these ideas with a contracted role for the state in cultural and language policy.

## Interests

In previous work (Lo Bianco, 2001) I have argued that changes in formal language education emerged from the variable interaction of initially three, and later four, policy interests. These were 1) policy consciousness among language professionals; 2) the political agitation of articulate second-generation immigrants and their Indigenous counterparts; 3) business, diplomatic and political elites spurred into action on language education policy by the concrete experience of accessing markets for Australian exports in Asian markets; and 4) the OECD-inspired but politically motivated pressure for improving standards in English literacy.

The relations among these four interests have been the principal dynamic in language education policy in Australia since 1970. Initially the coalition of the three interests led to a comprehensive approach to language education planning, stressing pluralism and diversity, and notable for its 'citizen-driven' character (Horne, 1994). Working together the otherwise disparate interests evolved a shared discourse that refused to locate the value of languages within the publicly available frameworks of trade, or traditional hierarchies of cultural value. In deploying a discourse that attached multiple values to languages, they came to represent multilingualism itself as a kind of national capital endowment whose cultivation could benefit the entire society. The values of bilingualism within their own communities, their distinctive languages plus English, produced a successful claim to a wider social multilingualism. In turn this process of language maintenance and language learning was attached, in broad and deliberately not narrow ways, to potential benefits for the whole society: children's enhanced intellectual functioning, harmonious cultural relations and enhanced internationalization.

During the 1990s this approach of 'multiple values' – in truth, a collective compromise – was challenged by the new rationality of governance, shared by both conservatives and social democrats, that elevated interests of economy above those of nation and community. A key device for realizing this, for dislodging the discourse of multiculturally based multilingualism, has been the crisis alleged (many say manufactured: Boreham and Mitchell, 1997; Raethel, 1997) in English literacy standards. This approach has abandoned comprehensive and pluralistic policy as expensive luxuries, gravitating instead around a consensus of *English literacy first*. Of decisive importance in bringing about this shift has been the work of the Organization for Economic Cooperation and Development, whose studies have connected success in the increasingly globalized trading economy with levels of attainment in education, utilizing assessed literacy performance data as a critical indicator (OECD, 1992, 1996).

## Dichotomies to hybrids: Italian and Japanese

This section discusses Italian and Japanese to illustrate changing fortunes and ideologies discussed above in relation to general languages education. Japanese is selected because it is the exemplar of the foreign Asian language of commerce that dominated the Asianism phase, and Italian because it is the exemplar community language of the multiculturalism phase.

Among the most dramatic language policy developments in recent decades in Australia has been the vast status change that both Italian and Japanese have enjoyed. Both languages have endured several complete transformations of esteem. Both are latecomer additions to foreign languages study in Australia, but today Japanese is by far the most widely taught language in formal education and Italian possibly the most studied second language overall if we aggregate all levels of formal, non-formal and community-based education (Lo Bianco, 1994). The fortunes of the two languages have a similar and intriguing pattern of esteem affected by relations first between cultural elites, then between nations, and then direct encounters between individuals.

### From British prisms to Australian perspectives

The foundation of the British colonies in Australia coincided with a wave of Italomania in Britain. In the 19th century, Italian visitors to the British colonies of Australia included many artists, singers, scientists and political revolution-aries. Educated colonists knew classical Italy, the 'triumphs of art and thought' (Pesman, 1994) of its Renaissance city-states, and were constructing monuments and public buildings 'claiming for this new place a continuity with the classical world and its values' (Malouf, 1998: 70). The Italians they encountered often confirmed their cultured view, but despite constituting a kind of cultural self-discovery for educated Australians, Italian remained absent from formal education.

The beginnings of Australian self-consciousness also coincided with the Meiji Restoration, the opening up of Japan to Western influence, and promoted Western fascination with its culture as 'exotic' difference. After Federation in 1901 Japan again entered Australia's European consciousness for its assertive, independence-minded modernization. Its defeat of a major European power, Russia, in 1905 caused consternation in British Australia. Both civilization and orientalism motivated the introduction of Japanese at the University of Sydney in 1917, and James Murdoch was appointed to Chair of Oriental Studies in 1918.

The first half of the 20th century joined Italian and Japanese in a perverse union of fortunes. From cultural self-discovery, and admired but feared exotic difference, they became the despised languages of political enemies. Interestingly, these developments stimulated attention to their teaching. For Japanese- and Italian- Australians, however, the conflation of ethnic background with presumed political allegiances that often occurs to minorities at times of hostility between source and host nations resulted in internment for some, deprivation of liberty for many, and generalized hostility (Douglass, 1994; Nagata, 1996).

The Second World War changed everything, intensifying proximity to feared Asia, distance from protective Britain, feelings of vulnerability, and tensions between history, culture and geography. A critical policy response was population increase and perversely, again, this connected Australia and Australians first to Italians, and later to Japanese. The post-war migration programme recruited as its largest non-British component of the population Australia's Italian community. The eventual post-war prosperity of Japan, and its pacifist constitution, transformed it into Australia's pre-eminent economic partner. In both cases Australian encounters with Japan and Italy, with Japanese and with Italians, and the languages, displaced British mediation.

As Australians encountered more Italians directly, prevailing views of Italian culture changed. Unlike its origins in the 19th century, later Italian immigration was family and region based, mainly of southern peasant origins, replacing the 19th-century northern pattern of travelling artists, scientists, liberal and revolutionary-minded individuals. The new immigrants, a sub-class, marginalized and alienated, spoke dialects and regional languages that education ignored or despised. Over the subsequent three decades a locally born, articulate and dual-identifying generation emerged, coinciding with new prosperity in both Australia and in Italy and ultimately transforming Italian culture, people and language, first into a kind of exemplar minority community, and later into the preferred non-British European cultural experience for Australian society and education.

Economics and regionalism combined to transform Australian–Japanese relations. Over time Japan became Australia's dominant trading partner. The

Australian direct encounter with Japanese was not through immigration, but initially trade, and later tourism. Australian commerce, strategic alliances and cultural interests produced direct and unmediated encounter with Japan and Japanese, people and language alike. And this too, as it did for Italian, produced a transformation of esteem and knowledge.

Travel was the critical medium. The encounters involved multiple flows in all directions over time. First, Italian culture travelled to Australia with Australia's largest non-British immigrant population component. Initially only the educated and moneyed few and then larger numbers of Australians travelled to the new and prosperous Italy, which during the 1950s and 1960s emerged as the world's premier tourist destination. From the 1970s, Australians commenced travel to Japan, seeking commercial relations and increasingly aware of Japan's burgeoning economy and increasingly anxious to attract its overseas direct investment. The emergence of an Australian tourism industry dramatically brought the intercultural encounter to Australia with mass Japanese tourism and investment in Australian tourism infrastructure. Japan rapidly became the major source for inbound tourism, producing a market for Australian competence in Japanese language and culture in an industry with a buoyant demand for guides, tour operators and thousands of ancillary jobs.

By the 1990s Japanese was also well on the way to becoming an Australian community language, though on a small scale by comparison with Italian, but nevertheless exhibiting the same classic pattern of settlement: adjustment (embrace and rejection), compromise and hybrid cultural practices, nostalgia and recovery, ongoing adaptation and eventual absorption.

Early 19th-century Japanese immigration involved pearlers in Broome, and the Torres Strait contemporary immigration is to Sydney and south-east Queensland: educated, business-oriented spouses and retirees. By 1996, 25,634 Japanese native speakers (Jupp, 2001) were living permanently in Australia, undergoing the standard pattern of language shift exacerbated by exogamous marriage, reduced by endogamous marriage, ameliorated by high education levels, relative ease of home contact, continuous same time-zone travel and the now booming Australian interest in Japanese language and culture. Some 1 million Australians have some Italian ancestry, whereas some 250,000 are Italian born (Jupp, 2001), but the scale differences only confirm similar patterns of settlement and adaptation.

Just as Japanese culture regained a pre-war esteem, so too Italian culture has recaptured the positive regard it enjoyed in the 19th century, though now for masses rather than small and educated elites. Today altogether new population categories, the Italo-Australians and the Japanese-Australians, sustain part of the continuing interest in education in these languages, investments in contemporary cultural knowledge, and explorations of the past. New dimensions include political and economic regionalism, an Italy integrating into a new Europe in which Britain is not dominant, and an Australian Asian regionalism led by Japan, the first globally prominent Asian economy in many centuries.

In addition, the remarkable attractiveness that contemporary Italian life, from cuisine to architecture, projects into the world signifies a cultural forming influence for the vast majority of Australians, who increasingly discover Europeanness unmediated by British prisms (Castles *et al*, 1992). Similarly, from cuisine to architecture, Australian direct encounter with Japan constitutes a globalization of Japanese aesthetics and life (Nagata, 1998).

Around half the Japanese programmes that currently exist in Australian universities were established during the 1960s and 1970s (Marriott, Neustupny and Spence-Brown, 1994). The all-time peak in student numbers was the tsunami of the late 1980s. At that time Japanese replaced French as the most popular foreign language at all levels of education.

Despite their different histories the stories of Japanese and Italian in Australian education show signs of convergence. Japanese has been the exemplary foreign language, studied by Australians without 'a background'. Italian has been the exemplary immigrant-community language, studied by Australians with 'a background'. But Italian, the heritage language, is undergoing a transformation into a language of universal cultural claims (Simone, 1990; Tosi, 1991; Haller, 1994), while Japanese, the trade language, is being transformed into a language with an immigrant community. Japanese is becoming, like Italian, though on a small scale, an 'Australian' language. Partly this recovers the original presence of Japanese and Italian in the Australian academic world, as languages of philological curiosity for scholars.

In formal education today Italian is a *community* language becoming *foreign*; Japanese is a *foreign* language adding *community*. To teach a language as foreign is to assume that its learners have little direct encounter with it, that it is not widely accessible to them in their immediate environment and that it has few psychological associations for them. Typically, a foreign language is not available for 'incidental' learning and commands few or no identity associations. A community language is one in which the learners are surrounded by native speaker contexts, from which they derive incidental language acquisition opportunities but also from which they come to derive personal and emotional associations and attachments. Though the classic community language, Italian is transcending its 'migrant' associations to function also as a language of culture in which the foreign is leavened with established familiarity.

In formal education today Japanese is the classic foreign language. It is also Australia's first, and so far only, language whose presence in education has effectively conveyed immense instrumental associations, the pre-eminent language of trade, career promise and practical utility in an increasingly anglophone world. Japanese is transcending these associations to become the Asian language of choice for Australians, functioning as a language of culture and, increasingly, of community as well. Though the classic foreign language, Japanese is transcending its 'trade' associations to function also as a language of culture in which the foreign is leavened with increasing familiarity.

In schools there is a sharp and interesting contrast between Italian and Japanese. Italian is holding its numbers very strongly at primary level, but is declining sharply at secondary level; at the points where vocationalism becomes a strong factor in choice, Italian is losing its candidates. Japanese is more closely associated with the secondary school, though the numbers learning it at primary school are increasing, but its attrition rates in school are low, at university high.

Perhaps there is emerging a tendency in the sociology of foreign language study that can throw light on these trends. The pre-eminent role of English in the world, and very strongly so in Asia, may have influenced Australians to see in language study not tools for immediate practical application, but training for internationalization: induction into kinds of difference alongside the traditional rationale of language study for cultural enrichment. English teaching will have to increasingly incorporate perspectives on cultural difference and communication, since English's success is the success of variation and diversity: world Englishes, varieties that carry multiple cultural values and histories. Perhaps in this emerging realization Italian appears to be evolving within the wider Australian cultural framework as a kind of *common second language apprenticeship* for large numbers of young learners, a relatively easily learnt second language with local presence, combined with prestige associations of past and present. By contrast, Japanese may be seen as the Asian partner in this compact, in schools where an Asian–European balance is desired, and in an Australia that increasingly imagines its cultural future in terms of an Asian–European fusion.

These education cultural functions of Italian and Japanese express an enduring European, and an emerging Asian, dimension to Australian identity: history and geography expressed though linguistic otherness. Italian appears to offer Australian education a bridging of anglophone monolingualism and Asian-language-knowing bilingualism. Japanese appears to be evolving a role of mainstream Australian encounter with 'Asian difference', via a prestige language highly esteemed in many parts of the world, but with sustaining economic and commercial dimensions (Hasegawa *et al*, 1995; Bramley and Hanamura, 1998).

## In conclusion

Economic globalization involves massive population transfers (Castles and Miller, 1993) and makes diversity, multiculturalism, mobility, and therefore difference, more rather than less salient (Giddens, 1999).

As *lingua mundi* (Jernudd, 1992), English, common English, actually makes possible multiple kinds of exploration of otherness in language education. As languages of national states, and national cultures, at a time of challenging post-nationalism, Japanese and Italian express cultures with wide recognition of their civilizations, but with limited utility for international communication. Neither is an international language other than among the vibrant and extensive Japanese and Italian diasporas. English-knowing bilingualism is becoming the dominant pattern of multiple language competence in the world today. The sociological functionality of English, the global meta-lect, provides and makes important space for languages of prestige national cultures offering cultural diversification dimensions to bilingualism.

In the formal education system of Australia, Japanese and Italian appear to represent experiences in which wide strata of previously steadfastly mono-lingual Australians have discovered Australian-specific motivations to study languages. While in the formal education system Japanese is dominant, Italian commands remarkable numbers if we add the informal settings of community-based schools. Collectively they epitomize two distinct phases of the history of language policy making: multicultural reconstruction of Australian identity on the one hand, and economically motivated regionalism on the other.

Australian cultural policy since the middle of the 20th century finds perfect expression in the continuing presence of Japanese and Italian in mass public education, one the vast nation-making experience of immigration, and the other the equally momentous re-orientation towards Asia. As a result, there is a specifically Australian experience expressed in *Italian-for-Australians* and *Japanese-for-Australians*: educational experiences that make contemporary sense for a nation reconciling history, geography and culture in an era of intense globalization.

The contemporary Australian regard for things Italian needs to be under-stood in the context of an Australia that by geopolitical, strategic and economic fortunes is inextricably tied to the Asia Pacific region and to Asian trading partners; while the contemporary Australian regard for Japan and its culture and language involves Australians in processes whereby national cultural diversity is an individuating possibility, signalling national distinc-tiveness from the United Kingdom and United States, locating Australia as a unique and multicultural presence in Asia. Expressing precisely the dilemma of national cultures, histories and geographies has been the ongoing debate between Australian attempts to join ASEAN (the Association of South East Asian Nations) and its repudiation by Malaysia's prime minister, Mohamed Mahathir: 'Once you become Asian, we will think about that' (Lyall, 2002).

Australians have embraced second language study more enthusiastically than is the case in other English-speaking nations, specifically the United Kingdom and the United States. Perhaps this reflects a search to reconcile and combine a politics of geography and region (Asianism) with demands for the recognition of diversity (multiculturalism) and respect for continuity (Britishism) in a global epoch in which distinctiveness (Australianism) is a considerable challenge.

The Canadian scholar of constitutionalism James Tully sees essentialized views of culture as 'no longer acceptable', because cultures are not 'separate, bounded and internally uniform' but 'overlapping, interactive and internally negotiated' (1997: 10). Constitutional change is on the agenda in Australia, and its most insistent demands are for the recognition of diversity, difference and pluralism within a framework of continuity and security: indigenous prior ownership of the land, their dispossession but continual presence; immigration and its transformation of both the population and its many and overlapping identities; histories of connection and derivation, the United Kingdom, English and the United States; and geography.

Contemporary education policy making faces immense pressures from rampant ideologies of marketization. The already evident pressure to increase assessed levels of English literacy attainments, in the context of widely shared political theories connecting education to the economy, will surely intensify. New discourses about national diversification and pluralism will need to evolve to account for identity and culture politics in the context of economically driven globalization.

## References

Boreham, G and Mitchell, B (1997) Ministers in bitter row over literacy, *The Age*, 15 September, p 3

Bramley, N S and Hanamura, N (1998) The Teaching and Learning of Japanese in Australian Universities: An overview, in *Issues in the Teaching and Learning of Japanese*, eds N S Bramley and N Hanamura, pp 1–10, ARAL Series S, no 15

Castles, S, Alcorso, C, Rando, G and Vasta, E (eds) (1992) *Italo-australiani: la popolazione di origine italiana in Australia*, Fondazione Giovanni Agnelli, Turin

Castles, S and Miller, M J (1993) *The Age of Migration: International population movements in the modern world*, Macmillan, Basingstoke, UK

Clyne, M G (1991) *Community Languages: The Australian experience*, Cambridge University Press, Cambridge

Clyne, M G (2001) Can the shift from immigrant languages be reversed in Australia?, in *Can Threatened Languages Be Saved?*, ed J A Fishman, pp 364–91, Multilingual Matters, Clevedon, UK

Dawkins, J (1992) *Australia's Language: The Australian Language and Literacy Policy*, Australian Government Printing Service, Canberra

Douglass, W (1994) 'Trionfo' in Ingham: the Italian community in north Queensland, *Studi Emigrazione*, Rome **113**, pp 43–64

Giddens, A (1999) *Runaway World*, Profile, London

Haller, H W (1994) From ethnic to cultural: Italian in the USA, in *Italian towards 2000*, ed A Bivona, pp 118–22, Victoria University of Technology

Hasegawa, T et al (1995) Bunkakenyuu no shoruikei kara mita 'Nihonjijoo', *Gaikokujinryuugakusei no tameno 'Nihonjijoo' kyooiku no arikata nitsuite no kisoteki choosa kenkyuu*, Report, pp 51–66

Horne, D (1994) Teaching our youth to be Australians, *Montage*, **20**, pp 19–20

Jernudd, B H (1992) Culture planning in language planning, in *Bilingualism and National Development*, vol 2, eds G Jones and C Ozog, pp 491–531, Universiti Brunei Darussalam

Jupp, J (ed) (2001) *The Australian People: An encyclopedia of the nation, its people and their origins*, Cambridge University Press, Cambridge

Lo Bianco, J (1987) *National Policy on Languages*, Australian Government Publishing Service, Canberra

Lo Bianco, J (1994) Italian the most widely taught language: how much is learned?, in *Italian towards 2000*, ed A Bivona, pp 149–56, Victoria University of Technology

Lo Bianco, J (2001) From policy to anti-policy: how fear of language rights took policy making out of community hands, in *Australian Policy Activism in Language and Literacy*, eds J Lo Bianco and R Wickert, pp 13–45, Language Australia Publications, Melbourne

Lo Bianco, J and Wickert, R (eds) (2001) *Australian Policy Activism in Language and Literacy*, Language Australia Publications, Melbourne

Lyall, K (2002) Hello again, I'm quitting: Mahathir, *The Australian*, 4 July, p 7

Malouf, D (1998) *A Spirit of Play: The making of Australian consciousness*, ABC Books, Sydney

Marriott, H, Neustupny, J V and Spence-Brown, R (1994) *Unlocking Australia's Language Potential*, vol 7, *Japanese*, Commonwealth of Australia and NLLIA, Canberra

Nagata, Y (1996) *Unwanted Aliens: Japanese Internment in Australia*, University of Queensland Press, Brisbane

Nagata, Y (1998) The study of culture in Japanese: towards a more meaningful engagement with Japanese language studies, in *Issues in the Teaching and Learning of Japanese*, eds N S Bramley and N Hanamura, pp 93–104, ARAL Series S, no 15

Organization for Economic Cooperation and Development (OECD) (1992) *Adult Illiteracy and Economic Performance*, OECD, Paris

OECD (1996) *Human Capital Investment: An international comparison*, OECD, Paris

Ozolins, U (1993) *The Politics of Language in Australia*, Cambridge University Press, Cambridge

Raethel, S (1997) Literacy crisis manufactured, say ministers, *Sydney Morning Herald*, 15 September, p 4

Rudd, K (chair) (1994) *Asian Languages and Australia's Economic Future*, Queensland Government Printer, Brisbane

Ruiz, R (1984) Orientations in language planning, *National Association for Bilingual Education Journal* (Washington, DC), **8**, pp 15–34

Simone, R (1990) Il destino internazionale dell'italiano, in *Lingua e cultura italiana in Europa*, ed V Lo Cascio, pp 62–71, Le Monnier, Florence

Tosi, A (1991) *Italian Overseas: The language of Italian communities in the English-speaking world*, Editori Giunti, Florence

Tully, J (1997) *Strange Multiplicities: Constitutionalism in an age of diversity*, Cambridge University Press, Cambridge

Turner, G (1991) Australian English and general studies of English, in *Linguistics in Australia: Trends in Research*, ed M G Clyne, pp 35–55, Academy of the Social Sciences in Australia, Canberra

# 13. The languages of Spain and Spanish language education

Clare Mar-Molinero

## Introduction

Major changes have taken place in the Spanish education system in recent years, beginning towards the end of the Franco dictatorship in the early 1970s and culminating with a sweeping reform law introduced in 1993. These changes reflect the radical political and social changes in Spain since the death of Franco and the introduction of a Western-style democracy. Such political reforms are characterized by an increasing awareness of Spain's cultural and linguistic diversity that is reflected in changing attitudes and legislation regarding the use and teaching of its languages. This in turn finds echoes in the education curriculum.

In this chapter I will start with a brief summary of the nature of the education reforms in Spain since 1970 followed by a thumbnail sketch of the linguistic situation there in order to give the background and framework in which the issues and debates surrounding the teaching and learning of languages in Spain operate today. While I will give a synthesis of the languages encountered and taught in Spain, I shall concentrate primarily on the situation of 'Spanish' languages. The terms 'Spanish' and 'Castilian' are controversial, as will be seen; here I am using the adjective 'Spanish' to refer to languages belonging to Spain. I will discuss the way in which the learning and teaching of languages other than Castilian have become symbolic of far wider political and national debates. In particular I shall focus on the case studies of Basque and Catalan to illustrate this. I will conclude with some discussion of the role of language learning in Spain in the context of Spain's relations with the European Union (EU) and the international community generally. The competition with English and its role in the curriculum will be considered.

## The Spanish education system

For centuries Spain's education system has been inadequate. A fundamental reason for this has been the failure by the modern Spanish state to take on the responsibility for education, preferring to leave it to private organizations, above all the Church. This bred inequalities and insufficiency. Well into the 20th century too many Spanish children simply did not attend school or experienced grossly inadequate school facilities. As José María Maravall (1984) says:

> The social consequences... were particularly grave, not simply in terms of thousands of children who remained without schooling, but because the same weakness predictably turned education into a site for the confrontation of opposed interest groups, manifested in spectacular, passionate, ideological debates. The scarcity of school places was thus linked to an ideological struggle to determine who should prevail over the system, and whose leadership should be imprinted upon it. (translated in Boyd-Barrett and O'Malley, 1995: 42)

Certainly during much of the 20th century this so-called leadership was assumed by a highly centralized, ultra-conservative Catholic dictatorship. It is reaction against this situation that has led to radical and much-needed reforms in the last quarter of the 20th century and the early 21st. It has been a slow and often contested process.

Even towards the end of the Franco period it was becoming apparent that Spain's education provision was inadequate for a modern, developed country, which, with the relative opening up to tourism and foreign investment, Spain now aspired to be. Illiteracy among adults was still very high and the curriculum offered a traditional and outdated view of society that failed to prepare children adequately to participate in the modern world. As a result, the Ley General de Educación (General Education Law) of 1970 was introduced, the most significant features of which were the making of education free and compulsory to the age of 14 and the introduction of the *Educación General Básica* (EGB – General Basic Education). Underlying these reforms was an acceptance at last by the Spanish state of its responsibility to provide education for all. However, an implication of this was the perceived squeezing out of the private sector, which, given its powerful voices, lobbied hard for state subsidies to maintain what it argued was the right of choice and 'freedom of education', the phrase coined to describe this.

In fact in 1984 the government introduced the *Ley Orgánica del Derecho a la Educación* (LODE – Law of the Right to Education), which sought to create an integrated state–private system by offering subsidies, not to prop up the private sector, but to give access to it for those who could not previously afford it. Many middle-class parents and teachers opposed this law vociferously.

After the death of Franco in 1975 Spain introduced a new constitution in 1978 that defined Spanish society and political configuration as an *Estado de las Autonomías* or 'state of autonomous regions'. This represents a considerably decentralized country with significant powers delegated to the regions, including many education powers. The implications of this for the teaching and learning of minority languages will be discussed more fully later on but is a clear example of a radical shift. Much of the ideology that recognized a more diverse and plurilingual Spain was hated by those who continued to wish to protect and promote separate and, generally, elitist private education.

As a result of these important social and political changes, symbolized by the victory of the Spanish socialist party in 1982, the scene was set for the debate on and introduction of sweeping educational reforms by the socialists with the new education law, the *Ley Orgánica de Ordenación General del Sistema Educativo* (LOGSE – the organic law of the general regulation of the education system), from 1993. This ground-breaking law was preceded by a period of debate and discussion as the government recognized that legal decrees alone would not be enough and that changes in attitudes and philosophy throughout Spanish society were needed. Boyd-Barrett and O'Malley (1995: 53) sum up the essence of this law well:

The reform is dedicated above all else to the needs and aspirations of individual citizens within the framework of a democratic, participative, consensual, pluralist, non-discriminatory society that is part of a wider Europe, and of a world of increasingly rapid change. The law facilitates the further realisation of aspirations embedded within the Constitution. It is fully compatible with the sharing of responsibilities between the State and the autonomous communities.

This last point is particularly relevant when we come to look at the implications of the LOGSE for regional education systems and their rights and responsibilities as regards the promotion of the teaching and learning of local languages.

## The situation of languages in post-Franco Spain

As we have noted, the death of the right-wing dictator Franco in 1975 and the subsequent passing of a new constitution in 1978 laid the seeds for a dramatically different Spanish society and state. This is reflected also in attitudes to and the use of language and languages in Spain.

Throughout Spanish history there have been tensions between the central state and its marginalized regions in the struggle to assert and establish 'Spanish' identity. Frequently this has been marked by the language issue. The existence over the centuries of many highly centralized (and often highly authoritarian) regimes governing from Madrid has led to the dominance and power of Castilian as the 'Spanish' language – the two terms becoming increasingly interchangeable in modern Spanish history. Nonetheless, the languages of significant minority communities have survived and even had periods of substantial importance (eg during cultural renaissances in the 19th century and the short-lived Second Republic of the 1930s). However, during the Franco period non-Castilian languages such as Catalan, Basque and Galician were proscribed and not tolerated. In the early part of the dictatorship sanctions against the use of these languages took the form of fierce oppression, censorship, fines and even prison sentences for those using them in public. In the latter period of his regime, however, the persecution was subtler and ostensibly more tolerant, with a policy of deliberate degrading and belittling that sought to ignore and downgrade the minority languages to the role of mere dialects (Mar-Molinero, 2000: 83–86). Throughout the 40-year dictatorship the non-Castilian regional languages were banned from being taught in state schools, and only tolerated in certain private establishments and, in the case of Catalan, as an exotic subject at university level, towards the end of the Franco regime.

One of the first and most visible changes in post-Franco Spain was the legalizing of the use of minority languages and their gradual introduction into the education system. The 1978 constitution played a major role in activating this. In its third article it lays out the legal framework for language planning and policies in modern Spain. This article refers to Castilian (rather than 'Spanish') as the official language of the Spanish state, but also refers to the 'other Spanish languages' as having official status within the regions (or *comunidades autónomas*) where they are spoken. Article 3 also makes reference to Spain's 'wealth of different linguistic varieties', which it describes as its 'cultural patrimony' to be given 'special respect and protection'.

These constitutional pronouncements have led many commentators inside and outside of Spain to point to an enlightened linguistic policy that identifies and supports multilingualism. In terms of enabling changes in attitudes and use through active language planning, particularly in contrast with the previous regime, there is no doubt that current Spanish language policy is supportive. However, the exact intentions and consequences of the legislation have been widely debated and received criticism from those who feel it has gone too far and those who feel it has not gone far enough (see, for example, Mar-Molinero, 2000; Salvador, 1987; Vernet i Llobet, 1994).

It has certainly been the case that in such regions as Catalonia, the Basque Country and Galicia, and to a lesser extent Valencia, Navarre and the Balearic Islands, much activity has followed the publication of the constitution in terms of promoting and encouraging the use of the local languages. This has manifested itself in public campaigns, in the incorporation into the local autonomy statutes concerning the status and rights of the minority linguistic community, the requirement for the use of the local languages in regional administration, the encouragement of their use in the media and local commerce, and, above all, through the education systems at all levels. The result has been a marked upturn in the use of non-Castilian languages, nowhere more so than in Catalonia. We will now examine in greater detail the language situation and its related education debate in Catalonia and the Basque Country.

## Language and education in Catalonia and the Basque Country: two case studies

Catalonia, in north-eastern Spain, and the Basque Country, in the north on the Atlantic coast, are the two regions that have historically most contested their separate identities from the central Spanish state. Language has frequently been a significant marker in this struggle. It is therefore not surprising that they have been the two regions to embrace most enthusiastically the possibilities opened up by the post-Franco constitution.

During the greater part of the Franco dictatorship the teaching of Catalan was prohibited. During the 1960s it became legal to include some teaching of Catalan in private schools. From 1968, Catalan philology was offered at Barcelona University. However, with the death of Franco and the *Transición* to democracy there was an immediate rush to bring Catalan fully into the education system as soon and as comprehensively as possible.

In July 1978 a decree was issued that Catalan should form part of the official state curriculum in Catalonia. It was now a compulsory subject in all Catalonia's state schools, to be taught at least three hours per week. Courses to train teachers of Catalan were also set up at this time. It was further recognized that some schools would want to move towards a curricular programme largely taught through Catalan, in which case at least five hours of Castilian were to be offered. In October 1979 the Catalan Statute of Autonomy was approved. Article 3 of this statute confirms the status of Catalan as the '*llengua pròpia*' of Catalonia (best translated as Catalonia's 'own' language).

The Catalan government, the Generalitat, issued another decree in 1982 making three hours' teaching a week of both Catalan and Castilian compulsory, plus one hour a week of a curricular subject taught through Catalan. No equivalent was stipulated for Castilian. With the drawing up of the 1983 *Llei de Normalització Lingüística* (Linguistic Normalisation Law) this anomaly apparently favouring Catalan disappeared.

Embedded in these articles are some interesting and potentially controversial principles. For example, the first clause underlines the recognition of the potential equal status of Catalan to its community by stating that it is Catalonia's 'own' language, whereas the third clause reminds us that Catalan is on no more than an equal footing with Castilian in terms of the duty to offer it in the state education system. Clause 2 enshrines the notion of the 'right to choose' in which language a child should be taught, but Clause 4 makes it clear that whichever language that might be, children must also eventually reach an equal mastery in both languages when they complete their basic (compulsory) education. Clause 5 is especially interesting as it stresses the idea that educational segregation should not be allowed to take place, and that children should be able to learn together regardless of their mother tongue and their language preferences. But it also implies that the expected expansion in the command of Catalan should be reflected by its being more widely introduced throughout the education system. Article 20 in fact makes it clear that Catalan should normally be the language in schools.

Catalan teaching had initially to face various problems of the sort familiar to minority language communities when trying to promote their language: a shortage of trained teachers, a low level of literacy skills in the mother tongue among teachers, shortage of materials, and the continuing dominance of the majority language throughout the Spanish state (and worldwide). A further problem was the uneven balance between private and public education in Catalonia. The former tended to be more Catalanized, and therefore tended to cream off the teachers and pupils who could provide the native Catalan-speakers' input into the state schools, which were attempting to integrate non-Catalan-speakers into a bilingual/bicultural society. The distribution of predominantly Catalan- and Castilian-speaking communities was uneven not only at the socio-economic level, but also geographically. Large concentrations of Castilian-speaking migrants from poorer parts of Spain meant that the pupils in schools in some areas (particularly in the industrial belt around Barcelona) were almost entirely Castilian-speaking.

The implementation of the new language education policy was therefore somewhat patchy initially. Nonetheless, the attitudes of parents to their children being taught Catalan were largely positive (Mar-Molinero, 1995), recognizing as they did that Catalan is the dominant language within Catalonia itself in terms of prestige, local culture and economic success. In order to meet this need to learn Catalan in those environments that were not always particularly conducive to it, the Catalan Department of Education decided to introduce immersion method schooling – that is, teaching children through the target language (Catalan) rather than their mother tongue (Castilian), from the start of their schooling, with bilingual teachers. This method, which is normally a voluntary choice on the part of parents and children, has been developed and expanded enormously over the years (Arenas, 1986; Artigal, 1993).

A few years after the mass introduction of Catalan teaching in schools the LOGSE (see p 191) was implemented by central government. One of the reforms implicit in it was the recognition that school curricula should be able to reflect more explicitly the features of their immediate environments and respond to their local community needs. The exact nature of the curricular goals and content was to be left to individual schools following basic principles outlined in the LOGSE. The Generalitat immediately interpreted this as encouragement for the promotion of Catalan culture, language and identity. The Generalitat issued a decree in March 1992 that underlined the link between Catalan as *llengua pròpia* of the region and the need to reflect this in the school curriculum. To this end it declared the immersion programmes to be an essential part of the community's education policy. As a result, these programmes have become the core of the local government's policy in setting out to extend the learning of Catalan more aggressively among predominantly Castilian-speaking communities in Catalonia. From the school year 1993–94, the Generalitat brought into force also its decree that Catalan 'would normally be used as the vehicular language and the language of instruction in compulsory infant, primary and secondary education' (cited in Milian i Massana, 1992: 352). This constitutes an important change in the apparent level of compulsion to learn Catalan. Of course, much depends on the meaning of 'normally'. In theory, under both the national constitution and the 1983 language law, children (or their parents) may choose the language in which they should be educated. This should mean that children can still demand to have the major part of their education in Castilian, as long as they learn Catalan and reach the necessary standard in it. However, in practice the Generalitat's main way of implementing the decree for this extended use of Catalan was through a far greater imposition of the immersion system. It seems to some that the voluntary aspect of this method has been discarded, despite that being one of the main cornerstones of the method (see Artigal, 1993).

It was inevitable that this change in attitude by the local government towards the teaching of Catalan would lead to some tension among non-Catalan-speakers in Catalonia. It also coincided with changes in Madrid, with the socialists first losing their overall majority and then being defeated altogether. These changes moved the tensions to a more centre-stage position in terms of Spanish politics. As a result of this marked change of attitude in the policies regarding the promoting of Catalan through the schools, various individuals and organizations began to campaign against what they regarded as an unacceptable level of obligatory Catalan teaching. Some of this opposition came from Catalans within Catalonia, but most came from non-Catalans, both within and outside Catalonia. Much of it can be seen as a direct consequence of national politics, while some is at a more personal or a more ideological and philosophical level.

There remained, nonetheless, a great deal of quiet support for the Catalan language policies. However, opposition, albeit from a – vociferous – minority, now existed towards the language normalization policy and the education programme in particular, and it was beginning to make itself heard. Among the opponents were various organizations usually made up of active parents, or, in one case, teachers who started to challenge the Catalan language laws through the courts (to date largely unsuccessfully). The contentions regarding the constitutionality of the language laws and the disquiet on the part of some in Catalonia as the education system became more Catalanized are based on various principles and beliefs. For example, the right to be taught in a child's mother tongue, as supported since the 1950s by UNESCO among other international organizations, was considered by opponents to be denied by the immersion method. The issue of individual rights versus collective rights was also important to the debate. The opponents of the language teaching policies believed that the individual right of the Castilian-speaking child should take precedence over the collective right of Catalonia to pursue policies that defined its territorial entity.

On 7 January 1998 the Catalan Parliament passed by a majority of 80 per cent of its deputies a new law on language policy, replacing the 1983 Normalization Law. This approval came after lengthy consultation and debate about the new law, including opposition from those groups who believed that the language policy in Catalonia was detrimental to their children's language education.

Articles 20–24 of the new law refer to matters of education and language. Article 21 is in fact very similar to the earlier Article 14 of the 1983 law. However, one substantial difference is the fact that not only, as in the earlier law, are children expected to reach a level of mastery in the two languages, but students will now not be given their secondary school graduation certificate unless they can prove sufficient competence in oral and written Catalan and Castilian (article 21, clause 6).

Article 20, clause 1 again states that as Catalan is the *llengua pròpia* of Catalonia, it is the language of education at all levels and in all types of school. While this echoes what was said in the 1983 law, the more explicit and coherent meaning given to *llengua pròpia* in the new law has greatly strengthened the interpretation that Catalan will be expected to be the language of all communications as well as instruction in Catalonia's schools. For this not to be the 'normal' situation now would need to be challenged and justified. Whereas previously schools had tended to reflect their local community's linguistic profile in terms of which language dominated, although frequently with a willingness to introduce more Catalan, now the default position is clearly that of Catalan-medium education. And it is for this reason that the opponents of such strong support for Catalan are unhappy and claim that children in Catalonia are losing their opportunities to learn Castilian effectively.

Since the death of Franco in 1975 there has been a marked change in the attitudes to and the provision of Catalan in the education system. From its tentative reintroduction in the 1970s it has been transformed into the principal language of the Catalan education system. Some argue that this has a detrimental effect on the learning and use of Castilian, and thereby infringes both children's constitutional rights and also their opportunities in the wider national (and international) arena. Those supporting the language education policies will argue that a 'normalization' of Catalan is the native right of Catalans and that it can be achieved only by relatively aggressive action if it is to compete on equal terms with the language of the central Spanish state. They argue that no child in Catalonia can possibly be deprived of learning Castilian since it is still the dominant state language, widely heard and read in the media and the mother tongue of nearly half Catalonia's population.

A further complicating factor in the tension between Catalan and Castilian is that of the increasing presence of North African immigrants. Until the 1970s Spain had virtually no experience of the non-European immigration that in other parts of Europe is so common. The relative economic buoyancy of Catalonia in the 1970s attracted particularly Moroccans to live mainly in Barcelona and surrounding areas, often illegally. The children of these immigrants often spoke neither Castilian nor Catalan and have presented major challenges to the local education policy makers in terms of curricular philosophy (Boogerman Castejón, 1997; López García and Mijares Molina, 2001). Whether Catalonia wants to, or can, offer a truly multicultural education to its citizens is acutely challenged by these newest arrivals, although, for the moment, numbers are small. It is a challenge that could potentially be very uncomfortable for the more aggressive Catalan-teaching policies. Those counter-arguments that used to dismiss demands for more mother tongue rights for Castilian-speaking children on the grounds that Castilian is the state's majority language and widely spoken and heard simply cannot be asserted in the context of demands for mother tongue teaching for Moroccan immigrants. Many international bodies are firmly committed to the teaching of such community languages as Arabic to the children of immigrants, and these are precisely the same international bodies to which the Catalans look for support and approval in their campaign to promote their own (minority) language.

The other area besides Catalonia where language planning has been most active since the death of Franco is the Basque Country. The Basque language had not originally been a major constituent of the sense of Basque national identity, but its potential elimination and the general hostility from the Franco regime to all things Basque persuaded many of the need to teach their children Basque before it was too late (Tejerina, 1996).

In response to this perceived need, and indeed as an act of political defiance towards the Franco dictatorship, a series of semi-clandestine Basque-medium schools known as *Ikastolas* were created in the 1960s (or in some cases reactivated from the Republican period). The popularity of these schools, which had eventually to be tolerated by the Franco government, can be seen in the increase in numbers attending them and the growth in such centres (Tejerina, 1996: 228). It must be remembered that although there was now greater political solidarity with the idea of teaching and learning the Basque language than there had been previously, there were still many, particularly among the urban middle classes, who were not convinced of the need to protect and use Basque. Less than a quarter of the population of the Basque Country spoke Basque, and this figure has increased only slightly since the death of Franco.

In 1979 the Basque Autonomous Community was given its statute of autonomy. In October 1982 the Basque government published its own language law, the *Ley de la Normalización del Uso de Euskera* (the normalization of the use of Euskera law). As regards education, it decrees that Euskera (the Basque word for 'Basque') and Castilian shall be compulsory subjects from kindergarten to pre-university studies. It also establishes three separate models of bilingual education from which parents and children may choose. These reflect the varying objectives of bilingual education ranging from a minimal provision of some second language teaching as part of the overall curriculum (Model A), to total immersion in the target language (Model D).

The challenges for the teaching of Basque are in many senses greater than for the teaching of Catalan, not only because the pool of native speakers is so much smaller and its prestige among the elites historically lower, but also because in the absence of a substantial literary tradition, the necessary materials for the education system did not exist. Even fewer appropriately trained teachers were available, necessitating a major retraining programme. Also, Basque is a much more difficult language for Castilian-speakers to learn than Catalan, with competence taking much longer to achieve.

Nonetheless, since the introduction of these types of bilingual education in the Basque Country from 1982 the most significant feature has been the decrease in students enrolling on the Model A programmes and the corresponding increase of those on Model B and D schemes (Artigal, 1993; Cenoz, 1998; Gobierno Vasco, 1990). In its own way this represents almost as dramatic an increase in the use of Basque as the language of education as the similar increase that we noted with Catalan in schools in Catalonia. Vigorous language planning activities in the region have helped. In particular, the need to pass exams in Basque to be eligible for certain desirable public sector jobs has been an important incentive. In general, too, a pride in the culture of the local region in an era where globally there is significant revival in awareness and respect for local identities has also encouraged parents to want their children to learn the local language, which many never had the opportunity to do themselves.

In both the Basque Country and Catalonia at present an impartial observer might wonder if the institutionalized power of the politicians and language planners is not directing the agenda to the exclusion of more grassroots-level popular support. It is a delicate balance, which appears still to be holding, and holding well in Catalonia in particular. But unexpected or unwelcome factors may shake this balance, be they the arrival of significant non-European immigrants with new language needs, or the pressure to learn English, which is increasingly challenging the language curricula in both regions (see, for example, Cenoz, 1998).

Meanwhile, to judge by the criterion of increased numbers of speakers of the two minority languages, both regions should claim success for their language education policies. Ninety-four per cent of Catalonia's population claim to understand Catalan, and 75 per cent speak it. In the Basque Country the figures for understanding and speaking Basque are considerably lower – approximately 27 per cent (Cenoz, 1998); the significant feature as far as language educators are concerned is the increase in the number of young people speaking Basque (Garmendía, 1994).

## Other non-Castilian language teaching in Spain

There are other non-Castilian mother tongue groups in Spain who have access to some language education, alongside the provision of foreign language learning and teaching as compulsory subjects in the school curriculum. Indigenous languages of communities such as, notably, the Galicians, as well as the Valencians and to a much lesser extent the Asturians and Aragonese, are also to a greater or lesser degree offered within the education system (as is the case of the Galicians and Valencians) or in extra-curricular activities. There are also significant communities of other linguistic minorities, such as Portuguese-speakers from Portugal, Brazil or Cape Verde; Arabic-speakers from the Maghreb, as well as the important Gypsy population, some of whom speak Caló as their mother tongue. In the case of all of these there is limited support for mother tongue teaching; in the case of the Portuguese this even extends to some teaching in Spanish schools where there is a significant population (López Trigal, 2001).

As regards foreign language learning, Spain shares many of the inadequacies of such European countries as the United Kingdom and Portugal in providing relatively few foreign languages in the curriculum (primarily English, followed by French and then German). However, some positive reforms that were indicated in the LOGSE are beginning to be implemented, such as the lowering of the age when children are first introduced to a foreign language (from 10 to 8 years). Also, in order to free up more time in the curriculum for the optional study of a second foreign language, under the new system foreign languages are taught for fewer hours.

There is a clear belief now in Spain in the need to learn languages, usually English, to a competent level in order to progress in job opportunities and for businesses to be successful. Consequently, many Spaniards attend a high-quality state-funded *escuela oficial de idomas* (they exist in most big cities), a private language school or evening classes to improve their foreign language skills. Spain's generally popular membership of the EU since 1986 has also highlighted the need to learn other European languages, although in reality this has usually meant English. The impact this preference for English is having on the linguistic situation in Spain is interesting, as it emphasizes yet again the dominance of English as the world language even when in competition with Spanish, a language spoken by nearly 400 million people across the globe. This puts pressure on the Spanish government to counter with resources and initiatives to promote and expand the use and learning of Spanish as a foreign language. One such response has been the creation of the network of Cervantes Institutes round the world, with a consequent marked upturn in the learning of Spanish as a second language in many areas.

This in turn can influence the status and future of the non-Castilian Spanish languages in Spain, speakers of which may fear being sidelined by efforts to enhance and promote the role of Spanish. The result may be even more committed campaigns to teach non-Castilian mother tongues to avoid being swallowed up by the overwhelming march of Castilian. Ironically, too, the learning and use of English as a 'neutral' language can be observed in such situations as Catalans wishing to avoid the use of Castilian when choosing a language of wider circulation for such purposes as publishing academic articles or contributing to Web sites.

## Conclusion

Language use in Spain is a hotly political issue, marking as it does regional and local identities and their relationship with the central state. Moreover, these roles are extended today beyond Spain's national borders to the language relationships found on the European stage and globally. The political significance of language use and language behaviour is thus reflected in the policies and legislation surrounding language education, as we saw particularly in the case of Catalan and Basque. Language frequently symbolizes other social and political tensions and emphasizes the over-lapping issues, be they the relationship between national (state) and regional identity, or that between national and international roles, or that between indigenous and migrant (minority) communities. Post-Franco Spain is a very different place from the old Spain of empire, dictatorship and ultra-conservatism, but it is still struggling to accommodate its multiple identities, as is acutely apparent in its language and language education policies.

## Note

For an excellent and comprehensive overview of the situation of linguistic minorities in Spain, including any educational provision for the learning of mother tongue languages, see Turell (2001). For further information on the teaching of foreign languages in Spain, including the training of foreign language teachers, see the section on Spain in Eurydice (2001).

## References

Arenas, J (1986) La inmersió lingüístivca, Llar de Llibre, Barcelona

Artigal, J M (1993) Catalan and Basque immersion programmes, in European Models of Bilingual Education, ed H Baetens Beardsmore, pp 30–54, Multilingual Matters, Clevedon, UK

Boyd-Barrett, O and O'Malley, P (eds) (1995) Education Reform in Democratic Spain, Routledge, London

Boogerman Castejón, A (1997) Educational policy, mixed discourse: responses to minority learners in Catalonia, Language Policies and Language Planning, 21 (1), pp 20–35

Cenoz, J (1998) Multilingual education in the Basque Country, in Beyond Bilingualism: Multilingualism and multilingual education, eds J Cenoz and F Genesee, pp 175–92, Multilingual Matters, Clevedon, UK

Eurydice (2001) Foreign Language Teaching in Schools in Europe, supplement on Spain, produced by Ministerio de Educación, Cultura y Deporte, Madrid

Garmendía, C (1994) El proceso de la normalización lingüística en el País Vasco: datos de una década, *International Journal of the Sociology of Language*, **109**, pp 97–109

Gobierno Vasco (1990) *10 años de enseñanza bilingüe*, Gobierno Vasco, Vitoria-Gasteiz

López García, B and Mijares Molina, L (2001) Moroccan children and Arabic in Spanish schools, in *The Other Languages of Europe*, eds G Extra and D Gorter, pp 279–93, Multilingual Matters, Clevedon, UK

López Trigal, L (2001) The Portuguese community, in *Multilingualism in Spain*, ed M T Turell, pp 344–55, Multilingual Matters, Clevedon, UK

Maravall, J M (1984) *La reforma de la enseñanza*, Editorial Laia, Barcelona

Mar-Molinero, C (1995) 'Catalan education policies: are Castilian-speakers persecuted?', *ACIS*, **8** (1), pp 49–56

Mar-Molinero, C (2000) *The Politics of Language in the Spanish-Speaking World: From colonisation to globalisation*, Routledge, London

Milian i Massana, A (1992) *Drets lingüístics I dret fonumental a l'educació*, Generalitat de Catalunya, Barcelona

Salvador, G (1987) *Lengua española y lenguas de España*, Ariel, Barcelona

Tejerina, B (1996) Language and Basque nationalism: collective identity, social conflict and institutionalisation, in *Nationalism and the Nation in the Iberian Peninsula*, ed C Mar-Molinero and A Smith, pp 221–37, Berg, Oxford

Turell, M T (ed) (2001) *Multilingualism in Spain*, Multilingual Matters, Clevedon, UK

Vernet i Llobet, J (1994) La regulación del plurilingüismo en la administración española, in *¿Un estado, una lengua? La organización política de la diversidad lingüística*, ed A Bastardas and E Boix, pp 115–41, Octaedro, Barcelona

# 14. Language education in Russia

Georgii Khruslov

## Historical and political background

Modern Russia, with its population of 145 million in September 2000, is a multi-ethnic state where people belonging to more than 150 ethnic groups speak a wide range of languages. This sociolinguistic situation has a long history behind it, with gains and losses during the periods of the Russian Empire, the Soviet Union and the current Russian Federation.

Since the late 16th century 'Russia' has expanded from Muscovy, the former principality of Moscow, to incorporate vast territories inhabited by people with different cultures and languages. Modern Russians anthropologically, culturally and linguistically are successors to different groups of Slavs who historically lived side by side with Turkic, Finno-Ugric, Caucasian, Mongolian, Tungus-Manchurian, Palaeo-Asian and other peoples.

Russians are still nevertheless the dominant ethnos, Russian is the dominant language, and Orthodox Christianity is once again the dominant religion in the present Russian Federation. However, in all regions of Russia there have also always lived people with different backgrounds, different religions (if they have any at all) and different languages. Language education in Russia has to deal with all the languages spoken in the country, and also to satisfy the need to learn the languages of other countries.

Thus, language education in Russia is to be understood as an educational sub-system designed to guarantee its citizens knowledge of their mother tongue, the Russian language (if necessary); any other official language of the Russian Federation (if it does not coincide with the mother tongue); and also one or more foreign languages. Language education is provided by the actions of state and society via educational institutions: through the training of language teachers, the designing of curricula and syllabuses, the publishing of course-books, dictionaries and other resources, and the evaluation of the language knowledge and skills acquired.

The statistics of language education in Russia are drawn from about 140,000 state educational institutions of different levels and types in which about 39 million people are being educated and professionally prepared (for further details, see the Web site of the Russian Ministry of Education, Current position and main tendencies in the development of the educational system in 2000).

## Aims and structures

Language education in Russia is regulated by the Law on Languages of the Russian Federation (1991, rev 1998), the Law on Education (1992, rev 1996), the Federal Programme of Development of Education (2000), the 'National Doctrine of Education' (2000) (a basic educational document approved by the government of the Russian Federation), the national curriculum, and the regulations and programmes, etc, of individual educational institutions.

Among the main goals of the state in the sphere of education are maintenance of the languages and cultures of all citizens of the Russian Federation, and the maintenance and development of the Russian language as a unifying factor in the multi-ethnic state. Learning different languages is seen as providing a basis for interethnic tolerance, contributing to better understanding of the spiritual cultures of other peoples, and discouraging chauvinism and xenophobia. Language education is intended to broaden learners' linguistic and cultural outlook, and to show not only the diversity of the human world, but also the underlying values of one's own language.

The 1998 draft national curriculum for the whole period of compulsory education has a special section on languages and literature. This section sets out goals for learning Russian and other mother tongues of schoolchildren necessary for work and social life: reading, writing, listening and speaking. The aims include acquiring meta-linguistic knowledge, and internalizing the laws and rules that make up linguistic, communicative and cultural competencies. The section also sets goals of a more general kind, such as the socialialization of children, the development of their logical thinking, and the acquisition of academic skills and habits (eg using dictionaries and reference books; making summaries).

The current curriculum has a special subject: Russian as the official language for schools in those republics of the Russian Federation where another official language has been legally adopted as the main medium of instruction. 'Other mother tongue' curricula are the responsibility of the different autonomous republics.

To summarize: language education in schools is made up of the following subjects:

- Russian mother tongue;
- Russian as the official language (sometimes referred to as 'Russian in ethnic schools' or 'Russian in schools with a non-Russian medium of instruction');
- Russian in schools with Russian as medium of instruction that are, however, located in areas of Russia with many ethnic minority students;
- other mother tongues – languages of a 'titular' nation (ie an autonomous region with a corresponding language) or any other non-Russian language spoken natively in the Russian Federation;
- foreign languages.

The number of hours allocated to learning Russian in minority ethnic schools with Russian as the medium of instruction and in minority ethnic schools using a non-Russian language of instruction is approximately the same. However, the level of Russian language proficiency is higher in the former type of schools where all subjects are taught in Russian, and the level of mother tongue proficiency is lower than in schools of the latter type – and vice versa – as demonstrated by the results of final exams in schools.

## Current practice and changes in progress in the teaching of Russian

The Russian education system in general is now under reform. It is moving to the provision of 10 compulsory years of basic education for everyone (instead of 9) and 12 years for a full secondary education (instead of 11).

Current practice in the teaching of Russian in schools is a matter of constant concern for parents, schoolteachers, academics, journalists and other social groups who are worried about the declining reputation of this school subject. The core of the discussion is about what steps could raise motivation in school students, and the main measure discussed is a proposed shift from the traditional teaching of grammar and spelling to more communicative and culture-focused methods.

To meet the new requirements the concept of a school subject called 'Philology' in the 12 years of schooling has been outlined. It is based on the creative character of the teaching, intended to develop children's memory, thinking and speech by using games, essays, conversations, role playing, etc, and in general making language learning more enjoyable.

The main goals of this newly conceptualized subject of 'Philology' are as follows:

- educating patriotic citizens of Russia who love their own people, language and culture but who also respect the traditions and cultures of other peoples;
- raising awareness of the values inherent in the national culture;
- learning the system of knowledge, skills and habits in the language subjects, and developing the verbal, intellectual and creative capacities of school students.

New programmes in Russian have been designed and new course-books have been published (including those for schools where Russian is taught as the official language), and in general primary and secondary schools both standard course-books and alternative books are in use. For schools and classes with extended study of Russian, and for specialized academic secondary schools with a humanities profile (the labels 'gymnasiums' and 'lyceums' have been revived from the pre-revolutionary era), special books have been designed. Students aged 17–18 can choose from among such special courses as Russian communicative syntax, specialist vocabularies, speech development, language in speech communication, language of belles-lettres, rhetoric, history of personal names, language and life, or language and society. In senior classes in schools of general education there is an emphasis on revision and generalization of the basic facts in the grammar and vocabulary of Russian, systematization of knowledge gained, and also extension of students' recognition of styles of speech and varieties of texts.

Many urban and rural schools hold annual contests for students of forms 9 to 11 – the final two years of secondary schooling under the existing system – for best knowledge of Russian. The winners participate in national contests in the subject. Assignments and questions during the contests test students' knowledge of linguistics as a science: of the work of outstanding Russian linguists such as Mikhail Lomonosov, Vladimir Dal' and Yakov Grot on the language system and the specifics of its functioning, and on the interrelationships between Russian language, history and culture. They also test skills and habits in different speech activities, and such contests are seen as a promising way to increase students' interest in Russian, to judge from the general atmosphere and attitudes both of teachers and students.

Among other measures still needed to raise the level of Russian language teaching in school are enhancing the academic training of future teachers, the creation of new course-books for all courses taught in colleges, the widening and deepening of courses in the history of modern literary Russian, with attention to changes in it during recent decades. New teaching technologies for Russian in schools are also needed urgently, as is integration between Russian language and literature lessons.

## Mother tongue teaching: alternative models

One of the main principles of state educational policy is the right of all the peoples of Russia to maintain their own mother tongue. This right is realized through a number of educational models.

### Model 1: 'ethnic' schools with teaching in the mother tongue and the learning of Russian as a subject

Model 1 has the following variants:

- tuition in mother tongue through the whole school, from Class 1 to Class 11: this model applies in Tartarstan, Bashkortostan and Sakha-Yakutia;
- tuition in mother tongue up to Classes 7–9 with a subsequent switch to Russian: this model is used in the rural schools of Tyva and Buryatia, and in a number of northern Caucasian republics, and in the urban schools of Tartarstan and Bashkortostan;

- tuition in the mother tongue up to Class 5 with a switch to Russian after that: this happens in the urban schools of Tyva, Kalmykia, Adygea, Kabardin-Balkaria, Karachay-Circassia and a number of other places.

There are also regions where teaching in the mother tongue gradually increases from junior to senior classes. For example, the realization of the 1990 Law on Languages of the Chuvash Republic stimulated the learning of Chuvash. New curricula have been designed with additional hours for learning the mother tongue; course-books in the main subjects have been translated from Russian to Chuvash for Classes 5 and 6; Chuvash has been introduced as a subject in Russian-medium schools; and new course-books about the Chuvash language, literature, history and culture, ecology and geography are being prepared. A number of national lyceums and gymnasiums have been opened, which extend the learning of Chuvash language and literature, music and other subjects.

## Model 2: 'ethnic' schools with Russian as medium of instruction, but with extended learning of mother tongue languages and cultures

This model is used in the schools of the far North and the far East. Taking into consideration the existence of writing systems, literature, maintenance of folklore, traditions and customs of certain peoples, it is possible to identify languages that are not endangered and are likely to develop in the future. These include Dolgan, Chukot and Nenets – provided that the teaching of them in schools is maintained.

An important part of this model is the 'nomad school' in the transpolar and other distant areas, where teachers follow reindeer-breeders' camps. Teaching is offered in this way up to Class 5. Local educational authorities work out recommendations on how to organize the teaching of younger children under such exceptional conditions.

## Model 3: the school of 'the ethnic diaspora' with a compact or dispersed residence outside the original territory of the ethnos

This model combines elements of the two previous models, in that teaching in the mother tongue is the foundation of the whole learning process, but effective learning of Russian is also provided. The specific features of these 'national' schools in multi-ethnic contexts are clearly illustrated by the arrangements in the Sochi area of the Krasnodar region, where the proportion of peoples who have their own historical motherland is high: mostly Armenians, Georgians, Adyges and Greeks. On the one hand, they remain committed to the all-Russia social and cultural context, but on the other hand, they do not want to lose their non-Russian identity. Thus, an educational sub-system is being built within the system of regional education which is designed to satisfy fully the ethnic and cultural needs of future citizens.

## Current problems in language education

The main academic and organizational problems of teaching Russian as the official language are as follows:

- a lack of course-books for the advanced stages;
- lack of alternative or parallel courses;
- insufficient continuity between elementary and middle school.

The main problems that preoccupy teachers of the other mother tongues are as follows:

- the lack of a common written standard in some languages;
- teacher supply, especially a lack of teachers of non-Russian mother tongues and teachers who could teach other subjects in these languages;
- the undeveloped terminology of the main school subjects in other mother tongues;
- a lack of modern course-books that would teach the norms, styles and genres in other mother tongues;
- disjunctures between secondary and higher professional education, since in the latter only Russian is used as a rule.

## Three case studies

Russian and other mother tongues are still not treated as interconnected and interdependent in school curricula. One basic requirement for dealing with these issues in education is the availability of empirical data on the language backgrounds and patterns of language use among pupils on the one hand, and pedagogic practices in multi-ethnic classrooms on the other hand. In the school years 1999–2001 a research group of Russian and Dutch specialists conducted a project in certain regions of the Russian Federation to collect and analyse data on family and school languages in Russian-medium and mother tongue-medium schools at primary level (Nederlandse Organisatie voor Wetenschappelijk Onderzoek (Dutch Organization for Scientific Research; (NOW, 2001) for its Interim Report; the Final Report is forthcoming).

Three research areas were selected: two 'titular' republics within the Russian Federation, the Republic of Altai and the Republic of Bashkortostan, and the City of Moscow. The former two are territories with Turkic-language populations, in which peaceful coexistence between Christian and Muslim cultures and civilizations is of vital importance for modern Russia. In Altai the proportion of 'native' population – an ethnic categorization used in the official census statistics – is 31 per cent, and these people's traditional religion is shamanism. In Bashkortostan the proportion of 'native' population is 22 per cent, and their traditional religion is Islam. In Moscow the proportion of the population that is 'native Russian' is 94 per cent, and the traditional religion is Orthodox Christianity.

Economically, Altai is a less advanced agricultural area, with strong nomadic traditions. Bashkortostan is a more industrially developed area where, as well as Bashkirs, Tartars make up 28.4 per cent of the population as a whole. Moscow is more like a Western-type multi-ethnic megalopolis.

## The Republic of Altai: an overview

(This section is based on the report by Oksana Pustogacheva prepared for the NOW 2001 project.)

Altai is in south-western Siberia, bordering on Kazakhstan, Mongolia and China. In total there are 202 schools offering general education in Altai, 95 per cent of them rural. In these schools about 40,000 pupils are educated. Sixty-four of the rural schools teach through the Altai language, and one rural school uses Kazakh. In 102 schools (10 urban and 92 rural) Altai is learnt as a subject, and in 14 schools (1 urban, 13 rural) Kazakh is learnt as a subject

The Law on Languages adopted in 1993 in the Republic of Altai proclaimed Altai as an additional official language alongside Russian, but the revival of interest in Altai language and culture has revealed many problems. In the former Soviet Union state schools in general were rigidly centralized, and Altai schools, like other 'national' schools, were not designed to form creative personalities, bearers of national values able to solve modern problems. So until the late 1980s Altai schools were obliged to use Russian as the language of tuition, and as a result of this the number of Altai national schools and the publication of educational materials decreased, thus hindering the use of Altai in education.

The need for revival of the Altai national language, and the broadening of its functions, and for development of the unique culture of the indigenous people of the republic required the revision of the whole system of education and training in national schools, as well as the training of teachers and other specialists. As a result, at the beginning of the 1990s the Plan for National Schools in the Republic of Altai was developed and adopted by the government of the republic. Its main principles are as follows:

- recognition of children's rights to be educated through their mother tongue, beginning in the family, until graduation from school;
- formation of the intellectual abilities and moral traits of children and young people, taking into consideration their specific ethnic and psychological features, and local traditions of education;
- acquainting the younger generation not only with the national culture of the Altai people but also with the cultures of other peoples, thus emphasizing their common humanity and preparing them for life and work;
- giving some priority to national and regional components in the structure of cognitive subjects and also in aesthetic, physical and vocational education;

- developing a variety of types of schools and pre-school institutions, and different curricula; starting specialist academic upper secondary schools – gymnasiums and lyceums again – and colleges and private educational institutions.

Since 1993 the educational institutions of the republic have been developing curricula following federal and regional basic curricula. To realize the Plan for National Schools of the Republic of Altai, draft national and regional and school components in the content of education have been prepared: in Altai language and literature, the history of the Mountainous Altai people, and Kazakh language and literature.

The main problems of school educational policy currently under discussion are as follows:

- how to achieve parity between the two languages in school when Russian is still the dominant language in economic life, trade, politics and higher education throughout the Russian Federation;
- how to build motivation for learning non-Russian mother tongues;
- which methods to choose for successful learning of two or three languages;
- at which age to switch from the mother tongue medium (Altai, Kazakh, etc) to Russian language medium.

## The Republic of Bashkortostan: an overview

(This section is based on the NOW 2001 Project Report by Flura Aznabaeva.)

Bashkortostan is on the borders between Europe and Asia, in and around the Urals, and in the Republic of Bashkortostan there are 3,259 institutions of general education, attended by more than 670,000 students. It is a multi-ethnic republic where special attention is paid to ethnic issues when designing laws and regulations, and such issues are fully considered in the republic's most recent Law on Education, in the Plan for the Development of National Schools and in the Programme of Development for Education in the Republic of Bashkortostan for the years 1999–2003.

A priority task for state national policy in the Republic is the provision of guarantees for the free development of all the peoples residing in Bashkortostan, and the 1992 Law on Languages of the Republic provides extra opportunities for this task by clearly defining the principles of language policy that contribute to the maintenance and development of different languages.

Fourteen languages are studied in the schools of the Republic: Bashkir, Russian, Tartar, Chuvash, Mari, Udmurt, Mordvin, German, Ukrainian, Belorussian, Greek, Yiddish, Latvian and Polish. Teaching is offered through the medium of the first six languages listed, and the other eight languages are learnt as subjects. Of the non-Russian mother tongue pupils, 62.4 per cent were learning their mother tongue.

Many measures are taken to stimulate children's interest in learning their mother tongues. For example, each year contests are held in the Bashkir, Tartar, Russian, Chuvash, Mari and Udmurt languages, with a traditional essay contest on the theme of 'My Motherland is Bashkortostan', dedicated to the annual Day of Sovereignty of the republic.

There has been a dramatic growth in teacher supply in the past decade, and in classrooms equipped for mother tongue studies, mainly with tape recorders, visual aids, etc. Education in the Republic of Bashkortostan is developing currently in three directions: to deal with national or 'ethnic' cultures, with the all-Russian dimension, and with world cultures. This dialogue of cultures in education contributes immensely to national development, harmony of cross-national relations and the overcoming of inter-ethnic tensions.

## The City of Moscow: an overview

Moscow, the capital, is the most multi-ethnic city in Russia. It has a demographic composition similar to that of a Western-type megalopolis, where representatives of all Russian nationalities, including many of Turkic origin, make their living as migrants in a diaspora.

There are about 1,500 schools in the city, attended by about 1.5 million students, and Moscow education is considered by experts to be the most developed in Russia, serving as a kind of model for the whole country. There are 27 schools there with a particular 'ethnic' component of education.

The content of education is governed by the Moscow regional basic curriculum, which is a variant of state educational standards, but in which the national and regional component has been specially modified for Moscow. In particular, the Russian language course takes the specific features of Moscow pronunciation into consideration, and Moscow Regional Studies is included as a separate subject.

There are some schools with extended study of Russian language and Russian culture, and an experimental Web site for the city called 'Pushkin Word' with which teachers try to increase children's interest in their mother tongue. Their goal is the development of Moscow schoolchildren in the field of humanities, and enthusiastic teachers strengthen the norms of modern literary Russian, increase interest and love for Russian, and form the language personality capable of maintaining appropriate spiritual values. The federal programme on Russian language has a city sub-programme aimed at the development of the oral and written language of learners, and the maintenance of the Russian language as a common national heritage.

Schools with a particular ethnic component of education are attended by children both from national diasporas that have been established in Moscow for a long time, and from families of 'new' migrants who have recently moved to Moscow from abroad or from other areas of Russia. In these schools they learn the languages, history, culture, traditions and crafts of different peoples

(Azerbaijani, Georgian, German, Jewish, Korean, Lithuanian, Polish, Tartar, Ukrainian and others). The Moscow Department of Education has adopted the Plan for National [in the sense of particular ethnicities] Education and the Programme of Development for National Education, and these two documents are the basis for this type of school. Education there is carried out according to curricula designed by school pedagogues and researchers from the leading research institutions and universities of Moscow. For children with a low proficiency in Russian, special programmes for linguistic and cultural teaching have been developed.

In the general schools most teachers try to see that children of different ethnic groups feel comfortable, whereas the 'ethnic' schools create special conditions for the self-determination of pupils as representatives of certain national cultures and traditions. The aim of the educational process is to build up the foundations of a general personal culture that will take into consideration the cultural traditions of a given people. The usual process by which a regular state-run school can be transformed into an 'ethnic school' is through the request of an ethnic minority community to the Education Department. Usually such schools continue to be attended by students from other ethnic groups too.

The interest in mother tongue and culture unites not only children but adults too, and many national schools also house Sunday schools and clubs for adults. National holidays and festivals are celebrated there, and again people of different nationalities often participate. Ethnic minority schools are not closed worlds but educational centres that aim to improve inter ethnic tolerance and mutual respect. Locally, within a town or a village, they can be important centres for bringing different groups into harmony, and a source of education and broader cultural activity. Within the country as a whole, these ethnic schools contribute to the foundation of a new concept of what it is to be Russian.

## Conclusion

To shape language education in Russia for the new century, decision makers have to establish the difficult balance between the many factors discussed above:

- the actual situation of language teaching in various regions;
- the fundamental role of teaching Russian in maintaining the unity of all-Russian federal educational, cultural and linguistic space;
- the role of mother tongue education in identity formation;
- social demands for learning foreign languages;
- the personal wishes of schoolchildren and their parents.

Given that the organizational and financial means of providing the many different types of language education that might be desirable are inevitably limited, this is a formidable task.

## Further reading

### In Russian

Аксянова, Г А 100 народов Российской Федерации: численность и расселение, язык, религия, традиционные занятия, антропологические особенности (справочные материалы). Москва: Издательство «СТАРЫЙ САД», 2001.

Государственные языки в Российской Федерации. Энциклопедический словарь-справочник. Москва: Издательство «ACADEMIA», 1995.

Красная книга языков народов России. Энциклопедический словарь-справочник. Москва: Издательство «ACADEMIA», 1994.

Многоязычие и преподавание родных языков. Москва: Издательство Института национальных проблем образования, 1998.

Национальная доктрина образования в Российской Федерации. «Поиск», 13 октября 2000.

Учебные стандарты школ России. М: Издательства «ТЦ Сфера» и «Прометей», 1998.

Языки семьи и школы. Москва: Издательство Института национальных проблем Образования, 2001.

### In English

Khruslov, G (1995) Multilingual Russia: gateway to Asia or passage to Europe?, in *Lust auf Sprachen. Beiträge zum Internationalen Fremdsprachenkongress Hamburg 1994*, Petersen, Hamburg

Khruslov, G (1998) Language policy in Russia, in *Modern Language Learning and Teaching in Central and Eastern Europe: Proceedings of the second colloquy of the ECML, Graz (Austria)*, 13–15 February 1997, Council of Europe, 1998

NOW (2001) Aznabaeva, F, Pustogacheva, O and Khruslov, G. Introduction to language situation and results of the family and school surveys in Altai, Bashkortostan and Moscow, in *Languages of Family and School* (in Russian: *Jazyk Semji i Skoly*), Report of the NOW Russian–Dutch Research Cooperation Project 'Multilingualism, Mother Tongue Education and Educational Policy: Russian Federation Case Studies', eds G Khruslov and S Kroon, pp 10–68, Institute for National Problems in Education, Moscow

## *List of electronic sources*

City of Moscow Department of Education – http://educom.ru

City of Moscow Experimental Site 'Pushkin Word' – http://pushinst.nm.ru/
rlc/doctr.htm

City of Moscow In-Service Teacher Training Institute – http://textbook.
keldysh.ru

City of Moscow Mayoralty – http://mos.ru

Ministry of Education of the Russian Federation – http://www.edu.html.ru

Moscow Ethnic Schools – http://www.1september.ru/ru/rus/2001/13/1.htm

Portal 'Russian Language' – http://gramota.rPushkin Institute of Russian
Language –http://www.pushkin.edu.ru

Research Institute for Informational Technologies – http://www.informika.ru

# 15. Language education and 'nation building' in multilingual Malaysia

Maya Khemlani David and Subra Govindasamy

This chapter details the multilingual milieu found in Malaysia, and the complex issues surrounding language policies that seem to be at odds with one another as the nation's leaders grapple with the need to balance nation building and the desire to be in line with globalization, a process that will shape the economies of the future. A discussion of language education-related issues in Malaysia may turn out to be reductionist in nature if historical roots and the political set-up of this multiracial nation are not foregrounded. The relevant background information is presented in the first section of this chapter. The second section contains an assessment of the language policies and other key issues related to language education. The concluding section recommends changes that can synergize the peoples towards greater integration and nation building.

## Malaysia: background to the setting

Malaysia is a multi-ethnic, multilingual country with a population of about 22 million people and at least 100 languages. It extends over two land masses: the 11 states of Peninsular Malaysia (previously known as Malaya) and Sabah and Sarawak on the island of Borneo. The British era in Malaysia began in Malaya in the late 18th century and ended when the Federation of Malaya became independent in 1957. In September 1963 Singapore, Sabah and Sarawak joined the Federation of Malaya to form Malaysia. Singapore left the union shortly afterwards, in 1965.

There are three main ethnic groups in Malaysia: Malays and other indigenous groups (61 per cent), Chinese (28 per cent), and Indians (8 per cent) (Khoo, 1991: 40). In 1991 there were 8.79 million Malay *bumiputras* (or 'sons of the soil') and 1.85 million other *bumiputras* (mainly indigenous groups from Sabah and Sarawak), 4.94 million Chinese and 1.39 million Indians. Within the different ethnic groups there can be found a variety of languages and dialects. The national language of the country is Bahasa Melayu (Malay), a language of the Austronesian family. Mandarin and many dialects of Chinese, Tamil and other Indian languages are also widely spoken.

Schools in the colonial past were set up along ethnic lines and conducted in different languages. According to Santhiram (1999: 35),

> The British superimposed a vernacular primary terminal education in Malay for the indigenous Malay masses within the Islamic traditions as a form of social control over the Malays, English education based on the principle of user fees for the immigrants and the Malay masses, but free for a select nobility and royalty, exemplify the classic ingredients of a divide and rule policy. For the immigrant populations, the colonial power tolerated an ethnically inspired and financed vernacular education for the Chinese; and an employer-initiated Tamil vernacular primary education for the Indians.

Malay schools, with a largely homogeneous Malay student population, were largely found in rural Malaya. Chinese schools were more often located in urban centres in the country; Tamil-medium schools were mainly in rubber estates. According to Omar (1982), the Chinese and Tamil schools had two things in common: both had homogeneous student populations and both oriented their curriculum towards another nation, China and India respectively. (Nation building was of no great concern in those days!) The relatively small number of English schools located in the urban centres offered an attractive alternative to the Malay-, Chinese- and Tamil-medium schools. The large subsidies given to them ensured adequate facilities for teaching and administrative purposes. They also groomed their students for positions in the government service as well as for obtaining tertiary education in Malaya, Singapore or the United Kingdom. As a result, parents with high aspirations enrolled their children in English-medium schools, and English education remained much sought after even after the country gained its independence.

With independence in 1957 and the consequent need for nation building, Malay was made the national language of the country. As English was, in 1957, the established language of administration and the language of education for urban children, it was necessary for the changeover to Malay to be implemented in an orderly fashion so as to avoid disruption and a drop in standards. The government did not rush the change. Omar (1982: 89) says it took 26 years (1957–83) to implement the National Language and National Educational Policies for the primary and secondary levels of education. The conversion of the English medium schools to Malay medium began in 1968 at a gradual pace and proceeded on a piecemeal basis. By 1976 all English-medium primary schools were completely converted into schools where Malay was used as the medium of instruction and by 1982 all the former English-medium secondary schools in Peninsular Malaysia were converted to national schools (Solomon, 1988: 46). The Education Act was extended to Sarawak (East Malaysia) in 1977 and the change of the medium of instruction to Malay throughout the entire school system was completed in Sabah and Sarawak (East Malaysia) by 1985.

However, the national-type schools – that is, the Chinese and Tamil primary schools – continued to function with Mandarin and Tamil as their medium of instruction respectively, but with Malay taught as a compulsory language. The content area subjects were realigned to reflect the syllabus taught at the Malay national schools. Unfortunately, these vernacular schools obtained only partial funding from the government, and therefore relied on parents and their ability to make contributions to provide their facilities. Furthermore, the only schools using Mandarin and Tamil as media of instruction that the government was obliged to fund were primary schools. Secondary schools using vernacular languages had to be self-supportive. As a result, on completing their primary education in the vernacular schools, a large majority of the Chinese and Tamil students continued their education in Malay-medium national secondary schools.

Language, ethnicity and educational issues are still closely linked almost 45 years after independence. Although in independent Malaysia, education is expected to play an important role in nurturing national consciousness, moulding national identity and achieving national unity in a multiracial society, education for the ethnic minorities is still, according to Santhiram (1999: 20), 'a modification of the colonial system of education'. The continuation of the Mandarin- and Tamil-medium schools alongside the more generously funded national schools today confirms this trend.

Over 24 per cent of the Malaysian school population is enrolled in Chinese or Tamil vernacular schools, with an apparently close relationship between ethnicity and type of school selected. According to Musa (2001), a former deputy prime minister, at primary school level almost 90 per cent of Malaysian Chinese are in Chinese primary schools while 90 per cent of Malays are in national schools. In addition, 88 per cent of Indian children choose to study in Tamil vernacular schools (Chok Suat Ling in *New Straits Times*, 17 January 2001).

Furthermore, 10 per cent of the Chinese students (52,000) who attend primary vernacular schools continue their secondary education in 60 independent private secondary schools that use Mandarin as the medium of instruction. The students from these schools sit for the Unified Examination Certificate, which is not recognized by any local Malaysian universities; consequently, many of these students continue their university education abroad in neighbouring Singapore or Taiwan.

In the national schools where a majority of Malaysian children are enrolled, Malay is the medium of instruction. English is a compulsory second language in such schools, and English lessons are conducted daily from the start of compulsory schooling in Standard 1. In addition, the teaching of Chinese or Tamil languages as a subject is made available if requested by the parents of at least 15 children in the school.

The education trend in the largest city in Malaysia, Kuala Lumpur, parallels that of the nation as a whole. However, as a result of the relatively large non-Malay population in this major urban centre, there are a significantly larger number of Mandarin- and Tamil-medium schools here.

In Kuala Lumpur, as elsewhere in the nation, English continues to be taught as an important second language in primary and secondary schools. However, students at the start of the English language course in schools differ in their levels of knowledge of and proficiency in English. In urban centres like Kuala Lumpur, many children use English as their first or dominant language in the home (see David and Faridah (1999) on the Portuguese community; David and Ibtisam (2000) on the Tamil community; David (2001) on the Sindhi community; David and Nambiar (2002) on the Malayalee community; and David, Ibtisam and Sheena (2003 forthcoming) on the Punjabi community). While these ethnic minority groups have been shifting to English, it must be emphasized that for about 60–70 per cent of the school-going population, mainly those living in rural areas in Malaysia, English is a foreign language (David, 2000).

## Contentious issues in language education: any feasible solutions?

As Malaysia is a multicultural nation with a strong presence of Malays, Chinese, Indians and other ethnic minorities, it may be expected to raise language-related issues. Some problems have been inherited from the colonial administration of the past, while others are related to unattainable national aspirations or policy shortcomings subsequent to gaining independence in 1957.

The medium of instruction at the primary level is a feature that has been inherited from the colonial past. On gaining independence, the Malay-medium schools were given a facelift by the Alliance government that swept to power in 1957. Full funding extended to these schools had ensured provision of better facilities. These schools also gained by the continual absorption of the English-medium schools into the system. Most Malay and non-Malay but English-educated parents continued to enrol their children in these schools, which are also known as national schools. The Mandarin- and Tamil-medium schools continued to exist, maintaining their form and identity largely as a result of support from communal-based political parties aligned to the Alliance and the subsequently enlarged National Front government. Only a minority of these vernacular schools received full funding, with the large majority requiring communal and parental support to provide adequate facilities. Fortunately for the Mandarin schools, they are well supported by an economically thriving society. In contrast, the Tamil community, largely consisting of plantation workers, does not have the financial clout to provide much-needed facilities to enable the same literacy levels to be achieved in the Tamil schools. Only 140 of the 526 Tamil schools in the country receive full aid. The remaining 386 schools are 'estate schools', sponsored by the managements of the large plantations. Of the 526 Tamil primary schools in the country, about 61 per cent are classified as under-enrolled schools, having a student population of below 150 pupils per school (Santhiram, 1999). Such under-enrolled schools tend to lack basic facilities such as libraries, proper school buildings, etc, and are characterized by multiple class teaching, where a single teacher is responsible for several classes. Husin Ali (1984: 272) describes the 'pathetic educational situation' found in such schools, where the poor physical facilities combined with the poverty of many of the homes produces an educational climate that has been described as hopeless (Marimuthu, 1983: 45). The (Malaysian) Works Minister who represents the Indians in the government has admitted as much: 'Partially-aided Tamil schools are unable to get the full support from the Government. The development of these schools and the quality of its education are sometimes questionable because they don't possess the money to do it' (*The Star*, 24 November 2001).

The greatest disappointment to the community was related to a recently released document on the Education Development Plan (EDP) 2001–10. It was expected to have put forward some strategies for the development of the Tamil schools but has prioritized other sectors instead. While Lim pointed out that 'Colonial education in Malaysia was partisan in nature and did not serve all the groups in society equally' (1984: 7), 44 years after gaining independence the problem of inequality appears to persist.

The situation is very different in the case of Chinese schools, where parents are economically more able to play an important role in the school's development. Though many of the Chinese primary schools are also partially funded by the government, parents and the community ensure that primary schools as well as 60 Chinese independent (or private) secondary schools are well supported. The secondary students sit for the Mandarin-medium Unified Examination Certificate, an examination conducted by the Association of Chinese Students, which is not recognized by Malaysian universities. To overcome this problem, some Chinese independent secondary schools conduct two sessions. The session in the morning uses Mandarin as the medium of instruction, and this leads to the Unified Examination Certificate. The sessions in the afternoon are in Malay and lead to the Malay-medium national examinations. Thus students attending such schools have the opportunity to become truly bilingual.

Malaysian educators Ng and Jomo (1984) and Rosnani Hashim (in 'Saturday Forum' in the *New Straits Times*, 31 March 2001) express the view that the continued presence of vernacular and other schools in the country may not contribute positively to national integration, arguing that such a school system segregates schoolchildren along linguistic and 'racial' lines as well as along religious lines. Ng and Jomo recommend a school system using Malay as the main although not the exclusive medium of instruction, with careful consideration given to the inclusion of English, Mandarin, Tamil and other minority languages as well. They argue that if these languages are given adequate importance in the national system, minority citizen groups will not continue to promote separate vernacular schooling facilities.

An 'inclusive education', according to Grainger and Todd (2000: 18), would necessitate a revision of curricular features as well, especially in subjects such as geography, history and other social sciences. These subjects should be broad based to include the achievements and contributions of all the communities. The distinction between indigenous and immigrant groups who have lived together for at least four generations in the country should be removed. The national aim should be to develop an education system in which all learners are valued.

A corollary of inclusive education is the development of true bilingualism. All learners should have at their disposal at least two languages, which would afford them more than one world-view. A multicultural and multilingual society such as Malaysia would emerge as a beacon for nations that have always advanced the 'melting pot' theory as the only means to national integration. Malaysia should promote bilingualism as a measure of achieving national unity and identity. Such a strategy may help the different communities to appreciate each other's aspirations and hopes. To achieve this, Malaysians must be competent users of the national language, Malay, and one other language, in addition to their mother tongue. The second language should be English, a common language to many Malaysians as a result of the British administration in the first half of the 20th century. There are also other compelling reasons for having English as the compulsory language in the school system. Omar puts it succinctly thus:

> It is with the full awareness of the importance and role of English the world over and with the determination that Malaysians cannot be made to undergo a handicap with the implementation of the National Language Policy, that the Malaysian government has chosen to establish English as 'the second most important language' in the country. This brings English to the second place, after Malay, in the scale of language priority... For a long time to come... there will be a sure need for materials written in foreign languages in the field of knowledge... there is no foreign language other than English that is more feasible for teaching to the Malaysians. (1982: 54–55)

## The role of English

The internal dynamism in the country has also ensured the continued survival of the English language in Malaysia despite its downgrading since independence. It draws its vitality from some of the following features: First, a need for English-medium schools both at primary and secondary level has emerged. There has also been a mushrooming of private schools that place more emphasis on English, even though Malay is the medium of instruction. The students from these schools sit for the same common examinations as candidates from government schools as they are competent in both languages. Second, in Kuala Lumpur a number of English-medium international schools cater to the offspring of mixed marriages, alongside the expatriate community. In addition, in the late 1990s the liberalization of education in Malaysia resulted in the opening of private institutions of higher learning, where English is used as the medium of instruction. Many of these institutions of higher learning have twinning programmes with foreign universities in the United Kingdom, the United States and Australia, all teaching in English. More recently, private universities have been set up in Malaysia, and in such universities English is the medium of instruction. Even in the older-established government universities like the University of Malaya and the National University, English courses are given great emphasis. While most of the older institutions of higher learning have Malay as the medium of instruction, one fairly old institution – the MARA Institute of Technology, a government institution (which has recently been given university status) set up to help the *bumiputras* as part of the government's affirmative policy – has traditionally used English as the medium of instruction, as a route to preparing students for overseas examinations such as the LLB (Bachelor of Laws) and ISA (Institute of Secretaries and Administrators). A further factor is the role of the media. There are four English daily newspapers in Peninsular Malaysia and countless journals and magazines. On television and radio, the airtime given to English is greater even than that given to Malay, and far exceeding that given to vernacular languages.

The revival in the learning and use of English is a fact. The use of English is quite extensive in urban centres such as in Kuala Lumpur. However, the worrying trend is that there is a failure rate of 50 per cent in English among rural students at the Sijil Pelajaran Malaysia (Malaysian School Certificate, equivalent to the former GCE O levels in the United Kingdom) (Matnor Daim, 1997). This trend is liable to lead to disastrous consequences for national aspirations because this group of students will be unable to access resources and acquire experiences that the more successful ones enjoy.

Matnor Daim explains that the Ministry's implementation of programmes to raise attainment in science and technology largely depends on students having a 'very high standard of English in order to exploit the sources of information that would be made available to them' (1997: 23). This rather high expectation is not compatible with what is being implemented in secondary schools in Malaysia. The English language test at the Malaysian School Certificate assesses only basic interpersonal language skills, not the higher-order second language skills needed to carry out more demanding academic tasks.

The only way of reaching this goal, Ng and Jomo (1984) suggest, is by making English an additional medium of instruction in Malaysian schools from primary classes onwards. While social sciences are taught in Malay, mathematics and core science subjects could be taught in English. The 11 years of exposure to both languages in the primary and secondary schools should make pupils proficient bilinguals and thus able to enjoy the positive effects of bilingualism (Cummins, 1982).

In 1994, national leaders, aware of the low proficiency of English among Malaysians, particularly among rural residents, made a proposal to allow the teaching of science through the English language. However, the criticism levelled against the proposal from a section of the population effectively curtailed any developments in using this strategy (Schiffman, 1997).

The lack of academic language skills is most felt among undergraduates who are pursuing their studies in institutions in which English is the medium of instruction. Govindasamy (2001), in his study on the use of learner strategies among engineering and law undergraduates at the International Islamic University Malaysia (where English is the medium of instruction), reveals that almost all of them resort to memorization of facts to overcome their limitations in using English. This is particularly evident with reference to language skills that help them to analyse, synthesize and evaluate information in their respective subjects.

## Malaysian English

So far the discussion has been on historical features, policy decisions and implementations that have brought about some unique problems requiring immediate attention from the Ministry of Education. There is one language feature, which has evolved particularly in urban centres such as Kuala Lumpur but which could well spread further, that calls for comment: the strong growth of English in its nativized form.

In Kuala Lumpur, English is seen as the means of communication in certain everyday activities and private sector job situations. It is not surprising, then, that there has emerged a localized variety referred to as Malaysian English (ME) (Baskaran, 1987) that has borrowed and assimilated from local languages. Local educationalists are slowly accepting the importance of nativized lexical items. While English is spoken fairly widely in its international form in the upper-class suburbs of Kuala Lumpur, the more nativized form is spoken in major commercial centres, corporate offices, financial institutions and large shopping complexes.

However, in the working-class areas of Kuala Lumpur English is seldom used. Consequently, within the metropolis of Kuala Lumpur, we find people with differing proficiencies in different languages, mainly Malay, Chinese, Tamil and English. The result is that it is fairly common to hear Kuala Lumpurians in discourse with each other using a bilingual mixed discourse that may consist of an English/Malay mix, English/Mandarin (or any of the other major Chinese dialects like Cantonese and or Hokkien) or an English/Tamil or even possibly a trilingual English/Malay/Tamil or English/Malay/Mandarin mix. At times, the mix can be of standard Malay and a regional variety of Malay (see David (2000) for examples of code switching in Malaysian service encounters). One reason for such a code-mixed variety of Malay and English discourse is because such a mix, especially English/Malay, is also used by teachers in the English-language classroom and this influences the input students receive (Lim, 1992). Such a phenomenon appears inevitable in a cosmopolitan area where people mix freely, but the legitimate use of this mixed code in learning across the curriculum and in the assessment of students' achievements in examinations is an issue yet to be addressed.

## Conclusion

The main issues in language education in Kuala Lumpur and the country have a long historical backdrop. Pragmatic policies could have averted the most contentious one: the existence of a vernacular schooling system alongside the national schools. The nationalistic fervour that followed independence removed English from its administrative and educational importance, giving Malay greater importance as the medium of instruction in the former Malay and English schools. At the same time, this encouraged the development of separate Mandarin and Tamil schools, resulting in a multi-medium schooling system that may have become an impediment to national unity and integration, segregating students along linguistic lines.

The way out of this malaise could be to make it extremely attractive to the various communities to merge into one system in which vernacular languages are supported, but where Malay remains the main medium of instruction. A main attraction to non-Malay parents, whose linguistic resistance to a Malay-only education is evident in their promotion of vernacular education, would be a system of education that also gave a significant role to English in the curriculum. It is in the national interest for students to have very high proficiency in English and as such the language could be given the status of an additional medium of instruction in the national schools, with subjects such as science and mathematics taught through this medium. An additional attraction for non-Malay parents would be an assurance that the education system would promote the teaching of minority languages as an inherent part of the national curriculum. In multicultural and multilingual Malaysia, integration is best achieved when citizens are proficient bilinguals with more than one world-view. We feel that this would be an acceptable proposition to most Malaysians as the older generation of all the communities went through such a system in the years preceding and immediately after independence.

In addition to this measure, language education and learning in general needs to become more interactive to bring about creativity among learners. The transmission model of teaching that is currently in vogue has not added to the quality of language learning. Students pursuing advanced learning need to be able to have the language skills to analyse, synthesize and evaluate information. The government's aspiration to be a nation in the forefront of science and technology will remain a dream if more innovative teaching models are not introduced into the education system.

The city of Kuala Lumpur, with its multilingual heritage and its array of international and private schools and higher institutions of learning using English as a medium of instruction, is in a position to contribute to national integration in Malaysia. It is already leading the country in turning out proficient bilinguals, with high levels of proficiency in both Malay and English as well as in their mother tongues. If this legacy carries on and if the rest of country is encouraged and helped to follow suit, the whole nation will be able to count multilingualism as one of its assets in a world that is fast becoming borderless.

# References

Baskaran, L (1987) Aspects of Malaysian English syntax, unpublished doctoral thesis, London University College, University of London

Cummins, J (1982) *Basic Principles for the Education of Language Minority Students*, Californian State Department of Education, Sacramento

David, M K (2001) *The Sindhis of Malaysia: A sociological study*, ASEAN, London

David, M K (2002) Code switching in Malaysian courts, paper presented at Regional Conference, International Sociological Association, Brisbane

David, M K and Faridah, N (1999) Language maintenance or language shift in the Portuguese settlement of Malacca in Malaysia?, *Migracijske teme*, **15** (4), pp 465–81

David, M K and Ibtisam Naji (2000) Do minorities have to abandon their languages? A case study of the Malaysian Tamils, *The International Scope Review*, **2** (3), pp 1–15

David, M K, Ibtisam Naji and Sheena Kaur (2003 forthcoming) The Punjabi community in the Klang Valley, Malaysia: language maintenance or language shift?, *International Journal of the Sociology of Language*, **161** (3)

David, M K and Nambiar, M (2002) Exogamous marriages and out-migration: language shift of the Malayalees in Malaysia, in *Methodological Issues in Language Maintenance and Language Shift Studies*, ed M K David, pp 136–45, Peter Lang, Berlin

Govindasamy, S (2001) Learning style preferences of IIUM engineering and law undergraduates, paper presented at the Department of English Language and Literature Colloquium, International Islamic University, Malaysia

Grainger, T and Todd, J (2000) *Inclusive Educational Practice: Literacy*, David Fulton

Husin Ali, S (ed) (1984) *Ethnicity, Class and Development: Malaysia*, Persatuan Sains Sosial Malaysia, Kuala Lumpur

Khoo, S G (1991) *Population Census*, vol 1, General Report of the Department of Statistics, Kuala Lumpur, Malaysia

Lim (1984) Colonial education in Malaysia, in *Key Questions in Malaysian Education*, ed S M Idris, Penang Consumers Association, Penang

Lim (1992) *Questions in Spoken Language Behaviour in ESL classes* (unpublished)

Marimuthu, V (1983) Schooling as a dead-end: education for the poor, especially the estate children, in *Ethnicity, Class and Development: Malaysia*, eds S Husin Ali, Persatuan Sains Sosial Malaysia, Kuala Lumpur

Matnor Daim (1997) Education policy for English in Malaysia, in *English Is an Asian Language: The Malaysian Experience*, eds M S Halimah and K S Ng, pp 22–25, Persatuan Bahasa Moden Malaysia and the Macquarie Library

Musa Hitam (2001) Memorial Lecture on Education and Excellence: Challenges of the 21st Century, Penang, 11 May

Ng, CS and Jomo, KS (1984) Schooling for disunity: education in colonial Malaya, in *Key Questions on Malaysian Education*, ed S M Idris, Penang Consumers Association, Penang

Omar, Asmah (1982) *Language and Society in Malaysia*, Dewan Bahasa dan Pustaka, Kuala Lumpur

Santhiram, R (1999) *Education of Minorities: The case of Indians in Malaysia*, Petaling Jaya, CHILD

Schiffman, H F (1997) *Malaysian Tamils and Tamil Linguistic Culture*, Nikos Drakos, Computer-Based Learning Unit, University of Leeds

Solomon, J (1988) *Bilingual Education*, Pelanduk, Kuala Lumpur

# 16. Linguistic complexity and the 'Three Language Formula': language and education in India

Amitav Choudhry

## Introduction

India presents a unique example of ethnic, sociocultural and religious diversity that is mirrored in linguistic diversity. Because of this, India is regarded as one of the 'sociolinguistic giants'. With a population of over 1 billion, having 1,652 mother tongues, 67 educational languages and 10 major writing systems, India is obviously one of the finest but most complicated laboratories for social research and action. Language academies as well as individual language reformers have played a notable role in politico-linguistic identity building over the past century, leading to the creation of linguistic states each with a strong cultural identity, the dangerous corollary of which is political fission.

The reorganization of the states of the Indian Union on a linguistic basis followed from the appointment of the States Reorganization Commission in late 1953. On the basis of the commission's report, several new unilingual states were formed in 1956. The main motivation for this redistribution of state territories was the reduction of the number of linguistic minorities by bringing together people who speak a common language. However, it is interesting to note here that still no state in India has fewer than 12 mother tongues; in fact, the number of mother tongues ranges from 12 to 410. The premise on which the states were reorganized as political and administrative units was the wish to reduce conflict among the major minority language speakers of India, and to induce a common spirit of nationalism among its people. In practice it actually gave a new dimension to conflict and provoked tensions among different minority speech communities who before the reorganization had enjoyed an almost peaceful coexistence. The resultant provocation of the multilingual masses made them rebel by forming language movements against the imposition of a homogeneity that seemed to derive from the needs of a centralized market economy.

Keeping in mind India's high linguistic diversity coupled with a comparatively low rate of development of indigenous languages, and the established use of a colonial language inherited from the past, issues concerning language policy and its implementation have been a subject of great debate and controversy, resulting in a constant tussle between politicians, educationalists and language planners both at union and state levels. At the same time, these dual authority structures mean that even the question of 'official language' has been marked by a continuing conflict in legislation, indecision and delay in executive action, as well as a lack of purposeful specificity in implementation.

As we will see later, this enormously hampers language policies in education. Although many of the languages share affinity in varying degrees, their interrelationships in recent times have been characterized by a constant rivalry for recognition at various levels, both political and social. The situation has been aggravated from time to time by the fact that English adds another dimension to the language conflict. According to Das Gupta (1970), the framing of the Indian constitution so that there is one official language for the entire nation provoked intense language rivalry among various language groups. When Hindi was chosen as the official language, Das Gupta adds that 'from the very beginning of the spread of modern education in India the nationally oriented intellectuals have been groping for a means of communication among the various regions and language communities' (1970: 39).

The Indian Union at present consists of 28 states and seven union territories, and some of India's salient linguistic characteristics are as follows:

- Different vernaculars of India can be grouped under four families: Indo-Aryan, Dravidian, Austro-Asiatic and Sino-Tibetan.
- The first two of these families dominate the linguistic scene in India and account for approximately 97.7 per cent of its total population.
- Eighteen major languages (ie languages specified in Schedule VIII of the Indian constitution) account for approximately 95.6 per cent of the total population.
- The two official languages of the Union – Hindi and English – together cover more than half of the entire bilingual population.
- There are only 240 mother tongues that have 10,000 or more speakers, and 1,248 mother tongues have fewer than 1,000 speakers. (This indicates that numerous dialects and pockets of tribal inhabitants exist with distinct identities and ethnic backgrounds and that they have not been integrated to form a larger superordinate group.)

## Language education policy

There are about 888,000 educational institutions in the country with an enrolment of about 180 million pupils and students. The elementary education system in India is the second largest in the world, with about 150 million children aged from 6 to 14 enrolled – about 82 per cent of the children in the age group – and 2.9 million teachers.

Underlying language policy in any particular state there remain always the wider principles of national policy, which have called for the following measures:

- strengthening the constitutional safeguards for linguistic minorities;
- promoting the regional languages mentioned in Schedule VIII of the constitution to official status;
- integrating India through two pan-Indian languages: Hindi (as a primary official language) and English (as an associate official language).

These measures led the national language policy makers to evolve the *Three Language Formula*, which stipulates the following language subjects for teaching at the school stage:

- the regional language and the mother tongue when the latter is different from the regional language;
- Hindi or, in Hindi-speaking areas, another Indian language;
- English or any other modern European language.

The three languages are not taught simultaneously throughout the school years. Although there is no uniform implementation of the Three Languages policy in educational institutions throughout the country, the first language is usually taught from the primary stage of education, the second language from the middle stage and the third language at the middle stage for a maximum of three years.

The educational policies and practices in India will be better understood if we keep in mind the hierarchy of status among the languages. At the top are the two official federal government languages, Hindi and English, followed by the official state languages. Then at the third level we may place languages that have no official government function at the federal or state level, but are spoken by more than 1 million people. Finally there are small group and tribal languages that not only are not recognized at any official level, but have scant hope of receiving anything but indifference and hostility from official sources (Fasold, 1990).

The medium of education has assumed fundamental importance in multilingual developing countries in the context of educational development and language planning. In India the Education Commission emphasized the vital role of mother tongue education for the massive revival of national life and the development of indigenous languages. It believed that the goals of industrialization and modernization could be achieved only through a wider dissemination of science and scientific material through these indigenous languages, stimulating in this way a steady flow of creativity vital for national development. A report published by the Union Ministry of Human Resource Development recommended among other things that

> the question of medium of instruction, particularly in early life, will not be fully resolved as long as our dominant and externally connected sections of society

continue to give more importance to elementary graces in a foreign language, than to intimate connections with the vernacular knowledge which our children gain during every week of their growing up, before they go to school. It is because of this reason that we have restrained ourselves from repeating the recommendation that mother tongue alone should be the medium of instruction at the primary stage. (Government of India, 1993: 1)

The provision of mother tongue education is a complex issue. Even if one leaves aside the problems of teacher training and materials development, the question of deciding what a 'mother tongue' is, is far from simple. If we look at two of the definitions that exist, the broader definition is that any language without a written tradition is automatically considered a dialect of the regional language; the narrower definition regards the home language of the child as being the mother tongue, irrespective of the level of development. According to Khubchandani (1977), the official policy is largely in favour of the narrower definition, with a very slow rate of implementation: some state governments are optimistically hoping that minority languages within their jurisdiction will actually die out before they get a chance to be used in education. Even under this narrow definition the problem still remains of which form of the mother tongue is to be used. First, different languages in a speech community have arrived at different developmental stages in their writing systems, literary traditions and extent of standardization for use in formal domains. The readiness of some languages for educational purposes does not purport to deny the possibility of using other less developed languages for the same purpose. Second, the internal differentiation within a single language may pose problems of linguistic description and development of an acceptable standard, and therefore make the application of the principle of vernacular education very difficult. Fasold argues:

> The pluralistic policy is often publicly justified on the pragmatic nationalist grounds that it is educationally more efficient. However... in education, more than in the selection of the language of government, the real threat to nationalism is not from the large number of indigenous Indian languages, but from English. Nationalistically, then, it is more important to reduce the reliance on English than it is to promote Hindi. (1990: 28–29)

The Central Institute of Indian Languages in Mysore has been helping to evolve and implement the language policy of the government of India and coordinate the development of Indian languages by conducting research in the areas of language analysis, language pedagogy, language technology and language use in society, with a bias towards problem solving and national integration.

## Problems of language standardization

Indian languages had shown significant development in the field of creative literature long before independence, and norms based on prestige varieties have emerged with a fair amount of flexibility for each language. Haugen

(1972: 107) talks about the form and the function of language, one representing codification and the other elaboration: 'As the ideal goals of a standard language, codification may be defined as minimal variation in form and elaboration as maximal variation in function.'

The Commission for Scientific and Technical Terminology was established by the government of India with the aim of developing all Indian languages as media of instruction. It was to do this by enriching and developing them to evolve a uniform terminology for Hindi and other modern Indian languages, and to produce university-level textbooks, supplementary reading material and reference literature in all disciplines of knowledge, except law, in order to facilitate a smooth changeover of medium of instruction in Indian universities. Krishnamurti (1988: 59) suggested that:

> In the context of the changed role of Indian languages there is need for developing supra-dialectal norms through planned codification and elaboration to achieve the following educational and national objectives; (1) to promote universal literacy (2) to serve as effective vehicles of administration (3) to spread modern knowledge through formal education (4) to facilitate inter-translatability with other Indian languages and (5) to promote multilingualism as a means of preserving national integration.

Most of the languages spoken in India have been cultivated in a societal atmosphere of plurality, and so have not been subjected to the pressures of standardization as practised in the West, and have not been explicitly codified through spelling and grammar manuals or dictionaries. For many major Indian languages norms and literacy drives have been introduced so recently that they have not yet seriously challenged implicit identity pressures. It is doubtful if standardization can be planned at the conference table, even where the policy makers are competent linguists or authoritative government representatives. Where widely accepted regional norms have developed long before their functional range has expanded, the only type of planning that can be shaped in terms of federal policies by the language planners is 'modernization', but at what cost and to what effect? The futile exercise of finding technical terms and the promotion of rigorous styles of writing for new technologies without the participation of users of modern knowledge in the creation of such terminologies are never likely to yield concrete results. In contrast to the traditional Indian accommodation to linguistic heterogeneity based on grass-roots multilingualism, which readily responds to the demands of the immediate situation, recent times have seen the emergence of sustained efforts towards language autonomy in the name of language development. Khubchandani (1985: 176), in generalizing the issue, states:

> Many processes of modernization in contemporary societies have been undermining the multidirectional, interactive, participatory processes in human communication as revealed by the current standards of language standardization and language teaching and by the overwhelming concerns of many media agencies at the global level.

Krishnamurti (1988: 73) while rejecting the notion of 'pressures from above', says, 'As long as regional variation in speech can be derived by systematic rules from the underlying spelling, the spelling should be adopted as norm. Arbitrary imposition of norms by academic bodies is bound to fail.' He is in favour of encouraging the bilingual style of instruction in schools and colleges without any bar on code switching, and believes that exploitation of the natural process of language growth could help technical terms come into vogue, through borrowing, through phonetic adaptation, through the coining of new terms from native components and by expanding the semantic field of existing words whenever possible. He is also in favour of a survey of occupational vocabularies in actual use, to provide the basis for coining new terms, and in terms of attitudes Krishnamurti advocates linguistic tolerance of regional variation in pronunciation, morphology and lexicon.

Ferguson (1968: 33) suggests that 'A technical vocabulary can be equally effective whether it comes from the language's own process of word formation or from extensive borrowing from another language.' He believes that there should be efforts to promote multi-modal standards for different roles. For example, he suggests that an 'area-centric' educated standard would be more suitable as the medium of instruction at the primary school level and in adult literacy programmes to facilitate a smooth learning transition for learners from their home dialect to the standard language (Bernstein, 1968).

For a proper encoding of the standard language, native creative writers should take the initiative to expand its comprehensibility. Khubchandani (1988: 72) reiterates that 'Standardization of language as a legitimizing activity prescribes correct and appropriate speech behavior.' On the other hand, there is a tendency in Indian languages to spread the net of tradition-inspired value systems of small elites over all domains in the entire speech community. Instead of allowing this process to proceed in a natural way, there seem to be a counter-productive sense of urgency to push forward an arbitrary standard through education and language planning programmes. Khubchandani (1988: 72) makes a valid point when he adds:

> One of the greatest obstacles to the speedy expansion of mass literacy in the country is the tyranny of urban standards imposed through text books. In standardizing languages for plural societies such as ours... what we need today is the inculcation of an entirely different set of values which can be built on the resources of tolerance and even the promotion of variation in a wide range of speech settings: this has been a significant characteristic of the Indian communication ethos through the ages.

In order now to have a close look at the actual situation in terms of education strategies, developments, policies, difficulties, etc in two different states in India, I have chosen first of all Andhra Pradesh, where Telugu is the dominant language, and then West Bengal, where Bangla (Bengali) is the dominant language.

## The view from within: the case for Telugu

Until the early 1950s, in Telengana districts Urdu was the medium of instruction at all levels. After Telugu was adopted as the official language by the Andhra Pradesh legislature in 1966, an autonomous institution called the Telugu Akademi was established in 1969 to facilitate the introduction of Telugu as the medium of instruction at pre-university level, and it was later progressively extended to undergraduate courses. With the help of the teachers of the three major regional universities, the Akademi produced a large number of textbooks for the pre-university courses and also for under-graduate courses. (Minority languages like Hindi, Urdu, Kannada and Marathi are still allowed, but on a limited basis, as alternative media, up through the first degree level, mainly in the Telengana districts.) By and large, however, Telugu as a medium has not yet become popular with the students or their parents, for many reasons. First, teachers who have themselves been educated through English are not psychologically prepared for the change. Second, because of constitutional constraints the state government has not developed any policy of preferential treatment for Telugu-medium graduates. Third, employers such as the banks, business houses and manufacturing industries still carry on their work in English, and hence prefer English-medium graduates. Furthermore, students and teachers complain that the style of writing in the Telugu-medium books and the Sanskrit-based termi-nology used in them make them more difficult to understand than English textbooks. Finally, at Master's degree level the medium continues to be English, and students who have used the regional language medium find it more difficult to switch over to English at this stage than at the pre-university level.

All through high school a quasi-classical style is employed in language as well as subject textbooks, whereas from the pre-university level onwards the style is based on the modern standard, as are the styles used in all other forms of spoken and written communication. The student is torn between the two conflicting styles used in these different contexts. Broadly speaking, there are in modern Telugu two social dialects: the educated and the uneducated. This is, of course, an oversimplification of a complex linguistic situation involving communi-cation among people of varying social, economic and cultural backgrounds. But with the spreading of education among the rural poor, these differences between the social dialects are likely to be accommodated in the direction of educated speech. Therefore, as Krishnamurti (1998) concludes, apart from the use of texts in a quasi-classical style at the undergraduate level, there is a tendency to move towards modern Telugu in the three regional language universities. At present modern Telugu is also used in every other form of formal speech and writing. The present guiding principle in terms of promoting the regional language is to achieve a higher degree of coordination between school and higher education by improving the standards of comprehension and

expression on the part of the students: if this can be achieved, it is likely to lead
to an overall improvement in the standards of education.

## The view from within: West Bengal

According to Dasgupta (1998: 54), there seems to be a consensus that the
broadest educational needs of West Bengal's population include at least:

- the construction of a solid knowledge base;
- the ability to acquire and apply knowledge across various contexts; and
- the enabling of mobility and flexibility.

And although 10 districts in West Bengal have substantial tribal populations
ranging from 21.0 per cent (Jalpaiguri) to 5.4 per cent (Uttar Dinajpur), there is
an overall acceptance of the fact that Bangla should be used as the general
medium of schooling, and this goal has been accomplished to a large extent.
Dasgupta emphasizes that there is now a need for a serious cultivation of
knowledge at higher levels in the medium of Bangla. He also points out that
West Bengal's educational system has long faced some 'calibration difficulties
on the national grid'. Language teachers there often use a rigorous scale to
evaluate students, with a general tendency to award low marks in the
language disciplines. 'One consequence is decreased national mobility for the
products of Bengal's schooling' (Dasgupta, 1998: 54).

A recent report on English in primary education (Sarkar, 1998) reported that
in rural West Bengal most children have a home language, usually a dialect of
Bangla that is more or less distant from school Bangla, ie the standard dialect.
They have to learn to read and write, and also speak, the language to some
extent, and in so doing they have to cross a dialect barrier to reach the
standard language. In such cases grappling with the Three Language formula
would prove a heavy burden.

For the promotion of the Bangla language, especially in the educational
field, the Bangla Academy, the Sahitya (Literary) Academy and the Rajya
Pustak Parishad (State Book Trust) are all actively involved, especially in
fundamental research on Bangla, and in translation of books into Bangla. They
all support publications in different disciplines, and at present at the under-
graduate-level Bangla books are available in arts subjects and subjects related
to commerce, with very few books publications at the postgraduate level.
Only subjects like folklore, philosophy and political science have books that
are adequate – though not good.

Even in West Bengal, Bangla-medium graduates still lose out in job situations to those educated through the medium of English. There are different
pressure groups like the Bhasa Sahid Smarak (Language Movement Martyrs),
Bhasa o Cetana (Language and Consciousness), and Nabajagaran
(Renaissance) that are constantly pressurizing the state government to

provide jobs to individuals educated through the medium of Bangla, but the process of change is very slow.

## Indian languages at the crossroads: looking for solutions

According to Krishnamurti (1998), Indian education has made huge strides since the 1920s, when the modern Indian languages became the media of instruction in schools. This was an objective that had taken seven decades to implement, following famous Wood's dispatch of 1854, in which the intro-duction of 'vernaculars' as education media was forcefully proposed (Naik and Nurullah, 1974: 286). The honour of having compiled the first school text-books in Indian languages goes to missionaries (1813–33) (Naik and Nurullah, 1974: 115). Talking about the educational scene in the pre-independence period, these same authors (as quoted by Krishnamurti, 1998) say:

> The problem of the medium of instruction received considerable attention during the period under review. The difficulties, real or imaginary, which had beset the adoption of modern Indian languages as media of instruction at the secondary stage in the earlier period (1921–37) now disappeared almost completely. Text-books of good quality were published in sufficient number; terminologies began to be evolved and made current, and although lacking in uniformity and universal acceptance in all parts of India, they paved the way for the preparation of common terminologies for use in Indian languages; the teacher got gradually used to teaching in mother tongue and even subjects like algebra, geometry, physics, chemistry or botany began to be taught through the Indian languages. By 1974, therefore, it may be said that the mother tongue became the medium of instruction at the secondary stage and the only problem that was left unsolved was that of the medium of instruction at the University stage. (Naik and Nurullah, 1974: 372)

Krishnamurti himself adds:

> Following this model, we should have gone on to extend the regional language media to higher education soon after Independence, with the preparation of text-books and terminologies developing simultaneously with the use and spread of the regional language media. A second major debacle in our educational policy has been to extend the regional language media up to the undergraduate level and to continue the English medium at the postgraduate level. The switch from a regional language to English was much easier between the stages of secondary and collegiate education than it is between undergraduate and postgraduate levels.

He also emphasizes the need for the use of the mother tongue to improve the quality of Indian education, appropriately supplemented with the use of other languages playing complementary rather than conflicting roles. He advocates functional multilingualism, with proper institutionalization to enable improvement in the quality of Indian education, while promoting national integration. With reference to linguistic minorities, Krishnamurti suggests that at the outset some hard decisions have to be taken at the political level, striking a balance between cost-effective planning and the political will to improve the educational standards of linguistic minorities.

First, there must be a constitutional provision to recognize all the minority languages with 100,000 or more speakers as 'languages for mother tongue education'. This should first of all apply to speakers who are concentrated in geographically contiguous areas.

Second, education being a concurrent subject, the central government should take upon itself the responsibility for the development of the education of the 'stateless' linguistic minorities (whose languages are not the dominant regional languages or the official languages of states or union territories). The provision for teaching 14 first languages, each spoken by a few thousand people in Nagaland, is a pointer to the fact that where an infrastructure exists, people prefer to have education through their mother tongue. Also, newspapers are printed in minority languages even though these are not institutionally taught.

Third, the special Directive 350a introduced into the constitution (Government of India, 1950) in 1956 can have a schedule attached to it giving the list of 'minority languages', which have to be declared as languages for 'mother tongue education' The directive reads:

> It shall be the endeavour of every state and of every local authority within the state to provide adequate facilities for instruction in the mother tongue at the primary stage of education to children belonging to linguistic minority groups, and the president may issue such directions to any State as he considers necessary or proper for securing the provision of such facilities.

Fourth, a modern Indian language should be introduced as a third language on a compulsory basis in the Hindi-speaking states, preferably choosing from the literary Dravidian languages or the other modern Indo-Aryan languages.

- Incentives can be created by providing free schooling and scholarships to those who opt for the study of these languages.
- Central government employees posted to non-Hindi states may be given two advance increments if they have studied the language of the state as the third compulsory language of the school.
- Educational tours may be financed by state governments for students learning the compulsory third language with distinction, so that they can spend the summer vacation in a state where their third language is the dominant regional language.
- Translation of scientific and creative writings from non-Hindi languages into Hindi by native Hindi scholars may be suitably rewarded.

Fifth, state governments, business houses, railways, industrial undertakings and nationalized banks may be persuaded to transact business in the dominant regional languages of the states in which they are located. A cell in each enterprise may be created for interstate correspondence through English and Hindi. The employees of most of these undertakings happen to be residents of the region who must have already studied through the regional language media up to the highest level. We must follow the example of Japan in this respect. This policy will encourage the extension of the regional language media to the university level, since employment potential will naturally increase. Some major industries in Karnataka have introduced Kannada in their day-to-day functioning, with a consequent increase in efficiency.

## Conclusion

In education in the Indian multilingual context the process of language development is progressing at a very slow pace, because of the monistic policies of unstable governments, academies constrained by rigid guidelines, pressures from above and the shortcomings of those organizations assigned the job of producing textbooks.

Because the linguistic landscape of India is extremely complex, it appears that we have not paid attention to the language problems in education in proportion to their primacy and functional importance in the entire framework. The infrastructure and the instruments of implementation have not been properly prepared and coordinated. No 'modernization' of the curriculum in terms of content and time allocation will make much of an impact on education as long as clear policies are not evolved on the medium of instruction, and on the study of different languages in schools.

Given the complexity of the Indian linguistic landscape, there have never been coordinated efforts to approach language problems in education rationally, in proportion to their importance at all levels: regional, national and global. There needs to be a uniform approach in education policy, so that the same language is maintained as the medium of instruction in college as in school. The current need is for a clear policy using the pluralistic option to promote and utilize different languages in schools and as medium of instruction, assigning them appropriate roles to enable a proper dissemination of science, to make knowledge in every known discipline available in Indian languages – especially in higher education – and to keep pace with rapid global technological developments.

## References

Bandyopadhyay, D (2001) *Linguistic Terrorism*, Rabindra Bharathi University, Kolkata

Bernstein, B (1968) Some sociological determinants of perception: an inquiry into subcultural differences, in *Language Problems of Developing Nations*, eds J A Fishman, C A Ferguson and J Das Gupta, pp 223–39, John Wiley, New York

Choudhry, A (1981) Language attitudes of a linguistic minority in a regional area, *Osmania Papers in Linguistics*, **7** (8), pp 116–30

Choudhry, A (2001) Linguistic minorities in India, in *The Other Languages of Europe*, eds G Extra and D Gorter, Multilingual Matters, Clevedon, UK

Das Gupta, J (1970) *Language Conflict and National Development,*: University of California Press, Los Angeles and Berkeley

Dasgupta, P (1998) Teaching English as a second language in West Bengal's schools, in *Report of the One-Man Committee on English in Primary Education*, Government of West Bengal, Calcutta

Fasold, R (1990) *The Sociolinguistics of Society*, Basil Blackwell, Oxford

Ferguson, C A (1968) Language development, in *Language Problems of Developing Nations*, eds J A Fishman, C A Ferguson and J Das Gupta, pp 27–35, John Wiley, New York

Government of India (1931) *India Report*

Government of India (1950) *The Constitution of India*, Ministry of Law, New Delhi

Government of India (1956) *The Report of the Official Language Commission*

Government of India (1993) *Yash Pal Committee Report*, Ministry of Human Resource Development

Grierson, G A (1927) *Linguistic Survey of India*, vol I, part I, Registrar General of India, Calcutta

Haugen, E (1972) *The Ecology of Language: Essays selected by Anwar S. Dil*, Stanford University Press, Stanford, CA

Khubchandani, L M (1977) Language ideology and language development, *Linguistics*, **13**, pp 33–51

Khubchandani, L M (1985) Language modernization in the developing world, in Interaction through Language: Sociolinguistic research, cases and applications, vol 99, *International Social Science Journal*, **36** (1), pp 169–88

Khubchandani, L M (ed) (1988) *Language in a Plural Society*, Motilal Banarsidass, Delhi

Krishnamurti, Bh (1988) Standardization of Indian languages, in *Language in a Plural Society*, : Motilal Banarsidass, Delhi

Krishnamurti, Bh (1998) *Language Education and Society: Language and Development Series 7*, Sage Publications India, New Delhi

Naik, J P and Nurullah, S (1974) *A Student's History of Education in India 1800–1973*, 6th edn, Macmillan India, New Delhi

Sarkar, P (1998) *Report of the One-Man Committee on English in Primary Education*, Government of West Bengal, Calcutta

# 17. Language education in Brazil: a focus on raising attainment for all

Luiz Paulo Moita-Lopes

## Introduction

To try to discuss developments in language education in Brazil is a complex enterprise. The very size of the country poses enormous difficulties for this task, in the sense that it is impossible to account comprehensively for the huge range of language education contexts. To give some sense of all the areas involved, even, we would need to sample the range from the indigenous population schools in the rainforests to some very affluent schools in urban areas. We would need to cover contexts such as Portuguese as a mother tongue, English as a Foreign Language, German as a Second Language, Brazilian Indian languages, Spanish in bilingual contexts, Brazilian Sign Language, Portuguese as a Second Language and so on. One feature, however, would make this enterprise unique: few nations in the world share with Brazil such high levels of social inequality, and these are clearly mirrored in language education.

Brazil was the last country to free slaves in the 19th century, and it has faced many different economic crises, a military dictatorship for some 20 years during the so-called Cold War and a neo-liberal government recently. In the context of the globalization we are now experiencing, and to keep the economy going, like most Third World countries Brazil devotes huge efforts to following the prescriptions of the International Monetary Fund (IMF). As a result, investment in social projects such as education is kept to a minimum. This is particularly damaging for language education, if it is true that we live in a reflexive society in which discourse is crucial, as linguists, sociologists and social geographers claim (eg Chouliaraki and Fairclough, 1999; Giddens, Beck and Lash, 1995; Santos, 2000).

Quality education in the public sector has virtually disappeared at primary and secondary level in recent years, except for the federal schools, although most education at these levels is in the public sector. At the university level the Minister of Education has recently said in an interview with a major Brazilian newspaper (*Folha de São Paulo*, 22 October 2001) that little will be left of the public sector within a few years' time. Curiously enough, however, it is in the public sector that virtually all the research, including research in language education, and the best-quality graduate and postgraduate programmes in the country are situated.

Governmental statistics,[1] nevertheless, show that there has been an improvement in education at the primary level, which covers the 7- to 14-year-old age group in which education is compulsory, although Brazil is at a disadvantage in educational terms if compared with countries at a similar level of development (see Ministério da Educação, 1998a). In 1997, 91 per cent of the children in this age group were at school, as compared to 86 per cent in 1996. However, 2.7 million children in this age group were still not in school. Illiteracy levels are said to have dropped, although 15.6 per cent of children over 15 are still illiterate and the rates vary dramatically in different parts of the country: in the south-east (the richest part of the country) the proportion is lower than 5 per cent, but for this same age group it is more than 30 per cent in the north-east.

Teachers at both the primary and secondary levels usually have two or more jobs, spending more than 40 hours a week in class to make up for their poor salaries. Only in the more affluent private schools can teachers afford to live on a single school salary, although, according to the last census, 91 per cent of teachers at the primary school level have secondary education or a university degree (Ministério da Educação, 1998a: 35).

In general, what this picture shows is the need for investment in the quality of the work that goes on in classrooms – that is, investment in teacher education, as well as the need to raise teachers' salaries so that they can dedicate more time to their professional work. These two requirements imply massive high-quality investment in education, which is problematic because of governmental policies that have given priority to the economic security of the private sector (companies such as banks and airlines) rather than to social development. This situation is not very different from what is going on in other countries; however, the dramatically different effects of this system in countries that have the kind of social problems that Brazil has need hardly be emphasized.

This is the context in which I want to situate and discuss recent changes in language education in Brazil. The picture I have drawn above is rather bleak; I note, however, two kinds of developments that may point to a better future if more investment is put into education. The first are initiatives taken by the Ministry of Education and the second are the research efforts in language education, which have increased during the past 10 years.

This chapter centres on a review of the initiatives of the Ministry of Education, and in particular, of the Brazilian National Curriculum Guidelines for Portuguese mother tongue and for foreign language education. First, however, I will say a few words about what I also consider a positive action on the part of the Ministry of Education, namely the National Textbook Programme.

## The National Textbook Programme

The main objective of the National Textbook Programme is the purchasing and free distribution of textbooks to all public sector schools at the primary level (first to eighth grades) for the subjects Portuguese as a Mother Tongue (PMT), mathematics, history, geography and natural sciences. The programme was established in 1985, but it is only since 1996 that particular actions have been taken for the systematic evaluation of the textbooks before they are actually bought by the government.

What is of interest in the recent developments in the National Textbook Programme is the system used for taking decisions on which books to buy. The Ministry of Education has set up groups of PMT specialists to examine the textbooks according to particular criteria: underlying language and learning theories, methodological approaches, editorial quality, teachers' manual, discriminatory content on race, gender, age, etc. A Textbook Guide, containing the results of the analysis and a star rating for each textbook, is published by the Ministry and sent out to schools so that teachers can choose those that most closely fit their purposes, their schools' objectives and the cultural characteristics of their communities. This system has affected for the better the quality of the textbooks published in Brazil.

Foreign language (FL) textbooks are not included in this system, which puts the FL teacher at a great disadvantage. At a time when there is a tremendous need for FL learning in the world and for building cultural plurality, FL textbooks are not issued free to pupils in public sector schools. This is extremely serious, since most pupils in the public sector cannot afford textbooks, and textbooks are virtually the only teaching materials both teachers and pupils normally have access to. As a consequence, teachers have to rely entirely on their own teaching materials. Although foreign languages are in the curriculum in the public sector, they seem not to be given the same status, implying somehow that FL learning is only for the middle and upper classes who can afford private FL schools. These private FL schools, which mostly teach English and, more recently, Spanish, are found everywhere in the urban areas.

## Brazilian National Curriculum Guidelines for language education

National Curriculum Guidelines (NCGs) for all school subjects were written for the primary and secondary levels of education and published in 1997 and 1998. This was the first time that such a project had ever been attempted in Brazil, and the main objective was to influence each school subject from a national perspective.

Although, ultimately, what happens in each state school system, in each city educational system and in each school is left to these levels of educational organization to decide, the NCGs are offered as a national reference instrument that can inform these decisions. They are not compulsory and could in fact not be so even if this were desirable, since it would be impossible to write up a document that could adequately deal with the existing language teaching constraints in such a diverse country.

The writing of the documents involved an enormous number of participants from all educational levels. Besides the authors of the texts – in the case
of the areas of language education these were university specialists – the
NCGs were evaluated by national and international consultants and by
Brazilian teachers at all educational levels.

The documents for each subject share the same sort of structure. Each
contains 'a conceptualization of the area followed by a definition of general
objectives for the area, which express the capacities that pupils have to
develop throughout compulsory schooling' (Ministério da Educação, 1998a:
52). Other sections of the documents contain a conceptualization of learning
and teaching, contents to be covered, evaluation criteria and teaching guidelines.

The main general objectives for primary school education may be summarized as follows:

- the understanding of citizenship as social and political participation;
- the critical positioning of oneself in different social situations through
  dialogue;
- awareness of the main features of Brazil in the social, material and cultural
  domains;
- consciousness of the sociocultural plurality of Brazil as well as of other
  nations and peoples;
- positioning oneself against any kind of cultural, social class, religion,
  gender, ethnic and other discrimination;
- the use of different verbal, musical, mathematical, plastic and body
  languages;
- the use of different sources of information and technological resources; and
- the questioning of reality in order to transform it. (Ministério da Educação,
  1998a: 56)

These objectives are to be achieved by making evident in all areas of education
the social dimension of learning in the process of the construction of
citizenship.

There are two other issues that characterize the Guidelines and that are in
my view crucial in the documents. The first is their concern with making clear
throughout the reasons why something is being learnt; this has the twofold
objective of enhancing cognition through metacognitive awareness and of
enhancing responsibility towards learning. Second, the so-called interdisciplinary themes occupy a central place in the documents. These themes are
socially vital topics such as ethics, health, the environment, sexuality, cultural
plurality, work and consumerism, which, because of their relevance in
everyday life, need to be addressed across all areas in the curriculum and
treated in an interdisciplinary manner so that their complexity may be more
adequately taken account of. These themes also help to connect the local with
the global, given their international dimensions.

I will begin by examining the PMT Guidelines and will then offer an appraisal of the FL document. For reasons of space I will focus my analysis of the PMT Guidelines on the fifth grade to eighth grade document, which is actually a development of the principles set out in the document for grades 1–4. The documents are too complex for me to do full justice to them here, so I will concentrate my analysis on the view of language that permeates both documents.

## Portuguese as a Mother Tongue Guidelines

The area of PMT is crucial in school education since difficulties in reading comprehension and writing skills are seen as responsible for pupils' failure in other school subjects. It is argued that the proposals set out in the document are in line with recent developments in language education in which language use is the focus of the work to be done in classrooms, rather than the traditional prescription of grammatical rules, in the sense that language use is both where language teaching starts and what it aims at. It is nevertheless acknowledged that in Brazilian society as a whole there is still much concern with language correction and, as a consequence, language prejudice against the less prestigious varieties of Portuguese. A tremendous concern with the correction of these vernacular forms permeates schools. In contrast to this, the focus of language education in the PMT Guidelines is on: 1) 'active reading comprehension and listening skills, and not decodification skills and silence'; 2) 'effective interaction in speaking and writing and not the production of texts to be corrected'; and 3) 'metalinguistic skills that can help pupils use language adequately in particular contexts with clear interactional purposes', and not exercises for their own sake (Ministério da Educação, 1998b: 19).

The capacity to use language is equated with full social participation, which is essential in the exercise of citizenship: pupils in the eight years of compulsory education need to learn to understand the variety of text-types that are used in society, and to be able to use language both orally and in the written mode. To do that, learners need to get involved with discourse under particular discursive conditions in which otherness and historical context are crucial. That is to say, 'when people interact with each other, they organize discourse on the basis of their objectives and intentions, of the types of knowledge and opinions they believe the interlocutor possesses, and of how they are socially and hierarchically related to their interlocutor' (Ministério da Educação, 1998b: 21). These issues will then inform the genres and linguistic structural choices that organize discourse.

When people use language, they do so by means of texts that relate to other, previously produced texts through intertextual relations and within genre restrictions. It is understood of course that there are restrictions on the production of discourses, and that genres are historically generated forms that are differentially available. It is clear, therefore, that the general theoretical framework is mainly inspired by Bakhtin (1929/1981, 1979/1992) and the Genevan sociohistorical view of discourse deriving from Bronckart (1985), Schnewly (1993) and others.

In view of this theoretical perspective the basic teaching unit is the text, which is organized according to particular thematic, compositional and stylistic constraints that in their turn characterize the particular genres. Accordingly, genres are to be considered as the objectives of teaching, in particular those that are typical of public oral and written modes of language use. Contrary to what has been normally aimed at in PMT teaching in Brazil, oral uses of language are also to be emphasized: learners need to learn how to use oral language in public contexts outside schools – that is, in other institutions, in professional tasks, in fighting for rights and points of views, etc. As regards written language, it is argued that since the only systematic access that most children and youngsters in Brazil have to written language is at school, it is essential that they be exposed to the variety of texts that characterize social practices, preferably the most frequently used genres, such as news, editorials, letters, encyclopaedia entries and literary texts. It is clear that in both oral and written uses preference is given to publicly used genres.

Tasks involving thinking about language are to be included to serve listening, reading, speaking and writing skills. This is quite a change from traditional PMT teaching in Brazil, which has emphasized metalinguistic exercises in which the so-called standard uses of written language grammatical rules are taught. Grammar teaching is to be included, but not to help pupils perform in language tests; its inclusion focuses on what learners need to learn to fulfil particular writing, listening, speaking and reading tasks. As part of the metalinguistic tasks, the document encourages language choices to be defined by the conditions of discourse production and genres as well as language use, planning and editing procedures. These tasks aim at making it possible for pupils to generalize about how their communities use language and about the nature of the texts they listen to, write and read. This feature seems to be related to what is usually referred to in the literature as the need for language teaching to develop 'language awareness'. Note, however, that the PMT Guidelines have no explicit concern with the development of what is known as 'critical language awareness' – that is, awareness of how people make particular choices within the language system according to who the interlocutors are and of how they are positioned in society. The document does refer to linguistic choice, to otherness and contexts of production, but there is no explicit concern with how language use is sociopolitically defined.

The last two points I want to deal with in this section relate to how language variation and the interdisciplinary themes are dealt with in these Guidelines. Language variation is presented as being constitutive of human languages no matter how much normative efforts are made. It is argued too that the idea that there exists only one variety of Portuguese, similar to the written language, does not stand up to any empirical analysis of language use. The Guidelines critique the view common in Brazil that 'nobody speaks correct Portuguese'. It is argued that the learning of written language – what is called 'standard Portuguese' – as the objective of school language learning is justifiable 'since there is no sense in asking students to learn what they already know' – that is, oral language (Ministério da Educação, 1998b: 30). However, it is suggested that schools need to get rid of a lot of language myths that are influential in Brazil – for example, that Portuguese is a difficult language, that a particular regional variety is better than other varieties, that teachers need to correct pupils' oral Portuguese so that they write it correctly. Instead, it is suggested that pupils need to be made aware that correctness is not the issue, but rather learning to use language that is appropriate to particular circumstances of use.

The document can be criticized for its lack of concern with a more sociopolitical view of language use. Presenting a range of varieties of language in class-conscious Brazilian society as equally acceptable is not enough for teachers and pupils to understand the reason why 'standard Portuguese' has to be learnt. It is necessary in my view to make clear in language education that the superiority of a particular variety is determined by social class power, which implies that the varieties most children in Brazil come to school with are inferior. In other words, social class oppression is the issue, which is not mentioned in the document at all.

The Interdisciplinary Themes are incorporated into language teaching in terms of topics that can be dealt with in classrooms and in terms of how particular lexical items chosen by language users are related to particular themes. Nevertheless, the articulation of this with the theory of language use that underlies the document is not very clear – as in the FL Guidelines discussed below. It is odd too that the document argues that some themes are more easily incorporated into language teaching than others: I would have thought that in language teaching any of the given themes could be dealt with. It is a question related to what we use language for in classrooms.

## Foreign Language Guidelines

FL Guidelines were written for the last four years of primary school, since such languages are included in the curriculum in Brazil from the fifth grade onwards. These inform in their turn the Guidelines for secondary education. The main concern of the document is with restoring the place of FL education in the school curriculum since, as discussed earlier, there is a general belief in the country that FL learning is only possible in private language school contexts.

The conditions prevailing in the private language schools – small classes, good technical equipment, imported textbooks, etc – are obviously not found in the schools in the public sector. However, from 1996, FL learning has also been compulsory in publicly funded schools from the fifth grade. The main objective of the FL Guidelines is to enhance pupils' perceptions of themselves as human beings and citizens, because by helping them to understand others and their otherness, FL learning helps pupils to learn about themselves by being exposed to a plurality of cultural values and different ways of organizing sociopolitical life. To make that happen, FL education has to aim at discourse engagement, in the sense that languages have to be learnt to provide pupils with ways of acting in the social context in which they are participants. FL learning is an instrument of social action in that it may help pupils to improve the conditions under which they live. Teaching therefore has to centre on pedagogic tasks that help the construction of pupils as discourse subjects, which is related to developing their ability to act on the circumstances in which they live through the use of communicative skills.

The crucial question is not the learning of a foreign language for pupils to do something with it in the future when needed; what is at issue is the learning of a foreign language for them to do something with it now, in the sense that it should help them to get through life in the social context in which they live. This has to be made possible by engaging pupils in foreign language learning through the use of at least one communicative skill – reading comprehension, for example. What is central is the engagement with meaning construction processes, which may in the future develop into other communicative skills if needed.

Another crucial aspect of the Guidelines is the concern with socially justifying the inclusion of a foreign language in the curriculum, and this directly relates to what most people in the country need a foreign language for. In general, this seems to be related to using it in reading comprehension: except for Spanish along the national borders, a few immigrant languages (eg German, Polish, Italian) and Brazilian Indian communities, the use of foreign languages orally is rare. Formal foreign language exams (graduate and post-graduate university entrance exams) only require command of reading comprehension skills. Furthermore, existing classroom constraints in the school system may make the learning of the so-called four communicative language skills virtually impossible. It is nevertheless suggested that when existing conditions allow the teaching of other skills, this should be done. What is at issue is providing an FL experience that is meaningful for learners in the sense that they get involved with meaning construction processes in the context in which they live. This suggestion of minimally focusing on reading comprehension has, however, been very strongly criticized in Brazil because the Guidelines seem to limit the possibilities for FL development rather than promoting access to FL learning in the school system.

What criteria should define the foreign language to be included in the curriculum? While it is desirable to have a policy that implements FL diversity in the curriculum, it is argued that economic pragmatism very often determines the need to select only one foreign language. The document lists criteria to be considered when deciding which FL to include: historical factors (which FL(s) is/are historically and sociopolitically relevant at a particular time in terms of the role that these languages play in international interaction), immigrant and local community factors, and factors related to traditional cultural relations. These factors are for the school community to consider when choosing the foreign language.

The Guidelines, however, explicitly draw attention to the need to consider the sociopolitical role that English plays nowadays as a hegemonic foreign language in most parts of the world, when the school system is selecting a foreign language to include in the curriculum. They also indicate that critical awareness of these factors should be considered as part of FL education. This is particularly relevant in a country that during the Cold War was subject to US imperialism and is still dominated by US multinationals and the IMF. The economic and cultural agreements in the context of Mercosul (the South American Common Market) have boosted the presence of Spanish in the school curriculum, although it is still very limited compared with English. This may in the long run help to counter the hegemony of English in Brazil.

The FL Guidelines follow a socio-interactional view of language, in the sense that language use is presented as dialogic, and is institutionally, culturally and historically situated. This implies that in meaning construction participants are acting on the construction of the social world on the basis of their social identities. When we use language, we do so as poor or rich, black or white, men or women, homosexual or heterosexual, speakers of stigmatized or prestigious language varieties, etc. The exercise of power, and resistance to it, are inherent in language use, so it is suggested that the critical awareness of these processes in language education is crucial in building a more democratic society. The Guidelines point to the need to incorporate both language awareness and critical language awareness into FL teaching. The theoretical underpinnings in these Guidelines, therefore, are mainly informed by the work of Bakhtin (1929/1981) and of Fairclough (1989, 1992a, b).

This view of language use, which clearly links discourse and the construction of social life, offers a way of theoretically articulating the Interdisciplinary Themes with FL teaching. It is pointed out that the analysis of written and oral interaction practices in FL classrooms is a useful way to focus on these themes by drawing attention to the linguistic choices participants make to act on the social world through language. These choices may be looked at from the perspective of the themes that are evident in these practices as well as of the systemic (the language varieties that are included) and textual organization choices discourse participants make in the light of who their interlocutors are, of where they are using language, when, why and so on.

These choices are to be compared with similar choices other participants in similar discursive practices in PMT and in FL use would make. This also offers a way of interculturally comparing meanings constructed in different languages. A special section on the theme of cultural plurality is presented and it is recommended that FL teaching should be used to deconstruct essentializing views of specific cultures, which are typical of FL classrooms, by drawing attention to the heterogeneous nature of cultures as sites of conflict. This, it is suggested, can also be used as a way of deconstructing stereotypical views of Brazilian-ness by bringing into focus the cultural complexity of Brazil too.

## A final word

Both the PMT Guidelines and the FL Guidelines include a body of knowledge that may be useful in informing decisions in the schools, notwithstanding the criticisms levelled at the documents above. However, their actual usefulness has still to be demonstrated. The main difficulty has to do with how the teacher in the classroom can make use of them, since so far there has been no investment in teacher education that could involve teachers in reflexive appraisals of the documents. To be fair, however, the National Guidelines themselves have made clear that only through policies that, on the one hand, improve teachers' salaries and, on the other, massively invest in both in-service and pre-service teacher education programmes, can the recommendations in the documents be in any sense realized (Ministério da Educação, 1998a: 38; 1998c: 109).

Language teacher education, one of the most frequent research topics in language education in Brazil, is the cornerstone of improvements in this area. It does not matter how excellent the National Textbook Programme, or the National Language Curriculum Guidelines, or the research projects in the universities are, if there is no serious investment in language teacher education in the public sector. This depends on policy decisions about where money in the country is invested, and in a country where less than 12 per cent of school-age students are in the private sector, these are policies that affect the immediate future of the whole country. Brazil simply cannot meet these pressing demands if more than 88 per cent of the school-age population is excluded from adequate education. And language education is crucial in this enterprise.

## Notes

I am grateful to Marlene Soares dos Santos for her comments and suggestions on a first version of this chapter.

1. The source here is the Brazilian Institute of Geography and Statistics (IBGE) and Ministry of Education (MEC) as presented in the Brazilian National Curriculum Guidelines, fifth to eighth grades (Ministério da Educação, 1998a: 24–35, 103, 115.

# References

Bakhtin, M (1929/1981) *Marxismo e filosofia da linguagem* (Marxism and the philosophy of language), Hucitec, São Paulo

Bakhtin, M (1979/1992) *Estética da criação verbal* (The aesthetics of verbal creation), Martins Fontes, São Paulo

Bronckart, J P (1985) *Le Fonctionnement des discours: un modèle psychologique et une méthode d'analyse* (The functioning of discourse: a psychological model and a method of analysis), Delachaux & Niestlé, Neuchâtel and Paris

Chouliaraki, L and Fairclough, N (1999) *Discourse in Late Modernity*, Edinburgh University Press, Edinburgh

Fairclough, N (1989) *Language and Power*, Longman, London

Fairclough, N (ed) (1992a) *Critical Language Awareness*, Longman, London

Fairclough, N (1992b) *Discourse and Social Change*, Polity Press, Cambridge

Giddens, A, Beck, U and Lash, S (1995) *Modernização reflexiva: política, tradição e estética na ordem social moderna* (Reflexive modernization: politics, tradition and aesthetics in the modern social order), Editora da UNESP, São Paulo

Ministério da Educação (1998a) Parâmetros Curriculares Nacionais, introdução, 5ª a 8ª séries (National Curriculum Guidelines, introduction, fifth to eighth grades), Brasília

Ministério da Educação (1998b) Parâmetros Curriculares Nacionais, língua portuguesa, 5ª a 8ª séries (National Curriculum Guidelines, Portuguese as a Mother Tongue, fifth to eighth grades), Brasília

Ministério da Educação (1998c) Parâmetros Curriculares Nacionais, língua estrangeira, 5ª a 8ª séries (National Curriculum Guidelines, foreign languages, fifth to eighth grades), Brasília

Santos, M (2000) *Por uma outra globalização* (A plea for another globalization), Record, Rio de Janeiro

Schnewly, B (1993) *Genres et types de discours: considérations psychologiques et ontogenétiques. Les Interactions lecture–écriture* (Genres and types of discourses: psychological and ontogenetic considerations. Interactions between reading and writing), Peter Lang, Geneva

# Part III
# City case studies

# 18. Hamburg

Ingrid Gogolin

## Introduction

Hamburg is the second largest German city, situated in the north of the country with 1.7 million inhabitants. It traditionally considers itself a liberal, hospitable, broad-minded town, and the official city motto reads, 'Hamburg – gateway to the world'. Because of its port, and its tradition of worldwide trade, Hamburg has always been a multilingual, pluricultural place, and the first part of this chapter presents some impressions of the kind of linguistic and cultural diversity that is to be found in Hamburg today.

In terms of hard data the question of what exactly linguistic diversity means nowadays is a long way from being fully answered. The next section explains the problem of presenting reliable data concerning the linguistic reality in Germany, although in this respect Hamburg is an exception in Germany, as it is the only German city where accurate figures about the number of home languages of primary school children are available.

The third section presents, first, the legal and administrative framework for the response of German schools to linguistic and cultural diversity among their pupils, and then the situation in Hamburg. The final section deals with the question of why immigrant children do not achieve more in the German school system: after more than 40 years of immigration, equal opportunities for immigrant children are still a long way off in Germany, as is very clearly shown by the results of PISA 2000 (see OECD, 2001). Some reflections on the question of how language education contributes to these results are offered.

## Linguistic and cultural change in German cities

Imagine we take a walk through the inner city of Hamburg and visit an average Hamburg school. We start our walk at the university campus, just opposite *Dammtor Bahnhof*, one of the three major railway stations of the city, and walk east. After crossing a park, which is on the site of the old town wall, and passing a big television tower, we reach an area called *Schanzenviertel*. The streets are getting narrower now. We pass the old slaughterhouse, *Schlachthof*, late 19th-century red-brick buildings. Originally the *Schlachthof* was a huge meat factory that supplied the whole north of Germany with meat products of all kinds. After it went bankrupt a few years ago, the buildings were transformed into spaces for cultural events, art galleries, lofts and expensive apartments, bars and restaurants.

Although gentrification is obvious here, the surrounding streets still show that we are walking through a former industrial, working-class area. Most of the houses were built at the beginning of the 20th century: five-storey buildings with neo-baroque fronts, some recently redecorated, but many of them pockmarked, the paint flaking off, the balconies about to collapse. The pavements are narrow with not many places for children to play. The children's space is in the back yards, and most of the buildings have two or more houses behind them. Many of the buildings show traces of the former industrialized area: workshops, small plants, loading ramps and ancillary industry for the *Schlachthof*. Today this business has been replaced by fancy restaurants and modest snack bars, tailor's workshops and greengrocers, hairdresser's shops, video-tape libraries and telephone shops offering cheap international phone calls. Some years ago many of the old houses were occupied by young radicals: at first students, later punks and other 'alternative' groups. An old music hall is still occupied today, the occupation condoned by the city and the owners. We can easily recognize these houses when we pass: they are painted in garish colours, the pirate flag flutters from the windows, and banners testify to the political opinions of the inhabitants.

As we walk through the district we see and hear linguistic and cultural diversity everywhere. Graffiti tell us, 'Beşiktas [a famous Turkish soccer club] ist [is] best of the world'– three languages in one sentence. Shop signs have names in Turkish, Greek, Chinese; the menus at restaurants use non-Roman scripts; the products are named in many languages – and in some cases, German is not one of them. We pass a hairdresser's with a special offer for Afro hairstyles; the music we hear through the open doors of the greengrocer's shop sounds North African; some windows are decorated with talismans against the evil eye. The people busily passing by talk to each other in German and many other languages, of which we can identify only a few.

The district we are walking through is not at all exceptional, but typical of many parts of Hamburg as well as of other big cities all over the world. Traditionally, urban areas attract difference; in fact, the existence of cities is a direct consequence of this attraction, and an important manifestation of this is that cities are the main targets of immigration from abroad. Although this is not new, the speed and dynamics of the demographic changes in urban areas as a result of immigration have increased tremendously in the past decade, and districts like the *Schanzenviertel* are a microcosm of this development. Here, more than a third of all the inhabitants, and roughly half of the children, hold a non-German passport. Richard Sennett (1998) suggests that most people will, sooner or later, live in areas where this kind of 'culture of difference' is dominant in everyday life.

Meanwhile, we have arrived at our school. The building has a white-painted front, four storeys high, originally with separate entrances for girls and boys. Today everybody enters through the boys' door. The school was built in the 1920s, and at that time roughly 1,000 children were taught here. Today, because of the drop in birthrates and other factors, no more than 200 children attend the school, so there is plenty of room for them. In demographic terms the children are a perfect reflection of the area. Roughly 50 per cent of them hold German passports, and the other half are of about 15 different nationalities; more than 20 different languages besides German are spoken. In the course of a research project in this school a few years ago (see Gogolin and Neumann, 1997), we audio-taped the following exchanges among three girls in a third-grade classroom:

Cynthia:   *Wollen wir uns morgen treffen?* (Shall we meet tomorrow?)

Sonja:     Ja. (yes)

Cynthia:   *Wann?* (When?)

Sonja:     Weiß nicht. (Don't know)

Cynthia:   *Um zwei?* (At two?)

Sonja:     Ja, ist gut. (Okay)

Cynthia:   *Soll ich bei Dir klingeln oder kommst Du raus?* (Shall I come to your house or will you come out?)

Sonja:     Ich komm raus (I'll come out). Támbén queres ir? (Will you come too?)

Carla:     *Eu só posso ir as três.* (I can't come before three)

Cynthia:   Está bem. (Okay)

This is a typical children's dialogue: as our data show, in informal situations, mixtures of German and many other languages are frequently used. The three girls here are a classic example of children growing up nowadays in urban areas in Germany. Cynthia was born and grew up in Hamburg: her family language is German because, although her father came from Argentina, he did not actively introduce his daughter to his mother tongue. Instead, Cynthia learnt to understand quite a lot of Portuguese in the home of her best friend Sonja, who was also born and grew up in Hamburg. Sonja holds a Portuguese passport, and – as for all the other members of her family – Portuguese is the most important means of communication, but German is also frequently used, especially by the children. Three afternoons a week Sonja visits a Portuguese class organized by the Portuguese consulate, so she is literate not only in German but also in Portuguese.

Carla, the third speaker, had been in Hamburg for less than a year when we made the tape. Her mother was born in Portugal, but grew up in Germany as a 'guest-worker's' daughter. When she was a teenager, her family went back to Portugal. Roughly 10 years later, now a mother of two children herself, she returned to Hamburg, where the family now plans to live for an indefinite period. This is an example of the increasingly common phenomenon of 'trans-migration' (see Pries 1997, 2000; Kivisto, 2001): the migration process is left unfinished, links to the former home country as well as to other migrants from there living in other parts of the world are actively cultivated, and social networks are created within which the language of origin is the best, if not the only, means of communication. These practices do not show the 'segrega-tionist' tendencies of the immigrants, but can be interpreted as the other side of the coin of modern integration processes: the dissolution of past and present into a newer, more mobile lifestyle.

Because of these developments, among other factors, the vitality of immi-grant languages in Europe is significant (Extra and Gorter, 2001). Thus, not only does new immigration promote linguistic and cultural diversity in European urban areas, it also promotes the growing practice of transmi-gration. And, as was shown in the little dialogue of Cynthia, Sonja and Carla above, linguistic and cultural diversity in their everyday life is an important aspect of the socialization of all children in urban areas today – including those who grow up in monolingual families.

## Demographic and sociolinguistic debates

The following section will briefly contextualize the *Schanzenviertel* and provide some more general data. Millions of people living in Germany now, many of them not German citizens, use one or more language(s) other than German in their everyday life. Yet no reliable statistical data about this were available until 2001; neither the number of speakers of other languages nor the range of languages spoken by them.

The lack of official data concerning the other languages of Germany is the result of the traditional concept that the German nation-state is a monolingual country, and not a country of immigration. Even the debate over new legis-lation concerning immigration which started in 1998 avoids the term *Einwanderung* (immigration). Instead, the term *Zuwanderung* (incomers) is used, which until that time had been unusual in German terminology. This indicates that it is still taboo to think of Germany as an immigration country.

Thus, official data are only available on non-German residents, and such data cannot be used to make statements about linguistic plurality in Germany, for two reasons. First, of course, the equation of state and language is untenable; and second, a growing number of people of immigrant back-ground in Germany have German citizenship.

These 'immigrant Germans' are a combination of two main groups. First, there are the *Aussiedler*, whose ancestors emigrated from Germany, in many cases centuries ago, but who were entitled to 'remigrate' if they were able to prove their German line of ancestry. Most of them – there were roughly 4 million between 1945 and 2000 – come from Eastern Europe, especially the former Soviet Union. Second, there are growing numbers of immigrants with German passports acquired via naturalization. As a result of the change in citizenship legislation that took effect in January 2000, these numbers will grow tremendously, because children of immigrant families who have been born in Germany since then can, under certain conditions, automatically acquire German citizenship if their parents so choose. All these Germans of immigrant background are simply not visible in the official data, so that information about the sociolinguistic situation in Germany today has to be based more on guesswork than on secure knowledge.

The proportion of 'foreigners' living in Germany grew from 1.2 per cent in 1960 to roughly 10 per cent in 2000, a total then of about 7.35 million people, from more than 100 states of origin. About 25 per cent of these are citizens of other European Union member states, and another 30 per cent or so are Turkish citizens. These 7 million people are distributed unevenly across the country: 5–15 per cent in the former Western *Länder*, no more than 2.5 per cent in the Eastern *Länder*. Most live in urban areas, and they constitute more than 30 per cent of the total population of Frankfurt am Main, for example.

The vast majority of children with foreign passports attending German schools were born or grew up in Germany, and by 2000 roughly 1.2 million pupils with non-German passports were enrolled in the state school system, about 10 per cent of the total. These were differentially distributed across the different secondary school types: whereas more than 30 per cent of pupils with German passports finish their school career in a gymnasium – gymnasia being the academically most prestigious schools, those that give access to university studies – fewer than 10 per cent of 'foreign' pupils' do so.

## Language education policy and practice: the national framework

Germany is a federal state in which the 16 *Länder* have cultural, including educational, autonomy at school level, coordinated by the Conference of Ministers of Education (CME or, in German, KMK). This body in 1964 decreed that the children of families who had migrated officially should be admitted to German state schools. The main countries involved at that time were Greece, Italy, Yugoslavia, Portugal, Spain, Turkey and the Maghreb countries; later other countries were added.

The CME recommendations said that foreign children in Germany should in principle receive the same educational opportunities as German children. Reception classes were set up to introduce pupils to the German language and school curriculum, and later to integrate them into 'regular' classes. If it was considered to contribute to equal opportunities, teaching of the languages of origin could also be provided. Whereas originally this option was only open for 'guest-workers' children' – that is, children from the above-named states of origin – recently this provision was extended to the languages of other immigrant groups. According to the CME's recommendations, this 'mother tongue teaching' is aimed at contributing to the social integration of the pupils 'for the duration of their stay in the Federal Republic of Germany' and at the same time at helping them 'preserve their linguistic and cultural identity'. The underlying agenda of these recommendations was, like policies in other EU countries, an 'assimilation or rotation perspective': the immigrants should either adapt fully to the host country's language, or return to their country of origin.

Most of this 'mother tongue teaching' has to take place outside the regular curriculum and school day, and should not exceed five lessons a week. Some *Länder* offer the pupils 'mother tongue teaching' instead of the first or second obligatory foreign language (usually English or French). This would imply a severe limitation of potential school success for a child, since a pupil who accepts this offer would either be excluded from the highest qualification or obliged to learn additional foreign languages later.

Within this framework two types of immigrant minority language teaching were developed until 1989 in the old West Germany. In five of the *Länder* this teaching took place under the supervision of the *Land* itself; in the remaining areas the teaching was placed in the hands of the countries of origin, and in these *Länder* the regional governments contributed mostly by providing free classroom accommodation. Apart from these official measures, plenty of unofficial mother tongue teaching happens.

## Hamburg: demographic information

Of the 1.7 million inhabitants of Hamburg, about 16 per cent have non-German passports, with the proportion in Hamburg schools more than doubling in 20 years to around 20.5 per cent in 2000 – a total of around 33,500 students. In addition, probably about 6,000 children had an immigrant background but a German passport. A recent study shows that 20.2 per cent of all grade 9 children in Hamburg schools are not German citizens. For 28.4 per cent of them, German is not their mother tongue, and 33.6 per cent speak a language other than German at home (Freie und Hansestadt Hamburg, 2002: 36).

By 2000 only four schools in the public school system in Hamburg had no 'foreigners' among their school population (Büchel and Bühler-Otten, 2000). Nearly 40 per cent of the 'foreign' children have passports from Turkey, with other large groups coming from former Yugoslavia, Iran, Poland, Albania and EU member states. Up to 80 other nationalities are represented. According to data collected since 1996 by the *Land*'s education ministry, some 90 languages are spoken by Hamburg schoolchildren, the largest groups in 2000 being Turkish (about 10,800 speakers), Russian (about 4,500 speakers), Polish and Farsi (about 2,300 speakers each), and Dari (about 1,900 speakers). More detailed and reliable surveys carried out among primary schools suggest that as many as 120 languages in addition to German may be spoken.

## Rhetoric and practice

Hamburg, with its long social democratic tradition, has traditionally fostered a strong policy of integration and equal opportunity for immigrant children in the regular school system. At first this was implemented using the principle of 'fairness'. Apart from there being different forms of reception classes for newcomers and some extra teaching resources allocated to schools with large numbers of immigrant children, they were treated in the same way as non-immigrants, with attempts made to teach German as a Second Language (GSL) only in reception classes or through extra support for children in regular classes. In the ordinary system, no GSL teaching was established, even if the majority of children in a school had an immigrant background.

The teaching of minority languages was at first not considered to be a task of the school system, and only in response to the EEC guidelines of 1977 (*Richtlinie 77/486/EWG* on the schooling of guest-workers' children) did Hamburg allow the countries of origin to establish classes for mother tongue teaching, with the respective consulates responsible for provision of teachers. In 1996, 104 classes for mother tongue teaching of this type existed, with 87 consulate teachers. The policy was heavily criticized by the political representatives of immigrant communities as well as by academic experts, and in response to this criticism a measure to help children of Turkish origin was established in 1986. To 'safeguard their linguistic and cultural identity' (Freie und Hansestadt Hamburg, 1986) the children were offered a maximum of five mother tongue lessons a week. In reality, these courses were offered mainly to Turkish children. For them, two of the language lessons a week were given over to Turkish-medium Islamic religious instruction.

The criticism of language education policy did not stop after the introduction of this new measure. In fact, it was now argued that Hamburg had created an additional inequality for immigrant children, one that offended the general principles of democratic education systems. But it took a decade for the arguments to be addressed politically.

In 1997 the preamble to the new school law stated:

> Because of their ethnic and cultural identity, children and young people whose first language is not German have to be supported in such a way that they can develop their bilingualism so that they can actively participate in the learning process, as well as in school life more generally. (*Hamburgisches Schulgesetz*, 1997, translated by the present author)

Hamburg's government, which from 1998 to 2001 consisted of a Social Democrat–Green Party coalition, started to put this into action by establishing a range of new measures, the most relevant of which was the intention to take over responsibility for all teaching of immigrant minority languages. Hamburg still allowed foreign consulates to make their contributions and cooperated with those who did so, but the *Land* started establishing a procedure to make itself responsible for this teaching, if necessary together with the countries of origin.

There were several measures taken to raise the legitimacy and public esteem of mother tongue teaching (see Neumann and Häberlein, 2001). As a first step, from 1999 the teaching was allowed in principle to take place within regular school hours, at least in primary schools. It was planned to extend this regulation also to secondary schools. Furthermore, it was declared that as a rule the teachers should be appointed and paid by the *Land*. However, most of the teachers were not to be regularly employed, but to work for hourly fees. In addition, the *Land* was willing to take over the inspection even in those cases where the consulates insisted on carrying on with their own classes.

In order to put the new policy into practice, an action programme was established on the following basis. Wherever possible, primary schools were encouraged to integrate the courses into the regular school day as part of the normal timetable. The opportunity for children to take part in this teaching was no longer dependent on citizenship of the country of origin. As a symbol of the growing official recognition of such teaching and of the pupils' bilingualism, the marks they received in their mother tongue classes were now to be mentioned in their regular school reports.

The number of languages taught in this framework since 1999 was extended beyond Turkish. In 2001, 13 languages were taught within this framework, including Albanian, Kurdish, Dari, Farsi, Romany and Russian. It was also planned to take over the teaching of other languages, such as Italian and Portuguese, from the respective consulates. Of course, the number of classes available means that only a fraction of children from bilingual families have any chance to participate. In 2001, about 5,200 children took part in these language lessons, and 96 teachers worked in this framework. Obviously there will remain a large number of languages in which no teaching at all will be offered by the *Land*.

To alleviate this injustice for the pupils a system of examinations in immigrant minority languages was established. This measure aimed at providing the chance for those who do not have access to mother tongue teaching within the Hamburg school system to receive officially recognized credits for their performance in out-of-school courses. There is no reliable information available about the number of such courses, the number of languages taught, the different bodies responsible or the financing of the courses. Many of them are private initiatives not supported by either a German official institution or one from the country of origin, but the number of languages in which these examinations can be passed is limited, since examiners are not always available.

In order to raise the quality of the teaching in these classes, several measures were taken, including in-service training courses. Most of the teachers were well-educated native speakers of the respective languages, but they were not necessarily qualified as teachers, nor familiar with the special needs of teaching an immigrant minority language in a multilingual context. The in-service courses were intended to introduce knowledge about language learning and about bilingualism, especially in immigrant situations; information about the school system in Hamburg and about the regular curriculum; an introduction to language teaching methodology; and, last not least, exercises about strategies for cooperating with the other teachers in a school.

Another field of activity is the development of a syllabus for mother tongue teaching in multilingual contexts. A specific feature of this syllabus is that it is not limited to certain languages, but designed as a framework for the teaching of minority languages as a whole. The reason for the development of such a conceptual framework was that mother tongue teaching was considered to be an element of 'intercultural education', which is accepted as a general goal for education in Hamburg schools. With this in mind, the teaching of immigrant minority languages is meant to aim at language awareness and reflexiveness about linguistic and cultural diversity in German society, just as the teaching of German or of other modern foreign languages should do. Additionally, mother tongue teaching is intended to support the children's bilingual competences and respect their bilingualism as a regular condition for overall learning. Consequently, the teaching goals do not include a national perspective of the countries of origin.

Some additional model projects were introduced in recent years, all aiming at a positive valuing of immigrant children's family languages and of their bilingualism. Two examples follow.

## Bilingual primary schools

All primary schools in Hamburg now have to teach English as a first foreign language beginning in Year 3. But as well as this, the *Land* in 1999 established a model project for primary schools with programmes in languages other than English, in effect starting a form of bilingual education in Year 1. The project started with one school, where German with Italian was offered, and since 2000 other schools have offered German with Portuguese and German with Spanish. From 2003 the programme was to be expanded to other schools and other languages, especially Turkish and Russian. The project is carried out in cooperation with the relevant consulates, which contribute to the programme by providing the teachers for the languages other than German (Gogolin, Neumann and Roth, 2001).

These bilingual schools start the teaching of both languages on the first school day, with the aim of producing coordinated bilingual literacy. The basic principle of school organization, following US and Canadian models, is that

50 per cent of those taking part are expected to speak the language other than German, which is also taught as a mother tongue. All the children take part in reading and writing courses in both languages, but the first steps in literacy have to be undertaken in the dominant language of each child. The syllabuses of both literacy processes are expected to be carefully adjusted to each other, and throughout the four years of primary schooling, subjects other than 'language' are gradually introduced in the language other than German. The children are expected to learn a second language more efficiently if it is taught through particular subject matter (see overview in Reich, Roth *et al*, 2001).

It is far too early for claims about the success of these experiments. In fact, the principle of organization, 50:50 monolingual and bilingual children, could not be realized in exactly the way intended. This is not surprising, since the schools certainly attracted families whose language was taught along with German, but it was not possible to exclude children with a bilingual background different from that. Therefore all the bilingual classes are in fact composed of linguistically mixed populations, in each case with a small excess of the language other than German which is being taught. First evaluations of the language development taking place in these classes showed an unexpected result, since it turned out that those children who had a bilingual background, but a family language different from the one actually being taught, made the best progress in the acquisition of both German and the second language (Gogolin, Neumann and Roth, 2001).

## The languages portfolio

The 'languages portfolio' was an initiative of the Council of Europe. It was created in response to the rising cultural and linguistic diversity in Europe, taking account of the fact that the role of the school system is changing as a consequence of this situation. Whereas traditionally the school was considered to be the exclusive site for the creation of bilingualism or multilingualism, it now has to be accepted that much of the language experience of children is a result not of teaching but of the social contexts of their lives, and not only in places like *Schanzenviertel*. In order to give official recognition to all the language experience and skills of children, tools other than traditional school reports have to be invented. The languages portfolio, initiated by the Council of Europe, is such a tool (see http://www.culture2coe.int/portfolio). It encourages the pupils, in cooperation with their teachers, to observe their developing language proficiency and describe the levels of their competences in a sophisticated manner. These documents receive an official validation by the school in which they are used; thus a pupil may profit from them, for example, when he or she starts applying for professional training.

Hamburg contributed to the further development of the languages portfolio, and designed its own version with special reference to linguistic diversity in the city. The portfolio was officially introduced in secondary schools in 2000; a version for primary school is in development. This is undoubtedly an improvement in Hamburg's language education policy, but unfortunately is only a half-measure: schools and children are not obliged to use the languages portfolio as an official part of school reports. So although this instrument is regarded as useful and interesting for both teachers and children, it is not accepted as a legitimate tool for the evaluation of children's abilities.

Considering the recent decisions and measures planned or already established, Hamburg is one example of a possible change in basic political attitudes towards multilingualism in the German *Länder*. At least some parts of the political spectrum are beginning to realize that linguistic and cultural diversity in German society is an undeniable fact, and that it is unwise to react to this fact only in a negative way. The new discourse on immigrant minority languages conforms closely with recent recommendations of the CME about intercultural education (KMK, 1996). It is stated there that immigrant minority languages represent a positive gain for German society as a whole, and for its schools, and that efforts should be made to ensure that both those children who live in bilingual or multilingual families and those who grow up as monolingual German-speakers benefit from the situation.

Thus a positive and promising picture about the prospects for the teaching of immigrant minority languages in Hamburg could be drawn, at least until the end of 2001 (which in Hamburg, as elsewhere, was celebrated as the European Year of Languages). Certainly, a comprehensive language education policy that reflects the contributions of all language teaching to multilingual education, including the teaching of both German and the traditional foreign languages, was still missing; and discussion of concepts of multiliteracies and multimodalities (see Cope and Kalantzis, 2000) was taking place for the time being only among academics. Nevertheless, a growing acceptance of multilingualism and of immigrant languages as resources could be observed.

Unfortunately, it is impossible to make any predictions about future developments. The new conservative Hamburg government that has held office since autumn 2001 may change course. There are several negative indications: the government argues, for example, that the promotion of bilingualism hinders success in German and that the recognition of multilingualism impedes the immigrants' integration into German society. Obviously, this argumentation is based not on research into linguistic diversity and language learning, but on political ideology, or on a monolingual habitus (Gogolin, 1994). Future language education policy in Hamburg may therefore step backwards to the *status quo ante*.

## Conclusions

As already indicated, immigrant children in the German school system are far from enjoying equal opportunities. The results of PISA 2000 show that immigrant children in Germany come out worse than all others in every area of achievement tested, and this still applies after adjustment of the data for social class. PISA shows that this is the main reason for their lack of success in mathematics and sciences too (Deutsches PISA-Konsortium, 2001).

For specialists working in the field of migration and schooling in Germany, none of these results was a surprise. Their research shows that conventional language education in Germany fails the needs not only of bilingual immigrant children, but also of those who do not grow up in a middle-class, standard German environment. The individual bilingualism of immigrant-background children as a potential basis for language learning and teaching is not systematically recognized in the teaching either of German or of other languages, let alone in the teaching of other subjects.

There is no tradition of teaching German as a second language, mostly because Germany has almost no colonial experience. A small and very specialized group of teachers is trained to teach German as a foreign language; but these teachers are not regularly employed in German schools. Teachers in general are not aware of the fact that bilingualism has a strong effect on all learning processes. Consequently, German language teaching is mostly carried out as if all the children were native speakers of that language, and in fact, teaching very often refers to the language intuition of the learners. This way of dealing with language can be shown by historical analyses and empirical research to be part of the teachers' habitus (Gogolin, 1994). As research on language acquisition shows, bilingual children develop intuitions that are different from those of children who grow up monolingually. Therefore, appeals to their language intuitions do not necessarily support their language learning. Studies show that many bilingual immigrant children appear to develop German very well at a surface level, and are able to communicate fluently in everyday situations. But as the complex structure of German is not systematically introduced to them, they do not achieve the variant of the language which is necessary for school success: cognitive academic proficiency (Cummins and Swain, 1986; see also Cummins, 2000). The PISA results give further support to this position.

One group of reasons for persistent lack of equal opportunities for immigrant minority children in Germany is, then, to be found in the teaching of German. Two further contributing factors can only be briefly indicated. First, with the exception of isolated cases such as the bilingual primary schools mentioned earlier, no efforts are being made to develop systematic, coordinated bilingual literacy for children who are growing up bilingually. As relevant research shows, literacy in both languages is an important contribution to successful comprehensive language development and has positive effects in coping with other subjects (see Reich, Roth et al, 2001). Second, there is hardly any traditional recognition of the linguistic demands of teaching and learning in subjects other than languages. Very often, the language instruction in these subjects is limited to the introduction and reproduction of a specialist terminology. This is not enough – and not just for bilingual learners – as there are crucial problems of understanding in the increasingly complicated, abstract structure of the specific vernacular of specialist school subjects.

As the case study of Hamburg, shows, Germany is a multilingual, multicultural country. But in terms of dealing with this reality, only a little progress has been made; Germany in this respect is still a developing country.

# References

Büchel, H and Bühler-Otten, S (2002) Hamburger Rahmendaten, in *Home Language Survey – Hamburg*, ed S Fürstenau, I Gogolin and K Yagmur, Behörde für Bildung und Sport, Hamburg

Cope, B and Kalantzis, M (eds) (2000) *Multiliteracies: Literacy learning and the design of social futures*, Routledge, London

Cummins, J (2000) *Language, Power and Pedagogy: Bilingual children in the crossfire*, Multilingual Matters, Clevedon, UK

Cummins, J and Swain, M (1986) Towards a theory of bilingual proficiency development, in *Bilingualism in Education: Aspects of theory, research and practice*, eds J Cummins and M Swain, pp 207–13, Longman, London

Deutsches PISA-Konsortium (eds) (2001) *PISA 2000: Basiskompetenzen von Schülerinnen und Schülern im internationalen Vergleich*, Leske & Budrich, Opladen

Extra, G and Gorter, D (2001) *The Other Languages of Europe*, Multilingual Matters, Clevedon, UK

Freie und Hansestadt Hamburg (1986) *Richtlinien und Hinweise für die Erziehung und den Unterricht ausländischer Kinder und Jugendlicher an Hamburger Schulen*, Behörde für Schule, Jugend und Berufsbildung, Hamburg

Freie und Hansestadt Hamburg (2002) *Aspekte der Lernausgangslage und der Lernentwicklung: Klassenstufe 9*, Behörde für Bildung und Sport, Hamburg

Gogolin, I (1994) *Der monolinguale Habitus der multilingualen Schule*, Waxmann, Münster

Gogolin, I and Neumann, U (1997) Grosstadt – Grundschule, Waxmann-Verlag, Muenster / New York

Gogolin, I, Neumann, U and Roth, H-J (2001) Modellversuch bilinguale Alphabetisierung in Hamburg. Erster Bericht der wissenschaftlichen Begleitung, mimeo, Universität Hamburg

Hamburgisches Schulgesetz (HmbSG) vom 16. April 1997, Hamburg GVBl 1997, pp 97–124

Kivisto, P (2001) Theorizing transnational immigration: a critical review of current efforts, *Ethnic and Racial Studies*, **24** (4), pp 549–77

KMK (Ständige Konferenz der Kultusminister der Länder, 1996) (1997) Empfehlung 'Interkulturelle Bildung und Erziehung in der Schule', *Deutsch Lernen*, **1**, pp 81–89

Neumann, U and Häberlein, J (2001) Länderbericht Hamburg, in *Schulbildung für Kinder aus Minderheiten in Deutschland: 1989 bis 1999*, eds I Gogolin, U Neumann and L Reuter, Waxmann, Münster

OECD (2001) *Knowledge and Skills for Life: First Results from PISA 2000*, OECD, Paris

Pries, L (ed) (1997) Neue Migration im transnationalen Raum, in *Transnationale Migration. Soziale Welt*, Sonderband 12, pp 15–36

Pries, L (2000) 'Transmigranten' als ein Typ von Arbeitswanderern in pluri-lokalen sozialen Räumen, in *Migration, gesellschaftliche Differenzierung und Bildung*, ed I Gogolin and B Nauck, pp 415–37, Leske & Budrich, Opladen

Reich, H H, Roth, H-J *et al* (2001) *Zum Stand der nationalen und internationalen Forschung zum Spracherwerb zweisprachig aufwachsender Kinder und Jugendlicher*, Behörde für Schule, Jugend und Berufsbildung, Hamburg

Sennett, R (1998) *The Corrosion of Character*, W W Norton, New York

# 19. Singapore

Anne Pakir

## Introduction

Language education in multilingual contexts is often confronted with complex realities, not least among which is finding the right balance between competing ethnolinguistic representations and urgent educational goals, including optimal human resource development. Multilingual and multicultural Singapore, a city-state republic of 639 km² with a population of 4 million, has faced this problem head-on and is an illuminating case study of what works and what does not in terms of language education and language management (Gopinathan *et al*, 1998). Educational practice and language policy have helped Singapore move from being a Third World to being a First World country, and its experience in language education may have some direct implications for language educators and policy makers elsewhere. Within the country itself, paradoxically, the success that it has achieved has brought about contradictions that have to be managed carefully. Some of this chapter is devoted to raising the issues that will matter for Singapore in the 21st century.

Reports examining the use of language in national development in East Asian countries, including Singapore (Pakir, 2000a), are provided by Ho and Wong (2000). Language education in Singapore involves 'social purpose language planning' (Kaplan and Baldauf, 1997: 122), with consistent attention paid to language-in-education planning and literacy-in-education planning. Corpus planning plays a role here, with the focus on the standards to be achieved for both bilinguality and biliteracy. Language management, on the other hand, involves a comprehensive approach to building linguistic capital out of the country's multilingual assets, by rationalizing, redistributing and prioritizing 'languages of importance' in the community and society. Status planning plays a role here, as the focus is on societal change and how to make the members of the society respond to the theme of relevance in a complex and increasingly interconnected world that uses English as the global locomotive (Pakir, 1999).

Singapore's aim of a having highly educated and creative workforce skilled in IT and familiar with international partners in business and geopolitics has been unwavering, and is a key goal for the 21st century. The country has achieved remarkable success in transforming itself into a harmonious multiracial, multilingual and multicultural nation that continues to look to the world for its living. Much of this has been achieved by policy planning and implementation, and by obtaining social consensus about language in society and in language education.

Having gone through phases of survival-driven, efficiency-driven and ability-driven education (see 'Educational drivers: survival, efficiency, ability', in the next section), Singapore currently focuses its attention on 'mother tongue' education (see 'Mother tongue' education, p 271) and the issues raised therein, including improved pedagogical and sociocultural approaches. Underpinning its educational thrusts is the goal of making bilinguality and biliteracy (see 'Bilinguality and biliteracy', p 272) achievable by all its younger population, and the goal of giving high achievers the opportunities to excel in two of the official languages, plus a third language of choice (mainly Japanese, French or German).

In Singapore, language-in-education planning and literacy-in-education planning revolves around the importance and future of English and that of the three other official languages of the country: Mandarin, Malay and Tamil, representing the 'ethnic mother tongues' of the 77 per cent Chinese-background, 15 per cent Malay-background and 7 per cent Indian-background population. The official bilingual policy practised and implemented in the national school system is that of an 'English-knowing bilingualism' (Pakir, 1992, 1993a; and see 'English-knowing bilingualism', p 274).

On this track, Singapore is an example where exogenous influences are critically felt, and, as a response, indigenized curricula are being developed. A form of 'glocalized' education (see 'Glocalized' education, p 275) – global in outreach but local in concerns and treatment – is being developed.

In a 21st-century 'borderless' world, people flows, econo-cultural flows and capital flows will feature prominently. 'Big' languages such as English are thus to be critically examined for their impact on spaces of identity, transnationalism and nationalism, cybernetics and technology. These are the issues faced by tiny Singapore, as well as other places in the Outer and Expanding Circles that allow important domains of use to English (Kachru, 2001).

## Educational drivers: survival, efficiency, ability

Education in Singapore is built on the five pillars of literacy, numeracy, bilingualism, physical education and moral education. Although pre-school education is not compulsory, there is universal recognition of its importance. Every child is enrolled for primary education at the age of six, but the majority have already gone through kindergarten and pre-primary experiences. Singapore's parents place a high premium on education, since as a generation some of them had not been given the same opportunities for value-added education. The evolution of educational excellence has been the study of educators and language specialists (Yip and Sim, 1990). For a review of the role of language planning in education from 1959 to 1989, see Pakir (1994a), and for language policy changes, see Gopinathan (1998).

There have been three distinct phases in education since Singapore's independence in 1965: a survival-driven education system (1965–78); an efficiency-driven education system (1979–91), and currently an ability-driven education system (1992–2001). For the first decade of the 21st century the emphasis will be on 'Thinking Schools, Learning Nation', where creativity, IT and innovation are in full focus. Three goals have remained constant: first, the aspiration to provide the best form of education in the different phases of Singapore's development; second, ensuring that education served the purpose of national cohesion; and third, ensuring that the schooling population had the opportunity to become bilingual and biliterate.

Singapore was founded in 1819 by Sir Thomas Stamford Raffles and became a British Crown Colony in 1824. When Singapore gained self-governing status in 1959 and later became a fully independent country, it inherited an educational system from the British that was designed to produce only junior-level clerks. Education for the Malays had been provided for, to a limited extent, and education for the rest of the multiracial population was the purview of the Chinese clans and individual Indian organizations. The laissez-faire attitude to education led to an assortment of poorly resourced schools. Singapore had four systems of education with different languages, standards, syllabuses, end points and certificates, and compounding the problem was the lack of schools to accommodate every child of school-going age. The government's decision to recognize all four systems and fund them had a quid pro quo: in exchange for government support, the schools had to adopt the same curricula and the same exit points on the educational ladder. Priority was given to centralizing and unifying the system, without treading on language sensitivities. This meant that four streams of education (English medium, Chinese medium, Malay medium and Tamil medium) were allowed to evolve but within one system.

However, the desired outcome of a centralized education system was achieved through the population's pragmatic choices. Parents were the 'invisible planners' (Pakir, 1994b), and as soon as they recognized that an English-medium education gave an advantage to their children in terms of employability and mobility, they decided the fate of the other media. From the 1960s to the 1980s, enrolment in English-medium schools increased dramatically, while enrolment in the other media declined. By 1976 no pupils enrolled in Primary One in Malay-medium classes; by 1982, no pupils enrolled in Primary One in Tamil-medium classes. By 1987 only four primary schools (Chinese medium) enrolled children for two 'first languages': English and Mandarin. During the survival phase of education, the priority was streamlining the different systems and curricula, building enough schools, and equipping them with teachers mainly to teach in English, although language teachers for Chinese, Malay and Mandarin were also in demand.

In 1987 a national stream of education with English as the main medium of education came into official existence. The introduction of an all-English stream did not affect the bilingual policy: a commitment to education that will produce students bilingual and biliterate in two of Singapore's official languages, the compulsory one being English. Bilingualism in Singapore is uniquely defined as 'proficiency in English and one other official language' (Tay, 1984: 5).

The efficiency-driven phase of education (1979–91) recognized that not all children were equally able to achieve their full potential in language learning, and that a streamlining of their use of language was urgently required. The problem was one of mismatch between home and school languages: in the late 1970s, 85 per cent of Chinese children did not speak either Mandarin or English at home. A follow-up survey in 1979 confirmed that those who spoke English and Mandarin at home did well in their first and second language examinations (as well as in science and mathematics). Those who spoke Chinese 'dialects' (such as Hokkien, Teochew, Cantonese, Hainanese, Hakka) at home fared the worst in both language and subject content examinations (Ang, 1998: 344). As a result of the 1979 survey, a policy change was made to allow those who are unable to master two languages to aim only for basic literacy and numeracy in English.

A key finding in the 1978 comprehensive critique of Singapore's language education was that 'too much was being demanded of too many in terms of language competence' (Gopinathan, 1998: 23). Various strategies that had been devised to improve language competencies had proved to be ineffective, including the increase in language exposure time. The conclusion was that there had to be a synchronization of school and home languages. At the macro level, an attempt was made to promote the 'ethnic mother tongue' of the Chinese in the nationwide Speak Mandarin Campaign (officially launched on 7 September 1979 and still going on). The belief of the then prime minister was that 'Without making Mandarin the mother tongue in place of the dialects, our policy of bilingualism will not succeed' (Lee, 1981, cited in Ang, 1998). By making Mandarin the intra-ethnic language among the Chinese community, as well as its home language, it was hoped that children would have less of a burden coping with two school languages, one of which was important to their future employability and the other for their Asian identity. At the micro level of the schools, 'streaming' based on bilingual ability was introduced in the primary and secondary school systems, placing pupils in different language ability bands on the basis of examination performance in the two school languages and in mathematics from the age of nine. The newly introduced system – although with its bias of double weighting for the first and the second school languages it was not perfect – worked to a remarkable extent to stop high attrition and failure rates in the major examinations that pupils took. This phase was designed to create efficiency in the system of education, to help towards the production of excellence.

In the ability-driven phase, individual achievement in bilingualism was a focus. A major change proposed was the redistribution of curriculum time from Primary One to Four: 33 per cent to English, 20 per cent to mathematics, 20 per cent to other subjects, and retaining 27 per cent for 'mother tongue' and moral education. The significant development was that schools were to be given 'flexibility and latitude in the allocations of curriculum time according to the needs and abilities of their pupils, especially taking into account the language(s) they use at home' (Gopinathan, 1998: 31).

A tally taken at the end of the century indicated significant all-round improvements from the three phases. The Advance Data Releases 1 and 3 of Census of Population 2000 report the following trends: a significant improvement in the education profile of Singapore residents with all ethnic groups showing upward progress; well-qualified young adults (the majority of whom have attained secondary or higher qualifications); and parity in educational attainment between younger males and females. Compared to the older population (55 years and over), who were less educated and of whom only 14 per cent had undergone secondary education, the youngest generation (15–24 years) had 86 per cent who completed secondary education. In tandem with the societal pressure to upgrade their educational status, those who were not university or polytechnic graduates, having missed out on earlier educational opportunities, acquired additional technical, commercial or vocational qualifications after leaving school.

## 'Mother tongue' education

The official policy in the schools has been consistent over the decades: give all children facility in English (so that they can engage with the larger world) and their ethnic 'mother tongue' (so that they retain their cultural roots and identity). Children in the Special Assistance Programme schools (10 former Chinese-medium schools with excellent educational attainment) study English as a first language and Chinese as a first language simultaneously (that is, increased exposure time to Mandarin at first language level as 'Higher Chinese' lessons). The top 10 per cent of the cohort leaving the primary schools at the end of six years is given the opportunity to offer a third (foreign) language: Japanese, French or German.

Language policy makers believe that English cannot help to preserve the core Asian values of a developing cosmopolitan Singapore, nor can it be a 'mother tongue' since it has been deemed a 'neutral' language not belonging to any of the three major ethnic groups. Linguistic identity in Singapore is therefore tied to ethnic and cultural identity, and 'mother tongue' is ethnically and officially defined. The ascribed ethnic mother tongue is Mandarin for the Chinese, Malay for the Malays, and Tamil for the Indians who form the Tamil speech community in Singapore (among the 7 per cent 'Indian' population in Singapore, 64 per cent are of Tamil origin).

One of the first paradoxes that observers of the Singapore educational system might note is that English is the first school language, and the second school language is a 'mother tongue' (Chinese, Malay or Tamil). Since the adoption by Singapore of English as the national medium of instruction in 1987, classes have been held in English and designed both for the development of effective language skills and for the learning of subject content. Second language classes concentrate on language skills and moral and cultural content. Chinese children learn Mandarin as a second language, Malay children learn Malay, and Indian children – if they are of south Indian descent – learn Tamil. Eurasian children, children of north Indian descent, children of mixed marriages and 'others' have choices in the second school language. Many Indians enrol for Punjabi, Hindi, Urdu, Bengali or Gujerati in community-held classes and offer them for examination.

As reported earlier, for several decades the mismatch between home and school languages had been evident: the majority of schoolchildren did not speak school languages at home. This applied especially to children of Chinese descent whose parents and grandparents spoke one of the 12 to 15 non-Mandarin Chinese dialects at home. A survey done in 1979 revealed that close to 90 per cent used these varieties in the home and with their friends. However, in recent years a discernible language pattern has emerged: a primary shift to English on the part of the entire population of Singapore and a secondary shift to Mandarin on the part of the Chinese sector of the population. It is becoming increasingly true that the school languages are better aligned with the home languages, so it is expected that children will have an easier entry into the schooling enterprise since their pre-school and home experiences match more closely the school's expectations in terms of language.

Singapore has kept pace with the improvements in approaches, designs and methodologies of effective language skills in English in tandem with the vast English language teaching (ELT) industry in the Western world. One of the spin-off benefits has been improvements in the pedagogical and sociocultural approaches to the teaching of the other school languages. For example, in the teaching of the Chinese language in Singapore (Ang, 1998), the adoption of simplified characters and *hanyu pinyin* (as a Romanized tool for the pronunciation of Chinese), the development of new language instructional materials to reflect current trends in language learning research and usage, and upgrading of the professional standards among Chinese language teachers are, at least in part, responses to the advances made in English language teaching practices.

## Bilinguality and biliteracy

Singapore in its early days experienced a societal multilingualism that reflected a vast linguistic repertoire drawing from Malayo-Polynesian, Sinitic,

Dravidian and Indo-Aryan language families, with over 20 languages and dialects used in daily interactions, and a form of Bazaar Malay as the lingua franca. However, there was a low level of literacy and limited educational opportunities in the pre-independence days. Currently, in a 'dramatically altered language environment', carefully engineered and successfully created, the majority of Singapore citizens have been 'streamlined' into using the country's two official languages, and at a much higher level of literacy and biliteracy.

The trends seen in the 2000 Census of Population are the following: rise in multilanguage literacy; a higher degree of literacy in English; more spoken English and Mandarin at home (although the most common languages spoken at home were still the vernacular languages); age differentials in home language use; more speaking of English among the better educated; and a positive correlation between socio-economic status and the use of English at home. English has also emerged as the lingua franca of the Singapore resident population. Data from the Department of Statistics over the past three decades show that English and Mandarin are gaining more speakers at the expense of the Chinese dialects.

For the Malay and Tamil communities, language use at home has remained consistent. Vernacular languages continue as the most common languages spoken in the home by the three main ethnic communities, although Mandarin has gained more speakers from among its 'Chinese dialect' speakers. In these communities the second most frequently spoken languages at home are also English and Mandarin, especially among the younger population. The effect of bilingual education on the home environment is clear: a decline in the use of the 12 to 15 once-prevalent Chinese dialects. On the positive side, Singaporeans are now in line to tap China's economic potential, as Mandarin has a new relevance in the changing geopolitics of the 21st century (Goh, 2000).

As the 2000 Census demonstrates, English 'appears to be emerging as the language of the young among the Chinese resident population.' At the end of the last decade of the 20th century, 36 per cent of the Chinese Singaporeans aged 5–14, 22 per cent of young people aged 15–24 and 25 per cent of those aged 25–54 used English most frequently at home. The implications of these figures include a likely effect on the language of socialization for the very young when those in the 5–14 years cohort reach childbearing age.

Literacy rates in Singapore continue their upward trend, along with the rising educational levels of attainment, across all ethnic groups. The current overall literacy rate is 93 per cent, with the proportion literate in two or more languages at 56 per cent.

It is clear that there has been a rise in multilanguage literacy. The Malays have the highest biliteracy rates: literacy in English and their native language (77 per cent), while the Indians have the next highest biliteracy rates (55 per cent) in the official languages, but a high 69.5 per cent if other languages are included. However, as the Chinese form the largest population group in the country, their biliteracy rate (English and Chinese) at 48.3 per cent contributes to the overall total of literacy in two or more languages at 56 per cent in 2000.

By the turn of the 21st century, bilinguality and biliteracy have become a norm in Singapore, arising from a situation of 'streamlining' a diverse community that in the middle of the 20th century had used more than 20 languages. By design, English-knowing bilinguals who are also biliterate have been created. This development brings with it a host of important issues that have to be resolved.

## English-knowing bilingualism

As is clear from the preceding sections, Singapore presents a unique case of English-knowing bilingualism created by an official language policy that defines bilingualism 'not as proficiency in any two languages but as proficiency in English and one other official language' (Tay, 1984: 5). English-knowing bilingualism is built on the assumption that it is crucial to Singapore's economic and political well-being.

This section deals with the issues faced by the English-knowing bilingual population of Singapore, who are increasingly using English in functional and controlling domains: educational, cultural, commercial, social and political, and in their homes (Pakir, 1993a). Besides extending into various contexts, 'English-knowing bilingualism' (a term first used by Kachru, 1983: 40–42), has also penetrated social levels beyond the elite. The functions served by English in the new developing contexts include the instrumental, the regulatory, the interactional and the personal (Halliday, 1975). The use of English in Singapore has become 'socially semiotic', allowing for interpersonal enactment as well as experiential reflection on more and more levels, and between more and more members of the diverse communities.

Singapore's special form of bilingual education, with English as an official language and the working language, does have some sociocultural implications. Although its language-in-education and literacy-in-education plans are being implemented successfully, with English as the key language of the bilingual policy, some complex questions need to be raised:

- As its global and local importance increases, can English serve as a language of national identity for Singaporeans?
- What is the sociocultural price to be paid for making English the premier co-official language?
- How strongly can the second school languages compete with an awesome language that is spreading so quickly throughout the Internet and globalized communities?
- How will increasing use of English erode traditional values among the majority Chinese population? (Pakir, 1991a).

Issues such as these will have to be resolved in the new century.

The complex and dynamic situation in Singapore has given rise to the 'ascendant bilingual' (see definition given by Li Wei (2000: 6): 'someone whose ability to function in a second language is developing due to increased use'). Societies like Singapore that are dependent on English-knowing bilingualism for survival, efficacy and relevance in the global economy begin to produce such 'ascendant bilingual communities'.

Ascendant English-knowing bilingual communities represent both an enigma and a dilemma to their nation-states. What is lost when whole communities give up their collective association with their other languages and shift over to ascendancy in English-knowingness? What can be done for language maintenance in the face of rapid shift to 'big' languages such as English and Mandarin? Does the ascendant English-knowing bilingual community operate with the same parameters and strategies irrespective of whether they are Malay and English-knowing, Chinese and English-knowing, Indian and English-knowing? Will new norms of interaction and interpretation emerge from this community, allowing a larger communicative integration than previously experienced?

English-knowing bilingual communities like Singapore are engaged in the new knowledge-based economy with the expectation that global interfacing will be done mainly in English and that some international 'standards' for mutually successful communication can be achieved. The juggernaut of English and the vast ELT enterprise that has grown around the increasing use of English throughout the world should take note of the significance of ascendant English-knowing bilingual communities.

## 'Glocalized education'

'Glocalized education' is a term that I use to describe the local responses to global developments in education, pedagogy and instructional materials. It gives 'insider' perspectives on developments within countries that look to established ELT research and scholarship but realize the need to develop their own language education because of their varying sociolinguistic contexts for teaching English. Some old assumptions cannot hold. An example would be a double assumption in the research on language teaching and learning:

- that the two languages in contact, as a result of the learning process, present a symmetric unity. They are examined as a pair: first language versus target second language;
- that the learner is equally considered as a homogeneous speaker of a particular language called his or her 'mother tongue' and at the same time exposed to another language, the target second language.

This double assumption has to be reviewed for the simple reason that with the spread of decolonization, globalization, migration, urbanization and multiculturalism, new learning situations in complex communities arise. The cultural experiences of the learner and the nation have become ever more complex. And, in the case of Singapore, it has been established that even the nomenclature (eg 'mother tongue', 'first language', 'second language') is used differently, as are targets such as bilinguality and biliteracy.

'Chains of control' regarding the teaching of English have been identified by Kachru (1996: 9). These chains are controlled by 'native speakers', who may wittingly or unwittingly strengthen 'the native speaker' myth, which is already powerful because it is propagated by a vast 'ELT empire' that has arisen to replace both the old colonial empire of Britain and the newer knowledge empire of the United States.

In 'glocalized education' the intellectualization of teaching English for dynamic cultural contexts might result in increased creativity and innovation in English language education (Pakir, 1993b, 1998). The Singapore experience of English-knowing bilingualism has produced a generation of language educators with sufficient confidence to teach reading and writing in English but based on Asian scripts, and to explore exogenous influences for an indigenized curriculum (Ho, 1998). They are also secure in the knowledge that while producing language syllabuses, evaluation measures and instructional materials, they are keeping in view their rapidly changing linguistic environments.

The global and local logistics of the 'glocalized education' arising in English-knowing bilingual communities can be run on the platform of reform, recontextualization, redefinition and reaffirmation, leading to a new literature on language education for the 21st century.

## Conclusion

This chapter has examined the implications of 'social purpose language education' for a city-state that has given premier status to English, although recognizing, at the same time, the importance of its three other official languages. It has attempted to analyse what has worked and what has not, keeping in view developments for language education in 21st-century Singapore. In terms of its language policy and language education practice, Singapore has had to accommodate English and achieve a kind of language balance in a synchrony of national goals and international participation.

The future of global English and its new forms and functions in Singapore and the question of mutual intelligibility in its use of English with the rest of the world is a key concern. Naisbitt acutely observed in the 1990s that one mega-trend would be the use of English as the language of the New World Order – but which English and whose (Pakir, 2000b)? The notion of a standard language and a standard variety of English (see Kaplan, 2000: 174) weighs heavily in a Singapore that has to remain plugged into the international grid of finance and business and the global economies of the 21st century.

The challenges confronting Singapore revolve round the future of English (Graddol, 1997), and the future of its other official languages, especially Mandarin (see Goh, 2000 on the rise of global Mandarin). Amid geopolitical and global economic developments taking place on an unprecedented scale in the 21st century, Singapore is seeking to develop its human potential to the fullest. To prepare for an uncertain future, the city-state republic is geared to attracting, recruiting, retaining and rewarding foreign talent while at the same time upgrading home talent. Both of these measures are based on the premise that speaking and using Standard English for effective communication and business is of the utmost importance. With extensive use of English for internationalization, there is an anxiety that Singaporeans may begin to speak a form of English that will not be universally understood (Gupta, 1998; Pakir, 1991b, c, 1998). Consequently, the approach to the promotion of Standard English has included a stigmatization of Singlish (Singapore Colloquial English with contact features from the country's background languages).

A social divide is seen to be emerging between the English-educated 'cosmopolitans' and other-language dominant 'heartlanders', a division closely related to the use of English among Singaporeans. An ascendant English-knowing bilingual community in Singapore with cosmopolitan values and aspirations is faced with the responsibility of articulating homeland visions in English. English education in Singapore has served several purposes but two are currently relevant: it provides a means of interaction with the global community but it has also – in the local context – become the medium of expressing the identity of an ascendant English-knowing bilingual community into the new century.

The changes to language education have been evolutionary rather than radical, but in crossing the threshold into a new century, a quantum leap is being taken in curricular and system changes to language in education. Whereas until now nothing has seemed worth fixing because 'it ain't broke', the notion of 'creative destruction' taken from one of the world's economic tsars (Thurow, 2000) is appealing in terms of analysing social-purpose language planning in Singapore. Making obsolete existing paradigms that have worked successfully in the past or destroying systematically in whole or part old beliefs and practices and replacing them with innovative ones is the way to improving quality and performance on a continuing basis (see an application of this economic idea in Rubdy's analysis of Singapore's Speak Good English Movement, 2001). The idea of creative destruction can be applied to ELT paradigms and methodologies for English-knowing bilingual communities such as Singapore's.

Clearly, Singapore's unique developments and experiences in language education and language management are worthy of examination – for all their successes and potential pitfalls. In having an ascendant English-knowing bilingual community, Singapore may be an excellent site for fresh perspectives and insights into the theory building and hypothesis forming among language education scholars in anglophone as well as non-anglophone cultures in the 21st century.

## References

Ang, B C (1998) The teaching of the Chinese language in Singapore, in *Language, Society and Education in Singapore: Issues and trends*, eds S Gopinathan, A Pakir, W K Ho and V Saravanan, pp 335–52, Times Academic Press, Singapore

Census of Population 1980 Singapore, Release no 8, Languages Spoken at Home, by Khoo Chian-Kim, Superintendent of Census, Department of Statistics, Singapore

Census of Population 2000, Statistical Release 2, Education, Language and Religion, by Leow Bee-Geok, Superintendent of Census, Department of Statistics, Singapore

Goh, Y S (2000) The rise of global Mandarin: opportunities and challenges, in *Language in the Global Context: Implications for the language classroom*, Anthology Series 41, eds W K Ho and C Ward, pp 304–11, SEAMEO Regional Language Centre, Singapore

Gopinathan, S (1998) Language policy changes 1979–1997: politics and pedagogy, in *Language, Society and Education in Singapore: Issues and trends*, eds S Gopinathan, A Pakir, W K Ho and V Saravanan, pp 19–44, Times Academic Press, Singapore

Gopinathan, S, Pakir, A, Ho, W K and Saravanan, V (eds) (1998) *Language, Society and Education in Singapore: Issues and trends*, 2nd (revised) edn, Times Academic Press, Singapore

Graddol, D (1997) *The Future of English? A guide to forecasting the popularity of the English language in the 21st century*, British Council, London

Gupta, A F (1998) A framework for the analysis of Singapore English, in *Language, Society and Education in Singapore: Issues and trends*, eds S Gopinathan, A Pakir, W K Ho and V Saravanan, pp 119–32, Times Academic Press, Singapore

Halliday, M A K (1975) *Learning How to Mean: Explorations in the development of language*, Edward Arnold, London

Ho, W K (1998) The English language curriculum in perspective: exogenous influences and indigenization, in *Language, Society and Education in Singapore: Issues and trends* eds S Gopinathan, A Pakir, W K Ho and V Saravanan, pp 221–44, Times Academic Press, Singapore

Ho, W K and Wong, R Y L (eds) (2000) *Language Policies and Language Education: The impact in East Asian countries in the next decade*, Times Academic Press, Singapore

Kachru, B B (1996) English as an Asian language, in *English Is an Asian Language: the Philippine Context. Proceedings of the Conference held in Manila, 2–3 August*, ed M L S Bautista, pp 1–23, Macquarie Library, Sydney

Kachru, B B (2001) World Englishes and culture wars, in *Ariels: departures and returns. Essays for Edwin Thumboo*, eds C K Tong, A Pakir, K C Ban and R B H Goh, pp 391–419, Oxford University Press, Singapore

Kaplan, R B (2000) Why is English a global language? Problems and perplexities, in *Language in the Global Context: Implications for the Language Classroom*, Anthology Series 41, eds W K Ho and C Ward, pp 268–83, SEAMEO Regional Language Centre, Singapore

Kaplan, R B and Baldauf, R B Jr (1997) *Language Planning: From practice to theory*, Multilingual Matters, Clevedon, UK

Li Wei (ed) (2000) *The Bilingualism Reader*, Routledge, London

Naisbitt, J (1982) *Megatrends: Ten New Directions Transforming Our Lives*, Warner Books, New York

Pakir, A (1991a) Bilingualism in Singapore: tradition and change among the Chinese, *Journal of the Institute for Asian Studies*, **18**, pp 117–45, Institute for Asian Studies, Asia University, Japan

Pakir, A (1991b) The range and depth of English-knowing bilinguals in Singapore, *World Englishes*, **10** (2), pp 167–79

Pakir, A (1991c) The status of English and the question of 'standard' in Singapore: a sociolinguistic perspective, in *Languages and Standards: Issues, attitudes, case studies*, Anthology Series 26, ed M L Tickoo, pp 109–30, SEAMEO Regional Language Centre, Singapore

Pakir, A (1992) English-knowing bilingualism in Singapore, in *Imagining Singapore*, eds K C Ban, A Pakir and C K Tong, pp 234–262, Times Academic Press, Singapore

Pakir, A (1993a) Two tongue tied: bilingualism in Singapore, *Journal of Multilingual and Multicultural Development*, **14** (1/2), pp 73–90

Pakir, A (1993b) Issues in second language curriculum development: Singapore, Malaysia, Brunei, *Annual Review of Applied Linguistics*, 13, pp 3–23

Pakir, A (1994a) The role of language planning in education in Singapore, in *Language Planning in Southeast Asia*, comp A Hassan, pp 151–75, Dewan Bahasa dan Pustaka, Ministry of Education, Kuala Lumpur

Pakir, A (1994b) Education and invisible language planning: the case of English in Singapore, in *English Language Planning: A Southeast Asian Contribution*, eds T Kandiah and J Kwan-Terry, pp 158–81, Centre for Advanced Studies and Times Academic Press, Singapore

Pakir, A (1998) English in Singapore: the codification of conflicting norms, in *Language, Society and Education in Singapore: Issues and trends*, eds S Gopinathan, A Pakir, W K Ho and V Saravanan, pp 65–84, Times Academic Press, Singapore

Pakir, A (1999) Connecting with English in the context of internationalisation, *TESOL Quarterly*, **33** (1), pp 103–14

Pakir, A (2000a) Singapore, in *Language Policies and Language Education: The impact in East Asian countries in the next decade*, eds W K Ho and R Wong, pp 259–84, Times Academic Press, Singapore

Pakir, A (2000b) The development of English as a 'glocal' language: new concerns in the old saga of language teaching, in *Language in the Global Context: Implications for the language classroom*, Anthology Series 41, eds W K Ho and C Ward, pp 14–31, SEAMEO Regional Language Centre, Singapore

Singapore Census of Population 1990, Statistical Release 3, Literacy, Languages Spoken, and Education, by Lau Kak-En, Superintendent of Census, Department of Statistics, Singapore

Tay, M W J (1984) *Trends in Language, Literacy and Education in Singapore*, Census Monograph no 2, Department of Statistics, Singapore

Yip, S-K J and Sim, W-K (eds) (1990) *Evolution of Educational Excellence: 25 Years of Education in the Republic of Singapore*, Longman Singapore, Singapore

# 20. Cape Town

Peter Plüddemann

## Introduction

The city of Cape Town is the product of a fractured history that goes back some 350 years. Historically, the area now known as Cape Town was inhabited by Khoi pasturalists. In the mid-17th century, seafaring Dutch traders led by Jan van Riebeeck took advantage of the friendliness of the Khoi and the bounty of the land to set up a refreshment station. By 1659 the Dutch East India Company was bringing in slaves from South-East Asia, Madagascar and the east coast of Africa to bolster the economy of a burgeoning settlement. The intermarriage of indigenous people (Khoi), Dutch settlers and their descendants, and slaves resulted in a group whose home language eventually became known as Afrikaans. This group was to become the majority population at the Cape. Over time the Khoi were dispossessed and driven into the interior.

Between 1795 and 1815 there was a change of colonial administration as the British took over the Cape from the Dutch. The arrival of British settlers in 1820 signalled the colonial power's longer-term economic and political interest not only in the Cape, but in the hinterland as well.

As the point of entry for the colonial enterprise, the Cape was the first region to bear the brunt of colonial language policies. These flowed from the imperialists' economic, political and cultural strategies (Alexander, 1989: 12). A defining feature of the British occupation was an aggressive Anglicization policy in which English was imposed as the main language of the civil service and education. Anglicization and the accompanying secularization of society was resisted by the descendants of the Dutch settlers and their (Calvinist) households in a *taalstryd* or language struggle (Heugh, 1987: 111) that was formally launched in Paarl near Cape Town in 1875 and culminated 50 years later in the recognition of Afrikaans (replacing Dutch) as the second official language alongside English in the Union of South Africa. The status of black people remained that of virtual non-citizens in the Union, as was the case subsequently under apartheid. Unsurprisingly, African languages were completely marginalized from use in high-status domains, including education.

Today Cape Town is the capital of the essentially trilingual Western Cape province. Afrikaans is the most widely spoken home language in the province

(59 per cent), followed at some remove by English (20 per cent) and Xhosa (19 per cent). However, the prevalence of Xhosa in the province, and in Cape Town, is increasing rapidly: between 1991 and 1996 there was an increase of 225,102, or 30 per cent, in the number of Xhosa-speaking people in the Western Cape. Corresponding increases for Afrikaans and English are 7.6 per cent and 12.5 per cent respectively.

**Table 20.1**   Home language speakers, 1991

| Language | Western Cape province* | | | | Cape Town |
| | 1991 | | 1996 | | 1991 |
| | Numbers | % | Numbers | % | % |
| --- | --- | --- | --- | --- | --- |
| Afrikaans | 2,138,821 | 63 | 2,315,067 | 59.2 | 47 |
| English | 695,474 | 20 | 795,211 | 20.3 | 31 |
| Xhosa | 522,875 | 15 | 747,977 | 19.1 | 20 |
| Other & unspecified | 60,492 | 2 | 98,620 | 1.4 | 2 |
| Total | 3,417,662 | 100 | 3,956,875 | 100.0 | 100 |

Sources: http://www.statssa.gov.za; Williams and Van der Merwe (1996: 58)
* Note: includes Cape Town

Well over half the province's inhabitants live in the vicinity of Cape Town. A distinguishing feature of the social stratification of the city from colonial times has been its arm's-length attitude towards 'African' people and hence to African languages. Described variously as 'the last outpost of the British empire' (B Rostron) and 'a nowhere city, neither part of Africa nor part of Europe' (M Nicol, both in a series of articles entitled 'The last outpost', *Mail & Guardian*, 3–9 August 2001), Cape Town is peculiar in that 'Africans' – for the most part Xhosa-speakers – form a minority. In 1991, 47 per cent of Capetonians spoke Afrikaans at home, 31 per cent spoke English and 20 per cent used Xhosa (Williams and Van der Merwe, 1996: 58). English is thus more widespread as a home language in the metropolitan area than in the hinterland. The other 25 language groups together account for no more than 1.3 per cent of the city's population (Williams and Van der Merwe, 1996: 58).

African-language speakers continue to form a social as well as a numerical minority. In 1991 Xhosa-speakers, who accounted for 20 per cent of the city's population, occupied only 13 per cent of the land; and Xhosa-speakers are largely segregated (segregation index: 96 per cent) in townships and vast shanty towns from English-speakers (60 per cent) and Afrikaans-speakers (57 per cent) (Williams and Van der Merwe, 1996: 59). More recent figures for primary school children (see Figure 20.2, p 286) suggest that internal migration of 'Africans', mainly from the impoverished Eastern Cape, has resulted in an increase in the proportion of Xhosa-speakers in the city to around 30 per cent.

## A brief note on theory

This chapter draws on certain concepts from social theories that have been influential in shaping the discourse of many of those committed to promoting multilingualism in the country, but which for reasons of space can only be briefly alluded to here. Collectively, these provide a framework for the analysis of language and power in society and in education. Antonio Gramsci's concept of *hegemony* is most helpful here. Hegemony is defined as

> [t]he 'spontaneous' consent given by the great masses of the population to the general direction imposed on social life by the dominant fundamental group; this consent is 'historically' caused by the prestige (and consequent confidence) which the dominant group enjoys because of its position and function in the world of production. (Gramsci, 1971: 12)

Or, in Roger Simon's paraphrase, hegemony is 'the organisation of consent' (Simon, 1982: 21). Tollefson's (1991) ideology critique of the hegemony of English is pertinent here, as is Phillipson's (1998) concept of *linguicism* or linguistic racism, which is deployed to good effect in a critique of the worldwide English as a Second Language enterprise. A closely allied concept to emerge is Gogolin's coinage of the *monolingual habitus*, or 'the deep-seated habit of assuming monolingualism as the norm in a nation' (Gogolin, 1997: 40). With reference to multilingual contexts, Gogolin avers that

> a 'monolingual habitus' is likely to be at work in multilingual nations as well, due to the fact that there is usually one language of power. This may be a national language, like English in South Africa, but it is not necessarily so. (1997: 41)

The challenge of resisting the internalized oppression that characterizes the hegemonic position of former colonial languages in African societies is encoded in Ngugi wa Thiongo's felicitous phrase 'decolonizing the mind'. Building on Ngugi and Gogolin, Alexander (2000) argues for the widespread use of African languages alongside the former colonial language, and for the strategic use of two Languages of Learning and Teaching (LoLTs) in education if democratization is to be achieved.

The remainder of this chapter focuses on the tension between official multi-lingualism[1] and the hegemony of English in education in contemporary Cape Town. The chapter highlights the continued marginalization of Xhosa and its home-language (HL) speakers in public schooling, teacher education and tertiary education. Official figures and survey findings are analysed to confirm the entrenchment of social stratification along language lines, despite the partial desegregation of schooling and a rhetorical commitment to democ-ratization. In the absence of government implementation plans for language policies, non-governmental organizations and university-based research units have shown the way with important pilot projects. Some of those concerned with the promotion of multilingualism and the enhancement of African languages in education are briefly reviewed. The chapter concludes with a set of recommendations for realizing language-in-education policy in Cape Town. Before then it is necessary to include a brief synopsis of the language-in-education policy for schools.

## Policy environment for schools

The national language-in-education policy (LiEP) since 1997 for public schools provides a useful context for the continued educational marginalization of Xhosa in Cape Town. The LiEP's defining feature is its endorsement of multilingualism and the parity of esteem it accords all 11 official languages. The policy endorses 'additive multilingualism' or 'an additive approach to bilingualism' in which 'the underlying principle is to maintain home language(s) while providing access to and the effective acquisition of additional language(s)'. No language is a compulsory subject, although learners are obliged to take at least two languages as subjects from Grade 3 upwards, one of which has to be an official language. Learners – in practice their parents/guardians – may choose their preferred LoLT and languages as subjects, within the bounds of practicality.

More recently, Minister Asmal identified '[putting] into place dual-medium education' as one of the 'two ways in which we can – and must – realise our Language in Education Policy' (Asmal, 2001: 5). Mother tongue education (MTE) would become compulsory for the first four years of schooling, including a proposed pre-school year or grade R, after which 'incremental bilingualism' would be introduced (as reported by Jorisna Bonthuys in an article entitled 'Asmal skop vas oor taal' published in Beeld, 24 May 2001). Thus far, however, neither government nor the schools have shown much intent to realize the LiEP, as the following section will show.

## Language profiles: what they tell us

### Home languages

Accurate information on language profiles of school populations in Cape Town is hard to come by. Despite repeated calls for such a database, beginning with LANGTAG (1996), the reliable baseline data essential for informed educational planning are sorely lacking.

With regard to primary schooling, 1999 WCED figures for Cape Town show that Afrikaans is the most-used home language, followed at some remove by English, with Xhosa not far behind. Such figures are potentially misleading, however, as they cater for only one home language per learner. A language vitality survey undertaken among some 3,500 primary school learners across 49 primary schools in Cape Town in 1999/2000 (Braam et al, 2000) revealed that fully one-third of learners (33 per cent) have two home languages, and that in the majority of cases these were Afrikaans and English in combination (Figure 20.1).

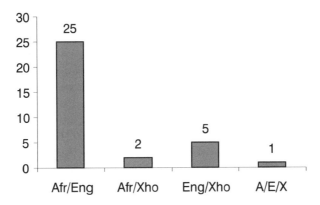

**Figure 20.1** Distribution of bilingual homes as a percentage (primary schools, Cape Town, 2000) (N = 3,452)                    Source: Braam *et al* (2000)

The discrepancy in findings raises the question of data collection methods. The WCED obtains its statistics from completed questionnaires submitted annually by the schools, whereas Braam *et al* relied on self-reporting data by primary school children. It is easy to see why the schools would opt for a one-language-per-person approach. Whatever the merits of the respective data collection methods, it seems clear that more triangulation of information on learners' home language profiles is required. This is especially critical in the light of the open-endedness of the LiEP, and the powers bestowed on school governing bodies to formulate their own policies.

## Language attitudes

The hegemonic position of English is well illustrated in the respective figures for language dominance and language preference in the survey by Braam *et al*. In answer to the question 'Which language do you speak best?', 47 per cent reported English, 32 per cent reported Xhosa and 24 per cent opted for Afrikaans. English is thus the dominant language of the three, by a considerable margin. When asked, 'Which language do you most like to speak?', 61 per cent of respondents indicated English, 30 per cent Afrikaans and only 16 per cent opted for Xhosa. The popularity of English probably has less to do with any inherent love for the language, and more with its perceived instrumental value in providing access to formal education, the job market and social mobility (see Vesely, 2000). Conversely, the low popularity of Xhosa is proportional to its perceived low instrumental value (Figure 20.2).

The high negative rating for Afrikaans (28 per cent) and Xhosa (24 per cent) in response to the question, 'Which language, if any, do you not like?' indicates either the perceived low instrumental value of these languages, or outright antipathy towards their (home-language) speakers. Given the

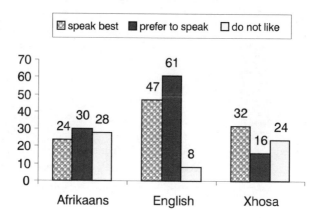

**Figure 20.2**   Language dominance and language preference, as a percentage
(N = 3,452)                                                 Source: Braam *et al* (2000)

overlap between language and colour ('race') in Cape Town, and the historical
association of Afrikaans with apartheid, the possibility of latent racism is
never very far from the surface. On the other hand, the largest group (40 per
cent) chose not to answer, indicating they might have had no particular
linguistic dislikes.

## Xhosa as a language subject

Research by Barkhuizen (2001) has documented the ambivalent attitudes
towards Xhosa as a matric[2] subject among home-language speakers in the
Western and Eastern Cape provinces.

> Respondents believe that it is important to study Xhosa as a school subject, but the
> reasons for its importance can be located in informal domains, such as community
> and culture, rather than in domains that are often associated with progress and
> success, such as further study and job opportunities (Barkhuizen 2001: 12).

Concerning the status of Xhosa as an additional language subject, statistics
obtained from the Western Cape Education Department (WCED) for
secondary schools in Cape Town reveal the low numbers of learners taking
Xhosa L2/L3. In 2000 a mere 5,302 learners, or 2.5 per cent of the eligible
number, took Xhosa as a subject. Proportionately, very few learners in traditionally 'white' schools (1,972 of 44,713, or 4.4 per cent), and even fewer in
former 'coloured' schools (2,328 of 127,198, or 1.8 per cent) and no learners in
'Indian' schools (0 of 2,862) took Xhosa. This points to the lack of prestige of
Xhosa as a language subject, and to the linguicism of both middle-class and
working-class Afrikaans- and English-speaking populations. The main
reason, derived from a preliminary study,[3] is the marginalization of Xhosa in
the school curriculum and in society.

## Home language v LoLT

The educational marginalization of Xhosa, and hence of Xhosa-speakers, in Cape Town is particularly stark when viewed against the discrepancy between home language and LoLT. Official figures for secondary schools for 2000 show that Afrikaans is the most widely spoken home language (101,122, or 43 per cent), followed by Xhosa (66,877, or 29 per cent) and English (62,708, or 27 per cent). However, English is the most widely used LoLT (53 per cent), disproportionately large in relation to its number of HL speakers. While Afrikaans is used as an LoLT by roughly as many learners as have Afrikaans as a home language, there is a dramatic drop-off in the case of Xhosa. A mere 16 per cent of Xhosa-speaking secondary school learners (or 5 per cent of the total learner population) receive instruction in their home language for the 'content subjects'. The vast majority of the remaining 84 per cent of Xhosa-speakers are taught in English. Home language (HL) speakers of other languages together constitute less than 2 per cent of the secondary school population. The majority of these are Sotho-speakers, who are catered for in a limited way through the use of Sotho as an LoLT (in at least two primary schools) and as a language subject (in a few secondary schools also).

## Analysis

Apart from the one-home-language-per-learner fallacy already alluded to, statistics such as these hide several trends that negatively affect the academic performance of African-language speakers in former DET schools. First, the use of English as an LoLT begins well before learners reach secondary school, with deleterious consequences. Research evidence (Macdonald with Burrows, 1991; Vinjevold, 1999; NCCRD, 2000) from around the country confirms that the vast majority of African-language-speaking learners experience a debilitating transition to English-medium teaching after three (formerly four) years of HL ('mother tongue') education. Despite the 'additive bilingual' intent of the LiEP, African languages continue to be 'subtracted' from curricular use before sufficient language development has taken place. Linguistically demanding 'content subjects' such as mathematics, science, history, geography, accounting and technology are (officially) taught and assessed through the medium of English from Grade 4 upwards.

Second, teachers in ex-DET schools make widespread (and unofficial) use of code switching to bridge the conceptual gap for learners struggling with English. Research conducted in township primary schools in Cape Town (Mati, 2000) has revealed the complexity of the code-switching issue. On the one hand, teachers display fine intuition in switching between Xhosa and English in geography classes. On the other, some teachers appear to use English strategically in order to mask their ignorance of science, switching to Xhosa only for classroom management purposes (Mbude, 2001).[4] However, the use of the African language in the 'content' subjects is invariably limited to the spoken domain, and does not extend to reading, writing and assessment. Most learners are thus not given the chance to develop advanced literacies in their HL.

Third, statistics such as the above mask the likelihood that the majority of teachers, themselves the products of an inferior system, have insufficient command of English to be able to provide high-quality access to what remains virtually a foreign language to most of their learners. The ultimate proof of the failure of what amounts to an English as a Second Language system (Alexander, 2000, following Hartshorne) is the high failure rate of African-language-speaking matriculants in the Grade 12 school leaving examination every year. Several years after the advent of the LiEP in 1997, matric exams can still only be taken in English and Afrikaans. The disadvantages accruing to African-language speakers has been tacitly recognized by the national Ministry of Education, which has artificially inflated the marks of African-language-speaking matriculants in each of the past two years. This disingenuous device to compensate African-language speakers for their language 'deficit' represents a paper-thin attempt to disguise the linguicism that still characterizes language practice in schooling. There are signs, however, that the Ministry of Education may soon make provision for the translation of matric exam papers into the official African languages. Such a move would have a significant 'backwash effect' on the rest of the schooling system, and might even animate the tertiary institutions to offer African languages as supportive LoLTs.

The major stumbling-block in the realization of the LiEP remains the lack of political will on the part of the national Department of Education and its provincial counterparts. There has simply not been the same heavy investment (in teacher training or production of learning support materials) as there has been for, say, the new national Curriculum 2005. Despite important findings that most African-language speakers prefer a strong role for the home language (alongside English) in their children's education (Barkhuizen, 2001), government for the most part continues to act as if English is the main language worth learning. The politically inspired open-endedness of the LiEP with regard to LoLTs has hindered, rather than helped, the promotion of additive multilingualism, as it has allowed schools to get away with assimilationist English-mainly policies.

## Implementing the LiEP

For reasons of space this section will focus on those organizations and initiatives that explicitly seek to promote additive multilingualism in the schooling and teacher education sectors. With regard to language policy formulation and implementation proposals, the Project for the Study of Alternative

Education in South Africa (PRAESA)[5] and, before it, the National Language Project (NLP)[6] have been particularly influential. Much of the discursive orientation around language policy and planning since the late 1980s has been shaped by the work of these two projects, whose joint publication *Multilingual Education for South Africa* (Heugh, Siegrühn and Plüddemann, 1995) remains a reference point in the field. The NLP's *Bua!* magazine, now available only online, has for years constituted an important source of information on language matters more broadly, including education.

Concerning teacher education, innovative on-site interventions promoting multilingualism have been carried out by NGOs such as the Scientific and Industrial Leadership Initiative (SAILI) and, more recently, the Iilwimi-Sentrum[7] at UWC. Both of these organizations work with a number of schools in working-class areas. The Primary Open Learning Pathways (POLP) Trust is an off-campus NGO that has offered a module in an in-service course at a teacher education college. The course trains teachers to develop literacy in out-of-school youth who are being integrated into mainstream schooling in working-class bilingual/multilingual contexts. University-based NGOs and research units have, unlike their off-campus counterparts, been able to run accredited courses for teachers. The Advanced Certificate in Multilingual Education constituted a path-finding initiative in this regard. It was a one-year course for in-service teachers offered jointly by PRAESA and UCT's Department of Education from 1997 to 2001. Uniquely for a course at this level, some teaching as well as assessment was done in Xhosa (alongside English) in the interests of students, a practice that amounted to a violation of the university's English-only language policy.

Other interventions by research units working in Cape Town schools and classrooms have demonstrated the difficulties of swimming against the tide of English hegemony, official multilingualism notwithstanding. PRAESA has been involved in a number of initiatives at primary school level in an attempt to demonstrate that the LiEP can be realized in practice, despite initial attitudinal resistance and material resource constraints. These include:

- piloting dual-medium (Xhosa/English) science teaching and assessment, with accompanying development of scientific terminology in Xhosa;
- producing a multilingual school newsletter featuring contributions by learners and teachers in two Xhosa-speaking schools;
- introducing biliteracy (Xhosa/English) development and Xhosa teaching in a multilingual English-medium school (Bloch, 2000) and promoting a culture of free voluntary reading in Xhosa and Afrikaans.

Progress on each of these initiatives has been bedevilled by the monolingual habitus on the part of stakeholders, who increasingly valorize English at the expense of Afrikaans and Xhosa. Furthermore, the heavy investment in on-site intervention has tended to limit research on these sites to action research.

Since its inception in 1998, Biblionef (SA) has played a key role in the promotion of mother tongue literacy in education in Cape Town. Essentially a depot for reading materials for children aged 3–18, Biblionef has donated books to children's organizations and schools in working-class areas all over the country. Its main focus in the Cape Town region has been to provide Xhosa-speaking and Afrikaans-speaking children with reading books in their home languages, clearly a vital investment in the context of under-resourced schools.

The Education Department has drawn on the experience and energies of local NGOs as well as developments in Great Britain in promoting literacy. A successful Literacy Indaba in 2000 was followed up by a national 'We are a reading school' campaign in 2001, in terms of which all schools were to introduce a literacy half-hour with the aim of improving on low literacy levels among learners.

Finally, the Multilingualism Action Group (MAG), an informal group formed in 2001 under the auspices of the Western Cape Language Committee, deserves mention for its pioneering role in promoting trilingualism in the province. The MAG's main purpose is to popularize multilingualism, and to promote respect among the various language groups in order to advance democracy and economic prosperity. A particular focus has been devising strategies to promote and enhance the status of Xhosa as part of a wider multi-lingualism awareness campaign in the Western Cape province.

## Universities and their language policies

The Western Cape has three public universities all within a radius of 50 km of each other: Cape Town (UCT), Western Cape (UWC) and Stellenbosch (US). While only the first two can be said to be in Greater Cape Town, the proximity of Stellenbosch and its historically white Afrikaner character make for an interesting comparison. In particularly, UCT and US have a demographic profile that reflects the historical marginalization of Africans in Greater Cape Town. UCT and US were established in the early 20th century as parallel-medium institutions designed to enable Afrikaans-speaking and English-speaking 'whites' to get to know each other, *inter alia* through the other's language (Giliomee, 2001: 5). Within 10–15 years of its founding, however, US went over to Dutch- and Afrikaans-medium tuition, while UCT phased out Afrikaans in favour of English. While legislation restricting access on the grounds of colour has long since been scrapped, both institutions have largely retained their white face, particularly with regard to academic staff. UWC, on the other hand, is a newer creation of apartheid-era legislation, and was established in 1960 as an Afrikaans-medium institution exclusively for 'coloureds'. Initially much despised for the fact, UWC radically changed its political orientation during the 'struggle years' of the 1980s and became a self-proclaimed 'intellectual home of the Left'. It opened its doors to increasing numbers of African students, the vast majority of whom had negative perceptions of

Afrikaans and preferred (and were more proficient in) English. With the partial exception of African-language departments, African languages have never been used for teaching, examination or administration purposes at any of the three universities.

Today, all three institutions have begun to move away from overt linguicist attitudes and practices by virtue of their commitment to multilingualism, at least on a rhetorical level. UCT remains primarily committed to 'scaffolding' students to academic literacy in English. With regard to admissions policy, South African undergraduate applicants to UCT must have achieved a pass of 40 per cent or more for English on the Higher Grade (First or Second Language) at Senior Certificate/Further Education Certificate level. Prospective first-year humanities students who have English as a second or third language, or as a first language with a matric result of E or lower, have to write the Placement Test in English for Educational Purposes. Those who do poorly on this test but are admitted to the institution have to take the English for Academic Purposes course, which is credit bearing (De Witte, 1998: 17). A subcommittee on language policy in 1998 recommended that

> urgent attention must be given to the development and provision of teaching and learning support materials in the other official languages, and that staff, as well as students, should be encouraged to become proficient in these languages with the ultimate aim of true multilingualism at UCT. (Cited in De Witte, 1998: 17)

While similar sentiments are expressed by progressive constituencies on campus from time to time, there appears to be no urgency in implementing these recommendations. The hegemony of English at UCT and the monolingual, Anglo-centric habitus of academics and management continue to retard nascent attempts at transformation.

The University of the Western Cape (UWC) has undergone considerable linguistic transformation since the mid-1980s. Unlike at UCT, prospective undergraduate students who fulfil the minimum entry requirements at UWC do not have to write a language proficiency test or a placement test. In 1998 a Working Group on Language Policy proposed a shift away from the Afrikaans/English bilingual policy towards a commitment to multilingualism in which English would be the main but not the only language of teaching and learning (De Witte, 1998: 16). Xhosa and Afrikaans should, where appropriate, be used as supportive languages of teaching, learning, and assessment. The university should commit itself not only to providing access to English, but also to promoting Afrikaans and Xhosa as academic languages. English should be the language of internal communication, while translations into Afrikaans and Xhosa should be made available 'wherever possible and practicable' (De Witte, 1998: 16). As in the case of UCT, not much progress appears to have been made in promoting multilingualism (as opposed to bilingualism) in practice at UWC. Isolated instances of the use of Xhosa in the

Department of Didactics and in the Department of History (the People's History Programme – see Du Toit, 1999) notwithstanding, mainstream academic and administrative life appears to be moving ever Englishward, with some allowance for Afrikaans.

The University of Stellenbosch (US) is at present caught up in a national controversy about the status of Afrikaans as a tertiary language medium. Historically an Afrikaans-medium institution serving the interests of the 'white' Afrikaans elite, the university has always made some allowance for assessment through the medium of English, alongside the official language medium (Afrikaans). In recent years, however, US has come under increasing pressure to decrease the use of Afrikaans in favour of English in order to accommodate growing numbers of non-Afrikaans-speaking students. A University Council resolution of 1996 reconfirms Afrikaans as the (sole) official language medium. The resolution stresses the need to accommodate English-speaking students (De Witte, 1998: 18), but makes no mention of Xhosa.

De Witte (1998: 21) concludes her review of the three universities by confirming that the 'proposed language policies have not been implemented in practice' for reasons of weak internal communication, lack of interest in the debate on the part of African languages and literature departments, a lack of genuine commitment to promoting multilingualism, and the absence of an 'active and central language debate'.

In 2001 a report on the language policies of higher education institutions to the Minister of Education recommended that US be one of the only two universities in the country to promote Afrikaans as an undergraduate language medium (the other being Potchefstroom). The Gerwel Report's recommendation represents something of a pyrrhic victory for Afrikaans and for multilingualism (Brand, 2001). While the future of Afrikaans as a tertiary language medium appears to have been thus secured, it has come at the cost of entrenching English as the language medium at all other universities in the country, the remaining three Afrikaans-mainly institutions included (Brand, 2001). A more sanguine appraisal of the recommendation is that it opens the way, in principle, for the establishment of Xhosa-medium, Zulu-medium and Venda-medium universities in the future (Alexander, 2001).

## Conclusion

The work of the Western Cape Language Committee, and its Multilingualism Action Group, is set to play a pivotal role in creating public awareness of the advantages of multilingualism. Should MAG succeed even modestly in galvanizing government to promoting full trilingualism in the province by enhancing the status of Xhosa, advocacy work in schools and universities will become more fruitful.

Until then, the language-in-education scene in Cape Town is one in which the performance is unlikely to match the script. Language policies seeking to promote access to and success within all public educational institutions in the city have yet to be realized in practice. Yet policy implementation cannot be a top-down process. It requires careful consideration, as it involves contestation and conflict since 'policy is made as much – or often a good deal more – in practice as by pronouncement' (Maharaj and Sayed, 1998: 2).

In the case of Cape Town, the ultimate proof of successful language policy interpretation in education will be a positive shift in attitudes towards home languages and the improved academic performance of the most marginalized constituencies, namely working-class Xhosa-speaking and Afrikaans-speaking learners at all levels of the system.

## Notes

1. South Africa officially has 11 official languages. The Western Cape province, of which Cape Town is the capital, has three official languages, namely Afrikaans, English and Xhosa.
2. Matric exam = school leaving exam at the end of Grade 12.
3. The study was conduced jointly by Project for the Study of Alternative Education in South Africa (PRAESA), the Department of Linguistics and Southern African Languages (University of Cape Town), and the Department of African Languages at Stellenbosch University.
4. Many teachers' conceptual weakness in mathematics and science has been identified by the president's Education Initiative report (Taylor and Vinjevold, 1999) as a key national concern.
5. See the Web site http://www.uct.ac.za/depts/praesa or e-mail praesa @beattie.uct.ac.za.
6. The NLP's Web site is at http://www.geocities.com/Athens/Delphi/4368/. E-mail: language@sn.apc.org
7. Visit the Iilwimi-Sentrum Web site at http://www.uwc.ac.za/arts/iilwimi/

## References

Alexander, N (1989) *Language Policy and National Unity in South Africa/Azania*, Buchu Books, Cape Town

Alexander, N (2000) English unassailable but unattainable: the dilemma of language policy in South African education, PRAESA Occasional Paper 3, PRAESA, Cape Town

Alexander, N (2001) A note on the demand for an Afrikaans-medium university, unpublished mimeo

Asmal, K (2001) Turning our Mogomotsis into Rutasetjhabas, Budget speech, National Assembly, Cape Town, 24 May

Barkhuizen, G (2001) Learners' perceptions of the teaching and learning of Xhosa first language in Eastern and Western Cape high schools, Summary Report, PANSALB Occasional Paper 3, Pan South African Language Board, Pretoria

Bloch, C (2000) Don't expect a story: young children's literacy learning in South Africa, *Early Years: An International Journal of Research and Development*, **20** (2), pp 57–67

Braam, D, Broeder, P, Extra, G, Mati, X, Plüddemann, P and Wababa, Z (2000) Language vitality and policy implementation: the Greater Cape Town primary schools survey, paper presented at the Applied Language Studies and Services into the Millennium Conference, University of Cape Town

Brand, G (2001) Opwinding oor die Gerwel-verslag, *Die Burger*, 7 September

De Witte, J (1998) Report: Practical training South Africa: language policy and language practice at the three universities in the Western Cape, unpublished mimeo

Department of Education (1997) Language in education policy, 14 July [Online] http://education.pwv.gov.za/Policies%20and%20Reports/Policies/Language.htm

Du Toit, M (1999) Telling tales: the politics of language in oral historiography, Paper presented at the South African Historical Society Conference, University of the Western Cape, July 1999

Gogolin, I (1997) The 'monolingual *habitus*' as the common feature in teaching in the language of the majority in different countries, *Per Linguam*, **13** (2), pp 38–49

Gramsci, A (1971) *Selections from Prison Notebooks*, edited and translated by Q Hoare and G Nowell Smith, Lawrence & Wishart, London

Heugh, K (1987) Underlying ideologies of language medium policies in multilingual societies with particular reference to southern Africa, unpublished MPhil thesis, University of Cape Town

Heugh, K, Siegrühn, A and Plüddemann, P (eds) (1995) *Multilingual Education for South Africa*, Heinemann, Johannesburg

Heugh, K (2000) The case against bilingual and multilingual education in South Africa, PRAESA Occasional Paper 6, PRAESA, Cape Town

Language Plan Task Group (LANGTAG) (1996) *Towards a National Language Plan for South Africa: Overview, recommendations and executive summary*, Part I of the final LANGTAG Report

Macdonald, C with Burroughs, E (1991) *Eager to Talk and Learn and Think*, Maskew Miller Longman, Pinelands

Maharaj, A and Sayed, Y (1998) Policy contestation and conflict in the democratisation of school governance in South Africa, *Eduforum* **1** (1) [Online] http://www.sun.ac.za/edupapers/volume1/Ysuf.htm

Mati, X (2000) Code-mixing and influence of English as a language of learning and teaching in the Western Cape township primary schools, paper presented at the Linguistics Society of South Africa Conference, University of Cape Town, 12–14 January

Mbude, Z (2001) Trilingualism in South Africa and the Dual-Medium Education Programme, paper presented at the International Third Language conference, Leeuwarden, the Netherlands, September

National Centre for Curriculum Research and Development (NCCRD) (2000) *Language in the Classroom: Towards a framework for intervention*, Department of Education, Pretoria

Phillipson, R (1988) Linguicism: structures and ideologies in linguistic imperialism, in *Minority Education: From shame to struggle*, ed T Skutnabb-Kangas and J Cummins, Multilingual Matters, Clevedon, UK

Plüddemann, P (2001) Teachers and their literacies: findings from a Cape Town survey, paper presented at the International Literacy Conference, University of Cape Town, 12–16 November

Simon, R (1982) *Gramsci's Political Thought*, Lawrence & Wishart, London

Statistics South Africa [Online] http://www.statssa.gov.za/

Taylor, N and Vinjevold, P (1999) Teaching and learning in South African schools, in *Getting Learning Right*, eds N Taylor and P Vinjevold, Joint Education Trust, Wits

Tollefson, J (1991) *Planning Language, Planning Inequality*, Longman, London

Vinjevold, P (1999) Language issues in South African classrooms, in *Getting Learning Right*, ed N Taylor and Vinjevold, P, Joint Education Trust, Wits

Williams, C and Van der Merwe, I (1996) Mapping the multilingual city: a research agenda for urban geolinguistics, *Journal of Multilingual and Multicultural Development*, **17** (1), pp 49–66

# Index